PRAISE FOR *Liberating Abortion*

"*Liberating Abortion* is an unabashed defense of abortion as an essential part of reproductive justice, inextricably tied to our right to parent on our own terms. Based on compelling stories of people of color who had and advocate for abortions, Bracey Sherman and Mahone contest the racist, sexist, and unscientific myths that stigmatize abortion, and they issue a no-holds-barred manifesto for abortion care—for anyone, anywhere, at any time, and for any reason. This book is the rebellious call for reproductive freedom we need right now."

—Dorothy Roberts, author of *Killing the Black Body* and *Torn Apart*

"In a deeply consequential moment in our struggle for abortion justice, our *Liberating Abortion* storytellers, Renee Bracey Sherman and Regina Mahone, meet the moment with powerful insight and testimonials. Abortion care is health care. And together, we will work to build a nation where anyone who seeks abortion care can receive that care with dignity and support."

—Congresswoman Ayanna Pressley

"Part manifesto, history lesson, and urgent call to action, *Liberating Abortion* is a powerful and razor-sharp road map to a just, liberated future where abortion is for all."

—Karlie Kloss, model, entrepreneur, and advocate

"To read this book is to be invited into a conversation with Black and Brown activists, artists, leaders, scholars, people who have had abortions, and people who have unapologetically provided this essential care throughout history. *Liberating Abortion* skillfully weaves together personal stories, political analysis, and practical advice to tell a story that's both unflinchingly candid and fiercely hopeful. In writing the book they wish they'd had, Renee and Regina have given a gift to future generations."

—Cecile Richards, author of *Make Trouble*

"Renee Bracey Sherman and Regina Mahone do the urgent work of mapping out history that many of us have never been taught, weaving in representational, familial, religious, racial, and sexual analysis that is in turns surprising, enraging, and hopeful. Centering voices who have too often been silenced, *Liberating*

Abortion provides a generously corrective view of our past and a compassionate glimpse of what a freer and more collective future might look like."

—Rebecca Traister, *New York Times* bestselling author of
Good and Mad and *All the Single Ladies*

"A visionary must read for people who have abortions and the people who love us. Using intersectional framework of reproductive justice, this book combines comprehensive structural-level analysis with a wealth of abortion stories told with unwavering care and respect. It is a balm against abortion stigma, and an antidote to white supremacist myth-making that ignores the vast wisdom and myriad experiences of the majority of people who have abortions. By centering Black and Brown people, *Liberating Abortion* replaces false histories and offers a clear vision for what people who have abortions should and can have, instead of what we can't."

—Becca Rea-Tucker, abortion storyteller, author of
Baking by Feel, and creator of @TheSweetFeminist

"*Liberating Abortion* combines experience and history, research and personal narrative. It gives its readers an honest understanding of human nature and leaves us hopeful. A must read."

—Molly Jong-Fast, author, special correspondent for
MSNBC and *Vanity Fair*, and host of *Fast Politics*

"*Liberating Abortion* is a path-breaking book and a work that we most need now. With great sensitivity, depth, and compassion, Renee Bracey Sherman and Regina Mahone do the finest storytelling by lifting up voices of those seldom heard. They are masterful. In doing so, they are building the future of reproductive justice by reframing the cultural narrative and setting forth a new agenda. In the process, they are reclaiming history and reigniting the power of storytelling."

—Michele Goodwin, author of *Policing the Womb*

"Prescient and beautifully written, this is the book we need at just the right time. Renee Bracey Sherman and Regina Mahone have created an accessible text that addresses the void often created by the pro-choice movement. This book is a primer on abortion and reproductive justice, a sex education manual, and history book all in one. This remarkable book is one of a kind and should be on your reading list."

—Alicia Gutierrez-Romine, PhD, author of *From Back Alley to the Border*

"In a crowded field of books about abortion after *Roe*, *Liberating Abortion* offers something totally new. Renee Bracey Sherman and Regina Mahone tell the whole history of abortion and reveal the racism behind antiabortion, and even pro-choice, political movements. The experiences and contributions of Black women and other people of color haven't been fully recognized and appreciated until now."

—Dr. Diana Greene Foster, author *The Turnaway Study*

"Renee Bracey Sherman and Regina Mahone have given us a beautiful, and crucial, history of abortion, told through the stories of Black women and people of color. By honoring the abortion experiences of Black and Brown folks, *Liberating Abortion* also serves as a glaring reminder that the predominant abortion experience we have been taught is from a white, often privileged, perspective. By giving us this rich history, this book offers the education and compassion we desperately need to achieve true reproductive justice."

—Lizz Winstead, author of *Lizz Free or Die*
and founder of Abortion Access Front

"*Liberating Abortion* shows us how to claim our bodies and our history through the essential lens of reproductive justice, especially now. This book is a must read in this era and beyond."

—Rabbi Danya Ruttenberg, author of *On Repentance and Repair*

"*Liberating Abortion* is an essential and transformative read that delves into the untold history and ongoing struggle for abortion rights among people of color. Renee Bracey Sherman and Regina Mahone's rigorous research and poignant storytelling bring to light the systemic racism and stigmas that have long plagued our communities. This book is a clarion call for justice, empowering readers to understand and fight for reproductive freedom. It is a crucial addition to the conversation on abortion rights and an inspiring guide for building a more equitable future."

—Carmen Perez-Jordan, civil and human rights activist and Chicana feminist

"A breathtaking manifesto and a warm hug of a self-help book all rolled into one. Reading it healed things in my heart. Bracey Sherman and Mahone snatch the past, present, and future of abortion out of the hands of politicians and men in white coats and hand it back to the people who it has always belonged to—people who have had and/or may yet want abortions, most especially people of color. If you're starved for abortion hope, abortion love, or abortion abundance, this is the book for you."

—Jaclyn Friedman, coeditor of *Yes Means Yes!* and author of *Unscrewed*

"There is nothing higher than authority and agency over ourselves—and for people of color especially, it is sacred. Renee and Regina understand this deeply—and are committed to ensuring each of us are champions of a free future. Make no mistake: this book is about abortion—and a blueprint for freedom."

—Brittany Packnett Cunningham, activist, social impact strategist, and founder of Love and Power Works

"Renee Bracey Sherman's and Regina Mahone's immense skill and generosity as storytellers make this book deeply personal, human, and real. *Liberating Abortion* is an exhilarating call to action and a celebration of the power of friendship, love, and community. What a momentous achievement. I can't wait for my daughters to read it."

—Heidi Schreck, performer and writer of *What the Constitution Means to Me*

"Abortion rights are trans rights. Shining a light on the untold history of some of the powerful voices who tirelessly paved the way for the abortion rights movement, *Liberating Abortion* is a rigorously researched and profoundly moving series of stories that serve as a reminder of our collective strength and resilience. With rigorous analysis and compelling personal accounts, this book is a clarion call to recognize the essential role that abortion access plays in the health and autonomy of every community. It's a blueprint for a powerful democratic future because there's no true freedom without freedom over our bodies."

—Imara Jones, journalist and CEO of TransLash Media

LIBERATING ABORTION

Claiming Our History, Sharing Our Stories, and Building the Reproductive Future We Deserve

RENEE BRACEY SHERMAN
AND REGINA MAHONE

AMISTAD

An Imprint of HarperCollinsPublishers

LIBERATING ABORTION. Copyright © 2024 by Renee Bracey Sherman
and Regina Mahone. All rights reserved. Printed in the United States of
America. No part of this book may be used or reproduced in any manner
whatsoever without written permission except in the case of brief quotations
embodied in critical articles and reviews. For information, address
HarperCollins Publishers, 195 Broadway, New York, NY 10007.

HarperCollins books may be purchased for educational, business,
or sales promotional use. For information, please email the Special
Markets Department at SPsales@harpercollins.com.

FIRST EDITION

Title page illustration © vector_ann/Shutterstock
Chapter-opening illustrations by Emma Hernández

Library of Congress Cataloging-in-Publication Data has been applied for.

ISBN 978-0-06-322815-3

24 25 26 27 28 LBC 5 4 3 2 1

For my mother.

—RENEE BRACEY SHERMAN

For my children.

—REGINA MAHONE

Contents

LIBERATING
ABORTION

Introduction

The waiting is what we both remember most about our abortions. Waiting for the tests to tell us our fate. Waiting for the clinics to answer the phone. Waiting for our appointments. Waiting in the waiting room. Endless waiting. For Regina, it was waiting to get an appointment after her ob-gyn turned her away matter-of-factly because that doctor didn't provide abortions. Then it was waiting one more day after Regina's initial appointment for her abortion because the Planned Parenthood clinic ran out of pills. The waiting turned to irritation, jealousy, and anger because the other patients who were called before her got their abortions. For Renee, the waiting was an excruciatingly emotional pain. Although she scheduled her appointment less than an hour after the pregnancy test turned positive, the week she had to wait for that appointment brought stress and sorrow. She considered throwing herself down the stairs or drinking a dangerous amount of Incredible Hulk (a mix of Hennessy and Hpnotiq; yes, it was 2005) in hopes of causing a miscarriage. That would save a few hundred bucks and have the whole ordeal over with immediately. When she made it to the clinic, the hours of waiting for her appointment moved to jealousy of a white teen who reluctantly sat beside her overbearing mother and inattentive boyfriend. At the very least, she had two people waiting with her, while Renee had none. It wasn't the abortions that made us feel this way; it was the less-than-ideal circumstances that made us feel unsupported and alone during a defining moment in our lives.

By all basic standards we had "good" abortion experiences: our clinics were nearby; we were able to afford them; we had thoughtful, trained providers; we weren't interrogated or questioned by anyone; we experienced no complications; and we had the abortions we wanted. Yet, both of our "good" experiences still felt harder than they needed to be.

What if, after the at-home pregnancy test turned positive, Renee could have gone back to the pharmacy where she bought the test and picked up abortion pills to take immediately, or what if she could have had the abortion at the pharmacy's walk-in clinic (similar to walk-in urgent care)? What if Regina's ob-gyn, who confirmed her pregnancy, had just provided Regina with the medication to take in the comfort of her home or performed a same-day procedure instead of sending her to an entirely different clinic? Or what if we had had abortion pills in our medicine cabinets before we needed them, similar to how we stock pain relievers in anticipation of a headache?

It can feel challenging or even frivolous to imagine what "good" abortion care should look like when so many people dream of the ease of care we accessed or, even worse, some never receive their abortions at all. But we have to push past that impasse and stop settling for good enough. We need to end the struggle altogether and build toward abortion liberation.

So much of our society tells us that abortions are bad and that people who have abortions did something wrong: from the protesters shouting at us and providers looking down on us when we need care, to insurance companies deeming coverage nonessential and governments dictating who has an acceptable enough reason for care. We can even feel it from our loved ones who may declare their support for abortion rights but bristle when we tell them that we are considering one ourselves. This phenomenon is called abortion stigma: a shared belief that abortion is morally wrong and socially unacceptable. It manifests in every imaginable way; it's the air we breathe. All of us, no matter what we believe about abortion, contribute to it. It lives in us, and it takes time to dismantle. Abortion stigma affected each of our abortion experiences. We felt stigmatized for needing and wanting an abortion, while also feeling the pressure to not let our families and ourselves down by continuing a pregnancy in a situation that wasn't ideal.

Despite being raised by a Black single mother, Regina felt pressure not to have a child within a new relationship that might not last and could lead to her parenting on her own. *Mama's baby, papa's maybe.* Even at twenty-nine, with a full-time job and her own apartment, she worried about societal judgment should she become a single mom on her own. As a nineteen-year-old, Renee knew she wasn't ready to become a parent, and she felt the judgment of political messages reprimanding teen parents, for ruining both their own lives and the lives of their children. Even though Regina and Renee knew loved ones who made different parenting decisions, such as becoming single parents or young parents, and, although some of them struggled, they were anything but unfit parents. But still these messages in the news, politics, and television impacted us. Black scholar Patricia Hill Collins calls these stereotypes "controlling images": the negative ideas that come into our heads based on racialized and gendered narratives and that influence how we as a society see these groups of people based on the ideas of the dominant group, white people.

For Black people and many people of color, our reproductive decisions aren't straightforward. They are compounded by racial stereotypes, in particular "misogynoir," a term coined by Black queer feminist scholar Moya Bailey to describe the prejudices and discrimination uniquely faced by being women and Black. These tropes include the "welfare queen," President Ronald Reagan's conjured-up image of a Black mother who doesn't contribute to society and lives with her children off of taxpayer dollars (read: white people's money). Stereotypes of teen parents or single mothers of color are portrayed as broken, undesirable parenting situations to be avoided at all costs, rather than an integral part of our society throughout history. No matter what, our reproductive decision-making is stigmatized, limiting our free will and community support, instead inviting judgment and isolation based on who we are.

What would it look like to create a society in which everyone receives unbiased, factual information about our options and support that affirms that we know what is best for our own lives? What would it look like if every pregnancy decision was met with support and understanding? That is the world we are building toward—a world in which we achieve reproductive justice, upholding the right to bodily autonomy that people of color deserve, regardless of our parenting decisions. This world doesn't yet exist, but it doesn't have to be a fantasy.

We believe liberating abortion is central to building that world.

Liberation is the act of freeing ourselves from repression. For us, it's a vision in which everyone is able to have their abortions, free from shame, stigma, oppression, and struggle. It's a vision where abortions are quite literally free—no cost, available to everyone, everywhere, whenever they need it. Our abortions are fully supported and met with unconditional love and understanding. But our vision is bigger than the abortion rights limited by the landmark *Roe v. Wade* and *Planned Parenthood v. Casey* decisions—two US Supreme Court cases that protected abortion access in the United States but not for everyone. As we will outline in this book, those rights were never enough, and not real for too many people—that was by design. Although the *Roe* decision legalized abortion during a portion of pregnancy, it never actually put the power of the decision in the hands of those of us who needed abortions, instead giving the legal right to perform an abortion to doctors and governments. Radical abortion activists of the 1970s and '80s argued that our liberation was never going to come so long as abortions were under the discretion of medical institutions and the government.

Unfortunately, since the conservative justices on the Supreme Court overturned these rulings in their *Dobbs v. Jackson Women's Health Organization* decision in June 2022, pro-choice Democrats have argued simply to "restore" *Roe*. If we re-create the same system, we will get the same outcome. That is not the future of abortion access we are demanding when we say "abortion liberation." What we know from our own abortions as well as our work organizing on behalf of people who have abortions (in Renee's case) and editing or reporting on abortion access (in Regina's case) is that even before the *Dobbs* ruling, and subsequent Supreme Court decisions, obtaining an abortion legally in the United States was hard.

We believe liberation will never come so long as certain types of families and types of parenting are privileged over others. It is not possible for us to receive our liberation from the Supreme Court, an institution that exists to maintain order and power structures. We cannot continue to beg the powers that be for crumbs when it's politically convenient for them; they've never gone above and beyond to act in our best interests, especially for people having abortions.

* * *

Abortion care today is available only to those who are physically able and can afford to travel to access it—with the support of abortion funds, community networks, or their own bank accounts. This system leaves countless people to fend for themselves while abortion activists fight like hell to get abortion pills and accurate information about available resources, legal or otherwise, to those who need it most.

This moment feels uniquely complicated for people of color. For us, access to most things has always been disparate and challenging. People of color are the canaries in the coal mines: whatever bad happens, happens to us first. While we were not always the face and leadership of the abortion rights movement, we have had to bear the brunt of the antiabortion rhetoric shaming us for having abortions and for having children. Yet few centered our needs in the fight for reproductive rights. What feels frustrating is that if advocates and policymakers had centered people seeking abortions—the majority of whom are people of color—we might have been more successful in maintaining and expanding access to abortion.

In the fifty years it took the antiabortion movement to overturn *Roe v. Wade*, just as activists promised to do, there were opportunities for pro-choice leaders and lawmakers to make abortion liberation a priority, but they failed to do so. Instead of dismantling the societal systems, which could free us all, they worked to *maintain* abortion stigma and hierarchies that upheld class and racial oppression. They scapegoated abortion patients, Medicaid recipients, teens, and people later in pregnancy to achieve short-term electoral wins. But abortion wasn't all they didn't defend. They said little when Black and Brown people were being criminalized for miscarriages, stillbirths, and substance use during pregnancy; had their families separated at border crossings; saw entire generations eradicated in genocide; and watched their children die at the hands of police, armed with budgets handed to them by pro-choice legislators.

Our belief in abortion liberation builds on the radical vision of reproductive justice, a human rights framework building a world where all of us can maintain personal bodily autonomy, and have the right to have a child or not have a child and parent our children in safe and sustainable communities. The twelve Black women who dreamt up this framework understood that our reproductive liberation would not be found in any court and that politicians would always wield laws harming our families to uphold white supremacy, colonialism, and capitalism. In *Liberating Abortion*, we are putting renewed focus on this framework as the nation comes to terms with not having a national right to abortion.

Protesters, one holding a child, stand around a placard reading "Free legal abortion" during a mass demonstration against New York State abortion laws, in the Manhattan borough of New York City, March 28, 1970. *Photo by Graphic House/Hulton Archive/Getty Images.*

Reproductive justice brought the two of us together ten years ago. We met when Regina became Renee's editor while Regina worked at *Rewire News Group*, a news outlet reporting about reproductive health, rights, and justice issues. Renee wrote for *Rewire* as part of Echoing Ida, a community of Black women and nonbinary writers who believe the "way to right wrongs is to turn the light of truth upon them," as their namesake Ida B. Wells put it. Renee and Regina bonded over their abortions. Regina was inspired by the way Renee was outspoken about her abortion, not long after Regina had her own; Renee was one of the first Black women Regina had known who spoke frankly about the connections between abortion access, stigma, and systemic racism, whether at rallies or in pithy op-eds criticizing pro-choice organizations for being ineffective or not centering the needs of people who have abortions. At the time, Renee was growing her work as an abortion storyteller, trying to meld her belief in storytelling narratives as liberation with racial justice. She was inspired by Regina's ability to use writing to help people envision ideas that had not yet existed and to unearth history and data to create a new way forward. When we talked with each other about our abortion experiences, we identified with each other's feelings of loneliness and isolation due to the lack of honest and positive narratives of Black people who had abortions. We wanted more, but we weren't yet sure what it was. Reproductive justice as a framework offered us a path forward.

Within reproductive justice, we could bring our whole selves to the conversation. We could interrogate the systems that made our abortions what they were and the internalized and competing feelings we had about our lives, and we could dream of a world in which we could be supported more on the next go-around. Reproductive justice invited curiosity. It encouraged us to research our histories, both in books and in our own families. When we had our abortions, we thought we were among the only women in our families to have had abortions, but it turned out that many other relatives had had abortions. It's just that few were talking about it.

We felt alone in our experiences, but we didn't need to.

As we delved deeper into reproductive justice research and storytelling, we became more curious about what other histories were being left untold. As more abortion restrictions swept the nation, mainstream news outlets were finally starting to cover the story of abortion in the United States but were doing so through a narrow lens that left out the whole stories of the people who have the majority of abortions. Context and history were missing. Abortion was framed as if it had always been a regretful, isolated act, despite overwhelming evidence that our ancestors were having abortions for thousands of years and did not see them as stigmatizing or shameful, and despite research showing that many people have abortions, for many different reasons, and their stories are not necessarily sad or traumatizing. Most of us feel relief after our abortions. And yes, there are people who can and do have complicated feelings—and even regret them—but in our experience (and according to research), the reason was that they didn't feel the abortion was truly their decision, they didn't have emotional support throughout their experience, or they did not have the social safety net support or resources to continue the pregnancy as they wanted. That's a lot of missing context and a different narrative that indicts our systemic inequities as a cause.

We also wondered about the names of the activists of color whose stories weren't being told because, as the thinking goes, "abortion is a white girls' issue." We found that the movement for abortion rights and the news media leaned too heavily on convenient, regurgitated stories rather than doing the work to tell the whole picture of the people of color who have abortions and what factors contributed to their decisions. This oversight becomes erasure of historic contributions and traditions. At least a dozen books have been written about Margaret Sanger, a white nurse who opened the first birth control clinic in the country in 1916, later founding the American Birth Control League, a precursor to Planned Parenthood, in 1921. Several have been penned on Ann Trow Summers Lohman, a white English immigrant midwife and entrepreneur, better known as Madame Restell, who created and sold her own abortion pills in the late 1800s in defiance of the burgeoning antiabortion laws. But, we wondered, where were the Black and Brown midwives, nurses, and healers who served our communities? And why weren't we told their stories?

We knew they had to exist. And they did. Over the course of our research, we read newspaper coverage on the trials of Mildred Campbell, a Black midwife in Washington, DC, who provided abortions in the late 1800s and was arrested half a dozen times but never convicted, even by all–white male juries. We sat at the feet of Marie Leaner and Sakinah Shannon Ahad, two Black revolutionaries who organized in Chicago and were the two Black members of Jane, a group of women who provided abortions in the late 1960s until it was legalized nationwide. We spoke with Dr. Toni Bond, one of the twelve founding mothers of the reproductive justice framework, learning about how her abortions brought her to this vision that guides our lives. Reproductive justice icon Luz Marina Rodriguez told us the stories of Puerto Rican women harmed by birth control experimentation and sterilization that brought her to this work. The connection to this pain in all of our communities grew the reproductive justice movement. We were honored to talk to four sitting members of Congress, three of whom had more than one abortion but hadn't talked about it publicly until this book. We learned from activists who are reviving Indigenous practices and building on traditions and lessons from around the world. We sifted through hundred-year-old archival documents, searched high and low for old magazines, and read more books than we can recall. We interviewed over fifty people of color, asking for the smallest of details so we could bring you inside their experiences to feel a connection. With very few exceptions, all of the scholars, researchers, lawyers, advocates, and television writers we spoke to for this book have had abortions. And we interviewed people like you—people who have and have had abortions and care for others seeking abortions. We anchor each chapter in stories because that's what connected us and that's what we must pass on from generation to generation.

Through these stories, we saw ourselves in history. We saw ourselves as leaders in the movement to liberate abortion—because it is *our* movement. It always has been.

Our goal with this book is to write our experiences back into the history and future of abortion liberation so that it is no longer a question of what our role is or has been. There is a whole spectrum of people of color who get abortions, and to overlook us is to erase not only the current generation but also our ancestors who had abortions freely, without permission or apology. This erasure creates another generation of people who are taught to be ashamed of their bodies and ignorant of their sexuality, and who are denied the nation's promise to its citizens that all are created equal and with the foundational right to life, liberty, and the pursuit of happiness. We invite you to join us in rejecting that behavior and rhetoric with love. This book is a love letter to all of you who have had abortions and haven't yet seen your stories reflected in books about abortion. It is an invitation to all who seek a better understanding of freedom and how you want to see it manifested in your life. It is a corrective to centuries of misogyny and racism, and a counter to the stigma flooding at us from all angles.

We also have an ask of the people of color reading this book: you, too, have a role to play in retelling the history of abortion by claiming your voice and writing yourself back into this movement. It's not always easy, but thankfully a number of us are already doing it, offering a path to follow, and new leaders are emerging every day, showing us what might happen if all our voices are offered equal weight.

In *Liberating Abortion*, we paint a picture of the reproductive future we deserve, and our vision centers the experiences of people of color who have had abortions. Over a dozen people share their personal stories in chapter 11 ("What to Expect When You're Expecting an Abortion"), bringing a collective voice. Abortion stories are vulnerable and powerful testimonies and they should never be thrown around to fit political agendas or talking points. We believe abortion stories are the key to unlocking the past and building a liberated future. When you hear someone's abortion story, you're bearing witness to their soul, listening to their struggles, and all they have triumphed. That's why we believe abortion storytelling is so critical to this work—it's a testimony that cannot be denied and forces us to reckon with the status quo that must be revolutionized. We feel so lucky that those who shared their abortion stories with us for this book did so with compassion and courage. All that they shared should be heard with an empathetic ear and held with a compassionate embrace.

* * *

White supremacy has intentionally blocked other possible paths forward, making it difficult, if not impossible, for people of color to imagine the world we are fighting for. But, as Charlene A. Carruthers pointed out in her manifesto *Unapologetic: A Black, Queer, and Feminist Mandate for Radical Movements*, it is within the tradition of our people that we continue reviving the Black radical tradition of dreaming and working toward the future we want. Enslaved Black people saw and fought for collective freedom and liberation. Indigenous people looked seven generations ahead toward a better future. Our book contributes to the canon of reproductive justice work by moving the conversation forward.

The book starts by getting back to basics. Because of unfounded fears about our bodies and sexuality, many of us weren't taught about the birds and the bees in medically accurate ways. We'll break down what happens when the egg and sperm meet, how fertilization goes down, the ins and outs of a spontaneous abortion (also known as a miscarriage), and how abortions are performed. Once we're on the same page about how pregnancies and abortions happen, we'll explore the history of abortion, discussing methods our ancestors used as far back as 6,500 years ago as part of natural fertility regulation and to gain liberation. Our ancestors drank teas, ate pomegranate rinds, and made concoctions of birthwort, pepper, and myrrh to cause abortions before and after the "quickening" (the moment you can first feel movement in a pregnancy).

We will also clarify how lawmakers have used restrictions on abortion to bar people of color from wielding their power, while relegating them to poverty and furthering racist and xenophobic stereotypes. This newfangled idea of restricting abortion has also been used to criminalize sex and pleasure, which we'll also get into later in the book. Throughout the book, we share the stories of people who've had abortions and are also experts on the history of abortion, political systems, and social change.

But it's not enough to know the facts and misinformation swirling around abortion; things operate differently for people of color. Abortion stigma multiplies when combined with racism, misogynoir, and xenophobia in a toxic stew. Once we understand how it all operates, stirred up by white supremacy, we can break it down and expand our vision for abortion liberation. The reproductive justice founders provided a framework for activists to bring into being a world in which every person has the ability to decide if, when, and how to become a parent, and pregnancy and parenting decisions are met with respect and are free from violence and coercion. With new eyes on this established framework, we will illustrate how and why it came to be and how it could make a more equitable world for all of us, and we will help readers envision what their reproductive justice future looks like. That vision is centered around actually meeting the needs of people who have abortions, including an allegiance to community care that operates outside of the current criminalized medical care system; a solidarity toward abolition of police, because we cannot have truly unfettered access to abortions, in all the ways people who have abortions want them, while in a police state; and complete access to self-managed abortion, free and available at pharmacies and grocery stores, in communities, and through the mail. In a world that has abortion liberation, abortion pills are as widely available as Tylenol or toothpaste. We also envision a culture in which people freely share their abortion stories, without stigma or shame.

We are working toward a world where we all are able to have safe and healthy pregnancies on our own terms, as well as pleasurable sex that affirms our bodies and beings.

This work is urgent at a time when history continues to repeat itself.

As two Black women who have had abortions and experienced the anti-Blackness of the "pro-life" movement, we have experienced much of what we are writing about. We write in a "we" voice to reflect our collective experience, and we speak as "Renee" or "Regina" when we are sharing from our individual perspective. In this way, we wanted *Liberating Abortion* to be an account of our decision-making and that of other people of color who have had abortions—a book that counters the dominant rhetoric. We wanted to write for those of us who've had abortions but have been too afraid to speak openly with family or friends because we are embarrassed or have felt ashamed. We want you to know that you are not alone—we have experienced the stigma you're feeling. There is a better world out there—a world that we can create together.

We are also writing for future generations of young people of color who will have abortions. This book is for you. It is the book we wish we'd had.

Renee Bracey Sherman and Regina Mahone
May 2024

What Is an Abortion?

As long as people have been able to become pregnant, they've sought ways to end their pregnancies or "bring on their menses." For much of history people didn't consider themselves pregnant until "quickening," the moment when the pregnant person can feel fetal movements. Because quickening could only be sensed by the pregnant person, it was up to them to identify and confirm the pregnancy. And even after quickening happened, pregnancy care was generally in the hands of pregnant people, with the support of their elders, healers, and midwives.

Some of the earliest known abortion recipes are from ancient China and involved ingesting mercury (very toxic!) and from Greek gynecological texts that prescribed strenuous activities or root of worm fern. Recommendations were found in the Ebers Papyrus, an Egyptian medical text; in Crow cosmology (the Seven Sacred Brothers); and in Indian texts, and included massaging the abdomen to cause a miscarriage; drinking and inserting combinations of herbs like rue, ivy, birthwort, pepper, myrrh, lily, and honey; eating pomegranate rinds and cabbage flowers; doing extreme amounts of hard labor; or even squatting over a pot of steamed or stewed onion.

Terminations were sought for any number of reasons, without question, in early societies. For the Crow people of Montana, "a woman utilized postcoital birth control methods when a pregnancy or child would be burdensome—for example, when a particularly brutal winter had left the tribe with inadequate resources, or if the mother was not in good health," writes Brianna Theobald in *Reproduction on the Reservation: Pregnancy, Childbirth, and Colonialism in the Long Twentieth Century*.

In many societies, abortions were regularly practiced by midwives, relatives, or the pregnant person. In *Theaetetus*, Greek philosopher Plato writes of Socrates explaining that "the midwives, by means of drugs and incantations, are able to arouse the pangs of labor . . . and they cause abortions at an early stage if they think them desirable." Today, midwives, along with broad range of contemporary healers, are essential to expanding access to abortion care.

So, what exactly *is* an abortion, and who has them today? Let's talk about it!

THE BASICS

Put simply, an abortion is the termination of a pregnancy. The termination of the pregnancy can happen either spontaneously such as a miscarriage or intentionally by medical intervention called an induced abortion. Throughout this book, when we use the term "abortion," we're referring to an induced abortion. Unless noted, the data refers to people who had clinic-based abortions because data on people who self-managed their abortions is limited.

Abortion is a common medical intervention that people need. All people, from all walks of life—including religious believers—have them. Yet, abortion is often thought about as something only secular people do. In fact, believing in a higher being is quite common among abortion patients in the United States, with 17 percent identifying as mainline Protestant, 13 percent as Evangelical Protestant, and 24 percent as Catholic. About 8 percent of abortion patients identify with another religion, such as Buddhism, Hinduism, Judaism, or Islam, while 38 percent of patients did not identify their religious affiliation. As atheist and abortion activist Anne Nicol Gaylor said, abortion is a blessing.

Abortion stigma forces us to judge a person's reason for their abortion as good or bad, deserving or undeserving, but the reality is that people have always needed and wanted abortions for myriad reasons, all of which are valid. It may be because they did not want their children to become property of a slave owner; because they were done having children; because they did not want any children; because they were abused or raped; because they could not carry a pregnancy to term due to health, desire, or another reason; because they did not want to be pregnant at that time; because they could not afford another child; or because the fetus they were carrying was no longer viable. Sometimes it is because of several of those reasons at different points in their lives.

Researchers continue to survey these reasons, and guess what? The responses are pretty standard. Three-quarters of people having abortions in the United States say that they are unable to afford a(nother) child; that they need to care for another individual in their life; or that having a baby would interfere with school, work, or their ability to care for their dependents. We want to be able to continue a pregnancy if and when we're ready to grow our families.

Factors unique to communities of color are frequently ignored in conversations about abortion. For instance, about half of those having an abortion say they do not want to be a single parent or describe an unstable partnership. This isn't a surprise; not only has our culture stigmatized single parenting, but the United States doesn't make it easy for single parents or families of color being paid low wages to survive, let alone thrive. Although many people may choose an abortion because they simply do not want to parent or do not want to have another child, we cannot deny the role that governments, here and abroad, and economic coercion play in pregnancy decision-making.

Several states still have "family cap" policies, which deny additional financial aid and resources to families who are enrolled in social service programs and have additional children. They're forced to make ends meet with less or "choose" to have an abortion because they cannot afford another child. Our nation's inability to provide for its pregnant and parenting residents forces their hand and removes the reality of "choice."

Our society mistreats people who become pregnant outside of a perceived perfect set of circumstances. Messages promoting households with two heterosexual parents who have children after marriage are pushed to punish and ostracize anyone who does not fit that norm. At the same time, older generations use these stories as cautionary tales to keep their grandchildren in line, and pop culture, through TV shows and movies, reflects these stories to create a narrative about who people are. All of these efforts attempt to control how we should think about and treat those seeking abortions. As a result, when faced with an unintended pregnancy, feelings of isolation are quite common, and the way people are treated no matter what path they choose leaves them feeling stuck. The ostracization amplifies feelings of fear and guilt in the face of a big decision.

While abortion is often described as an option sought to delay parenthood, in reality, abortion is often a parenting decision. More than 60 percent of abortion patients are already raising at least one child, and another third are raising two or more children. Despite the fearmongering of politicians, news media, and TV shows in the 1990s, only 9.9 percent of people having abortions are under 20, with 2.4 percent between the ages of 15 and 17. In reality, the majority (60.4 percent) of abortion patients are between the ages of 20 and 29.

In fact, there is no one type of person who has abortions. Although the overwhelming majority of those who do are cisgender women, the fact is that trans men and nonbinary people have abortions, too. And so do people of all sexual orientations. A 2023 Guttmacher Institute study found that as many as 16 percent of people who have abortions identify as queer or trans, with 12 percent identifying as bisexual and 1 percent identifying as nonbinary or trans masculine. A 2021 study of nearly 1,700 transgender, nonbinary, and gender-expansive people found that, among the 12 percent who had ever been pregnant, 21 percent had abortion experiences, of which 61 percent had a procedural abortion, 34 percent had a medication abortion, and 5 percent used another method such as herbs.

News and pop culture representations of abortion overwhelmingly show white women as the primary beneficiaries of *Roe v. Wade*; however, in the United States, the majority of people who have abortions are people of color. Structural barriers preventing marginalized communities from receiving comprehensive sexual and reproductive health information and consistent access to preventive care such as contraception has led to a disproportionate number of people of color seeking abortion services. Yet, we are rarely the face of abortion conversations . . . unless it's to stigmatize or degrade our decisions and lives.

Even the casual terms our communities use—phrases like "getting scraped," "getting Hoovered," "going to the chop shop," and "flushing it"—are intentionally stigmatizing. By repeating violent language, we keep those who need abortions from understanding that it's a safe option, a standard medical procedure, and historically a widely used and accepted form of birth control.

Cultural norms and lack of information prevent people of color from learning about our bodies, genitals, menstrual cycles, gender identities, sexuality, pleasure, contraceptives, sex, pregnancies, and other basic reproductive health issues. Everyone deserves medically accurate, accessible information about pregnancy and abortion. We deserve to know how our bodies work and the histories of our people, who were also sexual beings and used contraceptives and abortifacients.

PREGNANCY

So *how* do pregnancies happen?

A pregnancy occurs after an ovum is released from an ovary following a hormonal change, travels down the fallopian tube, and is fertilized by a sperm approximately two weeks after a person's last period. When the fertilized egg (or zygote) implants in the wall of the uterus, implantation has occurred. A person may begin to *feel pregnant*, experiencing swollen breasts or bloating that *feels different*—but not everyone has this experience. Bodies and symptoms can vary a lot month to month. It is also around this time that the developing pregnancy begins producing the hormone hCG, or human chorionic gonadotropin. A pregnancy is calculated from the first day of your last menstrual period (LMP) even though you aren't really pregnant until implantation occurs.

Some pregnancies are created using intrauterine insemination (IUI) or in vitro fertilization (IVF). With IUI, sperm is placed directly into the uterus during ovulation. With IVF, eggs are retrieved from the ovaries using medications and procedures, and then joined with sperm in a lab to become a zygote. A few days after fertilization, the zygote becomes an embryo and is placed inside a uterus for implantation.

If life were a movie, someone would figure out they're pregnant after first hugging the toilet all morning. Since life isn't a movie, it's important to note that queasiness isn't guaranteed and that many first discover they are pregnant after a missed period. Renee didn't have regular periods because of the birth control she'd been taking, so that wasn't unusual for her. But when a co-worker at the lingerie store where Renee worked noticed that her breasts had been filling out her bras a bit more, she realized something was up. Come to think of it, she had also been feeling tired, so she decided to take a test ASAP. Like Renee, someone may choose to take an at-home (over-the-counter, or OTC) pregnancy test to be sure. But unless they are tracking their cycle closely, many people do not find out they are pregnant immediately. Renee didn't find out for nearly two months.

Let's talk about pregnancy tests for a sec. It can take until you're five weeks pregnant—meaning one week after your anticipated missed period—for you to have an accurate urine test result. (Tip: If it's positive prior to five weeks, you can generally trust the accuracy. But, if it's negative, it may be too early to detect the pregnancy.) This is the anticipated timing for when your body is producing a sufficient amount of hCG to impact a pregnancy test stick. (If you think about that in the context of six-week abortion bans, your brain might implode, so we don't recommend it.) Some may find out sooner through a blood test at a doctor's office, which can detect pregnancy earlier and more reliably because it can detect lower levels of hCG than a urine test. But a positive urine test is enough to confirm the news.

When one is facing an unintended pregnancy, it may seem as if it happened very easily, but that isn't exactly how pregnancy works. A series of actions must occur and succeed in a specific order for a pregnancy to take: A person must ovulate in order to produce an egg. Sperm must be present in the fallopian tube to fertilize the egg. A fertilized egg must successfully attach to the uterus; however, if it implants in a fallopian tube, or somewhere else that isn't the uterus, it results in an ectopic pregnancy, which can rupture and cause irreparable fertility harm or even death unless the pregnancy is disrupted. And once implantation in the uterus occurs, the environment must be just right for the pregnancy to succeed. If fertilization or implantation doesn't happen correctly, a miscarriage—medically known as a spontaneous abortion or early pregnancy loss—is likely to result.

Miscarriages are incredibly common, especially when they happen before people even notice they are pregnant. Sometimes a miscarriage shows up as an abnormally heavy or out-of-sync period. There are many factors that contribute to miscarriages, including internal ones (such as uterine, genetic, or chromosomal abnormalities or irregular hormone levels) and external ones (such as exposure to environmental hazards). Miscarriages are most common in the first trimester of pregnancy. More than one in four pregnancies may end in miscarriage. After twenty weeks, if the fetus is no longer viable before or during delivery, it is called intrauterine fetal demise, more commonly known as stillbirth.

If a pregnancy does not end in a spontaneous or unexpected way, the pregnant person may choose to continue or abort the pregnancy. Overall, nearly 15 to 20 percent of pregnancies in the United States end in abortion. Of the pregnancies that are labeled unintended—about half of all pregnancies—35 to 40 percent end in abortion. Recent data indicates that the abortion rate is increasing in the US since the *Dobbs* decision.

When a person is pregnant, they should have access to unbiased, accurate information about the full spectrum of their options, which should include resources for continuing or terminating the pregnancy. Unfortunately, due to the presence of misinformation and prevalent misperceptions about abortion, or clinic staff concerns about potentially violating a state ban and "aiding and abetting" abortion, pregnant people don't always seek out or receive that information.

Tracking Your Period

Numerous apps exist to help you monitor your periods and symptoms. These apps can help establish a baseline for your menstrual cycle, prevent an unintended pregnancy, identify any irregularities that might require additional consultation with a provider, or track the times of the month when you may be most fertile to start or continue your parenting journey. We believe it can be empowering to keep tabs on your cycle and fertility, no matter where you are on your journey, including for those going through perimenopause or menopause.

Some abortion rights activists and groups have raised very legitimate concerns about period tracker apps and surveillance or data privacy—meaning that the information provided in these apps might be used by a partner or law enforcement agent, or shared by a tech company without the user's consent and in a harmful way. We love the Euki app, which was developed by reproductive health researchers and doesn't store your data beyond your phone.

The good news is that you don't need a fancy app to track your period. Here is a basic overview of how to chart your menstrual cycle:

1. Mark on your calendar (either in your calendar app, notepad, or on a hand-drawn or printed calendar) when your period starts with your first day of blood. You can use stickers, emojis, or give your period a nickname. Get creative!

2. Throughout your cycle, you may want to note which days are heavy, medium, or light flow; whether you experience any symptoms such as cramping or headaches; how your emotions change, if at all; and any food cravings. This can help you to prepare for future periods and also take note of any unwanted symptoms that you can address with a health care provider.

3. Write down when your period ends, aka your last day of spotting. If it ends and then starts up again or has a super light flow (spotting) for a few days, write all of that information down, too.

4. Repeat these steps for two to three months to set a baseline, which may shift as the months change because cycle lengths can be affected by big life events, exercise, and stress.

5. Once you have a couple of months or more tracked, you can start to count

how many days your typical period lasts; usually, periods last 2 to 7 days, and the duration varies based on the contraception you might be using. You can also track the length of your periods—the time between the first day of your period and the last day before your next period starts—which can range from 21 to 35 days.

6. Continue to track your cycle even as you begin to anticipate when it will arrive. Notice whether there are any commonalities or inconsistencies based on your schedule, moods, or life.

7. Speak to a provider about any concerns you might have if you notice irregularities or changes that don't feel right. You know your body better than anyone else does. If your provider doesn't listen to you, search for one who does (or get recommendations from friends or family).

One important note about fertility: If you are tracking your cycle to get pregnant or to avoid pregnancy, it's crucial to know that people are most fertile on days 12 through 14 prior to your next cycle. These are the days when an egg releases from your ovaries, a process called ovulation. If you have had unprotected sex or experienced contraceptive failure around this time and would like to avoid pregnancy, you can obtain over-the-counter emergency contraception, commonly called Plan B, which prevents ovulation or fertilization, or have an intrauterine device (IUD), inserted. If you miss a period and think you might be pregnant, it is a good idea to take a pregnancy test. In chapter 11 ("What to Expect When You're Expecting an Abortion"), we provide more guidance about next steps should you decide to get an abortion.

You may have heard adoption posed as the solution to abortion; in fact, many states spend millions of dollars on campaigns promoting this narrative. That couldn't be further from the truth. Abortion is a solution for someone who doesn't want to be or cannot be pregnant. Adoption—a more complicated issue that we'll discuss in chapter 6 ("Abortionsplaining")—is an outcome after someone continues a pregnancy. Everyone should be able to receive the information they need to make the pregnancy and parenting decisions they want, without coercion or misinformation.

INDUCED ABORTION VERSUS SPONTANEOUS ABORTION

Although society treats abortions and miscarriages as very different pregnancy circumstances, medically, they're quite similar. In fact, when someone has a miscarriage, they may receive the exact same procedure or pills that a person would use to induce an abortion. For Regina, the *physical* experience of a miscarriage and an abortion occurring early in her pregnancies were the same. Prior to conceiving her first child, Regina experienced a miscarriage at five weeks of pregnancy. She knew this intended pregnancy had ended as soon as the miscarriage started, because the feeling was the same as it was when she had terminated an unintended pregnancy six years earlier.

It's important to avoid talking about abortions in isolation because doing so only serves to divide and isolate us from one another. We're also not a monolith; some people mourn their spontaneous abortion, and others are glad to move forward from it. Regardless of how you ultimately feel afterward, the grief, the sadness, the fear, the pain, the joy, however brief, are real and represent the termination of what might be possible, whether intended or not.

The most common induced abortion methods are procedural abortion (what Renee had) and medication abortion (what Regina had). A person seeking a procedural abortion meets with someone who provides the abortion using medical tools, whereas a person seeking a medication abortion can either make an appointment at a clinic, receive the pills from a provider via the mail or a pharmacy, or obtain the pills outside of the health care system. The latter option is called a self-managed abortion (SMA), though pills are not the only form an SMA can take. Abortions using herbs, for example, are also considered self-managed abortions.

Abortions can happen at any stage of the pregnancy prior to labor, depending on the availability of a provider and state regulations; since the *Dobbs* ruling overturned the national right to abortion, state lawmakers can ban or severely curtail abortion care in their states. Most states where abortion remains legal restrict abortion care after a fetus is potentially viable, which is medically recognized at around 24 to 26 weeks and depends on how a pregnancy is progressing. Although it might be possible for a fetus to be viable, survival at this stage is not guaranteed. Several states allow providers to perform abortions later based on medical necessity or at the provider's discretion, which does not always take the patient's situation into account.

Historically, the majority of abortions in the United States have occurred during the first trimester—the first 12 to 13 weeks of a pregnancy. However, in some places the number of second- and third-trimester abortions is rising due to delays in a person's ability to access care. Because there are fewer later abortion providers and people often have to travel out of their communities for care, the cost of the procedure increases and takes longer to complete, making it more difficult to receive.

PROCEDURAL ABORTIONS

Procedural abortions are performed in clinics, hospitals, and a few doctor's offices. These used to be called surgical abortions, which is an inaccurate term because no actual surgery is performed; therefore, we use the term "procedural abortion" instead. These abortions are performed using medical instruments to extract the pregnancy from the uterus.

Before the procedure begins, you will get an exam at the clinic, hospital, office, home, or place where your abortion will be performed. First, providers may check your vitals (weight, blood pressure, and so on) and perform a few lab tests if needed. Then, if everything is normal, you may attend a counseling session, where the clinic counselor (or other clinic staff, depending on the state requirement) asks a series of questions to ensure that you are certain about your decision and aren't being coerced, explains the possible abortion methods, and in some states reads government-mandated statements. Often these statements perpetuate the myth that abortion is linked to breast cancer (it isn't) or that abortion causes depression and suicide (it doesn't). These patronizing statements are designed to convince you not to have an abortion, not inform you of medical facts or hold space for your feelings.

Next, some providers perform an ultrasound—over the lower abdomen on the outside of the body or via a transvaginal ultrasound during which a device is inserted into the body—to measure the size of the pregnancy, which confirms the gestational age, and check the uterus shape in case there's anything they need to be aware of before performing the abortion. In some states, the provider is required to show and describe the ultrasound. This is based on the assumption that the patient needs to be reminded that they are terminating a potential life and that they might change their mind, as if they haven't already been thinking about the decision for days or months—in other words, it is state-mandated abortionsplaining. Research has found that viewing an ultrasound very rarely changes a person's decision. In fact, a study from Advancing New Standards in Reproductive Health (ANSIRH) at the University of California, San Francisco, found that of those who chose or were mandated to view the ultrasound, more than 98 percent still went on to have an abortion. Many people want to see the ultrasound in order to feel informed in their abortion or even to keep the image as a keepsake. It's all about what feels right for that person and their experience.

The Process

When it's time for the abortion procedure to begin, the provider will have the patient lie on a medical table and place their legs in stirrups, similar to a general gynecological exam. The provider then inserts a speculum—an instrument shaped like a duck bill—into the vagina to allow them to view the cervix and start dilation. They'll also apply local anesthesia to the cervix to reduce the feeling of pressure and pain. The provider will dilate the cervix using metal rods called dilators to create an opening to the uterus that allows for the pregnancy to be removed. (If you've ever had an IUD inserted, you may have experienced a similar dilation process, but typically without being offered any pain medication.) If the cervix needs to be opened more, particularly for later abortion procedures, the provider will use medication like misoprostol or insert small sticks of either a synthetic material or dried seaweed that expand as they absorb moisture from the cervix (we bet you'll never look at sushi the same way again!). An abdominal ultrasound also may be used to help the provider see the uterus and ensure they've removed all of the pregnancy tissue.

With a manual aspiration abortion, the provider uses a small tube, called a cannula, attached to a syringe that creates suction, inserting this into the uterus through the cervix to empty the uterus. Some providers prefer this method, as it can be quieter for the patient. With an electrical vacuum aspiration abortion, the cannula is attached to a suction machine that, when turned on, loudly hums as the abortion is completed. Both procedures take about five to ten minutes. Aspiration abortions can be performed anytime during the first trimester of pregnancy.

With both procedures, patients experience cramping and pressure as the uterus begins contractions to return to pre-pregnancy size. Providers often offer oral or intravenous (IV) medication to help reduce the pain, which is different for every patient.

◇◇◇

Renee

When I had my abortion, it was a vacuum aspiration abortion. I don't remember much about it aside from putting my legs in stirrups and the injection of sedation in my left arm. (I paid an extra $100 to have anesthesia. I have a high pain tolerance but figured this wasn't the moment to test it. Even though I didn't really have the money, I felt it was worth it.) The nurse, an Orthodox Jewish woman, stood to my left and held my hand as she asked me to count backward from ten. I distinctly remember her and her kindness because at that moment I realized that religious people do support abortion; she was there because her faith called her to be. I remember dozing off to the sound of the aspirator and looking at pages of butterflies cut from National Geographic magazines and taped to the ceiling. I was told the procedure took only a few minutes. I have vague memories of being helped off the examination table and into a wheelchair to another room where I could rest as the sedation wore off.

◇◇◇

Sometimes the abortion aspiration procedure is called a D&C, or dilation and curettage. However, that procedure involves scraping the uterus with a thin medical instrument, which is usually performed after 10 weeks. After the first trimester, providers use a procedure called a dilation and evacuation, or D&E. With this procedure, the provider uses the vacuum aspirator and medical instruments like forceps to remove the pregnancy in pieces from the uterus. This can be a two-day procedure and involve receiving laminaria, mifepristone, or misoprostol the day before to prepare the cervix.

◇◇◇

Renee

Since my own abortion, I have seen dozens of abortions performed to better understand the different types of experiences people have and to gain more insight into the care people truly need. The very first abortion I observed, with the patient's consent of course, was at twenty-two weeks. The provider removed the pregnancy from inside the patient's uterus with forceps after removing the pregnancy fluid with a manual vacuum aspirator. All of this was done using an ultrasound to see inside of the uterus. The provider turned to me to make sure I wasn't going to vomit from the smell of blood. I was completely fine. I paused and processed what I was a witness to. As I reflected, I reaffirmed my commitment to the person on the exam table and their future—to this stranger and their decision.

A lot of feelings and emotions raced through me at really seeing an abortion— what it was and how it was performed. Seeing the abortion reaffirmed my commitment to abortion access.

◇◇◇

Prior to 2003, some providers also used a method called dilation and extraction, also known as a D&X, for some abortions after sixteen weeks' gestation. During this procedure, the cervix is dilated and the fetus is removed intact. However, the procedure is no longer used in the United States. Using scare tactics, antiabortion advocates made up the term "partial-birth abortion," which had the effect of further demonizing and stigmatizing later abortion care. Antiabortion Congress members introduced the Partial-Birth Abortion Ban Act in 2003, and the Supreme Court upheld the law banning the procedure in 2007.

MEDICATION ABORTIONS

Medication abortions, sometimes referred to as medical abortions, are abortions with pills. In 2000, the US Food and Drug Administration (FDA) approved mifepristone for medication abortion using a regimen combined with misoprostol. Patients may receive the pills directly from their providers, through telehealth or a clinic, or through a community support network. As of publishing, the pills are widely available via tele-medicine and pharmacy dispensing, despite an unsuccessful challenge by antiabortion groups to undo the FDA's approval of mifepristone in the Supreme Court's 2023–24 term. The science is on our side!

Since 2000, medication abortions have become increasingly pop-ular, accounting for nearly two-thirds of all abortions in the United States, according to a March 2024 analysis by the Guttmacher Institute. Medication abortion is also a method preferred by trans and nonbinary people who have abortions. A 2020 study found that they preferred a medication abortion over a procedural abortion because a medication abortion was less invasive for their bodies and more private. Globally, the World Health Organization considers medication abortion pills "essential" medicine, and the pills account for more than half of all abortions in countries where they are accessible.

How the Pills Work

Mifepristone, the first pill taken orally, blocks progesterone, a hormone the body produces to thicken the uterine lining to nourish an early pregnancy. The mifepristone pill causes the embryo to detach from the uterus due to the lack of progesterone. The second set of four (some-times more) misoprostol pills—dissolved buccally (between the gums and the cheeks) 24 to 48 hours after the first pill causes the uterus to contract and the cervix to dilate and expel the pregnancy. Misoprostol can also be taken without mifepristone, as it can expel a pregnancy on its own. While medication abortion is usually used during an early pregnancy, globally some people use this method to cause an abortion throughout pregnancy.

At the onset of childbirth, a pregnant person may be given misoprostol to induce labor, as was the case for Regina when she had her first child. Used alone, misoprostol is about 88 percent to 95 percent effective, according to a 2023 study. When used in combination with mifepristone, it's around 97 percent effective at termination. In some cases, if a medication abortion doesn't work, a person could try again or have a procedural abortion.

The medication can take up to eight hours to begin working, and the patient may experience anything from light to intense cramping, contractions, and bleeding as the body expels the pregnancy. Some patients prefer to have a medication abortion to ensure they can take time off work, secure childcare, have the abortion at a time that allows them to meet other obligations, or have loved ones and friends nearby throughout their experience.

Regina

I had my medication abortion at around 6 or 7 weeks. I took the dose of mifepristone at the clinic and the dose of misoprostol in the comfort of my apartment. I recall experiencing intense cramping for about two hours, though my memory about that period is a bit fuzzy. I remember experiencing lighter bleeding than I had expected. Two weeks after my abortion, I had a follow-up appointment with my provider to make sure it was successful. At the appointment, my provider did an ultrasound to confirm the abortion was complete. I did not experience any complications or prolonged symptoms. I did experience a roller coaster of emotions following my abortion. Looking back, I realize these emotions might have been caused by the pregnancy hormones. But thanks to a network of friends and a supportive partner, in time I was able to process all of those emotions and move on to the next chapter of my life.

SELF-MANAGED ABORTIONS

As access to abortion clinics becomes increasingly difficult, more people are seeking out medication abortions as an at-home remedy, because the pills are available at pharmacies, in communities, and on the internet. But some have always preferred to self-manage their abortions regardless of the political climate.

Historically, this is how Black and Brown communities have "restored the menses" for thousands of years—on our own, often surrounded by people who care about us. Because of US laws criminalizing abortion in the nineteenth and twentieth centuries, many people associate self-managed abortions with "back-alley abortions" and think of them as dangerous procedures. That history is very real and something we never want to return to. At the same time, that association represents a misunderstanding of self-managed abortion.

Abortion has always been something we can choose on our own, reflecting our cultural practices. When we deny that history, we perpetuate misinformed beliefs that we can't do this and have never done this before. Back in the day, it was common for people to self-manage their abortions with teas and other plants or through physical treatments, including abdominal massages. In the 1960s, the Abortion Counseling Service of the Chicago Women's Liberation Union, also known as "Jane," provided safe abortion procedures to those who needed them while abortion was criminalized. In the 1980s, Brazilian abortion seekers and pharmacists realized they could use misoprostol for abortions. The drug was initially an ulcer medication and it was forbidden during pregnancy as it can cause a miscarriage. Today, some people may choose to self-manage their abortions using herbs, or on their own with mifepristone and misoprostol pills or solely misoprostol. We'll explore all of this in the next few chapters.

While self-managed abortions are generally safe today, it still carries a risk of prosecution; some states require that abortions take place in the physical presence of a doctor while self-managing an abortion is a legal gray area in others. Several people, women of color in particular, have been arrested for allegedly performing their own abortions with pills.

Whether a person has taken pills to cause an abortion or is experiencing a miscarriage, if they were to go to the emergency room, the providers would treat both the same way, and there's no way to test for ingestion of the pills. If a person found themselves in this situation, they could just tell their provider they believe they are having a miscarriage and leave it at that.

<><><><><><><><><><><><><><><><><><><><><><><><><><><><><><><><><><><><><><>

Renee

Before I had my abortion at nineteen, I was worried about how I would pay for it and whether I could even wait the several days until my appointment. Each day at the top of the stairs I looked down and wondered how much it would really hurt if I threw myself down them to end the pregnancy. I knew this method would save me $450, nearly two weeks of my retail wages. I'd heard comments here and there on TV shows and from friends that fall-ing down stairs worked, particularly pre-Roe, but it would leave a lot of bruises. I was a figure skater growing up, so I was used to falling on hard ice. I thought I could probably handle the fall, but in the end I decided against it. I took emergency contraception one day, a handful of birth control on another, and drank Hennessy and Hpnotiq (two alcoholic beverages) until I blacked out on yet another day, thinking that I could cause a miscarriage. At the time, I didn't really understand how pregnancy and abortion worked. I assumed it could happen along the lines of fetal alcohol syndrome causing a spontaneous abortion. (Alcohol consumption does not cause a miscarriage. That's not how that works!) As an adult with more information about preg-nancies and abortions, sometimes I chuckle at my younger self's ridiculous line of thinking. Sometimes I cry, recalling how terrified I was and what I was willing to do. I wish I could reach out and hold Renee then, because she was scared, determined, misinformed, and strong-willed. Teenage Renee knew what she wanted, and nothing would stop her from getting it; the abortion couldn't come soon enough. The truth is, when you're desperate to get out of a difficult situation, any method that comes to mind sounds rational—no matter how dangerous or unrealistic it is.

<><><><><><><><><><><><><><><><><><><><><><><><><><><><><><><><><><><><><><>

HERBAL ABORTIONS

Herbal abortion is the oldest method for "slipping away" a pregnancy, dating back thousands of years. Although not studied as extensively as modern medication and procedural methods, herbal abortions are still trusted among some Indigenous, Black, and Brown communities and by some who are unable to access care due to abortion restrictions. While there is less of a guarantee of the effectiveness of herbal options, some people still prefer to use natural herbs to try to pass their pregnancy and connect with their ancestral methods. We explain more about the herbal methods that our ancestors used for thousands of years—and that some still use—in the next few chapters.

DANGEROUS METHODS

When people refer to abortions during the pre-*Roe* days, they're usually warning of the time when abortion was illegal and well-trained abortion providers were even more difficult to come by than they are today. This meant that some people who wanted an abortion were not able to get one, and they or an unskilled provider used dangerous methods.

The coat hanger became the go-to symbol of unsafe "back-alley" abortions, as it was one tool used to open the cervix and dislodge the pregnancy, causing a miscarriage. However, other common household items, such as pencils, hatpins, bleach, and Coca-Cola, as well as other means of self-harm, have been and are still used to try to cause an abortion. In April 1973, *Ms. Magazine* published a photograph of a then-anonymous white woman and mother of two daughters who died in the former Norwich Motel in Connecticut following an unsafe abortion. The woman was Gerri Santoro, twenty-eight, who had separated from her abusive husband and begun dating another man. She checked into the motel with her lover, a catheter, and a textbook, and they attempted to perform her abortion at twenty-six weeks. She began hemorrhaging and her lover fled the scene. Gerri was found the next morning by a maid, dead, naked, and kneeling on the floor over bloody sheets. The image of her was taken by police who investigated her death.

Ms. Magazine printed the image of Gerri Santoro's vulnerable, desperate, determined, naked body with the words "Never Again" in 1973 and again in 2016 after the election of President Donald Trump. We have very complicated feelings about the use of this image. So does Gerri's family, who did not consent to the release of the photo and was not notified of its release until they saw it in *Ms. Magazine*. Joannie Griffin, Gerri's youngest daughter, was seventeen when she saw it—which was also the moment she learned her mother had died from an abortion. "How dare they flaunt this. How dare they take my beautiful mom and put this in front of the public eye. I was pissed," Joannie says in *Leona's Sister Gerri*, the 1995 documentary about Gerri's death.

No one seems to know how the photo surfaced, but it's possible it was from medical examiner files shared by pro-choice organizations or the police. "We had no knowledge of any of the personal details around it. I don't even remember knowing where it was . . . none of that seemed relevant. I don't know that any of us asked. It was so gruesome, I don't think any of us wanted to know," Roberta Brandes Gratz, coauthor of the article, says in the documentary. "I wish I could remember, if I even knew, where the photograph came from. . . . I was horrified by it and yet, it said so much of what we were trying to say." *Ms. Magazine's* cofounder Patricia Carbine felt that it wasn't an infringement on Gerri's privacy because "she was unrecognizable."

The image has been circulated for decades, and Brandes Gratz believes "the power of the picture has proven itself in ways we never dreamed."

Gerri's daughter Joannie saw it differently. "Now, it's still every bit as tragic of a picture. . . . I would still want people to still remember her as beautiful and I wouldn't want anyone to have an ugly image of her." Although Gerri's sister Leona was upset about the image being circulated without the family's permission or knowledge, she has come to terms with it. "It was good that it was printed. People should see this."

While it did force people to confront the impact of abortion criminalization, it was an infringement of Gerri's privacy to print it; it put a hyperfocus on her death and worst moment, when she deserved to have her whole story told and be remembered by her daughters, and all who loved her, as she lived, not solely by how she died. In fact, outside of the documentary about her death, *Leona's Sister Gerri*, it is difficult to find a photo of her face in lieu of this disturbing image of her death. Still, we recognize that the image is a stark reminder that when someone needs an abortion, nothing will stop them from obtaining one—not the law, not fear, nothing.

ABORTION VERSUS CONTRACEPTION

You may have heard the debate about whether abortions are birth control and whether some contraceptives cause abortions. It's all designed to be confusing and to keep us from understanding our bodies and demanding access to health care, as well as to further stigmatize abortion. The simplest distinction between abortion and contraception is that an abortion *terminates* an established pregnancy, whereas contraception *prevents* the pregnancy from occurring in the first place. You cannot just take a handful of birth control or emergency contraception pills and cause an abortion. (Learn from Renee's advice!) Contraceptives, in the form of pills, IUDs, or barrier methods such as internal and external condoms, can only stop a pregnancy from occurring. The name is quite literally "contra," meaning "against," and "conception," a nonmedical term used to describe fertilization. Abortion, on the other hand, can happen only when a pregnancy is established.

Emergency contraception is medication taken soon after unprotected sex—sex without the use of birth control or a barrier method—or a contraceptive fails to prevent pregnancy, usually before 3 to 5 days, depending on the method. The most common emergency contraception is a synthetic progesterone (commonly known as Plan B), which stops ovulation from occurring. It is available over the counter in the United States. The second type of emergency contraception is ulipristal acetate (brand name ella), and it works by disrupting a fertilized egg. A prescription is required for this medication. If a person can get an appointment soon enough, IUDs can be used as emergency contraception, too! There are two types of IUDs—hormonal and nonhormonal. They work by stopping the implantation of a fertilized egg in the uterine wall, preventing pregnancy.

Unfortunately, not all emergency contraceptives work for all bodies. Some forms of emergency contraception are less effective for users who weigh more than 165 pounds and do not work as well for those who weigh more than 176 pounds. As of this writing, the emergency contraception method that is effective for users over these weight limits requires a prescription and is not available over the counter. Fatphobia in action!

Access to reproductive health care includes the ability to receive not just care, but care that is effective for our bodies along with medically accurate information about what we can do to protect ourselves.

As part of a long-term campaign to misinform the public, anti-abortion advocates have intentionally blurred the lines between abortion and contraception. By redefining "life" as the meeting of an egg and sperm—conception—they are attempting to ban certain extremely effective types of contraception by claiming they cause abortions. In fact, an egg and sperm can meet, and the egg can become fertilized but not implant in the uterus, sometimes due to chromosomal or uterine abnormalities, so that a pregnancy never takes place.

That hasn't stopped antiabortion groups from fighting attempts to expand access to contraception. In 2014, the Supreme Court heard a challenge to the Affordable Care Act's requirement that employers cover certain types of contraception at no additional cost as part of their employee health benefits. In *Burwell v. Hobby Lobby Stores*, the owners of the craft store chain challenged the requirement as a violation of their religious freedom because the law mandated they cover IUDs and emergency contraception, which they argued cause abortions. Ultimately, the Supreme Court ruled that "closely held" private for-profit companies could indeed deny insurance coverage for certain types of contraception to their employees based on the personal religious beliefs of the company owners, even if that belief is not based in basic science about reproduction. Wild, right? This is why it's critical we understand our bodies and the facts.

Moreover, if a pregnancy is legally redefined as the meeting of an egg and sperm, as in some "fetal personhood" bills and court rulings, rather than being defined as the implantation of the fertilized egg, many would be left unable to receive treatment for miscarriages, infertility treatments such as in vitro fertilization could be halted (as we saw in Alabama in early 2024), and people could be criminalized for things they do with their bodies before they know they're pregnant. This is one reason it's important not to separate abortion access from other reproductive health services. All of these services and treatments are related, and patients deserve access to the full spectrum of quality, affordable reproductive health care.

THE FUTURE OF ABORTION PROCEDURES

Although abortion has been around for 6,500 years, the technology and practice has changed quite a bit. No longer must we search for the right herbs in hopes they will work. Nowadays we have options including using some pills or the right herbs to cause an abortion in a few hours at home. Or we can go to a clinic where an abortion is done in a matter of minutes, albeit with some waiting. But what does the future of abortion access look like? What does it look like to liberate abortion so that care centers the full needs and desires of people who are having the abortions? Well, that's up to our imaginations. Or, we can borrow ideas from our friends and ancestors around the world.

For many advocates in the United States, the future of abortion would look like what many global organizers have pushed for: medication abortion pills, available over the counter at any pharmacy, grocery store, gas station, or drugstore or sourced in the community, to have on hand and take whenever they are needed, and for free. Having the pills available before they are needed makes it less necessary to travel out of our communities and possible to have an abortion as soon as the decision is made, much like we do with other medications and ailments.

One exciting way providers are working to increase access to in-clinic abortions is by allowing certified nurse-midwives, nurse practitioners, and physician assistants—also known as "advanced practice clinicians"— to provide early procedural abortions and dispense medication abortion pills. Having these clinicians provide abortion care is just as safe as when a physician provides care. This allows more patients to get appointments and for physicians with greater technical expertise to provide later abortions or travel to areas where access is more challenging for people.

In Latin America and throughout the United States, there is a movement of "accompanimiento," which translates in English to "accompaniment" or support for someone having an abortion. In this model, a person supports the person self-managing their abortion in several different ways, from procuring the medication abortion pills for them to sitting with them throughout the entire process—whatever fits the abortion seeker's needs. The person accompanying may bring snacks, heating pads, pain relievers, or anything else to make the abortion experience as comfortable as possible. The movement's goal is to create a supportive, nonstigmatizing community surrounding the person who needs the abortion and to allow the process to be led by their needs.

When Renee was in Barcelona, she learned from a local activist about the way they've been able to bring the accompaniment model into public and private hospitals in Spain and France, providing patients with a support person, paid for by the government. Similar to the doula model in the United States, where a support person assists a pregnant person during labor and delivery, these abortion support activists can spend 4 to 8 hours per day at the hospital supporting people during their abortions with comfort, massage, and even translation services. The activist told Renee that it's critical for breaking stigma, especially for immigrants who do not speak the local language and seek abortion services in isolation.

One thing that struck Renee as profound is how often global activists ask, "How many accompaniments do you do a month?" so that they can gauge an activist's involvement with the abortion movement. The question isn't asked in a judgmental way; rather, the assumption is that if you are committed to doing abortion work, sitting with and supporting someone during their abortion is a foundational and core aspect of the work.

Over the years, advocates have come up with innovative ways to bring abortion pills to patients. In March 2024, a small robot roved in front of the Supreme Court during oral arguments for the case challenging the FDA's approval of mifepristone, giving out medication abortion pills. Activists have flown drones from Germany to send pills to Poland, where abortion is banned, and from one part of Ireland to another for the same reason. Organizations have used boats to pick up abortion seekers from different ports, taking them out into international waters and then giving them the medication abortion pills. In Nigeria, where abortion is severely criminalized, local organizations operate hotlines offering medically accurate information to callers and provide resources about safe medication abortions, while other groups provide abortion pills through the mail or pass them along in the community. Activists are passing abortion pills around in communities in the United States, too.

What connects all these innovative strategies is the idea that people who have abortions get to have a method that fits their needs, schedule, and lives. The care comes to and centers them. It's not a one-size-fits-all model. The methods are attempts to liberate abortion from the local government and antiabortion zealots. It's not perfect by any means, but the abortion communities are putting abortion seekers first. Historically, that's how abortions have been performed for thousands of years, and even as the methods and medications may change, centering us—people who have abortions—must be at the core.

While many of these methods involving pills are innovative and creative, they cannot be the sole solution. Abortions must be available throughout pregnancy, at any time and for any reason, anywhere. We cannot create solutions prioritizing people who can or want to use pills. People who need abortions should not be limited by the availability of a method or forced to travel because the abortion method they need is not available. As we envision our future where abortion is liberated, it must include innovation for all people who have abortions, no matter where they are in their pregnancy or life journey. Anything less is not liberation.

"Jane . . . never left me": The Black Women of Jane

When Marie Leaner had her abortion, years after helping dozens of women have theirs when it was a crime, she was surprised at how simple it was. "It was no big story," the eighty-year-old described over the phone from her nursing home on the North Side of Chicago.

"We'd made such a big deal out of it. I mean, we all had made such a big deal out of what the abortion experience was," she admitted. "But my experience was fine. I wouldn't say it was a pleasant experience, but I certainly didn't have a traumatic experience."

When Marie had her abortion in the 1980s, it was legal and her insurance covered it—just as abortion activists across the country had envisioned for decades.

"This is what we fought for. But I wasn't thinking about that. I was thinking, *I'm having somebody go inside my body and mess around.* So I was really present to that experience," Marie shared with us. "I'd been sexually molested when I was a kid. And so all those traumas took precedence over any other concerns."

We've always known that Black and Brown women were part of the historic abortion liberation movement prior to the national legalization of the procedure in 1973, because people of color have always supported one another during pregnancies, including having and providing abortions. But most—let's be real, nearly *all*—of the books, films, and news articles about the early reproductive rights movement erase Black and Brown organizers. This erasure has led many to believe that people of color haven't played a critical role in the fight for abortion access in the United States, which could not be further from the truth. From the time Indigenous people lived free from white imperialism and before Black people were brought to the shores of the United States, we have had abortions and done what was needed to survive and care for our kin. Our abortion advocacy can't be disconnected from this country's struggle for Indigenous and Black liberation.

Marie was one of two Black women we interviewed who volunteered with the underground Abortion Counseling Service of the Chicago Women's Liberation Union, known then as "The Service" or "Jane" but colloquially known today as the "Jane Collective" (even though, as we learned from the women of Jane, they were never a collective because there was a hierarchy and they never called themselves "The Janes"). The other, Sakinah Shannon Ahad, had not shared her full story publicly about her time working in Jane, while Marie, who was interviewed in a feature-length documentary (called *The Janes*) about The Service, had not shared her abortion story until we interviewed her. We believe their presence made a major difference for the women of color in particular who sought abortions through The Service. We know from our own experiences that being in the presence of other Black women in an otherwise white-dominated space or risky situation can put us at ease, because often we only have each other. We share their stories not only to write them back into the annals of abortion history, but also to show how women of color have always been part of the movement for abortion liberation. To overlook our contributions is to tell incomplete stories and to prevent other people of color from seeing themselves in this work, when we have been here all along.

We felt instantly at ease when speaking with Marie and Sakinah. They felt like the abortion grandmothers we always knew existed, despite being overlooked in reporting of that era. When we first spoke to Marie by phone, in February 2022, the stories poured out, her Midwestern accent soothing us for hours. She often apologized for forgetting certain dates or specific details because she's living with multiple sclerosis and long COVID has impacted her memory. She took long pauses as she audibly shifted in her wheelchair and began to open up more about her own abortion and her multidecade work on behalf of Black women and families in Chicago.

Marie is an elder Black woman from the South Side of Chicago through and through—checking Renee's potential familial ties as we got acquainted, she requested we drop the "Miss Marie" formalities and just call her "Marie" because that was the name she chose for herself, by herself, in kindergarten, despite her mother's confusion. (She is still very proud of this first act of defiance and independence, more than seventy-five years later!)

As a volunteer with the Abortion Counseling Service around 1970, Marie offered her three-bedroom apartment as one of the locations where abortions were performed on people who would not otherwise have been able to terminate their pregnancies, which The Service referred to as "The Place." Marie could not recall roughly how many people would pass through her apartment in any given week, but in the 1995 book *The Story of Jane: The Legendary Underground Feminist Abortion Service*, author and former Jane member Laura Kaplan notes that over the group's four-year history they performed an estimated eleven thousand abortions. (In the book, Marie is identified as "Ricky," which is similar to her nickname, Mickey.)

Growing up, Marie pressured her parents to send her to Catholic school to expose her to different communities and faiths. She credits the Girl Scouts for putting her on the path of social justice organizing from a young age. At Loyola University, she organized a walkout after she was unable to use a pool in one of the school's buildings because of her race. The Illinois Club for Catholic Women managed the pool, which was supposed to be open to all the women students at the university. But when Marie swam in it they told her, "We're sorry, but you can't use the pool." So she decided to do something about it.

Rather than allow Marie and other Black students to swim, the women's club shut the pool down—a common response to integration across the country. Marie was eventually kicked out of Loyola because of her activism. But being kicked out hasn't stopped her from returning to the university. In 2021, Loyola students invited her to speak to the local Sunrise Movement chapter, which called on the university to sever its relationship with the fossil fuel industry and the Chicago Police Department.

During the 1960s, Marie, who was in her twenties, organized alongside the Black Panther Party, although she never officially joined as a rank-and-file member because she smelled the stench of misogyny in her first interview. "The Panthers were on the rise. Angela Davis, Huey Newton, Bobby Seale—those were people that I had to look at because these were influencers in our community. And since I was someone who was into social movements, I was certainly paying attention to them," Marie recalled. "I went back and forth about whether it was someplace where I wanted to put my energies. Their militancy was attractive, and I very much wanted to participate in that." On the other hand, there were aspects that Marie didn't like. In 2022, when Marie was interviewed by WBEZ, a local Chicago public radio station, she said, "Our men were getting beat up and shot up [by police, but] there was nothing about how the men were treating the women." Marie told us that she often felt objectified and devalued when organizing in Black spaces because of the extremely sexist and derogatory things men said to her and other Black women, with one man demanding that for her to be a real radical she would need to "suck their dicks." "A lot of people say that a number of women in the Panther Party were very much willing to subjugate themselves to the men in the party," she contended to us. There were exceptions, she explained, and when she was offered an "Angela Davis in Chicago"–like role, she was told that she wouldn't be subjected to overt sexism and sexualization in that position. But she decided not to join because "you can't make exceptions like that." The pain of that moment is still very real for Marie, as a Black woman and survivor, especially in a space supposedly dedicated to the uplift and liberation of *all* Black people.

"I certainly supported . . . and admired the work," Marie continued.

"I never condemned them or anything like that publicly. But I was honest when people asked me what I thought about them."

Marie continued her activism in many different spaces. Inspired by the first Black Supreme Court justice, Thurgood Marshall, Marie enrolled in law school classes but dropped out after a while because of the cost and lack of family encouragement. That didn't stop her from educating others about the law and how it could be used to change Black women's lives. Marie worked for a union of clerical workers and organized with Albert Raby, a civil rights activist, for reform within Chicago Public Schools. She encouraged her neighbors to create tenant unions in their public housing to ensure everyone had safe access to housing and fair rents.

"It's all about Black liberation," Marie explained about the relationship between these different overlapping issues. "I mean, my grandparents emigrated from Madison, Georgia, to Chicago, [as part of the] Great Migration. You know, that's Black liberation. I don't see these things as separate from each other. They're all the same to me."

Prior to her volunteer stint with The Service, Marie participated in a smaller group within the Chicago Women's Liberation Union called HERS (Health Evaluation and Referral Service), which advocated for more access to sexual and reproductive health information in communities. She hung around but was weary of getting involved. "It was the old Black-white tension," Marie said of her hesitancy and the lack of trust she felt around white women. She questioned what oppression they actually faced given that their whiteness gave them latitude not extended to people of color. "White women and Black women thought of themselves as not having mutual interests, and there was a dividing line. And if you were Black, why were you joining an organization of women who didn't seem friendly enough to invite you?"

When Marie became involved with The Service, she was already supporting pregnant Black women. She ran a teen mothers program and a youth program on Chicago's West Side, supporting them through healthy pregnancies and as they raised their children, in addition to advocating for incarcerated people. She understood how important it was for a pregnant person to have someone in their corner during the decision-making process, and she knew how few Black women and girls were championed by society or loved ones.

As Marie recalled, she knew Jody Parsons, one of the cofounders of the Abortion Counseling Service, through the Chicago Women's Liberation Union. Many of the early women of Jane were organizers with the group and were also involved in antiwar protests, voters' rights actions, and the civil rights movement. Marie was hesitant to join because, she said, "It was sort of like, that was a white woman's thing. It wasn't something that pertained to me as a woman of color, and so I was somewhat snobbish about the whole thing." Marie debated whether she should join or not and based her decision-making on her feminist values and the lessons of sisterhood she had learned from Girl Scouts, even though she dealt with racism there as well. "A Girl Scout is a friend to all and sister to every other Girl Scout."

As Marie described it, she didn't *join* Jane through an orientation or volunteer recruitment; it was "a set of groups within a group," part of her Chicago Women's Liberation Union work, and she just became part of it. She never attended a formal Jane meeting. Marie explained that she and some feminist organizing friends were hanging out one afternoon when a Jane member mentioned a need for more houses to perform abortions in. Marie offered her three-bedroom apartment, which she shared with friends in a building where everyone was a radical political activist in one way or another. "We were sort of hippies, you know? That was the conventional way you lived."

At the time, she was being monitored by the FBI and the Red Squad, which was an arm of the Chicago Police Department that surveilled Chicago organizers, including labor organizers, immigrant organizers, socialists, communists, and racial justice organizers. Marie was under suspicion of being "subversive" for her involvement with Weather Underground, a left-wing political organization that sought to overthrow US imperialism. The Weathermen, as they were called, began as a faction of the Students for a Democratic Society, and they demonstrated against and occasionally bombed US capitalist institutions to protest racist, imperialist wars.

Marie was always afraid that her loved ones, especially her mother and grandmother, would be policed for her organizing efforts. Her suspicions were well-founded: once her grandmother was called into a police department, interviewed, and told about what the police had on Marie via their phone taps and monitoring of her. Marie said the incident took a toll on their relationship and on her grandmother's relationship with Marie's mother. But Marie was still very committed to liberation, organizing for the most marginalized of communities no matter what. Marie saw abortion as connected to her advocacy work for prisoners. "I didn't see any difference between working for the rights of women in prison and working for our rights on the outside when we're in this kind of prison."

* * *

The Abortion Counseling Service operated between 1969 and 1973 in Chicago and provided roughly three thousand abortions annually. It comprised an ever-changing number of 20 to 25 volunteers and some paid workers. Originally The Service counseled and connected people seeking abortions with "doctors" who could do the procedures, but later the women of Jane learned to do the procedures themselves to ensure that members could care for more women for free and provide holistic, educational experiences.

The vision of the Abortion Counseling Service was simple: to ensure all who needed abortions were able to get them safely and affordably and hopefully learn a little something about their bodies along the way. Some of the women of Jane were inspired to get involved because of their own experiences, either mistreatment during their abortions or what they witnessed when supporting a friend seeking care.

People found Jane through word of mouth or flyers on street lamps, college bulletin boards, and referrals from religious leaders and sympathetic medical providers who wouldn't offer abortion services in their own clinics. "Pregnant? Call Jane," flyers read. Those in need of Jane's services called the phone number listed on the flyer, and, in the early days, Jane would answer to hear the callers' stories and assess whether or not they could be helped. Later, Jane purchased an answering machine, and callers would leave a message explaining their situation in hopes that a stranger would call back.

When a Jane called back, volunteers would listen to their clients thoughtfully and assess what support they needed—never pushing abortion or any option on a woman. The women who called Jane were encouraged to talk about all of their pregnancy experiences, and in turn, The Service educated women about their bodies and the abortion procedure itself. The women Jane cared for were fully involved in their abortions.

As Ruth Surgal, a former Jane who provided abortions, explained in a 1999 interview, "It was one of the things we talked about a lot, that we were not doing something *to* this woman, we were doing something *with* this woman and she was as much a part of it and part of the process as we were." That feeling is still very much with the former Jane members when they talk about their work today. Laura told us, "This was a process. This was an experience that you went through, not in a place you went to or something that was done to you."

Because of the care and attention the members of Jane placed on the experience, no one who received an abortion through The Service died from their abortion. This fact is pretty remarkable considering that women who sought abortions at that time were being abused by chauvinist providers and were dying by suicide and unsafe abortions. Others experienced sexual assault and financial extortion, being charged well over $1,000 for care. The women had very few options, and abortion specialists—particularly those of color—faced criminal sanctions for providing safe procedures to their clients. Jane sought to offer a service that protected everyone involved.

A pamphlet distributed by the Abortion Counseling Service detailed what an abortion is; what services they offered; what someone having an abortion could expect before, during, and after the procedure; terms of the loan fund to help people afford their abortions; and information about the efforts to end the societal abortion stigma that impacts all of us. "If you are interested in giving your energy and time to help bring about a better life for yourself and your daughters and sons, get in touch with Jane," it read.

Generally, to become a member of Jane, you had to know a member of Jane. Recruits were brought in by an already vetted and trusted

Jane member, were vetted themselves, and then attended training to get started. We spoke with Judith Arcana, who was a member of Jane between fall 1970 and fall 1972. She said that newbies were often assigned the tasks of "Call Back Janes," which meant they listened to the answering machine messages or called women back: *Hi. This is Jane from the Abortion Counseling Service of the Chicago Women's Liberation Union.* "Call Back Janes" took notes on index cards denoting how far along in their pregnancy the callers were, how many previous pregnancies they had had, how much they could afford, and what callers needed. Those index cards were passed around during weekly meetings, where the members determined who they could work with.

"Big Janes" focused on coordination and administration work: scheduling appointments and apartment locations; organizing materials; and taking care of the finances. The work was grueling, as the need always grew, and Jane burned through volunteers as a result. Many of the middle-class white women who volunteered with Jane had families to care for while taking on their two-week shifts on the callback line. The Front, the home where clients first arrived for their appointments, was often full of children playing and entertaining themselves while their mothers volunteered as Jane members or had abortions through Jane. The Front was so vibrant that some clients and neighbors assumed the Jane women were running a day care center.

Although the Abortion Counseling Service advertised all over Chicago to reach as many people who needed care as possible, not everyone could be helped. The high operational costs meant that only women who could pay at least the bare minimum could have one of the appointments the providers offered, while wealthier women who could pay more subsidized the overall costs. Some who were unable to contribute were, unfortunately, turned away. The "counselees" of Jane, as they were called, represented all ages, races, ethnicities, classes, and communities of Chicago and beyond. However, when New York legalized abortion in 1970, women who could afford to do so, usually those who were white and wealthier, began to fly there for legal care. It cost them about $300 round trip, including the abortion at $125. This reduced some of Jane's subsidies. As one woman recalled in Leslie J. Reagan's seminal book *When Abortion Was a Crime:*

Women, Medicine, and Law in the United States, 1867–1973, after New York's law changed "about 70 percent were women of color[,] most of whom were living on subsistence wage or welfare with very poor health care." Judith estimates that "anything from 60 to 80 percent of women who came to us were Black women and girls."

Initially, the founders of Jane partnered with several doctors to provide safe procedures. Most were trusted gynecologists, including a Black chiropractor and civil rights movement leader Dr. T. R. M. Howard. All of the providers were men, and a few weren't medical providers. But by 1970, they worked with only one "doctor," Dr. Kaplan. "Mike" was a white man trained as a union construction tuck-pointer who learned how to do abortions from a real surgeon in Detroit. To this day, Mike maintains that he never told the women he was a doctor despite having them call him by a code name, Dr. Kaplan. "I thought he was a blow-hard," Marie said in the documentary *The Janes*. "I thought he was a con man and a wise guy, and I thought he had a heart."

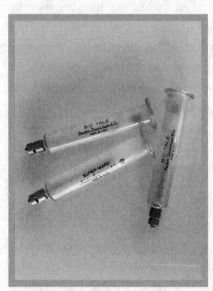

Photograph by Renee Bracey Sherman of original syringes used by members of Jane, the Abortion Counseling Service. *Courtesy of the Martha Scott Papers regarding Jane: The Abortion Counseling Service, Sophia Smith Collection, Smith College, Northampton, Massachusetts.*

At first Mike charged around $500 per abortion, but once New York legalized the procedure and the abortion and a flight totaled $300, he recognized that he no longer had a monopoly on pricing. The lead members of Jane worked with him to lower his price to $350 per abortion with $25 added on to the loan fund Jane started.

The work had to be done in secret, because abortion was a crime in most states, and police had been known to raid clinics and arrest abortion providers. Jane paid high rates to the providers for each procedure, and they in turn paid off the Chicago Police Department, as well as Chicago mobsters and others to keep them from ratting Jane out. As was mentioned in *The Janes*, at one point the Abortion Counseling Service was servicing the wives and mistresses of Chicago politicians and police at their behest. *Everyone*, it seems, found value in the services of Jane.

As Laura wrote in her book, *The Story of Jane*, two women in Jane, "Jenny" and "Miriam" (actually Jody and Ruth) persuaded the "doctor" to allow more Jane members to help. Several of the more experienced women of Jane attended the abortions Mike performed and held the hands of the counselees. They wanted more Jane members to take on this role; however, Mike resisted at first, as he was very slow to relinquish control. The members of Jane realized that Mike may not have been a doctor and there was a slight uproar about the safety and transparency for the women who called Jane and were told they were being seen by a doctor. Judith, however, begged the question, "Well, if he can do it and he's not a doctor, then we can do it, too."

The idea was brushed aside, as women were rarely allowed roles like that at the time and there was a taboo surrounding touching the abortion tools. But eventually, at the insistence of Mike, Jody reluctantly learned how to provide abortions. They started by injecting shots of Ergotrate, a drug thought to cause contractions and control heavy vaginal bleeding, to the counselees. The women were gradually performing more and more aspects of the procedure until they realized they could do all of the abortions themselves. Mike did the abortions for the money and if the money was going to be less, he saw it as beneficial to train the members of Jane and get out. Eventually, Jane operated the entire service.

* * *

When Sakinah Shannon Ahad found Jane in 1971, it was for her childhood friend who needed an abortion. Sakinah, who went by Paulette Myers at that time, started asking around to find a safe abortion provider. "I put feelers out. I got a call from one of my other friends who had went to Jane and she says, *Listen, I went to the women there, it's wonderful. I only paid $50.*" Sakinah had heard about women using coat hangers to cause abortions and bleeding out in Cook County Hospital's septic ward because of an infection, so naturally she was scared for her friend. Sakinah double-checked whether calling Jane was actually what she wanted to do, and her friend replied that she trusted Sakinah with her life and her babies' lives, so she trusted her on this. But Sakinah, who is Black, had one warning to pass on: "I want you to know it's Caucasian women."

Sakinah remembers the day vividly. She wore a colorful top with bell-bottom pants and her hair picked out to a perfect 'fro. The two women took the "L" train from the North Side to The Front on the South Side of Chicago, in Hyde Park, that The Service was using for the day. By this time, the women in Jane were doing the entire process, including the abortions, themselves. Diane, a Jane member, was doing counseling, and she sat with Sakinah and her friend to explain the entire process—the medicines they would use, the tools, who else would be there—and then prepped her friend to travel to The Place for her procedure with the other women having abortions that day. Sakinah waited at The Front with the other women, biding her time. A young woman of color, about sixteen or seventeen years old, approached her, Sakinah said, asking, "What do I do next?" Sakinah was confused. She wasn't a Jane, yet because she was a Black woman, the young girl assumed she could help her. Sakinah explained that she was there with a friend and what the next steps were to check in with the Jane members. This moment was also an epiphany for Sakinah: "My mind is racing, still thinking about my girlfriend, praying that she's safe, but also thinking, *Really? Are we [Black women] at this point in our life that we're not involved?*"

A bit later, Sakinah's friend returned from her appointment, unpregnant, sharing how wonderful and nice the experience was. Sakinah was moved. The young woman who needed help navigating the experience stuck with her. "I had it set in my mind and said, *Okay, I know this is illegal, but it's something that I needed. I felt a responsibility to my sisters. I felt this deep debt and responsibility.*" So she went up to Diane and asked what she could do to help. Diane promised to call her soon.

As for Marie, Jane was not Sakinah's first encounter with community organizing. She had been organizing in the late 1960s for Black liberation and idolized the teachings of Malcolm X. While her older sister Lois was involved with the Congress of Racial Equality (CORE) and attended the March on Washington, and her cousin organized with the Student Nonviolent Coordinating Committee (SNCC), Sakinah was less interested in nonviolent protest. "You guys are talking about turning the other cheek, but that's not gonna work for me," she explained. She also considered spaces such as Operation Breadbasket, an organization led by Reverend Jesse L. Jackson, appointed by Dr. Martin Luther King Jr. to encourage companies operating in Black communities to hire Black people, elevate Black-owned businesses, and boycott companies and stores that wouldn't hire Black workers. Sakinah attended a few of the trainings for Operation Breadbasket and SNCC, but a shift occurred in her, and she felt that many of the white and Black attendees were too interested in dating rather than the pro-Black organizing and community she was looking for. Malcolm X's call for militancy—*by any means necessary*—was a draw for her. Although she appreciated Dr. King's work, she believed the moment needed to be met with action *and* aggressiveness. "I felt like things moved with Malcolm X. He gave people of color a sense of power that we never had before."

Sakinah felt at home with the Black Panthers, volunteering at a church that hosted the Panther breakfasts. Jane was another opportunity to do something radical for Black women because of whom she could reach, even though it meant organizing with all white women. "Men have always been at the forefront, no matter if you're Black, white, or whatever," she started as we asked how she went from Black militancy to organizing with white women. "What I saw was women in power. Women taking chances . . . I'm talking about a chance that you might spend years in jail. This was way more than a felony . . . and I'm a risk-taker."

Before Jane had a chance to call Sakinah back to volunteer, she called first, a month later: she was pregnant. She was in her late twenties, attending college, mothering three kids, and contemplating divorce. "When I found out I was pregnant, I thought, *Oh, shit*. I was happy that I knew about Jane, but I was sad at the same time. But it gave me an option." So she called Jane to set up an appointment for herself.

Once again Sakinah took the "L" train to The Front of the day on the South Side, did her intake, and rode in the car with a Jane member to The Place for her procedure. She was only slightly nervous because her friend had already told her what to expect, and because the Jane in the car was so kind, so Sakinah felt aware of her surroundings. "There was a sense of companionship and sincerity," she explained. Yet, when the abortion-providing Jane examined her, she realized that Sakinah was over twelve weeks, so the usual dilation and curettage procedure couldn't be used. The abortion-providing Jane could only induce an abortion by breaking the amniotic sac and causing a miscarriage. Sakinah's procedure couldn't be finished that day, and it could take a day or two before the pregnancy passed. Sakinah had to wait until all of the other women had their procedures before she could go back to The Front, because everyone traveled back and forth together. It was then that her curiosity piqued. "Do you mind if I sit in on one of these procedures?" she asked. The Jane member who was providing the abortions didn't have a problem with Sakinah sitting in, so long as it was okay with the counselees. "I ended up holding legs and talking to the women, hand-holding," Sakinah told us, her voice cracking as the emotion overflowed. Barely two days later, she passed the pregnancy, completing the abortion at home by herself. "After that, I called Jane back and said, *I'm ready. What is the initiation?*"

Sakinah went to her first meeting a few weeks later and instantly bonded with the other Jane women—her sisters, as she calls them. Sakinah described everyone as white and dressed very bohemian, and she walked in full of color, platform shoes, bell-bottoms, big hair, and big earrings to match. "I fit in only because of my big mouth," she said. "I added some color to the joint. Not necessarily just my skin color but in general. And we all had big mouths, so we really connected." It's true. Sakinah is so very fly. On the day Renee met her in person, she floated in the café using a bedazzled cane, wearing huge pearls on her ears and draped around her neck. Her rosy cheeks and bright smile lit up the room. It was clear how she easily put counselees at ease.

Although she never met Sakinah during her time in The Service, Marie, too, volunteered as a Jane because she knew that her presence as a dark-skinned Black woman would make other women of color comfortable. As a former counselor, Marie knew people tended to trust her, and she deeply believed that because women of color were disproportionately in need of abortion care, The Service should reflect the identities of the people they served. "What it should look like, is that on either end, either the abortion provider or the abortion provider group should be inclusive," she explained. "That means you can have a variety of people participating, you can't just have white people, because it won't work."

Marie thought carefully about what it must feel like for people seeking abortions to walk into the homes of some of the Jane members, especially those who were wealthier and white. "I know, especially poor people and people who don't have means, they're going to be afraid of going to somebody's house. . . . I don't know that people realize how afraid people who have been marginalized and isolated from other groups are to be near those groups of [wealthy, white] people." Marie wanted people to feel safe during their abortions, so she offered all that she could, including her home and her warm smile. She knew a wider range of communities, especially Black women, would feel comfortable in her home—but, she laughed as she continued, "I didn't know whether white women would be." Sakinah doesn't remember the look or feel of the homes that she went to the day of her friend's or her own procedure. It wasn't overly crowded, she recalls; she noted only a handful of other Black women, several teenagers sitting in the living room, which made her feel comforted.

For a variety of reasons, including the privileges afforded to them because of their race and class, white women largely ran Jane, particularly Jewish women. Judith, who is white, explained that she recalled Jane did no outreach to recruit women of color to participate because specific racial justice recruitment wasn't a focus and they were already stretched to capacity fulfilling the abortions. She was clear that it was wrong not to reach out to women of color. Laura, who is also white, agreed that more could have been done. Sakinah, however, said that her experience was a very positive sisterhood. Marie described her kinship with the white women as supportive, and even when they disagreed at times, including about racial issues, they worked through it because they had a job to do. "[The other Jane members] had a deep, abiding passion for this work of reproductive freedom. That is what kept me coming back," Marie said.

* * *

The Abortion Counseling Service wasn't the only group connecting people to abortions. Activists in other parts of the United States—and the world—were training one another to perform safe abortion procedures so some who needed care could receive free or low-cost abortions. One such activist was Patricia Maginnis, a white medical laboratory technician based in San Francisco who founded the Society for Humane Abortions, originally named the Citizens Committee for Humane Abortion Laws, in 1962.

Maginnis was a true radical; she called for the full abolition of all abortion criminalization laws and spoke out against the power the medical industry held over women who needed abortions through medical review boards and reform efforts. She believed deeply that people having abortions should hold all of the power. The former Jane members we spoke with said they hadn't known about Maginnis or anyone else who was doing this work at the same time.

Determined not to repeat the experience of traveling to Mexico for care as she had done for her first abortion, Maginnis began holding informational trainings explaining how people could perform their own abortions or offer terminations to others in their own communities. And she did this openly, even deliberately giving event flyers to the police in hopes they would arrest her so she could challenge California's abortion bans. "I am attempting to show women an alternative to knitting needles, coat hangers, and household cleaning agents," Maginnis told a gaggle of reporters outside of San Francisco's Federal Building in 1966. Maginnis later performed her second and third abortions on her own and encouraged others to do the same on their own or abroad in Japan, Mexico, and Sweden. She critiqued reform efforts that worked with hospitals and physicians because she believed they would simply share power with the state and choose which circumstances merited care while denying abortions to others.

As states began legalizing "therapeutic" abortions, which are abortions permitted in certain health circumstances, the power was given to doctors to determine who was a sympathetic and worthy candidate for an abortion. Activists such as Maginnis considered this a reform effort that would allow providers to control who was able to access an abortion based on whether the providers agreed with the reason. She and other activists believed people who needed abortions should have that power themselves. For its part, Jane created a health care network outside of the inefficient and ineffective medical system that empowered their clients and centered their needs and care. After the *Roe* decision, many of the Jane members felt the medical establishment could never replace the experience they offered through The Service. As Laura Kaplan wrote in *The Story of Jane*, although *Roe v. Wade* demonstrated society's changing attitudes toward abortion, it also "undermined the grassroots efforts to confront the social authority that had kept women in their place and the medical profession firmly in control of women's health."

Some organizations responded by helping to connect people seeking abortions to clinics or trusted providers in their community, ensuring the people who wanted abortions maintained control of the decision of if, when, and how to have children. One such organization was the Clergy Consultation Service on Abortion, which operated a network throughout the country that offered information and resources for people who needed abortions and referred people who needed abortions to providers and clinics in states where it was legal and to trusted networks like Jane in places where it wasn't. Founded in 1967 by twenty-one Protestant ministers and Jewish rabbis, the Clergy Consultation Service on Abortion operated networks, eventually creating chapters in thirty-eight states with more than three thousand clergy members and helping an estimated 250,000 people seek abortions by 1973. When abortion became legal in New York in 1970, the local chapter opened an abortion clinic charging only $25 for those who couldn't afford care.

Hundreds of thousands of women received referrals for abortion care through the Clergy Consultation Service on Abortion, including sisters (and Renee's aunts) Shelley and Diane Sherman. Shelley and Diane had a nomadic childhood, moving from place to place—Michigan, Minnesota, Massachusetts, Tennessee, Texas, and Pennsylvania, to name a few. Their mother, Sulochana, was biracial, Indian and Swedish, and their father, Hal, was white and Jewish. Sulochana and Hal were politically progressive, raising their five children somewhat in the Unitarian Church and often criticizing the anti-feminist teachings of the Catholic Church that had a hold on some of the communities they lived in. Shelley, the eldest, said their family did not talk about sex or abortion much, but Sulochana did air her beliefs that Catholic women were being forced into having children and that the Church was determining family sizes no matter what people wanted for themselves. But, despite their family's progressive values, the parents supported neither Shelley nor Diane when the sisters needed abortions.

Over the Christmas holiday in 1969, Diane's boyfriend hitchhiked from Texas to Pennsylvania, and although she'd never tried any drugs or alcohol before, they tripped on acid and had sex. A few weeks later, seventeen-year-old Diane went to the doctor to figure out why she had been passing out. The doctor pulled Diane aside, wondering if she could be pregnant. When she said that she had missed periods and might be, he asked what she would do. She stated that she would seek an abortion. The doctor ordered some more tests and said he'd let her know the results. But rather than confirming the pregnancy with Diane, the doctor called her parents and told them that she was pregnant.

"Oh, God, Mom woke me up. I was asleep. She's yelling at me and . . . she and Dad were sitting in the living room and told me they'd gotten a call from the doctor," she told us. "I was pregnant. What the hell was I going to do?"

According to the sisters and Shelley's diligently kept journals from the time, on February 16, 1970, Shelley received a letter from Diane, who suspected she was pregnant. The day after receiving the letter, Shelley asked around for resources at her school, Macalester College, and even took out a $200 loan from the financial aid office. Eventually, Shelley connected with a chaplain named Al. (Given the time period, we assume this was some connection to the Clergy Consultation Service on Abortion.) Al walked Shelley through the process of talking to their parents and getting them on board with an abortion. He said he could set up an abortion in Chicago, which would cost $400, so long as Diane was under ten weeks. (Diane was seven weeks pregnant at the time.)

By the time Shelley called home with this information, their parents were already in the process of arranging an abortion for Diane in Colorado, which had recently liberalized its abortion laws to allow for therapeutic abortions in the case of health indications. Their mother's sister worked in the psychiatry field and knew about the recent changes. Diane would have to see two psychiatrists, who would each write a letter to a board of three men, who, based on what they read in the letters, would decide whether Diane could have the abortion.

Within days her parents concocted a story about her being ill and needing to travel for treatment, then she was shipped out to her aunt in Denver for two weeks and in front of the two psychiatrists for evaluation. The first psychiatrist was horrible, Diane told us. "He basically called me a slut." He asked why Diane didn't want to continue the pregnancy, and she said because she was seventeen and didn't want to be with her boyfriend anymore. "Oh, so you just sleep with anybody? So having sex was just nothing?" he retorted. Diane was so upset she threw up on her way out of the office. The second psychiatrist was much nicer and asked her about her life, what was going on, and how she was holding up being so far away from home. "He was very soft, very sweet, very supportive," she said. Diane told him her situation, how she would be shamed for becoming pregnant in their small town, how it would impact her brothers, and she said that if she couldn't end the pregnancy, she would attempt suicide. Diane wasn't sure how she knew this, but she knew she needed to explain that she would attempt suicide if she was forced to continue the pregnancy. Thankfully, her abortion request was granted, and on Monday, March 23, 1970, she was admitted to the hospital's maternity ward for the procedure.

She didn't remember much from the procedure because she had sedation, but she does remember staying overnight and the awkwardness of sharing a room with an older married woman who was being treated for a miscarriage. The next day, she went back to her aunt's home; her aunt had been very supportive and protective, especially after the shaming encounter with the first psychiatrist. Diane rested for a few days and then flew to Minnesota to visit with her sister.

Two years later, Shelley was able to hide her pregnancy and first abortion from her parents because, unlike Diane, she was in Minnesota, not living at home. Shelley, who was twenty-one, had been traveling throughout India for a language program and reconnecting with relatives during the summer of 1971 and into the following year before returning to Minnesota. Shelley told Renee the story over tea one afternoon fifty years, almost to the day, after her first abortion. "I did get involved with my pottery teacher who was just really good looking . . . and I was never looking for a commitment but I really liked him." She wasn't using birth control (or maybe was using "some weird method"); her mother had warned her against using the pill because breast cancer ran in the family. It wasn't an opposition to contraception, just concern about the pill, but this complicated Shelley's choices, given the few options available at the time. "Honestly, we had sex, and I just knew I was pregnant. I was in the middle of a cycle, I was tracking cycles. And in fact, I was."

Shelley knew immediately that she didn't want to continue the pregnancy, but abortion was illegal in Minnesota. "Having a baby was not in my plans. That was not even a consideration. I did feel sad like, this is a baby that I am saying no to, but I was just like, no way." She wanted an abortion but didn't have the money to pay for it because she was working a temp job. The procedure, she recalls, cost about $100 or $150 on top of the flight to New York. She didn't have the cash, so she borrowed it from a former roommate, who had taken her on a European vacation freshman year and was the only wealthy person Shelley knew.

Shelley went to Family Tree Clinic, a local independent health center (which still operates today and provides abortions in Minneapolis) that had connections in New York. Her flight was arranged near the Thanksgiving holiday weekend. She was given a phone number to call once she landed in New York City. It was all a bit nerve-racking. She traveled alone, without luggage, and when she arrived no one was there to pick her up. She called a few times, but only got the answering machine. She didn't know what to do: get to the abortion herself or find something to do with her time until her flight home that evening. She traveled into the city and walked around Central Park for hours on an empty stomach because she didn't have extra cash for food, and she couldn't eat before the procedure. She used the little change she had to call the clinic and Family Tree Clinic repeatedly throughout the day. Finally, several hours later, a receptionist answered. She met up with the driver who took her to the clinic. The clinic was plain and nondescript; there weren't very many people there because it was late in the day. "The procedure itself, I don't remember very much about it. It was easy. It wasn't painful." She said she does remember that everyone was very, very nice. "I remember this big feeling of relief and thankful that abortion was legal in New York."

After her procedure, Shelley rushed to the airport and boarded her flight, relieved that it was all over. Once the plane landed, she was greeted by her pottery teacher and friends, who welcomed her home with hugs.

* * *

By the end of 1970, the Abortion Counseling Service was a self-sustaining operation. With the fake Dr. Kaplan (aka Mike the construction tuck-pointer) gone, Jane members were providing abortions on their own and could change their financial operations. In the new formation, Jane offered abortions to as many people as possible, accepting full payment— which was $100, although the average paid about $40 or $50—from those who had it to cover supplies, advertising, and other operational costs, while offering free abortions to those who did not have the cash. Jane rarely counted the money from each client. During the counseling, Sakinah would say, "Whatever you have is fine, but if you can give more, that helps the organization for somebody who doesn't have [the money]."

At the weekly meetings, index cards—each one listing a woman's name, her situation, and how much she could pay—circulated around the room, and the Big Janes took cards and passed them out to counselors who coordinated the abortion work days. "Lots of women lied to us about how pregnant they were because they were afraid," Laura told us. "They lied about medical issues they had, they lied about whatever they thought they needed to lie to us about in order for us not to say no." If the women were far enough along that the Jane members were concerned they would give birth to a live fetus, Ruth, one of the Jane members, who was also a parent to a child with a disability, was called upon to talk to the woman about her options and the significant risks to the fetus should they perform the abortion and to suggest that she probably should continue that pregnancy.

When we asked Laura and Judith, both were clear that The Service didn't really have a process for selecting people for abortions depending on how far along they were. At the weekly meetings, the question would arise, and someone might say that The Service shouldn't do abortions after fifteen weeks or so, for example, and someone else would disagree. But the conversations always ended with an agreement to disagree and to not impose a gestational limit. The members of Jane who did the abortions decided for themselves individually how far along in a pregnancy they felt comfortable doing the procedure, so each had her own limit.

Judith was taught by Mike and the experienced women of Jane how to perform an abortion after 12 weeks, by rupturing the amniotic sac and expelling all the fluid. This was a relatively simple procedure to learn but was tough on the woman having the abortion because she had to go through labor and deliver a dead fetus. This method, however, allowed the members of Jane to provide abortions well into the second trimester.

When we asked Judith and Laura what The Service did with the pregnancy tissue, particularly when they had done a later abortion procedure, they were both very open. For early procedures, they would flush the pregnancy tissue down a toilet. For later procedures, Laura said they used to wrap up the pregnancy tissue, including the fetus, in newspaper and plastic bags and place the bags in public trash cans in parks in the middle of the night, hoping that no one would go through the trash before it was picked up the next day. "It was part of the deal for us. It's what we took on to do," Laura said bluntly. "If we were going to engage miscarriages, we were going to have to deal with the consequences. And that was just the way it was. That was just reality." Judith said that although she doesn't know what the other Jane members did, she had an easy option near her home. Her apartment was located across the street from Grant Hospital, and she could see their medical disposal bins from her windows. "I would wrap up anything I needed to dispose of, and because I was so angry with the medical industry anyway, I thought, *They're dealing with appropriate medical refuse. Here's appropriate medical refuse that they refuse to touch.* And I took it there and stowed it with their stuff."

As Laura explained to us, some women completed the abortion with a member of Jane at The Place while others did so at home, as Sakinah did. And some were encouraged to go to the hospital and act as if they didn't know what was going on, because the hospital assumed women knew nothing about their bodies. At the hospital, the providers would complete the abortion, thinking they were treating a miscarriage or still-birth. This is still a suggested method in places where abortion care is illegal today.

* * *

Sakinah was in Jane for a year and a half. She started out as a "Call Back Jane," doing intake for the women who wanted abortions and passing it on for scheduling. Though she eventually began to learn how to do the procedures, when she did assist she usually only injected the Ergotrate into the patient and held their hands to make them feel comforted. After a while she needed more income, given that it cost money for her to travel to The Front and she was raising three children while un-sure of the future of her marriage. She enjoyed counseling women in person before they headed to The Place, so the other Jane members suggested she counsel from her South Side home. When her home be-came one of The Fronts, she had no commute so it helped alleviate some of the money she spent traveling, but it brought a whole new set of risks because women were coming to her home—which she shared with her three kids, her husband, and the young adult daughter of a family friend. We asked Sakinah whether there were any risks she refused to take, and, without missing a beat, she said, "None."

Sakinah's home was full of people seeking abortions three days a week. They'd take the elevator to the tenth floor of her high-rise build-ing and enter her three-bedroom apartment through the front door and hallway; the kitchen on the left could be closed off by accordion doors. The bedrooms were on the right side, the living room was at the end of the hall, and the children had adequate space in their bedrooms where they could do their homework.

Providing abortion support quickly became a family affair. On a few occasions, Sakinah arrived at the house a little late, so her eldest daughter, who was ten years old, passed out vanilla sandwich cookies and strawberry- and grape-flavored Kool-Aid and picked up the intake index cards with the names and details from the women sitting in a circle. "These are women that are in need of help," she explained to her daughter, "and Mommy's there for them."

Sakinah said she never felt any fear about running the Abortion Counseling Service out of her home until one day when she was returning to her apartment with her daughter in tow. As they walked in the building, they were followed by another woman.

"Hi," the woman said. Sakinah replied hello politely and kept walking.

"You don't remember me, do you?" the woman inquired. Sakinah wasn't going to admit to anything and said she didn't.

"I owe you. I owe Jane."

"Oh, okay, that's fine," Sakinah replied as her daughter looked up at her, recognizing the name Jane as part of her mother's work.

"What apartment are you in?" the woman asked. She had been in Sakinah's home but couldn't remember which apartment it was.

Sakinah relaxed a little and said it was the tenth floor. The woman acknowledged this and then left. "She slid under the door every week $10 until she paid $100," Sakinah said. (Yes, we were crying at this part of the interview, too.) "Those are the kind of women that we were dealing with. We were trusting them, and they were trusting us. She didn't have to do that, but her gratitude was so intense that she wanted to."

During the counseling, the women Sakinah cared for would sit on the deep, dark-purple shag couch or the matching shag rug. The whole living room was decorated in shades of purple, with small black block tables, rattan throne chairs, and a Parsons table behind the couch. A record player sat in the corner with the family's vinyl collection and a stacked television set. "We were young and enjoying ourselves. Life was still going on." Sakinah knew that her home made the women feel welcome.

Despite the process becoming a routine, each day and each person was different, and Sakinah gave the women individualized care for their needs at the moment. "It might be 10, 20, 30, 40 women depending on the day that you service," Sakinah explained. "Your main thing was the connection . . . the humanity, woman to woman, holding hands, talking, taking their minds away from the process itself, just encouraging, *You made a decision, it's okay, we're going to get through this*, those kinds of answers." No one was questioning a person's decision—solely sharing information so the women coming through The Service would know what to expect and could calm their anxieties.

Because Sakinah opened her home to them, the women had the opportunity to meet other women—particularly women of color—who were having abortions and sharing their stories. It was a risk, because the procedure was illegal; nevertheless, Sakinah said they built camaraderie sitting together on the floor learning about one another. "To me, it was a healing process for them; we talked about the procedure, but we talked about everything before the process, from family relationships to social injustices." Sakinah saw firsthand how the ability to sit together and just be open and honest had an impact on women's abortion experiences. Although the work was rewarding, Sakinah's biggest fear was what would happen to her children if she was arrested. Still, she maintains that there were no risks in Jane that she wouldn't take.

Because Jane rotated through a series of volunteer homes and apartments, the mornings started early, explained Laura. They would begin the day cleaning the apartments to make sure they were ready for clients. "Oh my God, some of these people hadn't dusted their spice racks in years!" she recalled Diane telling her. We suggested it was because they were busy organizing, and she quipped, "Or smoking a joint. I mean, come on. We weren't organizing 24/7, that's for sure!"

The Service was always looking for cars to borrow for rides and apartments with at least two bedrooms to use for procedures. Sometimes they'd use a place once and never get to use it again because of blood and other cleanup issues. Laura said that a few times a woman would get blood on her shirt during the procedure, so a Jane would go into a closet and pull out a shirt for her to wear home, but then the shirt's owner would come home and notice the missing article of clothing, and The Service wouldn't be invited back. "Marie was extremely generous with her place. We used her apartment a lot," Laura said.

When it was Marie's week, for example, the members of Jane prepared the bedroom in the back of Marie's third-floor apartment with medical supplies and plastic sheets on the bed where the abortion would be performed. Then, on service days, sometimes Marie greeted people who came for abortions, escorted in small groups by the driver Jane from The Front to The Place.

After they arrived for their abortions, the women would be welcomed into the living room and offered tea or coffee while they waited. The wait usually lasted 20 to 30 minutes, depending on how the prior appointment went. The living room, by Marie's account, was simple yet cozy, furnished with a couch, upholstered chairs, and an antique rocking chair in the corner that Marie and her roommate had picked up at the secondhand store around the corner from their apartment building. "It was college dorm stuff. Nothing fancy," she said. Though Marie and the other Jane members always removed identifying information and pictures from view to keep everyone safe, the women's thoughts and worries could get lost in wood carvings and posters by Black women artists hanging on the walls.

In between appointments, Marie would hang out in her dining room, working on her political activism, reading books, or making calls, and she would periodically check on the women waiting in the living room to make sure they were comfortable. When it was each woman's turn, Marie remembers that she or another Jane would accompany the woman down the apartment hallway past the other larger bedrooms, bathrooms, and kitchen to the smallest bedroom in the back. The smallest bedroom was vacant after one of Marie's roommates moved out, so it was turned into a procedure room.

The one-window room was bright and sunny. It was small but big enough to hold everyone necessary for the operations: the client, a Jane member trained to perform the abortion, and another Jane member who assisted. There was a small, sink-only powder room separating the procedure bedroom from the bedroom on the other side. "People who were involved in The Service could wash their hands after each operation," Marie said. The bed would be prepped with clean sheets covered by a plastic sheet for easy cleanup, and the speculum, syringe, gynecological tools, and medication would be laid out and ready. The Jane trained to provide abortions would start out supporting the woman having the abortion by holding her hand, while the assistant Jane began the injections. Once the injections were finished, they would switch roles and the abortion-providing Jane would do the procedure. This was to upend the medical industry's tradition of the trained doctor leading everything.

Like Sakinah, Marie never conducted any abortion procedures herself, but she was in the room to comfort nervous women. Marie remembered one woman of color who cried that she was scared, questioning whether she should proceed with the abortion because she didn't know anyone involved. "I would not let anything happen to you if you were my daughter," Marie whispered calmly as she took the young woman's hand in her own. "I am treating you like my sister. Nothing is going to happen to you. You're going to be fine." Marie said her words calmed the woman; she stopped crying and was able to relax for the procedure. "I would have said smoke a joint," Marie laughed, "but that would not have been approved of, so I didn't say it."

* * *

The Service was eventually raided on the afternoon of May 3, 1972. Marie was going about her day as usual, listening to Chicago's local NPR station on the radio, when the newscaster announced that The Place and then The Front had been raided and seven Jane members, all white women, had been taken into custody by a homicide unit of the Chicago Police Department. The police were acting on a tip from a woman who wanted to stop her sister-in-law from seeking an abortion. The police followed a Jane who was driving that day from The Front to The Place a few times and later went inside the building behind her. They approached that Jane, later identified as Judith Arcana, standing by the elevator doors with a young woman who had just had an abortion and asked her whether she was having an abortion. The young woman started crying and confessed. Judith told the young woman that she had done nothing wrong and did not need to speak to the police. They were both taken into custody. Judith was not able to warn the other Jane members inside the apartment that police were in the hallway. The police knocked on the door and Madeleine, a Jane member, opened it thinking it was someone they were expecting. When they saw it was the police the other members of Jane gathered as many people as they could in the bedroom until the police breached the room.

When the police entered the apartment, they were reportedly confused, unable to find the abortion doctor, because there were no men in the apartment. Records found at the apartment indicated that twenty-three women had received abortions that day, three women were in recovery from their procedures, and another seven were waiting at The Front for their procedures. The truth is, we don't know how many people received abortions that day, because the arrested Jane members ripped up their intake notecards and ate the pieces of paper in transit to the police station to protect the identities of the women they served, and they flushed their money to prevent the police from taking it. Diane, Judith, Madeleine, and four other Jane members, Abby, Martha, Sheila, and Susan, were held in jail overnight, and each was charged with eleven counts of conspiracy to commit abortion, with possible sentences totaling up to 110 years in prison. Judith Arcana, who had a six-month-old baby, was still nursing and had to expel her breast milk in the dirty sink in the jail. Because of her status, she was released first. The rest of the "Abortion 7" were released the following morning on $2,500 bond—nearly $19,000 in 2024 dollars.

A *Chicago Tribune* article describing the arrests led with the fact that the women were feminists active in women's liberation groups and provided the care because "feminists believe women have the right to control their own bodies, which includes the right to abortion." A radical opinion, for sure!

When we asked Laura what was most important about that moment, she was defiant and clear: it was that every single woman who went to Jane to receive an abortion that day still got her abortion. The Abortion Counseling Service raised money to purchase flights and bus tickets for the women with appointments they could not keep to go to Washington, DC, and New York City, where abortion was legal, and the providers there were willing to do the women's abortions free of charge. "We didn't abandon the women who were relying on us," Laura said.

But the Abortion Counseling Service didn't end with the arrests. Word of the arrests spread quickly. Some Jane members left, but others doubled down on their work as the calls for services increased. Sakinah learned about the arrests from Laura and went back to work counseling. Sakinah said those who stayed changed their daily routes, assumed that they were always being followed, and made changes to tighten up security measures.

After the arrests, Sakinah was not deterred from her work at Jane. She knew the police could come for her if they wanted to, but that risk did not stop her from doing the work that needed to be done. "I was concerned about the seven women who were arrested, but I still felt the need and the responsibility to continue doing what I was doing." Marie, however, was convinced that the police would come after her for weeks and months, because she assumed the police knew her house was in the rotation. As it turned out, the police knew next to nothing, and higher-up officers were surprised that there was even an investigation, as they had not been interested in taking down The Service. Still, Marie kept a low profile while going about her daily life, worried about being approached by police but also trusting that none of the Jane members would ever tell who else was involved—no matter what. In return, she knew she needed to get the Jane women legal support, and fast.

"I needed to get to work to get a lawyer there to deal with the situation," Marie explained. "I could imagine they were scared and that we needed somebody there to represent them, to tell them what to do and what not to do. So that's what I needed to be concerned about."

Marie used her connections and charm to convince Jo-Anne Wolfson, a flamboyant white woman and lawyer who had defended members of the Black Panther Party, to represent the Jane members in court. In the documentary *The Janes*, Judith describes Wolfson as a very tanned white woman who came to court to defend them dressed in canary-yellow pants and a canary-yellow sleeveless sweater with a canary-yellow patent leather briefcase and silver bangles.

At first, Wolfson refused to take the case. "She really didn't want to do it," Marie told us, because Wolfson hated hippies. "And I was like, Jo-Anne, you know they can't go in there with men representing them. Come on. They took all these risks. You got to do this. And she goes, *I can't. They don't wear deodorant, they wear these Birkenstock shoes, they sit on the floor and eat their granola, they don't sit in chairs*, and blah, blah, blah." But Marie was persistent in asking Wolfson to defend her friends and stressed the importance of the case. "They have children just like you. You know? How is this gonna look?" Eventually, Wolfson agreed to take on the case.

According to Laura, Wolfson learned that the police raid was a bit of a mistake and that if certain higher-ups in the Chicago Police Department hadn't been on vacation that week it probably would have never happened. Knowing this made people feel more comfortable coming back to The Service. Wolfson's legal strategy of stalling and delaying, with motion after motion, drew the case out for months until the Supreme Court had time to rule in the *Roe v. Wade* case legalizing abortion nationwide, eventually making the Jane members' murder charges pointless. The case was ultimately dropped.

As legal proceedings stalled, Marie's involvement with Jane fizzled out. "After the arrest, the whole network was exposed, and I didn't want to go to jail. I was out at that point."

Judith told us that she continued "Jane-ing" for several months after the arrest but eventually discontinued her involvement due to her responsibilities with her new baby and transitioning family. Laura said that several of the arrested Jane members came right back to work and that Madeleine said "she wasn't going to have the Chicago police tell her what to do with her life." The women who needed The Service weren't deterred, either. Laura said there were thirty spots open each week and more than three hundred women waiting for those spots. Laura's main message to anyone who learns about the Abortion Counseling Service is clear: change happens when ordinary people work together, which is why it's important not to make them into heroes.

The Service operated until the spring of 1973, after *Roe* legalized abortion and the first clinics opened in Chicago. Laura said that some felt that shuttering The Service was a mistake and they should have kept it open, but she believed that the goddess was on their side—and they were all extremely burned out.

Even though Marie was never arrested for her work with Jane, she was frightened of that possibility, particularly because she was already under government surveillance. Her volunteer prison work teaching women about the law and filing grievances also allowed Marie to see the horrible conditions facing people who were incarcerated. "I was in a group called the Women's Prison Project that was also a part of the Chicago Women's Liberation Union. We went to Dwight [Correctional Center] every other Saturday for five years. And I was scared to death. I mean, I had nightmares that at some point I was going to be trying to leave the prison, and . . . I wouldn't be able to get out because they would lock me in. I mean, those were weird-ass times back then." Despite her nightmares, Marie continued to advocate for the liberation of the most marginalized people in our society. When we asked her to reflect on her activism days, she bluntly declared, "Well, they're still occurring."

After the case against the members of Jane was dismissed, many women in Jane were ready to get back to their lives, especially now that they weren't facing one hundred years in prison. Sakinah, on the other hand, knew that she wanted to continue providing abortions. After abortion was legalized in January 1973, she and the other Jane members were recruited to work at a new abortion clinic, Midwest Population Center. "I wasn't ready to let it go, and now I have an income that's legally on the books." It was located on Michigan Avenue near a millionaire's club, and the goal was to reach all kinds of people; the clinic provided not just abortions but also gay health workshops, vasectomies, and gender identity counseling. She took many of the skills that she learned from The Service over to the clinic to create a cohesive system of care for the patients there.

After leaving that clinic, Sakinah went to the Michigan Avenue Medical Center and worked there for ten years, doing everything from counseling to marketing. Eventually, the owner of that clinic died, and

Sakinah moved on to another clinic, a small facility owned by a doctor with one procedure table and a few recovery chairs. After an abortion provider was murdered in California, the doctor's wife pressured him to stop providing abortions, and Sakinah took over the clinic at Eighty-Third Street and Dante Avenue. She opened more procedure and recovery rooms, hired a few doctors as contractors, and began providing abortions full-time.

The work wasn't without its challenges: white antiabortion protesters followed her to her new clinic, shouting her name over the bullhorn. She wasn't deterred. Like the living room counseling Sakinah did with Jane, this was a family affair. Her eldest and youngest daughters ran several of the clinics and Sakinah's son did the marketing. Once Sakinah's youngest daughter went outside to the white protesters to tell them to leave. "After they saw we had security, they never did show up again."

Over the years, Sakinah and her family ran several abortion clinics on the South Side of Chicago, with so many different doctors of color (African American, Nigerian, Asian, and Latinx) that, she said, they were acknowledged by the National Abortion Federation and the Chicago Abortion Fund, two abortion advocacy groups, for having a diversified clinic. The doctors, including at one point a Black woman, would make the rounds between the abortion clinics and the other ob-gyn patients they had to see. Sometimes, after all of the clinic rotations, they'd stay as late as eleven o'clock at night to make sure that every patient was seen.

SABS Medical Group, named with the initials of Sakinah and her three children, was "a caring confidential service for women," as listed on ads all over newspapers and bus benches in Chicago and northern Indiana. Sakinah's clinics thrived for another ten years, but the stresses of the crack epidemic in the 1980s that shook Black communities across the country, including Chicago's South Side, changed things for her. "Grandmothers were coming in with the grandchildren they were raising who were 13 or 14 and were pregnant," she explained. "In counseling the whole initiative was that you were never there to make a decision [for someone]. You could be 12 and make a decision to have a termination of pregnancy. I found myself not necessarily pushing, but feeling so terrible for the grandmother that was raising [the children] because either the dad was in jail or the mother was on crack or vice versa." Sakinah felt for the young girls, most of whom said that they wanted a baby because they wanted someone to love, but she had a hard time separating her feeling for the girls from her empathy for the grandmothers who were already struggling to raise the girls themselves. As she burned out, she realized she could no longer offer the abortion services in the way she wanted to. Sakinah closed the clinics and switched fields to care for people experiencing addiction.

Of all the women who volunteered with Jane, Sakinah says she was the only one who stayed in abortion provision over the long term, for nearly two decades. "I was just following the process of Jane because it never left me," Sakinah told us. This isn't surprising because, as we explain in the next chapter, people of color have been providing care in our communities for thousands of years—and will continue to do so.

"We took the tea": Abortion Methods Throughout History

In the Supreme Court's *Dobbs* ruling, Justice Samuel Alito declared, "The Court finds that the right to abortion is not deeply rooted in the Nation's history and tradition." Obviously, we disagree with the justice's position on abortion overall, but when it comes to the history of this nation, he is just plain wrong. Abortion is deeply rooted in every tradition and culture. People around the world have had abortions for thousands of years—including during the colonization and establishment of the United States.

In 1785, before he became president, slave owner, alleged rapist, and deadbeat daddy Thomas Jefferson published *Notes on the State of Virginia*, a book detailing his thoughts on slavery; the government; white supremacy; his dislike of miscegenation, aka the mixing of the races (unironically); and life in Virginia. In a section describing his observations of Native Americans, he noted that their culture's gender views were more egalitarian than white people's, because both men and women partook in labor; for this reason, Jefferson labeled Native men as weaker. Aside from his casual racism, he clearly noted that abortion was the reason that women were able to engage in these duties:

The women very frequently attending the men in their parties of war and of hunting, child-bearing becomes extremely inconvenient to them. It is said, therefore, that they have learned the practice of procuring abortion by the use of some vegetable; and that it even extends to prevent conception for a considerable time after.

Jefferson went on to compare the procreation of Native Americans to animals in nature, explaining that based on the "certain bounds, those of labor and of voluntary abortion," they tended to have abortions and to have fewer children than white families.

This wasn't his only commentary on abortion; in 1792, his daughter provided one.

In September of that year, twenty-year-old Martha Jefferson Randolph, Jefferson's eldest daughter, traveled to the Bizarre Plantation to visit her eighteen-year-old cousin Nancy, who had recently moved to live with her cousin and brother-in-law, Richard, and his wife. When Martha visited, she realized that Nancy had been impregnated by Richard. In 1793, Richard stood trial for "feloniously murdering a child delivered of the body of Nancy Randolph"; Nancy was tried as well, but subsequently acquitted. Martha testified in court that she gave Nancy gum guaiacum, an abortifacient originating in the Caribbean, "to produce an abortion." Two weeks after Nancy took the plant she became ill and was found with bloodied sheets; evidence suggests she was in the second trimester. An enslaved Black man later found the deceased fetus on a shingle pile, but he was not allowed to testify because he was enslaved. After learning of the situation through rumors and the newspaper, on April 28, 1793, Jefferson wrote to his daughter that he believed there was only one guilty person in the case, alluding that it wasn't Nancy. Jefferson then offered words of kindness to his daughter, the abortion provider:

Never throw off the best affections of nature in the moment when they become most precious to their object; nor fear to extend your hand to save another, lest you should sink yourself. You are on firm ground: your kindnesses will help her and count in your own favor also. I shall be made very happy if you are the instruments not only of supporting the spirits of your afflicted friend under the weight bearing on them, but of preserving her in the peace and love of her friends.

It would seem that a Founding Father was aware of his daughter's medical knowledge and approved of her providing the herb for the abortion.

Even the inventor, creator of the post office, and Founding Father Benjamin Franklin knew that abortion was an essential part of family planning and that white American colonists would need to know its recipe. In 1748, Franklin reprinted a British textbook on arithmetic, writing, and other important tasks for the American colonies. *The American Instructor, or Young Man's Best Companion* omitted several portions of the British edition, which were replaced with more relevant and updated information, such as excerpts from a Virginia physician's medical pamphlet from 1734, which contained a recipe for an abortion. In the section titled "Suppression of the Courses," the text notes a "common Complaint among un-marry'd Women" and how to solve this "Misfortune." The weeks-long recipe calls for a purge with highland flagg (also known as bellyache root), a morning drink of pennyroyal water, and a mix of mustard, nutmeg, horseradish, and garden cress turned into a beer or tea. The recipe concludes with a reminder to be "cautious of taking Opiates too often" and to abstain from sex: "nor must they long for pretty Fellows, or any other Trash whatsoever." (Yes, it actually says "Trash.") Similarly, an 1813 brochure entitled "The Indian Doctor's Dispensary" has dozens of common Native American recipes, including a recipe for curing obstructed menses, and it sold widely.

We aren't new to this, Justice Alito. We're true to this.

Abortions are one of the oldest medical interventions—they're a normal way to end a pregnancy. Herbal concoctions and teas are listed alongside other medicines and treatments in ancient texts and scriptures. People have been having abortions for as long as people have been getting pregnant, and people have been getting pregnant for as long as people have been having sex. What has changed over time is how abortions have been used by people in power as a tool for reproductive oppression rather than continuing to be seen as a critical part of family planning.

Medical, religious, and historical texts—including the Jewish Talmud, Egyptian papyrus documents, and Chinese and Arabic medical writings—illustrate the use of abortifacients and the prevalence of abortion in ancient times. These texts also describe the situations in which different abortifacients were used and their efficacy. The Sushruta Samhita, a Hindu medical and surgical text in Sanskrit that is believed to have been written before 600 BCE, identified abortion as an option to preserve the pregnant person's life during labor. Some of the earliest texts also listed emmenagogues (a term for herbs that stimulate menstruation) commonly used by people with late or irregular menstruation or to terminate a pregnancy, and which are still used by communities all around the world today. Abortion was so common that it's mentioned in the Sumerian Code of Ur-Nammu (c. 2100–2050 BCE), Middle Assyrian Law, and the Code of Hammurabi from 1750 BCE.

The earliest recorded pregnancy test is an Egyptian method detailed in the Brugsch (Berlin) Papyrus, which in 1827 was "acquired" for the Berlin Museum, where it remains today. The medical document, written around 1350 BCE, detailed a method of pregnancy testing using barley and wheat; a pregnant person would urinate on the seeds, and if they sprouted, a pregnancy was detected, with wheat indicating a female fetus and barley indicating a male fetus. The test was re-created by scientists in 1963 and found to be about 70 percent accurate in detecting a pregnancy, but not so accurate in revealing the fetus's sex.

During more modern times and with medical advancement, the "you're pregnant" notification started coming earlier and earlier, and the authority of determining pregnancy and abortion options shifted from the pregnant person to medical providers and the government. What was often referred to as an abortion was usually what we would consider a *later abortion*, as it would take place during the second or third trimester, post-quickening. Anything prior to the second trimester was generally considered to be simply bringing a body back to its norm. As we mentioned, many religions throughout history have believed in some form of delayed ensoulment, meaning that the pregnancy did not have a soul or was not a being until after the first 40–120 days. In addition, these ancient documents have been open to interpretations and translations, which can vary by region, by time period, and, most important, by the intent and eye of the reader.

The point is that in most ancient societies, abortion, as we think of it, was normalized: it was about bringing down menstruation to set a body back to a regular, timely cycle. Many of the herbs and methods were used to unblock menses, rather than to terminate a pregnancy. Usually, weeks or months of missed menses would bring a suspicion of pregnancy, as would the moment of quickening, when the pregnant person could feel fetal movement. Prior to the invention of the pregnancy test, pregnant people were the sole and trusted authority on whether they were pregnant or not. It's important to know that even in ancient societies where ending a pregnancy was not fully culturally supported, abortion was practiced and generally not punished as a crime.

THE *OLD* OLD WAY

Some of the earliest recognized medical records of abortion are believed to have been made by Emperor Shen Nung in Chinese mythology. He recorded an abortion recipe using mercury 4,600 years ago. In the sixteenth century, Confucian physician and medical scholar Li Shizhen compiled the Bencao Gangmu (Great Pharmacopoeia), a medical text detailing Chinese medical traditions over time—and to this day, it's a standard reference. The text outlined seventy-two "drugs for dropping the living fetus," including safflower, sloughed snakeskin, leeches, lizard, crab's claws, musk, and mercury. The best herb, it noted, was a beautiful yet toxic purple plant called aconite, also known as wolfsbane. Acupuncture and massage methods were also recommended to terminate a pregnancy.

It's important to remember that the borders of Greece, Italy, and other places today were not the same as they were back then (and neither were their racial and ethnic categories); empires sprawled across parts of present-day Europe, Southwest and West Asia, and North Africa.

In some communities, information can be sparse because traditional methods were documented and passed down orally, rather than preserved in a written record. Some of the oldest medical information we have is found in Egyptian medical papyruses, which described recipes for abortion concoctions. According to John M. Riddle's *Contraception and Abortion from the Ancient World to the Renaissance*, the Kahun Medical Papyrus of 1850 BCE listed recipes that called for making a paste with crocodile feces or sprinkling honey in the vagina to prevent pregnancy. Other recipes of the time suggest inserting elephant feces into the vagina in the form of a suppository (also called a pessary). The Egyptian god Seth was depicted as trying to harm Isis during her pregnancy, and historians have noted that uterine amulets from ancient Egypt depict Seth to denote miscarriage or abortion.

Another Egyptian medical document, the Ebers Papyrus, listed prescriptions of herbal medicine from around 1550–1500 BCE. The papyrus, named for George Ebers, the German novelist who purchased the document in 1873, contained more contraception and abortion methods. Translations of the papyrus chronicle recipes for "loosening" or "stripping off" the fetus: for example, "one part fresh beans and one part honey are pressed together and drunk for one day," and "one part onion, beer, fresh beans one part, bird dung one part: made into a suppository and placed in her vagina." The Ebers Papyrus showed that Egyptians used many different ingredients, such as juniper, celery seed, leeks, Egyptian salts, resin, pottery, and teas. We know many were effective because, as demographers and anthropologists have found, birth rates could not be low solely as a result of outsize factors such as war, scarce food supplies, or catastrophic illness or economic decline, but because of intuitive interventions.

One of the most famous ancient Greek physicians was Hippocrates of Kos. You've probably heard of him referred to as "the father of medicine," one of the great thinkers of ancient Greece, or even as the creator of the Hippocratic oath. The modern version of the Hippocratic oath is taken by physicians today. Hippocrates lived circa 460–375 BCE and is credited as the first physician to decouple medicine and religion, identifying that diseases were caused by environmental factors and viruses, rather than punishment by the gods. As such, his writing was highly revered and is held in high esteem now. He documented many herbs and insect recipes that served as emmenagogues, including cantharidin beetles, cuttlefish eggs, squirting cucumber, head of boiled garlic as a suppository, and misy, which is a copper compound and used as a contraceptive today—copper IUD, anyone?

Side note about Hippocrates and abortion: Antiabortion advocates have argued that doctors should not provide abortions because they violate the Hippocratic oath to do no harm and operate by ethical standards when caring for patients. Those who are antiabortion have taken this interpretation—particularly the call for a doctor to protect the life of the patient—and the phrase in the oath "not give a woman a pessary to cause abortion" to mean that doctors cannot provide abortion care. In late 2022, one antiabortion lobbying group calling itself the Alliance for Hippocratic Medicine sued the FDA to take mifepristone (the first pill in one medication abortion regimen) off the market. The group chose that name to claim that medicine, in its ancient written form, was antiabortion, and thus abortion should be illegal, inaccessible, and not practiced now.

Why would a man who didn't believe in offering suppositories to cause abortions document and share tons of recipes explaining how to create suppositories to cause abortions? This is a problem with translation, according to John M. Riddle's book *Eve's Herbs: A History of Contraception and Abortion in the West*, and in fact, Hippocrates might not have actually written the oath. Riddle argues that the phrase *pesson phthorion*, which means "abortive pessary" (suppository), was changed during the Roman Empire era in the Latin copies of the oath to address *all* abortions, rather than a specific method. In addition, physicians hold that the Hippocratic oath deters them from not assisting a patient with physician-assisted dying, but suicide was acceptable in Greek and Roman culture. Riddle also explains that some scholars concluded that the writers of the oath applied it to Hippocrates, although they may not have been within his lineage of teaching. Riddle writes, "The popular understanding of the text, not the oath's original text, became the historically influential factor." This is why it's always important to fact-check people in power.

Aside from his recipes recommending contraception and abortifacients, we think Hippocrates was pretty clear on the subject in his treatise "On Generation": "When a woman has intercourse, if she is not going to conceive, then it is her practice to expel the sperm from both partners whenever she wishes to do so." And that's that on that.

Although Hippocrates's writings have been mistranslated, misunderstood, misappropriated, and downright mangled, the reality is that he wrote about the abortion methods of his time, and others wrote about them as well. These recipes were two of many found in Hippocrates's De mulierum affectibus *(Diseases of Women). As fascinating as they are, we do not recommend using these recipes.*

Ecbolic (Abortive) Suppository

Egyptian salt
Mouse dung
Wild colocynth

Pour in a fourth-part honey, boiled to a half.

Take a drachma of resin and put into the honey and mouse dung, grind all together well. Make suppositories and insert in the uterus, until the proper time.

Another Abortifacient

Shake her under the armpits and give her to a drink [sic] the petals of the chaste tree in wine, or grind an obol of Cretan dittany, or a handful of spikenard in leek juice with a large shell of oil of bitter almonds.

In some cases, ancient Greek and Roman writers documented their own methods as well as methods they learned as they met and traded with foreign medical providers and botanists in the course of their travels.

Over time, different methods were continuously used, and others were discarded as new ones were learned and shared. For example, savin, also known as juniper, was one of the most commonly used herbs to procure an abortion. The Ebers Papyrus described Egyptian uses of juniper mixed with pine resin, which could be made into a suppository to cause an abortion. In the thirteenth century, Muslim physician and botanist Ibn al-Baitar wrote that juniper "caus[ed] bloody urine, killing the living embryo, and expelling a dead one." Tribes indigenous to the Great Plains in North America, such as the Crow, used juniper, as well as tansy, horsetail, calamus, and bear root, to cause abortions.

Savin also had some wild (and honestly, kinda accurate) nicknames such as "abortion tree," "tree of life," "lucky herb," "bastard killer," "plant of the damned," *kindermord* (German for "child murder"), and *jungfernpalme* (also German, meaning that a woman using the plant could pass as a virgin at her wedding). Carl Linnaeus, a Swedish botanist who is known for giving Latin names to plants (despite the names already given to them by the communities living among the plants), was a bit of a hater when he stated that those who used juniper were "women who are whores, and though they think their sin is secret, God sees it." Whatever, dude.

Greek physician and botanist Pedanius Dioscorides lived during the first century in the Roman Empire, in present-day Turkey. Dioscorides documented the use of herbs such as cabbage flowers, ivy, myrrh, and pepper, which were taken orally or vaginally as a suppository to prevent or end a pregnancy. Laurel and buttercup had been used in India as abortifacients, which Dioscorides confirmed. In his writing, he noted that parts of the chaste tree, a small shrub with seeds, could be taken orally or made into a tea with pennyroyal and drunk, which "destroys generation as well as provokes menstruation." Myrrh, which grew in East Africa, was popular in ancient times as an abortifacient when combined with other herbs; Muslim physicians preferred it as a contraceptive, and midwives and gynecologists in the Middle Ages made it into abortion pessaries.

Dioscorides included a few wines to cause abortions that were very popular and sold by merchants. Here's one of the recipes:

Abortion Wine

Hellebore, either white hellebore or black hellebore
Squirting cucumber
Scammony

Give the wine mixed with water to a woman who has fasted and vomited, in the amount of eight cups.

According to more modern research we found, the wines would have worked. Honestly, we think abortion medication wine is something we should bring back, although we are definitely not recommending this recipe.

Dioscorides's list of ways to end a pregnancy was extensive, including the use of flowers such as daphne, lily, and iris. He also recommended allowing the fumes of sulfur or onions to enter the vagina to cause an abortion. Some of his recorded methods, such as the use of Queen Anne's lace, rue, and mints including pennyroyal, thyme, and sage, have been the most commonly used, because these plants grow all around the world and have since forever.

While visiting San Basilio de Palenque in 2022, Renee held rue for the first time. San Basilio de Palenque is known as the first free Black town founded by escaped enslaved Black people in Colombia, and one of many *palenques* that Black people set up to escape the horrors and violence of slavery. Pedro, a medicine man who cared for all the people in the community, explained the uses of herbal medicines both as part of their culture and because of the Colombian government's disinvestment from and ignorance about their community. After Pedro spoke of how the community weathered COVID-19 with traditional medicines, declaring that no one died, and the ways that cane could be used to help people who were experiencing infertility, Renee asked him whether they had methods for abortion. He took her around to see several herbs from the dozens of dried plants he had hanging up that he would offer to someone to "interrupt a pregnancy." Pedro explained that *la ruda y albahaca* (rue and basil) could be used in a tea, and the leaves of the totumo bush, a plant he pointed out by the side of the road, could be mixed with milk and other herbs to create a syrup that causes an abortion. Holding abortifacient plants for the first time felt powerful to Renee. It was so different to feel the natural power the Earth creates for us and touch a living connection to history. These oral traditions are alive despite colonizers' attempts to eradicate them—which we'll get to in a minute.

Nevertheless, even in ancient times, abortion stigma existed. Although Dioscorides extensively documented many ways to end a pregnancy with herbs and potions, he did not champion using surgical methods to remove a pregnancy. Soranus, a Greek practitioner and early medical writer on gynecology who lived in Alexandria and Rome during the second century AD, also meticulously recorded various methods for contraception and abortion. Like ancient Indian texts, Soranus's writings recommended,

Renee Bracey Sherman holding abortifacient herbs in San Basilio de Palenque, Colombia.

to end a pregnancy in the first month, pomegranate rinds or physical activities such as horseback riding, exercising, jumping, carrying heavy things, and drinking wine and eating pungent foods before a bath.

One of Soranus's recipes, Cyrenaic juice, called for silphium, a fennel plant that grew on the shores of the Mediterranean Sea in Cyrene, a Greek colony in North Africa, present-day Libya. The plant was used to treat coughs and headaches, to spice up lentil dishes, and, by Roman chefs, to garnish a dish of scalded flamingos. It was so well-known for effectively causing abortions and preventing pregnancy that its cost was driven up. Pliny the Elder, a Roman medical philosopher, recorded the plant as a menstrual regulator and said it was worth more than its weight in silver. The plant was so popular that Cyrene depicted its image on coins, both as the plant itself and as a woman seated pointing to the plant growing at her feet with one hand as the other hand is holding her stomach. Attempts were made to transplant silphium to Greece and Syria, but they were unsuccessful. It went extinct because of its immense popularity and inability to be grown outside of its natural region. Reportedly, the plant became extinct shortly after Soranus's era and, as Pliny the Elder claimed, with Emperor Nero eating the final stalk.

But silphium could be making something of a return. In 2022, *National Geographic* reported that a plant with similar medical potential to the ancient plant was discovered by a researcher in the foothills of Mount Hasan in central Turkey in 1983. He's been researching *Ferula drudeana* ever since. The only other documentation of the plant was in 1909 from a source about 150 miles from the site where the researcher collected his first specimen. Nature always finds a way to provide us what we need.

DOING IT BY HAND

Other early abortion techniques have been found depicted in Cambodian sculptures and Indonesian temples. Cambodian bas-relief carvings that date back to the ninth and twelfth centuries AD show thirty-two representations of Hell (a process of atonement), with women appearing around twenty weeks pregnant piled on one another receiving a belly massage, a manual method of abortion. Similarly, the Indonesian temples of Borobudur and Prambanan, dating back to the eighth and ninth centuries AD, respectively, depict abortion as part of afterlife or underworld scenes. The Pāli Vinaya, a legal text from India dating back to the fifth through first centuries BCE, discusses abortifacients and massage as a method for termination. The text includes the story of a pregnant woman who turns to a monk for an "abortive preparation," and he in turn tells her to "destroy" the fetus using a word that translates to "crush" or "bruise." In late imperial China, physical methods, such as "using the horizontal beating bar . . . to strike [the] abdomen," were also documented. Today, manual methods are sometimes used throughout Southeast Asia, including Myanmar, Thailand, Malaysia, and the Philippines, using fingers, elbows, feet, or rice pestles.

As we mentioned earlier, the Bencao Gangmu, a sixteenth-century medical text, outlined herbs as well as animal parts and minerals that could be used to induce an abortion. Researchers have attempted to identify the documented methods from that time period as well as methods people continue to use or have passed along as traditions and in folklore. Snails, fish, bird eggs, striped blister beetles, donkey meat, and herbs such as ox knee, musk, mercury, camphor, and cinnamon were among the supposed abortifacients, with some deemed dangerous or ineffective. Some Chinese medicine traditionalists and physicians still use smaller doses of ox knee grass to dilate the cervix when administering mifepristone for a medication abortion or when performing a procedural abortion.

When we spoke with actress Dawn-Lyen Gardner she told us her mother's story about her grandmother's abortion in China. She'd heard the story often: Her grandmother used their family's last dollars to purchase a gift for a friend when visiting their home, per the cultural tradition, with the hope of borrowing a larger sum of money from the friend. As a child, Dawn-Lyen's mother remembers the pain and stress on her mother's face when, facing the family's empty funds, her friend denied the loan request after all. A few years ago, Dawn-Lyen asked her mother what the money was for; it was to purchase herbs for a tea that would terminate the pregnancy. Her mother explained that this process was common, and her grandmother shared that she had experienced it twice. Dawn-Lyen realized that her abortion support had been passed down through generations of family decisions, from that of her great-grandmother, grandmother, mother, and her own: "My orientation to this issue is not just American."

Avicenna (Ibn Sīnā in Arabic), a Muslim writer who wrote a very popular and widely circulated medical text, *Canon of Medicine*, documented many herbal methods used in Southwest Asia during the tenth and eleventh centuries. He advised that medical caregivers prescribed abortion and contraception as they were necessary to save the lives of pregnant women. He documented cases in which the patients' health would have been worsened by continuing the pregnancy, as well as ways to prevent pregnancy with herbs and physical methods. Of course, there was the timeless pull-out method—that is, removing the penis from the vagina just before ejaculation—but also a method of jumping: "Jump backward from seven to nine times forcefully so that the sperm may come out . . . or to sneeze." We can assume this method was a little less reliable.

HOW COLONIZATION CHANGED ABORTION

During the Middle Ages, as early Christianity took hold of Europe and the rest of the world, abortion became more stigmatized, and the roles of midwives and women became more subjugated based on Church teachings. The Greek and Roman churches, among others, declared that sex was primarily for procreation, and other engagement constituted a sin. The use of birth control methods was curbed. There were punishments of lashings, determined based on social status and equal to those for stealing livestock. "If a woman gives to another a drink so that it makes an abortion," as seventh-century Bavarian Code noted, "if she is a slave, she should receive two hundred lashes."

Religious practices that diverted people away from Christianity were condemned. Anyone who refused the teachings and doctrines of the Church could be ostracized, at the very least, or burned at the stake. Witches were blamed for everything, from the weather to infertility. Women were accused of casting evil spells that tied an invisible string around a penis so men could not become aroused or be fertile. Pagan women were rejected and denounced for abortion "drugs [that] extinguish the beginning of futureman." Midwives, the most common practitioners of herbalism and pagan traditions, were deemed heretics. Their medicine was called witchcraft, and they were investigated and burned to death. Midwifery was a tradition taught orally through apprenticeship over generations of family; any records or recipes midwives did have were destroyed. An estimated 40,000 to 50,000 witches, women and some men, were executed across Europe to quell the spread of their beliefs and lessons. With their lives went the oral histories, recipes, and lessons for contraceptives and abortions. They didn't get to document their work, which appeared later on, around the seventeenth century, in midwifery books written by men.

Doctors were aware of what herbs and medicines could cause abortions and prevent pregnancies but would sometimes refuse to offer their patients help. Some women attempted abortions by getting an operation to prevent smallpox. There's documentation from as early as the sixteenth century of warnings to apothecaries, doctors, and midwives about unmarried women who sought any medication or cures that could be used as abortifacients. A German doctor reported "tricking" one of his patients who he believed wanted an abortion: instead of giving her care, he gave her a laxative. Many doctors focused on the dangers of abortion, dissuading patients from it after seeing those who had bad outcomes; however, this would have been an inaccurate assumption because patients who had safe outcomes wouldn't have needed to see a doctor after handling the abortion themselves. Other doctors did provide care, using medicines and traditional manual methods such as douches and bloodletting or prescribing intense activity like horseback riding. During the seventeenth century, a French surgeon documented a method used as early as the first century, in which a patient lay on her back with nurses helping to keep the patient's knees on her chest as the fetus was removed by a doctor whose hand was greased with butter, oil, or unsalted lard as he opened the cervix, ruptured the membranes, and removed the fetus and the placenta.

Still, some women of the Middle Ages provided and procured abortions. Saint Hildegard of Bingen (1098–1117) is believed to have been the first German female doctor. She recorded uses of plants gathered from her friends and neighbors, including those that were emmenagogues and abortifacients. Her classification of tansy as an abortifacient is the first known in Western medicine. Between the twelfth and thirteenth centuries in Salerno, Dame Trotula, a female gynecologist, did similar work creating recipes for contraceptives and early abortifacients. Dame Trotula's abortion recommendations included artemisia, hemlock, pennyroyal, savin, and other common herbs of the time, sipped in wines, followed by baths to unplug the menses.

Medieval Midwife's Abortion Recipe

Take half a pound of iris roots and half an ounce of savin, boil them in white wine, and add to half an ounce of powder of ground ivy, 1 ounce of honey; with 1 measure of the boiled proceeds, take 1 drachm of bull's gall, and make a pessary, and give a pill of 2 drachms of myrrh with this liquid. Take 1 ounce each of bishop's weed, wood-ruff, parsley seed, balm, caraway, dill, iris, artemisia, and 3 pounds of white wine. Boil them; then chop up 1 ounce of savory, hyssop, woodruff, and dittany in equal amounts, dilute with 4 drachms of the liquid, etc.

* * *

Eventually, after conquering one another, European empires began looking for new lands to colonize. They sent ships and soldiers to Asia, Africa, and the Americas, to rob, enslave, and murder the vibrant communities of people, plants, and animals who lived there. It is from the writing of the violent colonizers that we have some of the early records of abortifacients used by Indigenous Black and Brown people in these lands. This is yet another painful and unfortunate reminder that white supremacy allows only the records of the oppressors to survive, and their view of history is all that is left for subsequent generations.

An early record of abortion plants used by colonized people was by Maria Sibylla Merian, a German woman who traveled with her daughter to Suriname to illustrate and catalog the exotic flora, caterpillars, butterflies, and moths of South America. Her book, *Metamorphosis insectorum Surinamensium*, published in 1705, contained a passage about the flos pavonis or "peacock flower," explaining how and why the Surinamese people used it:

The Indians, who are not treated well by their Dutch masters, use the seeds [of the peacock flower] to abort their children so that their children will not become slaves like they are. The black slaves from Guinea and Angola have demanded to be well treated, threatening to refuse to have children. In fact, they some-

times take their own lives because they are treated so badly, and because they
believe they will be born again free and living in their own land. They told me
this themselves.

The peacock flower (*Poinciana pulcherrima*) is a dainty red-and-orange flower that grows throughout the Caribbean and South America and was exported by European colonizers. Whereas a French Antilles general used it to cure fever in his troops, Indigenous people and enslaved Black people in Suriname crushed its seeds to terminate a pregnancy; other communities used the flower or even the bark to end theirs. Although Merian was clear about the connection between slavery, abortion, and the reasons the Indigenous Surinamese people used the flower, physician and botanist Sir Hans Sloane, who recorded the plant in Jamaica, seemed unfazed by the violence of slavery. He chronicled the brutality Black enslaved people experienced, such as being burned for attempts to escape, yet refused to treat women he suspected were pregnant and were making themselves sick to cause miscarriages. When they turned to him for care, he refused to give them abortifacients, or he gave them medicines that would not help them. In 1799, a French doctor in Haiti, Michel-Étienne Descourtilz, documented that strong doses of peacock flower could end a pregnancy; he wrote that "ill-intentioned Negresses use it to destroy the fruits of their guilty loves." This wasn't the first documented instance of slut-shaming women who have abortions, but it shows the clear connection between misogynoir and abortion stigma, considering that he refused to even recognize in what situations Black enslaved women were becoming pregnant.

The story of the peacock flower is a fascinating example of the spread and uses of abortifacients throughout the Americas and over thousands of years. According to *Plants and Empire: Colonial Bioprospecting in the Atlantic World*, by Londa Schiebinger, some of the earliest records of the plant are credited to the Saladoid people who, over a century, traveled from Venezuela to the Guianas and then to Grenada and Puerto Rico, where they predated the Taíno, an Indigenous people of the Caribbean and Lesser Antilles, as early as 4000 BCE.

The Taíno lived throughout the islands of the Caribbean and were the first people to encounter Christopher Columbus. They faced extreme genocide and colonial violence, including being attacked by Spanish dogs and suffering mutilation of their extremities, faces, and breasts, according to a Spanish priest who wrote about these events. He also confirmed that the Taíno were known to use peacock flower to cause abortions, alongside suicide and infanticide, as resistance to colonization and enslavement, writing that they "took herbs to abort, so their fruit was expelled stillborn." In 1541, an Italian colonizer traveled to Hispaniola (now Haiti and the Dominican Republic) and documented the Spanish Genocide of the Taíno: "Many, giving up hope, went into the woods and hanged themselves from trees, having first killed their children; the women, with the juices of some plants, interrupted their pregnancies so as not to give birth."

This may sound similar to the stories of enslaved Black people throughout the Americas who chose abortion or infanticide rather than turn their children over to a lifetime of slavery and violence. Historians believe that the Taíno taught enslaved Africans about the benefits of the peacock flower for their own liberation.

Historians have identified that the peacock flower also has roots in Africa, including Saint Jago, Cape Verde, and throughout West Africa, but it's not widely used as an abortifacient. It is possible that kidnapped West Africans brought the flower with them as well or that they recognized it when they arrived in the Caribbean.

Many Africans have used herbal methods to procure abortions as part of birth spacing and pregnancy health. Aside from the ancient Egyptian methods, little is recorded about the abortifacients used in the precolonial era, although some African tribes still use the traditional methods today.

Colonizers in the early twentieth century documented that the Meru (or Amîîrú), a tribe in Kenya, caused abortions by inserting sharp objects in the vagina or brewing drinks made of plant roots and seeds to initiate bleeding, followed up by pressure on the abdomen to pass the pregnancy. The Hausa people in West and Central Africa concocted a drink of indigo and henna, which caused illness and miscarriage. The San, a hunting and foraging tribe in southern Africa, used a combination of plants and physical methods, such as riding a donkey, to "ruin" a pregnancy, as well as for infanticide.

These traditional methods were carried with enslaved Africans to the Americas during the more than 350 years of slavery. The colonizers recorded and monitored the methods that tribes used in order to cast suspicion on those who possessed the tools or herbs that could produce an abortion. The ability to plan and space births was a threat to population growth, leading to a shortage of labor and people to enslave. The colonizers considered many of the reproductive and sexual practices of Africans to be anti-Christian and pagan, and they pushed modesty and puritanism. Colonizers objected to postpartum practices including sexual abstinence, abortion, and prolonged nursing that kept people out of the workforce. This is how the criminalization of abortion lives on today and grows, as the US antiabortion movement sends missionaries to Africa to push evangelical beliefs and policies criminalizing abortion, queer relationships, and transgender identities, with penalties including death.

Despite the current illegality and restrictiveness of abortion in most of Africa's fifty-four countries, people still have abortions using traditional methods and modern medication, or a combination of the two, known as "method shopping." According to a World Health Organization official in 2014, 80 percent of health care in the world is provided by women in their homes through traditional remedies. Those traditional techniques are generally passed through apprenticeship or through family generations, overwhelmingly to daughters. A 2011 study in the *Journal of Ethnopharmacology* found that 45 percent of rural Tanzanian women use plants to induce abortions, and the study counted twenty-one plants known as abortifacients.

We spoke with some activists and providers in Africa about the methods that people use—and several that they themselves used—to self-manage their abortions. Maganya, a Kenyan activist, explained that a mix of leaves and roots of plants, such as cassava, rubia cordifolia, blackjack daisies (*Bidens pilosa*), and *Commelina africana*, are brewed into a tea or chewed to begin the abortion process, and some are inserted in the vagina near the cervix to begin contractions. Some pursue more dangerous methods that shouldn't be used, such as douching with juice or laundry detergent, overdosing on painkillers, or inserting a sharp object or hammer to terminate the pregnancy. Maganya explained that people who want abortions will use as many herbs as they can until the abortion is complete.

Jacqueline, a Black Liberian woman and advocate we spoke with, had three abortions and used a variety of methods: almond tree bark mixed with lemon for her first abortion at sixteen weeks, Prussian blue (a pigment made from oxidized salts) and baking soda for her second at four weeks, and abortion pills for her third at six weeks. These methods, she said, have been passed down for generations within families and communities since at least the 1900s; she learned the methods from her mother, who also had abortions.

Okra might be a familiar vegetable served today, but it was also used as an abortifacient. Originally okra grew in the mountainous region of Eritrea and Ethiopia, but it arrived in the Americas with enslaved Africans in Brazil and Suriname in the mid- to late seventeenth century. Okra can easily be dried and could serve as food on long travels. Edward Bancroft, a US physician and chemist, traveled to Guiana and documented instances of enslaved women causing abortions by "lubricat[ing] the uterine passages by a diet of these pods" and then inducing their abortion with "sensitive plant" or gully root. Both gully root (also known as garlic weed) and sensitive plant (*Mimosa pudica*) were found throughout the Caribbean and Brazil, and could be mixed to cause abortions, according to enslaved Africans and the local Indigenous communities.

The deep-seated misogyny and racism of the white colonizers toward the Black and Indigenous people of the Caribbean clouded their understanding of why people had abortions, resulting in language that has direct ties to stigma hurled at people who have abortions today. White colonizers wrote that Native women used abortion as a way to space their pregnancies to delay childbearing and maintain their "freshness and beauty" and that abortion was common among Africans because they were sexually loose and had sex with white colonizers through prostitution and temporary relationships, ignoring the Africans' status and inability to consent as enslaved people. Sir Hans Sloane wrote that the caraguata-acanga plant "causes abortion in women with child of which Whores being not ignorant make frequent use of it to make away their children."

Once again, some of the nastiest language came from the records of the French doctor Michel-Étienne Descourtilz. He documented herbs such as *Aristolochia bilobata*, which was similar to ancient birthwort and used by Haitians to cause abortions, as well as *trichilie à trois folioles* or the "tree of bad people." He explained that enslaved Caribbeans used the root to end pregnancies and "wreak vengeance" on their enslavers; he went on: "The women who have been miserable enough to resort to its use are punished by it; most of them lose their life in atrocious pain and uterine hemorrhages that nothing can stop." He also confirmed that enslaved Black midwives provided abortions, referring to them as "negresses."

Colonizers also used enslaved women for medical experimentation because English "women of fashion" (read: white) would not consent to the procedures, while enslaved women had no choice. To "bring on the menses" or cause abortions, doctors compressed the crural artery in the thigh with tourniquets to the point that the women revolted in pain and had difficulty breathing. The doctors also experimented using steel filings, hellebore, and electricity.

These narratives formed the understanding in research, medical science, and politics about when and why colonized and enslaved people—namely Black and Brown people—had abortions and have become the myths that are regurgitated to convince us that having an abortion is unnatural, even though abortion is part of our and the rest of the world's history. The ancestors of all of us practiced abortion. All of them faced the decision of if, when, and how to grow their families and sought remedies of the time to prevent and end pregnancies. But this isn't the story we're told. Colonization does that: it gets in our minds and rewrites history to benefit those with all of the power—unless, of course, we tell our stories ourselves.

* * *

Over the past century, researchers have written about and connected with Indigenous people of South America to identify the herbs they use to cause abortions. The Abipón, a precolonial tribe that lives in present-day Paraguay and Argentina, made a drink of mixed fruits, sugar, and the caraguata plant. They also engaged in infanticide as a part of family planning. Another Indigenous tribe, the Chamacoco, drank a decoction of the roots of menispermaceae, a plant with blueberry-like fruits. They also prepared a decoction of *Prosopis ruscifolia Gris* tree leaves in the afternoon, which was drunk the following morning before breakfast and a day of fasting. The Chulupí people, also known as Nivaclé, ate the flowers and green fruit of the shakeshake plant (*Crotalaria incana*) two to three times per day and then expelled the pregnancy by using manual pressure on the stomach.

Nearly six million Africans were trafficked to Brazil for enslavement between 1500 and 1875, so of course many of the traditional methods came with them. Plants such as savin, rue, windflower, and ergot were employed to cause contractions well into the twentieth century, and emmenagogues such as lemon verbena, chamomile, cinnamon, parsley, oil, and jalap were used to unblock the menses. Sharp objects such as crochet needles, whalebones from corsets, and metal hairpins were used to puncture the fetal tissue and force the pregnancy to pass but ran the risk of perforating the uterus as well. There is evidence that all these methods were used throughout the United States. Enslaved people, particularly midwives, used bundles of collard greens or other vegetables to expand the cervical opening and remove a pregnancy. Today, abortion providers use laminaria, small dried seaweed sticks, to absorb the vaginal fluid and expand the opening.

Prior to colonization, Native Americans had abortions as a common practice before their tribe migrated to a new land, because they knew it wasn't the right time or because they didn't have the food supply to care for another child. In the book *Reproduction on the Reservation*, historian Brianna Theobald chronicles the reproductive practices of several Native American tribes, including the Crow (Apsáalooke), a nomadic tribe in the northern Plains. The Crow believed that women had the autonomy to make their own decisions about abortion for their own reasons, which might include the tribe's nomadic way of life, the burden of an additional child, being unmarried, a weak fetus or unhealthy pregnancy, and hard winters leading to a need for food rationing. Calamus, tansy, juniper, horsetail, and bear root were on hand in case of need, but manual methods such as kneading the uterus were also used.

Sometimes an abortion was done by an elder who was the keeper of medicinal knowledge. In some tribes at the time, it wasn't considered an abortion in the way we think of it today; remember, it was just bringing your body back to a state of normal. Access to abortion became essential when the US government forced the Crow and other tribes onto reservations, diminishing their ability to travel with buffalo herds and hunt for food to feed families.

Taté Walker, a queer nonbinary Lakota writer and poet, told us that it is still common for people to use plant medicines to bring back a moon cycle or cause *hoksihiyuyekahiya*, the Lakota word for abortion. Knowledge of plants such as pennyroyal has been passed down for generations in Native American tribes. Although Taté had their abortions in a clinic, they explained that sacred plants such as prairie sage can be used for smudging because it increases blood flow in the body; a small amount brewed in tea can relieve a headache while a massive amount can cause an abortion.

Some Indigenous tribes engage in traditional practices alongside in-clinic abortion procedures. Indigenous Women Rising, an abortion fund based in the Southwest, has offered assistance for Navajo abortion patients who request their pregnancy tissue or fetal remains for burial traditions or need help affording sage for the ceremony.

Rachael Lorenzo, a queer nonbinary Mescalero Apache / Laguna Pueblo / Xicana activist who founded Indigenous Women Rising, said that they didn't have a relationship to traditional methods of abortion until they had their own abortion. There were a few discussions of abortion when they had their puberty ceremony, a two-week process of living in the woods with an elder from whom they learned about plants and Apache traditions. Abortion was always discussed as restarting a period. They learned that their ancestors had abortions for reasons similar to those of the Crow, such as being a nomadic tribe, trying to survive harsh winters, experiencing war, or because hunts weren't successful in bringing back enough food. Abortion was a very practical and pragmatic decision that people made based on what was happening in their lives at different times of the year. And in some tribes, if a woman did not want to have her husband's children, she could have an abortion and send him back to his mother and family. On their Apache side, Rachael said all of this medicinal knowledge would be shared by medicine women and midwives. "That's why we have our puberty ceremony . . . because we know what our bodies do and what they're capable of."

THE MYTH OF MISOPROSTOL ABORTIONS IN BRAZIL

For years, we'd heard the story of the Brazilian activists who realized that misoprostol, an ulcer medication developed in the 1970s as Cytotec, could cause abortions and heralded this use of the medication throughout Brazil and Latin America. But Brazilian activist Sonia Corrêa set the record straight: "I am telling you this story as somebody who was the witness."

For decades, women seeking to end a pregnancy would go to a nurse or midwife who inserted a *sondas*—a rubber tube—or a papaya tree stem into their cervix and injected an acid to cause an abortion. When Sonia needed an abortion in 1971, she did what most women of the era did: she went to a pharmacy and asked for something to help bring down her period. The vendors would set aside medications that were dangerous for pregnant people to use and offered them as options to try. A few of the methods were so toxic that women would bleed out and die in their homes and in hospitals. Unfortunately for Sonia and many women of the era, the recommended medications did not work. She spent a month trying to find an abortion provider because the new police chief, who was antiabortion, decided to stop taking bribes from the providers and wanted to end abortion in the city. Eventually, she traveled a few hours outside Rio de Janeiro to one of the safe providers that wealthy women used. The provider performed Sonia's sixteen-week abortion without anesthesia so she wouldn't be drowsy in case the police came and they had to run. She said that is a common scenario for Brazilians, and it is what turned her into an abortion activist.

In 1986, Brazil approved misoprostol for over-the-counter sale for ulcers. Sonia said that the drugstore vendors would put the suggested drugs to the side, but returning customers would tell the pharmacists that misoprostol worked the best. Word spread fast among the favelas and among low-income women and communities of color in Brazil, as they didn't have the money to visit the network of safe providers, and misoprostol worked better than any of the other medications. The word continued to spread to the point that the Brazilian government enacted policies in 1991 banning the sale of misoprostol, causing the supply of the vital medication to dwindle.

The myth that lionizes the role of activists comes from the game of telephone and a need to tell and retell the story. Sonia considered it critical to tell the true story of how misoprostol came to be known. This knowledge came to us through the ingenuity of the drugstore vendors who recognized its additional uses and the women they recommended it to, who risked their lives to test its consistency and spread the word throughout Brazil. Sonia said feminists did not discover the medication's use and were late to join these efforts.

SELF-MANAGED ABORTIONS CONTINUE

Even though the *Roe v. Wade* decision legalized the provision of in-clinic abortion procedures in 1973, some still sought care in their communities; they did so because they wanted to use traditional methods to feel control over their experience, because they knew how to take the medications on their own, because a trained caregiver could offer them a procedural abortion in the tradition of Jane, or because they simply couldn't afford the cost of care in a clinic. This was Mississippi reproductive justice activist Michelle Colon's abortion experience in 1995.

Michelle, a Black woman, grew up in Chicago and learned everything about her body and the birds and bees from her grandmother: "She was a retired registered nurse and she did not lie to us." Michelle said that her grandmother's desire to tell her children and grandchildren about their bodies stemmed from her experience of being surprised when her vagina started to bleed when no one had told her about her period. Thinking that she should treat the bleeding as she would any other wound, she used the old tradition and put salt on her vagina to clean and treat the "wound." Michelle's grandmother taught Michelle about her body and used herbal medicine for everything, including making her own cough syrup and using tobacco for stings. Although she didn't know this for a fact, Michelle was pretty sure her grandmother offered herbal abortions to the community.

When Michelle was twenty-three, she became pregnant and wanted an abortion but couldn't afford to go to a clinic. Already used to traditional medicine and on the recommendation of classmates, she went to the flea market to pick up some herbs. "They had herbs to make your hair grow. Herbs that make your dick bigger. Herbs supposed to make you lose [weight]. It was just everything." She found a stand that was tended by a Black Caribbean woman offering herbs for fertility; Michelle told her she wanted the opposite. The woman nodded and went to work pulling herbs from glass jars on different shelves and mixing things together in various bags. They included rosemary, either blue or black cohosh, parsley, mugwort, and various green and brown herbs: "It looked like a bunch of weeds when you think about it." The bag of herbs cost $25, which was affordable for Michelle.

When Michelle went home, she boiled some water and started making her tea. A slip of paper she was given instructed her to drink eight ounces of the tea three times a day for a week. But when she tried the tea, she thought it was disgusting and knew she wouldn't be able to do the full regimen. After the second day, she decided to brew the tea in bigger doses, drinking it out of a Big Gulp cup from 7-Eleven, over three days. Soon afterward, she started bleeding as though she had her period, with cramps and passing clots. She knew the tea was working but worried because she didn't know what to expect. After the bleeding didn't stop and she ran out of pads, she decided to go to the hospital, where they evaluated her and finished the procedure with a dilation and curettage. "I don't know how far along I was, but suffice it to say, the tea worked." Now, Michelle knows that she was actually fine and wasn't in any medical danger; she just worried because she hadn't known how much bleeding and cramping to expect. Her abortion was complete, and she was able to move forward with her life.

It wasn't until she became an activist that Michelle learned that what she had was formally called an herbal abortion. "We didn't call it [that;] it was like, *We took the tea.* That was it. *We took the tea, girl, we drank the tea, we drank the tea.*"

These days, with the invention of medication abortion, people who choose to self-manage an abortion usually do so using two regimens of pills, either a combination of mifepristone and misoprostol or a heavier dose of misoprostol on its own. It's the same FDA-approved medication that a person would receive when going to a clinic, but some choose to source it in their communities. In 2020, medication abortion rose to become the method for more than half of eligible abortions (before ten weeks' gestation) in the United States. The uptick was attributed to the coronavirus pandemic, which increased the use of virtual telemedicine. As procedural abortions became more restricted, more clinics began to offer abortions via telemedicine. As of 2023, the majority of abortions are via medication.

Of course, some people choose to use herbal methods at home despite having financial and physical access to clinical abortion care. Queer artist and climate change activist Favianna Rodriguez self-managed her third abortion with a combination of medication and herbs because she wanted to do womb healing and be more connected to her body during the experience. Her first two abortions in 2000 and 2012 were in-clinic procedures in Los Angeles and Oakland, respectively. She felt those experiences weren't holistic or helpful in terms of how she made those decisions based on generations of reproductive trauma. In the years afterward, she sought to use plant and somatic medicine to have a better relationship with her body.

"I need ancestral, decolonial wisdom to be held in this experience. There's something in my body and my fucking soul that needed to shift. I felt I was repeating old cycles," Favianna told us. So she contacted a friend who was a birthworker, and they talked through how to set up the best container for her to process the experience. With a friend and the doula, Favianna had her abortion at her home. The doula prepared a yoni steam, herbs that Favianna could put in her bath, and she rubbed a warm spoon of mugwort on Favianna's abdomen. She also placed laminaria, dried seaweed sticks, in Favianna's cervix to open it up over time and misoprostol to insert in the vagina as well. Favianna began to cramp but was soothed by the presence of her friend, the candles, and the mushroom bath prepared for her. "I remember being in my bed and the candles were flickering. I was starting to sweat a lot and getting these visions of my grandmother and my mom and the choices that they didn't have but also how their trauma affected how they raised me and how their trauma made me see my pussy as something that I could commodify or use without really reflecting on who I am allowing in there, literally. I needed to reconnect to the power of my womb and heal my generational trauma."

A small case study published in 2022 found that those who engaged herbs as part of their abortion regimen needed to use four or more plants to complete the process. Seventy-five percent had to change and adapt the herb formulas throughout the multiweek process to ensure that the formulas worked for them, and others had to engage medications to complete the abortion. Herbs such as cotton root, ginger tea, pennyroyal, black cohosh, and sprigs of parsley inserted near the cervix were used, just as our ancestors had used them for millennia. Others have used home manual vacuum aspiration methods with midwives or doulas, completing the at-home patient-centered care that Jane envisioned.

That's exactly why we decided to look into the history that's been stolen and hidden from us in favor of a whitewashed history in which the stories of our ancestors are told through the racist lens and journals of colonizers. Our communities have always resisted colonialization so that we could maintain control of our families and bodies. Our ancestors used plant medicine and ancient practices to care for themselves. Amid a calculated effort to erase our history, it is quite radical to write ourselves back into the story. Even as medical advancements change how most people have abortions, we can still work our ancient traditions into the process by, for example, adding an herb-filled bath or tea. We can liberate ourselves by reclaiming abortion traditions.

The First Time Abortion Was a Crime

When sixteen-year-old Donna needed an abortion in 1964, it was because the contraceptive foam her best friend recommended failed the very first time she used it. Contraception wasn't widely available to Black women, especially unmarried Black teens. What was more available to her, even though it was illegal, was abortion—so long as you knew whom to ask. Donna knew exactly where to go to.

Donna first learned about abortion the way many children learn about grown folks' business: overhearing conversations. Growing up in Pittsburgh, Pennsylvania, in the 1950s, her mother and all of her friends hosted a card game for a little cash every other weekend. Her mother sold fish sandwiches and dinner plates, and Donna tried to make a little pocket money putting the plates together and changing the vinyl records so she could stay near the action. "I liked being around grown people, listening to their conversations, because that's the only way you gon' learn it," she told us.

Donna was supposed to be in the kitchen washing dishes when she heard the grown folks talking. "We were kids and we knew that Miss So-and-So is who the young women went to go and get an abortion."

It was an open secret that the docile white woman in her forties who lived on Frankstown Avenue provided abortions in her home. The Abortion Lady, she was called. No fancy hair or diamonds, Donna told us. She kept to herself, but every once in a while Donna said folks in the community would catch glimpses of her at the grocery store or the drugstore. Everybody knew who she was, but no one knew her name. To this day Donna couldn't remember it. "She was just known as the Abortion Lady. We didn't even know she had a fucking name."

The community trusted her, and she trusted them right back. No one wanted to get in trouble. This made access more convenient for Black women who needed abortions, despite illegality and the very real medical risks that could accompany a questionable provider. "We didn't have to travel to West Virginia or way out somewhere [the way my white friends did]." Few Black families had cars or additional money, so they stayed close to home, but Donna's white friends traveled to West Virginia and other cities for a week or two to secret abortion providers known in various circles. "They went away because it was the taboo of these white families not wanting people to know what they were doing."

Donna was sure about her decision, but her mother took some convincing because she didn't think they could afford an abortion and she was afraid. "She had been told by friends, 'If you do some shit like that, your daughter's gonna die and you're going to jail.' I literally had to talk my mother into doing this." At the time, Donna's father had left and her mother was on public assistance, so there wasn't much money left over to pay for the abortion. They sold extra dinner plates of fish, potato salad, and greens and hustled at the card table to make the $200.

The Abortion Lady's house was big, although Donna didn't see inside past the entry alcove as she headed down the basement stairs, lit by a dim, flickering lightbulb. "If the abortion don't kill you, falling down these steps will," Donna laughed heartily recalling the scene. When she reached the basement, she saw jars of medical equipment and gauze placed around the room. A small corner with a light was the Abortion Lady's workspace. The room was dark and seedy-looking, she remembers, and instead of the bed she expected, there was a single chaise lounge covered with a sheet placed near the table. "And I'm like, *Am I getting on a chaise lounge? What the hell? It ain't even a bed!* But I'm just a kid. I'm thinking, *Damn. Black girls don't get nothing, do we?*"

Donna lay on the chaise lounge, and the Abortion Lady began the procedure. She picked up a long metal tool with a small hook on one end out of a plastic bag. She had Donna spread her legs, and she inserted the tool. The procedure was over in less than a minute. The Abortion Lady told Donna and her mother that she was going to bleed, experience cramping, and begin passing the tissue, which she should flush down the toilet, and to go to the hospital if the bleeding didn't stop. "So that's what I did and then I was fine."

Donna did have some additional bleeding over the following days, which worried her mother, so she took her to the hospital. But when the white doctors asked what happened, assuming that she'd had an abortion, Donna would only say she fell off her bike. She didn't want anyone to get in trouble. She never told. Nobody did.

* * *

As we've explained, throughout history, abortion was everywhere. In Donna's Pittsburgh community, people knew who could provide abortion care, and it was up to the community to keep the providers and their patients free from criminalization. Illegality has never meant unavailability. But alongside the fear of being arrested for having an abortion and potentially losing your freedom, an even stronger fear of shame from the community for carrying an "illegitimate" pregnancy while being unwed, or too young, forced people to risk criminalization. No one wanted to be the local example of an unplanned pregnancy or have their family embarrassed if something went wrong and their death was cause for an investigation of the provider. Fear of criminalization and stigma was stronger than the fear of a dangerous procedure and was pervasive enough that everyone kept quiet.

Until the nineteenth century, white people in the United States lived with an absence of abortion laws, both because there weren't any statutes against the procedure after quickening (when the pregnant person could feel the fetus move) and because terminating a pregnancy or "unblocking the obstructed menses" wasn't considered an abortion until quickening took place. The fetus was not recognized in common law, and when the potentiality for life began was a debate left to philosophers and religious leaders, not the law. Legally, white women were free to abort with abandon prior to quickening, but they still faced morality standards and shaming due to their lack of chastity. And, given that they were the pregnant ones, only they could say whether quickening had occurred. Even after quickening, abortion wasn't exactly legal, but it also wasn't illegal.

The abortion bans that Donna lived under in 1950—and that many of us are living under today—have roots in English law. Lord Ellenborough's Act was the British law that criminalized abortion prior to quickening in 1803. The United States at the time had recently and consciously uncoupled from the British Empire, and did not immediately follow suit and criminalize abortion; most court cases at the time held that if quickening couldn't be proved, there was no crime. The first wave of US abortion restrictions began in 1821, when the Connecticut General Assembly enacted a statute declaring the use of "any deadly poison or noxious destructive substance" to cause a miscarriage in a woman whose pregnancy had quickened to be a crime worthy of imprisonment. Afterward, several states enacted similar policies. In the 1820s, abortion also began to appear in the crime pages of newspapers. Arrests of both women and men who procured abortions were featured. The cases were a mixed bag, with some resulting in fines and short prison sentences and others ending in not guilty verdicts. Other stories announced the deaths of women who sought abortions; some were named, and others, especially Black women, went unnamed. Around this time, newspapers in Europe and the United States began to advertise French pills promising a cure for gonorrhea and other venereal diseases, so it wasn't a surprise when ads for abortion pills appeared in the late 1830s. Women who had been drinking tansy tea to keep their periods regular or savin oil to cause an abortion were increasingly able to open the morning newspaper and find ads for female monthly or French periodical pills that promised to regulate their menstrual cycles without harming their health, right next to ads for all the other medications a druggist offered.

New York changed the game, in a bad way. The state's 1830 law banned all abortions after quickening, adding a second-degree murder charge and punishing the provider with a sentence of up to a year and a fine of up to $500, with an exception for health necessities based on the recommendations of two physicians. The definition of a physician at the time wasn't clear, because a lot of people called themselves physicians but had little to no formal medical training. Medical schools were private businesses and generally were not open to white women, Native Americans, or freed or enslaved Black people. In 1910, the Flexner Report, funded by the American Medical Association (AMA), sought to delegitimize Black doctors and led to the closure of all but two Black medical schools, narrowing the pathways for Black and Brown people to learn the practice of medicine and elevating white providers. Essentially, abortion was allowed only at the discretion and approval of at least two white men.

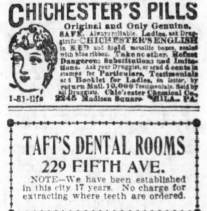

Various ads for abortion pills in the *Pittsburgh Press*, December 29, 1900.

Despite the fact that the laws criminalizing abortion generally weren't enforced, states kept enacting more anyway and inciting fear. Over the decade following New York's 1830 ban, of the twenty-four states that were then part of the United States, a handful rendered abortion a misdemeanor offense and added the use of instruments as a banned method. As states joined the union, they made it their priority to ban abortion, with Arkansas and the Iowa territorial legislature criminalizing abortion after quickening in their first legislative sessions. Maine revised its code to criminalize abortion "whether such child be quick or not," punishing providers with up to a year in prison and up to a $1,000 fine.

In 1831, a British white woman named Ann Trow Summers Lohman immigrated to the United States from England and developed an interest in women's health. By the end of the decade she'd changed her name to Madame Restell, announced herself as a "Female Physician for improving the breed of men and beauty of women," and ran long ads in the nation's top newspapers written "to married women" about their destinies, poverty, and being overwhelmed with mothering. Those who agreed with her vision could write to her to receive her new pills and

New York Daily Herald ads for Madame Restell and Portuguese abortion pills, September 22, 1842.

powder, which cost one dollar and five dollars per package, respectively, nearly $45 and $200 today. Madame Restell became the most famous abortion provider at the time, known for her skill and because she flaunted her work in the streets through the luxuries she purchased, directly in the faces of suffragettes and free-love feminists who believed her work set their cause back. But Madame Restell didn't care. Restellism, as the moment was dubbed, swept the nation.

In August 1839, the *Baltimore Sun* ran a short death notice titled "Danger of Self-Medication" about an unnamed "colored female servant in New York" who died after taking a half ounce of oil of tansy. Instead of aborting, she convulsed and died within an hour. Her story wasn't uncommon. Women of all races were using the pills, but the inclusion of their race stoked sensationalization of their deaths. During Restellism, the crime sections of newspapers carried both local stories and stories from other cities, spreading the narrative that abortion was dangerous and criminal, while several pages later the ad section featured advertisements for abortion pills. Medical providers competing for clients were popular based on their willingness to provide these pills, and for some providing the pills was their entire practice.

Salesmen and druggists sold Madame Restell's abortion pills, along with other popular brands such as Mott's, Chichester's, and Madame Dean's. Doctors, chemists, and druggists crafted pills made of various compounds and herbs such as savin, pennyroyal, cohosh, and tansy. Madame Restell, however, offered an additional guarantee: if her pills didn't work, her customers could go to her clinic in New York City for a termination procedure. Those who couldn't make it to her clinic or used other pills were left to continue the pregnancy or find a midwife in their community willing to provide them with an abortion, often later in the pregnancy.

Pregnancy fell in the domain of *women's problems*, so the medical care at the time tended to be provided by grandmothers, aunties, community elders, and midwives—or in Donna's case, the Abortion Lady. On plantations, on reservations, and in free communities, Black and Indigenous women ushered new babies into the world as well as concocted abortion remedies. In an effort to record the narratives of formerly enslaved people, researchers conducted interviews in the 1930s. In one interview, Lu Lee explained that women could "unfix" themselves using calomel and turpentine. She told the interviewer, "In them days the turpentine was strong and ten or twelve drops would miscarry you. But the makers found what it was used for and they changed the way of making turpentine. It ain't no good no more." To avoid becoming pregnant by another enslaved man with whom her enslaver paired her, Mary Gaffney told the interviewer that she "kept cotton roots and chewed them all the time." She said she never had any children until after slavery had ended. The secrets of abortion had to be kept close; otherwise the following generations might lose their traditions. Moreover, as William Coleman told an interviewer, enslavers beat Black women for having abortions. Elders, granny midwives, and neighborhood caregivers of color were known to provide abortions to kin and white women alike. Friends supported friends in seeking out a trusted provider. Anna Lee, a formerly enslaved Black woman, said that the use of cotton root was so common that it was impacting the birth population on plantations. "[They] got to chewing cotton roots to keep from giving births to babies and they finally made a law against that but it did not help much," she explained. "If slavery had lasted much longer they would not have been any slaves . . . we had done quit breeding." As criminalization proliferated, abortions later in pregnancy had to be done in secret for fear of prosecution. The second wave of abortion restrictions was on its way.

A combination of the impending emancipation of enslaved Black people, resistance by Native Americans and Mexicans defending against settlers stealing land, and the influx of Catholic, Chinese, and eastern and southern European immigrants stoked the nativist fears of white men in power in the United States. They feared not having the numerical population to maintain political control. Medical journals published a few case studies and data sets about patients doctors saw who needed abortions. Increasingly, they noted that the demographics of who was reportedly having abortions were changing; rather than the "wayward," "licentious" unmarried young women engaged in affairs, white, married, Protestant, US-born, middle- and upper-class women were having abortions. They were using pennyroyal and tansy pills to delay child-bearing or to declare their family complete.

This development struck fear in white doctors. It had been happening under their noses because they were not engaged in pregnancy health care. Medical schools limited enrollment to wealthier white men, while membership to the newly created medical associations barred midwives, Asian medicine practitioners, and medical school graduates from unrecognized institutions such as Black schools. Doctors maligned midwives as "unscientific" and "uneducated" for using learned African, Indigenous, Chinese, and rural European herbs and healing methods. The care midwives provided was based on patient needs and health, whereas white Western medicine was driven by capitalism and the needs of slave owners. Discrediting midwives' services served two purposes: removing women from the medical field and forcing low-income people, immigrants, and communities of color into the burgeoning medical system.

During enslavement, Black midwives held domain over childbirth, for Black and white babies alike. Although data from that period is sketchy, an estimated 70 to 90 percent of white women enslavers' births were attended by midwives (enslaved Black or white). After emancipation, some Black women continued to offer their midwifery services to the Black community and white women for nominal fees. The new field of gynecology, led by the white physician Dr. J. Marion Sims, practiced barbaric methods on enslaved Black women and published results in medical journals, gaining notoriety. The AMA, founded in 1847, went out of its way to bar the participation of women and Black doctors and eventually became the epicenter of antiabortion fervor and policy. The AMA sought to elevate white male physicians as the sole bearers of medical authority at the expense of midwives and community providers. Physicians began to refer to abortion using derogatory terms such as "murder" or "antenatal infanticide." And they portrayed abortion providers as incompetent quacks who were only in it for the cash. Physicians wanted total control of reproduction.

Separating white women from midwives was easier than separating communities of color and immigrants from midwives. As white settlers and the US government forcibly removed Native American tribes from their lands and onto reservations, they also forced tribes into substandard medical care. White medical providers believed that Indigenous women, like Black women, had pain-free births and disparaged their birth and infant-rearing practices, such as body feeding, saving umbilical cords, and carrying babies on cradleboards. As part of tribal agreements with the US government, Native American tribes were promised access to health care; that's where the Indian Health Service and other programs come from. The government placed hospitals on the reservations but rarely employed midwives to participate in birthing, leaving the direction of the care in the hands of white doctors whom Native American people neither trusted nor felt respected by. Additionally, the campaign to dehumanize midwives as providing inferior medical care eventually left Native Americans with few birth attendants, because the government viewed midwives and traditional healers as a hindrance to their plan for assimilation. The government dispatched white field matrons to further push Native American women into assimilationist health practices. Infant and maternal deaths were blamed on midwives, not on the obviously devastating impact colonization had on the tribes.

Being restricted to living on reservations caused malnourishment among many tribes. Some were relocated to lands they weren't accustomed to, and nomadic tribes were unable to follow herds of buffalo for food. The tribes became dependent on the US government for food rations, which were provided at the discretion of local authorities. As food sources dwindled, Native Americans became malnourished, and the infant mortality rate rose. Tribes such as the Crow were already accustomed to using abortion when food rations were low. But as abortion bans made their way west, the procedure became a crime on reservations as well.

In *Reproduction on the Reservation*, Brianna Theobald writes about the government employees who reported on the sexual practices of the Crow and other Indigenous tribes, including abortion. These government agents used the alleged sexual promiscuity of the tribes to substantiate the government's involvement in reproductive monitoring. In the Montana Territory, Agent Samuel G. Reynolds, a superintendent of the Crow Reservation, took it upon himself to identify abortion as his crusade, tying its prevalence to the Crow's land allotment. In 1905, he argued that if the Crow continued to have abortions, he would allocate smaller land lots for families and the tribe overall. It was a vicious gaslighting cycle: government officials blamed abortions for Native Americans' loss of their land while actively stealing the land and causing unhealthy pregnancies that led to a need for abortions.

Although the Crow were still able to provide one another with abortions, government agents such as Reynolds took to watching women's bodies and recording their pregnancies closely. He engaged police, as well as Native American men, to spy on those who had abortions and exact punishment on all who did not comply with the abortion ban. He reached out to Native American men to "use their influence to eliminate the practice." Even before the white colonizer insistence, colonial pressures had, decades earlier, prompted a council of Cherokee men to enact a law criminalizing abortion and issuing a punishment of fifty lashes. Theobald also argues that the forced conversion to Christianity may have played a role in the declining use of abortion.

As the Supreme Court was poised to recriminalize abortion based on decisions devoid of consideration for historical analysis, some white people in the United States called for abortion clinics to be set up on federal lands to avoid being governed by state abortion restrictions. Knowing the history of colonization makes this opportunistic and exploitative proposal excruciatingly painful. Native sovereignty is just that—sovereignty, not the convenience of white people in the United States.

INSUFFERABLE WHITE MEN AND THEIR COMSTOCKERY

As the prevalence of the abortion business grew during the nineteenth century, so did the frustration of physicians, legislators, and nativists. Their consternation was stoked by one doctor in particular: Dr. Horatio Storer.

Dr. Storer was a Boston-born white physician and the son of a prominent physician, Dr. D. Humphreys Storer. Both father and son specialized in gynecology, documenting diseases women suffered from and focusing their work on the ills of abortion. The younger Storer railed against abortion at all points during a pregnancy harder than anyone else had at the time. Given his prolific writing, he quickly became the leader of the AMA's campaign to rid the nation of abortion.

Storer hated everything abortion afforded middle- and upper-class white women and the demographic shift it was creating. He worked within the AMA to create a committee to investigate and eliminate abortion, and by 1859, the AMA passed resolutions condemning the procedure and delegitimizing doctors who provided care. Storer didn't believe the nation's laws went far enough, and he organized doctors to make theirs the singular profession responsible for "shutting the great gates of human death."

In his book *Why Not? A Book for Every Woman*, he wrote that, for healthy women, "occasional child-bearing is an important means of healthful self-preservation." For those who couldn't physically carry a pregnancy, he believed they should receive medical attention for their ailments but remain pregnant no matter what. Mostly, he was deeply concerned with US white birth rates. In 1868, with slavery abolished and Black people legally free to procreate on their own terms, immigrants moving to the country, and hordes of white soldiers dead, Storer saw banning abortion as the solution:

> All the fruitfulness of the present generation, tasked to its utmost, can hardly fill the gaps in our population that have of late been made by disease and the sword, while the great territories of the far West, just opening to civilization, and the fertile savannas of the South, now disinthralled and first made habitable by freeman, offer homes for the countless millions yet unborn. Shall they be filled by our own children or by those of aliens? This is a question that our women must answer; upon their loins depends the future destiny of the nation.

The Chinese Exclusion Act of 1882 fueled anti-Asian sentiments, barring Chinese immigrants from entering the country, separating those who were already here from their families. Newspapers underlined the connection between nativist and antiabortion arguments. Similarly, in

1888, the *Chicago Times* raised concern for the nativist reproductive beliefs of US Protestants by asking, "Is the Anglo-Saxon-American race to be driven out by the healthy sons and daughters . . . of Celtic, Teutonic [German], and Latin origin?"

Storer used his abortion campaign to deride women's desire for freedom in society and declared abortions as "unchristian, immoral, and physically detrimental." He deplored the newspapers that ran abortion providers' advertisements.

Sharing Storer's thoughts on eradicating abortion—after being disgusted by the prevalence of brothels, sex toys, pornography, and abortion pills—a young Anthony Comstock dreamed up a plan to destroy the vices of the nation through the mail system.

When Comstock was ten years old, he found his mother dead of a hemorrhage after giving birth to his youngest sister. Unfortunately, that had no impact on his understanding of the overall dangers of childbirth. Comstock's abhorrence of the lewd behavior of his fellow Union soldiers began during the Civil War and multiplied as he walked New York City streets. He believed that birth control, free love, and abortion advocates of the mid-nineteenth century were the root of all evil and spent his early twenties investigating saloons illegally operating on Sundays and printers of pornography. He grew upset that he was unable to shut these vices down because they paid handsome bribes to police and judges. He found like minds in the membership of the New York Young Men's Christian Association (YMCA) and met with government leaders and legislators interested in coming up with a potential law that would solve the problem. The YMCA members pooled their money, creating the New York Society for the Suppression of Vice (NYSSV), which had governmental power to investigate, search, and seize newspapers, books, photos, sex toys, and other items used as part of illegal vices.

Comstock was obsessed with maintaining a Christian society. While we weren't able to find much on his explicit views on people of color, he maintained detailed NYSSV records identifying the nationality and religious affiliation of the people he prosecuted. Historian Amy Werbel explained his records for the "Negro" category were light. At the time, refugees from Eastern Europe, including Jews, were coming to the US.

He considered the rise of immigrants to be a problem and praised the "noble" Commissioner of Immigration in "his heroic efforts to keep undesirable classes from our shores." Additionally, the rate of Jews he prosecuted tripled. He had deep pronatalist views that shaped his opposition to reproductive freedom and sexual liberation. "Comstock may have been uninterested in the salvation of America's Black community," Werbel writes in a chapter from *The Cambridge History of Sexuality in the United States*, "but his arrest blotters make clear that he worried very much that Jewish and other immigrant communities threatened to undermine his dream of a Christian nation."

Eventually, Comstock took his pleas for abstinence to Congress, which responded with An Act for the Suppression of Trade in, and Circulation of, Obscene Literature and Articles of Immoral Use (18 U.S. Code §§ 1461 and 1462), commonly known as the Comstock Act of 1873, which gave states a renewed push to criminalize abortion in every way possible. The law made it illegal to use the postal service or other interstate transport to give out "obscene, lewd, or lascivious" material or publish any information on how to use contraception, prevent sexually transmitted infections, or obtain an abortion. The law also gave Comstock the power, as a special agent of the US Post Office, to arrest anyone he found to be in violation of the law. He went after everyone, making enemies everywhere, even to the point that an assailant cut him with a pocket knife, severing four facial arteries (prompting his enemies to call him Scar-faced Tony). Comstock often conducted the raids himself, posing as a husband looking for birth control pills for his wife and at one point arresting Madame Restell when she supplied them in 1878. Arresting Madame Restell was a career get for Comstock and a huge hit to the abortion movement. But Restell would never let a man like Comstock take her down. Rather than finish the trial, Restell died by suicide the same year she was arrested.

As the nation became more conservative, living under the puritanical Comstock laws, the tolerance for vices fell. White suffragettes called abortion a "symptom of a more deep-seated disorder of the social state" and decried the men who used abortion providers to cover up their transgressions. In 1920, however, the former Soviet Union legalized abortion, which was a cornerstone of feminist efforts throughout Europe and a practice midwives brought with them when they immigrated to the United States. There were efforts to legalize the procedure in the United States, but they faced opposition from physicians and little support from birth control advocates who wanted to prioritize contraceptive access to avoid the need for abortion altogether.

Comstock's continued vendetta against sex didn't stop abortion pill providers from advertising in newspapers. They just had to be slicker and more vague. Their clients knew what to look for to order their pills, but many still needed procedures. Newspapers increasingly ran articles covering the stories of women who died from procedural abortions and the arrests and trials of their providers. *If it bleeds, it leads*, as they say. Rather than common death announcements, some contained salacious details of illegal operations, sex scandals, and the questionable skill sets of doctors and midwives whose race—"negress" or "colored"—was overemphasized.

THE EARLY CRIMINALIZATION OF BLACK PROVIDERS

The story of Mildred Campbell, a Black midwife at the turn of the century, captured newspaper headlines for years even though she was never actually convicted of a death related to abortion. Her story was one of the earliest we found of a Black midwife who was reported on so expansively, and her race was mentioned often. Mildred was described as a "mulatto, intelligent looking, and about middle aged" Black woman who provided midwifery services and operated a boardinghouse offering rooms to many young women traveling to Washington, DC. In August 1897, she was arrested after Abbie Compher, a white mother of four in her midthirties, died of blood poisoning, allegedly as the result of a procedural abortion. According to newspaper coverage of the trial at the time, Abbie had ordered abortion pills, but they didn't work, and she asked Mildred, who had delivered her fourth child, to provide her with an abortion. Abbie's husband claimed that Mildred had come to the grocery store he owned looking for Abbie and then went upstairs to care for her, and after she left Abbie was in more pain and eventually

RENEE BRACEY SHERMAN AND REGINA MAHONE

A SERIOUS CHARGE

Midwife Arrested for an Alleged Operation.

Deputy Coroner Glazebrook Making an Investigation—The Witnesses and the Case.

A colored midwife by the name of Campbell, who resides on 8th street northwest, below Grant avenue, was arrested today about 2:30 o'clock and lodged in the eighth precinct station, charged with criminal abortion, at the instance of Deputy Coroner Glazebrook.

The woman whose death is charged to her was Mrs. Abbe Coruther, thirty-four years of age, who died last night at her home, 2500 7th street northwest.

Her husband is G. W. Compher, a grocer of the same number. There were attending Mrs. Compher when she died, having been called in after the operation had been performed, Drs. W. T. Winter and H. H. Barber. They were summoned a week ago, after the criminal operation had taken place.

Dr. Glazebrook started in to investigate. Two witnesses will be Miss Bessie Chazeen and Mary J. Welch, a sister of the dead woman. Miss Chazeen is a trained nurse. The two physicians will also appear.

The woman stated before she died that the Campbell woman had given her drugs to prevent a birth, and then when they did not operate had performed an operation.

Dr. Glazebrook, with a sergeant of police and two officers from the eighth precinct, visited the Campbell woman's house, but she was absent. She was arrested later.

An autopsy was ordered by Dr. Glazebrook, and performed in his presence by Dr. Ruffin. A jury of inquest will meet at the eighth precinct station tomorrow at 11 o'clock, when the witnesses will appear.

Dr. Glazebrook stated that he had determined to see that the law in regard to criminal abortions in the District should be strictly enforced.

Newspaper coverage of Mildred Campbell's arrest from the *Evening Star* in Washington, DC, August 3, 1897.

died a few weeks later. Mildred was arrested and her home was searched, turning up a pocket surgical case with instruments used in an "illegal feature of midwifery" that were determined by the coroner as "having no place in the legitimate profession of nurse or midwifery."

At the inquest, doctors testified that there was internal evidence of decomposing matter and evidence that a child had been born and thus that a later abortion had been performed. One of her lawyers, John Mercer Langston, was a multiracial (Black, Pamunkey tribe, and white) abolitionist who helped free enslaved Black people via the Underground Railroad and served as the first Black congressman representing Virginia. (He was the great-uncle of the poet Langston Hughes, and several historic landmarks in Washington, DC, are named after him.) At trial, Langston questioned the doctors, getting them to admit that it was possible Abbie had performed the abortion on herself and noting that her husband was confused when Abbie became ill.

The newspapers reported that Mildred was "a fleshy mulatto" who "sat calmly" during the inquest, but "most of the time she picked her teeth with a straw." Her behavior seemed to point to her guilt. Although

116

the inquest jury found Mildred responsible and remanded her to jail on $2,500 bail (over $90,000 today), she was able to pay her bail, and at the trial the following year she was vindicated. The case hinged on the testimony of Black community members, such as doctors who testified that Mildred was too ill to have attended to Abbie and a young Black woman at the boardinghouse who contradicted Abbie's husband's story about hand-delivering a note to Mildred, who was illiterate, asking her to come care for Abbie. The jury deliberated for a short time, and Mildred was acquitted of manslaughter.

We assume Mildred went right back to providing abortions, because she was again arrested in 1901 after the death of Hattie Coxen, a Black schoolteacher in a nearby town who told friends she was going to Washington, DC, and ended up at Mildred's boardinghouse paying $7 for a week of lodging. The coroner determined that the cause of Hattie's death was an inflamed abdomen and blood poisoning, and that a child had been delivered a week before her death. Mildred was arrested, but because of testimony from a Black guest who confirmed that the timing of Hattie's arrival didn't match up with the coroner's account, Mildred was exonerated and discharged. She had the same outcome in 1904, when she was arrested for the death of Georgie Alexander, a Black woman in her thirties whose deathbed statements led to the accusation, and again in 1905, when Emma Pratt, an eighteen-year-old Black girl, presented at the hospital with complications from an abortion. With each case, the coverage dwindled, and patients kept showing up for "rooms" at Mildred's boardinghouse.

Was Mildred an abortion provider or just a woman running a home offering room and board? Was she a bad abortion provider? Honestly, it's hard to tell. Our guess is that she was indeed an abortion provider and most likely a skilled one, whose reputation spread around town. Deaths from medical procedures were more common then. It wasn't until the mid-1800s that doctors even realized that patients were dying during childbirth in large part because doctors didn't wash their hands before and between deliveries. The spread of germs was still a newer concept, and handwashing among the general public was just starting to become a thing. In *When Abortion Was a Crime*, historian Leslie J. Reagan argues that Dr. Lucy Hagenow, a white doctor who provided abortions in an office in the late 1800s and early 1900s, had at least six patients die over a decade, which was a "stunning" number of deaths for one provider. Reagan does note that records at the time tended to overemphasize abortion deaths.

Still, it seemed incredible to us that all–white male juries would so often not hold a Black woman liable for deaths arising from alleged abortions. When we looked at newspaper coverage of trials of the times, in general the response was mixed; some providers were acquitted, and for those who were not or who pleaded guilty, the fines could be steep, and these providers served a few months to several years in jail. The cases certainly weren't uniform. Nancy Plowden, an "aged negress abortionist," pleaded guilty to the blood poisoning death of fifteen-year-old Maud Viola Worley in 1907. Maud had admitted to having an abortion but did not give up Nancy's name. A police investigation eventually led to Nancy's arrest; the judge pitied her elderly age, saying, "I greatly dislike to punish an old woman like you, but I cannot see any other course to pursue," and sentenced her to a $10 fine ($340 today) and two years in a penitentiary.

Police were more likely to investigate midwives and physicians of color, as well as those who were immigrants or working-class, because that's what the police were set up to do when they originated as slave-catching patrols. After emancipation, municipalities set up police departments to scrutinize residents and protect the property and capital of the wealthy. Reagan believes that some wealthy white women and physicians may have been able to sidestep investigations into their abortions due to relationships with connected individuals and the ability to bribe police officers to look the other way. Their whiteness and wealth offered protection that some midwives were never afforded. When we talked with scholar Alicia Gutierrez-Romine, author of *From Back Alley to the Border: Criminal Abortion in California, 1920–1969*, she said the lack of coverage could be a combination of the Black, Indigenous, and immigrant midwives being very skilled, thus losing fewer patients; that perhaps they operated in midwifery networks or communities where they were trusted; and that their patients and neighbors rallied around them, as we have found in several cases.

These cases also illustrate how some early abortion stories made it into the public conversation, unfortunately not by choice. Police and doctors coerced women, fearing for their lives, into telling all they knew about the providers they had seen. Physicians were encouraged to refuse medical care until the patient made a statement, a policy endorsed by the *Journal of American Medical Association* (*JAMA*) in 1902. Other physicians would outright refuse care to patients they suspected of having an abortion or miscarriage so as not to be involved in any way. Deathbed confessions could be used to seek out arrests or surveillance warrants for suspected abortion providers and the names of the men who impregnated these women. Patients found during raids could be compelled to testify.

Most, it seems, didn't reveal the names of their providers, ensuring that access to care remained available for others. Some said little on the stand so they could not be used to put their provider behind bars, much like the clients of Jane who refused to talk. Gutierrez-Romine's research found that women generally resented speaking in open trials, but some used the moment to speak their truths. As Reagan documented, one New Yorker refused to talk, saying, "She was the only one who would help me, and I won't tell on her."

The demonization of abortion continued as police stepped up the surveillance and raids of clinics during the 1920s through 1940s. The intense criminalization took longtime midwives and doctors out of service, due to prison sentences and fear of criminalization and losing their licenses. Talking about abortion became a distinctly taboo subject, and newspapers continued to publish lewd headlines about women's deaths and arrests. Although abortion wasn't uniquely dangerous, the pervasive stigma made it seem that way.

The back-alley stories served as a warning to young girls about what could happen to them if they were too fast and didn't adhere to abstinence. That's the story Renee's aunt Vera learned about Bessie Lee, an auntie and mother of five who bled out after an unsafe abortion in the 1940s. Vera first heard the story when she was playing with her cousin, listening to grown folks talk on the porch about the family updates. Later, when she was sixteen, her mother told her about Bessie, explaining that if she wasn't careful around boys, she could end up dead because of pregnancy and a "tabletop abortion." Anytime something is illegal and unregulated, the market price is high, but with abortion, money, sex, and the added risk of death bolstered the narrative of an unsavory provider. Of course, safe providers like Donna's Abortion Lady existed, but they didn't make headlines if they were never caught and their patients made it home safely to their families. The absence of safe abortion stories sealed the notion that unsafe, back-alley abortions were all that existed.

In some cases, abortion providers who could escape the clutches of the law became public villains, like Virginia King, a Black woman from North Carolina. In early May 1921, Delsey Middleton took the train to Harveytown with her friend Maggie Hill for the day. The sixteen-year-old Black girls took a cab to the home of Virginia King, who, according to newspapers of the time, had an extensive clientele of both Black and white women needing her "considerable skill," which had served her in a "long career marked by comparatively few deaths." But during the spring of 1921, Virginia had been under the surveillance of police for several months and stood accused of causing two deaths, that of Delsey and another unnamed Black girl months earlier. In the case of Delsey, she arrived at Virginia's house and went into a room with her but never emerged; several hours later, she was reported dead, seated in a rocking chair, having died of a hemorrhage. Witnesses said they saw the girl visibly ill and fainting before going into Virginia's home, whereas her friend maintained that she wasn't ill and that Virginia told her it was a heart problem. The police took the arrest as an opportunity to confiscate all of Virginia's tools and medicines but found no evidence of blood on Virginia or anywhere in the room. The case ended in a mistrial and was retried the following year.

After Virginia was acquitted at the second trial, the local newspaper editor was furious, besmirching her by citing her Blackness and age. "She is a menace to morality," the editorial read, continuing that the

KINSTON NEGRESS HAS NUMEROUS TROUBLES

Kinston, May 27.—The authorities here are seeking clues to firebugs believed to have burned the home of Virginia King, in Harveytown, Thursday night. That the house was fired was the general belief 'n official quarters here today following an investigation.

Virginia King, elderly negress, has seen more trouble than any other person of her race in this section in recent years. She has been tried for murder in connection with alleged criminal surgery. She was convicted of abortion a few days ago and was in the county jail awaiting sentence when her home was burned. She has spent many weeks in prison.

Some weeks ago she received what purported to be a "K. K. K." warning to leave the section. This is believed to have been sent her by negroes desiring to rid the vicinity of her presence. About two weeks ago she was robbed by negro highwaymen, who shot her husband, Frank Howard, when she failed to produce $250 additional demanded by the robbers. Virginia King has never taken her husband's name. Her savings have been dissipated by the employment of counsel to defend her in many court actions growing out of her alleged malpractice.

Newspaper coverage of an alleged arson at the home of Virginia King from *The News and Observer* in Raleigh, North Carolina, May 28, 1923.

"aged negress" was "guilty of one of the most diabolical and abominable practices that it is possible to perpetrate." The following week, the paper railed against Virginia and how she caused the county to "expend a lot of money in trying to convict her of murder." The newspapers loved a story like Virginia King's because they could profit from it: the salacious court coverage and vilifying editorials warning about the dangers of abortion caught the attention of readers on the front pages and sold newspapers, adding to the revenue from ads for abortion pills in the back pages.

Virginia became a pariah, but like Mildred, people continued to see her for abortion services. Matilda Kennedy, a seventeen-year-old girl (whose race wasn't mentioned), gave a sworn statement that Tom Stroud, a married father and local Baptist preacher, took her to Virginia's house for an abortion on two separate occasions. Stroud's 1922 trial for prostitution and registering at a hotel with a woman who was not his wife made headlines and confirmed that Virginia King was still providing abortions to the community; she was convicted in May 1923 and sentenced to four to five years in jail. But this time, she would be punished by the community as well. Her home was set on fire, and the Ku Klux Klan sent her warnings to leave town (although the newspaper assumed that Black people were actually behind these actions). She and her husband were also robbed by highwaymen who demanded $250 in addition to the cash they had already been paid, and when the two refused, the robbers shot and wounded Virginia's seventy-year-old husband, Frank. It wasn't uncommon for abortion providers to pay for local protection or to be robbed due to their business. Her husband, an "elderly negro, almost blind," was arrested less than a month later when he asked neighbors to borrow a shovel and was seen carrying a Black woman's deceased body to their outhouse.

News stories like these justified the criminalization of abortion in the public's eyes. Gory and salacious details distracted readers from thinking about why someone would need an abortion and under what circumstances safe care could be offered. Instead, the media spread the idea that abortion was uniquely dangerous and disturbing, and that those who provided it were notoriously evil. News outlets also questioned the financial motives of abortion providers. The November 1947 issue of *Our World*, a Black magazine, ran a multipage article on the "Abortion Racket" with contrived images of a seedy, cigarette-smoking Black male abortion provider in a pressed clean white apron putting on latex gloves as he hovered over a Black abortion patient draped in pristine white sheets. Despite what the image showed, the caption identified the apron as soiled, the instruments as unclean, and the room as sordid. "It's ruthless! It's risky. It's a crime. Every abortionist opens the door to painful death, sterility and infection," the article warned. The article went on to identify some of the reasons why four thousand Black women had abortions the year before but dismissed these reasons as not worth risking sitting in the "death chair." *Our World* concluded that the "safest immediate solution is giving birth to the baby" and going to welfare agencies or Planned Parenthood Federation offices for support. Similarly, a January 1951 issue of *EBONY Magazine* featured a series of images purportedly documenting a Black woman meeting a "contact man" in a dark room and police standing over a bed where another woman allegedly died after an abortion.

Some of the more public criminalization cases of the twentieth century involved Black male physicians whose race and politics fueled their desire to provide care for Black people, as well as inflaming the animosity of their prosecutors. As Gutierrez-Romine writes in *From Back Alley to the Border*, Black providers "had little social or political clout in the event of an indictment." It was on the community to show up for the providers.

In late spring 1905, Jean Maxwell, a twenty-nine-year-old "handsome blonde woman of culture" was engaged to be married and was pregnant. Before she died that year, she told her parents that she sought an abortion to hide her ruin. After her death, the family's pharmacist, F. William Hermann, and Dr. J. H. Tompkins, a Black physician, were both arrested. Dr. Tompkins's race was always mentioned, but only once was it mentioned that Hermann was a "mulatto of fine physique." Despite having his bail set at $10,000 and wishing to remain in jail, Hermann was released first, bailed out by family members, while Dr. Tompkins remained in jail until Black people in the Cumberland, Maryland, community were able to raise the $8,000 to secure his release.

Similarly, in California, Black communities rallied around Dr. Mathew Marmillion when he was imprisoned. A Louisiana native, Dr. Marmillion set up his practice in the racially segregated Central Avenue district of Los Angeles in the mid-1920s just before the Great Depression of the 1930s—a time when Black residents "increasingly turned inward to care for and protect their own." In February 1933, Dr. Marmillion was charged with the murder of an eighteen-year-old Black girl, Margaret Scott, who died of shock on his operating table. The case hinged on whether Margaret went to Dr. Marmillion for a tonsillectomy after the abortion or whether he provided a tonsillectomy to cover up the abortion he provided that led to her demise. Dr. Marmillion argued that Margaret's boyfriend, twenty-seven-year-old medical student Archie Hairston, had provided the initial abortion, but Hairston pointed the finger back at Dr. Marmillion.

A jury found Dr. Marmillion guilty of second-degree murder and sentenced him to five years to life in prison. Unlike white providers who were convicted around the same time, Dr. Marmillion and another Black physician, Dr. Oscar W. DeVaughn, had their race specifically denoted in medical articles. While he was imprisoned, organizers rallied around Dr. Marmillion, with twenty thousand people demanding that the California governor release him, highlighting the doctor's religiosity and integrity. The *Los Angeles Sentinel* came to his defense as well, and some Black journalists began to question the need to criminalize abortion overall. Like they did for the midwives whose stories we explored earlier, Black communities leaned into support for alleged abortion providers facing prosecution to ensure their safety and ability to provide safe care in the neighborhood.

Even Dr. Martin Luther King Jr. found this strategy enticing, citing in his October 1959 article "The Social Organization of Nonviolence" the community release of Dr. Albert Perry, a physician accused of providing an abortion to a white woman in October 1957. In response to critiques of his "turn-the-other-cheek" strategy, Dr. King pointed to the way the people of Monroe, North Carolina, entered the jail and refused to leave Dr. Perry's cell until he was released. Dr. Perry admitted the woman had approached him for an abortion, but the community believed his arrest was in retaliation for desegregating a local swimming pool. It was quite common for white women to go to Black physicians for treatments, particularly those they wanted to keep secret, such as treatment for sexually transmitted infections and abortions. Dr. King wrote about nonviolent direct action strategies communities have used: "Many creative forms have been developed—the mass boycott, sit-down protests and strikes, sit-ins—refusal to pay fines and bail for unjust arrests—mass marches—mass meetings—prayer pilgrimages, etc." That he chose to focus on a community solution to free an alleged abortion provider is pretty radical, given that there were a lot of examples at the time that did not involve abortion.

* * *

Over the past half century, Black providers were able to document their own reasons for providing care and the anti-Blackness they waded through in their work. During medical school, Dr. Edgar Bass Keemer Jr. referred more than a few students to a local provider in Nashville who charged $25 per abortion for medical students; so when his wife, Beatrice, needed one during their medical internship in Washington, DC, he knew what to do. Dr. G performed her abortion in a large brownstone on P Street, charging $35, far less than the $300 to $400 he charged wealthy white women. Yet in 1938, when the daughter of the local preacher named "Margie X" came to the Richmond, Indiana, practice Dr. Keemer ran with his wife—also a physician—he refused to provide Margie with an abortion. "I won't have this baby. I won't shame my father," Dr. Keemer recalls Margie telling him in his memoir, *Confessions of a Pro-Life Abortionist*. "I'll kill myself first. It's my life, it is my choice." Over dinner that hot August Saturday night, Dr. Keemer said he preached about the immorality of abortion while Beatrice furiously countered with hypocrisy, reminding him of their own abortion a few years before. Upon returning home from church the next morning, Beatrice screamed and cried when her husband told her of Margie's death, an "accidental" drowning. Dr. Keemer said he was beside himself, realizing he had inadvertently caused her death, and he vowed to provide an abortion to anyone who wanted one from that moment forward. Reflecting in his memoir, Dr. Keemer said that he didn't perform the abortion because he was afraid of being imprisoned or even lynched, a fate his family had seen before.

Soon after, the Keemers were again presented with a patient, Clare, a Black woman who described being unable to fend off her husband and not wanting to be pregnant with her eighth child. She promised that she would do her own abortion if the doctors wouldn't help her. Dr. Keemer hopped on the evening train to Washington, DC, and spent several days being trained by Dr. G. Clare and her seven children brought a sweet potato pie and $15 to the Keemers on Christmas as a thank-you.

The Keemers eventually relocated to Detroit—and separated—but Dr. Keemer maintained a practice in the area, offering abortions for $15 and a sliding scale or free care to those who couldn't afford the fee. If the patient needed hospitalization, he would cover the bill and their lost wages, a practice inspired by the malfeasance of a white provider who wouldn't acknowledge patients who returned still pregnant. He even knew of providers who raped their patients while unconscious or demanded sex as part of the final payment. The thoughtfulness of his practice—including providing aftercare—helped shield him from complaints and made him a hero in the Detroit community.

Some of the providers of the time knew one another. Dr. Keemer details visiting the clinics of other physicians, including Dr. Theodore Roosevelt Mason Howard, based in Chicago, who goes unnamed in Dr. Keemer's book. Dr. T. R. M. Howard, as he was known, was a physician and prominent civil rights activist who counted Malcolm X, Fannie Lou Hamer, and Stokely Carmichael among his friends. Dr. Howard led the charge calling for an investigation into the disappearance of fourteen-year-old Emmett Till and escorted Mamie Till, Emmett's mother, to the courthouse every day in hopes of getting justice for her son's lynching. While Dr. Howard was a very prominent voice for Black liberation, it was an open secret in the movement that he also provided abortion care in Mississippi and subsequently in Chicago. As Dr. Keemer recalls, Dr. Howard operated a clean surgical suite; he said that he was proud to provide abortion care and would be a "full-time abortionist, law or no law."

Dr. Howard began providing abortions in the 1950s, receiving referrals from other doctors and the Clergy Consultation Service on Abortion, and he even served as the first abortion provider to connect with the Abortion Counseling Service, aka Jane. Heather Booth, a founder of Jane, was referred to him through the medical arm of the civil rights movement. Although she doesn't remember much about her very first call to him, she told us she remembered him being "pretty wonderful" and willing to answer questions for her and patients in a warm, direct, and factual manner. Once she set up an appointment, women who needed an abortion would meet up with a man holding a red carnation; they put a scarf over their eyes and rode to his clinic, Friendship Medical Center on the South Side of Chicago. Eventually, as Jane started sending more patients to Dr. Howard, they worked out deals so that for every three patients who paid $500, he would do one abortion for free. Dr. Keemer, a militant socialist, criticized Dr. Howard's fees in his memoir, writing that he thought charging as much as $700 made the procedure unattainable for those who needed it most. But Dr. Howard had claimed that he charged white women with money more than Black women and told Dr. Keemer that he couldn't afford to take on free cases because he needed the extra cash to pay off local, county, and state officials. Dr. Keemer, who also made "contributions" to the police, didn't buy that story, citing Dr. Howard's expensive vices.

Whether the payoffs were necessary or not is arguable, because both doctors were arrested for providing abortions. Dr. Keemer's clinic was raided by Detroit police in August 1956; everyone in his office was arrested, and police seized his patient records, using them to compel women to testify. Dr. Keemer sought to use his 1958 trial to challenge the abortion law, having doctors and patients testify to the necessity of therapeutic abortions—care provided at the approval and discretion of a panel of doctors—and the dangers of continuing an undesired pregnancy. He was also indirectly told that for $25,000, it could be arranged that none of his witnesses would show up. Dr. Keemer knew that his case could push the legalization movement forward, so he knew what was riding on it.

In his memoir, Dr. Keemer recounted the prosecution questioning one of his white patients and the way he repeatedly overemphasized for the jury that Dr. Keemer, a Black man, had touched the "private parts" of the white patient. "I looked at the pitiful young lady as she stepped down from this dehumanizing ordeal. I looked at the jurors. They were looking hard at me," Dr. Keemer wrote. "I knew then that justice was not to be done." The racist line of questioning raised age-old tropes about Black masculinity and sexual aggression, and Dr. Keemer was convicted, serving fourteen months in prison. He was arrested again in 1972 in yet another raid on his clinic; this time the police took in every person of color they saw on his clinic floor. He was later vindicated in court.

When Dr. Howard was arrested in July 1964, he was also fighting a tax evasion case; however, his abortion charges were dismissed in September, when the accuser failed to show up for court. He returned to provide abortions that same month and was arrested in a sting operation. After the assassination of Malcolm X, Dr. Howard gave a speech that the Red Squad (a unit in the police department tasked with monitoring and infiltrating social justice movements) determined dangerous, so a woman and a deputy wearing a wire posed as a couple in need of an abortion. When Dr. Howard quoted them $500 and took the woman back for the procedure, he was arrested. At his trial in 1968, he was found not guilty because, as his lawyer pointed out, the woman in the sting was not pregnant; therefore, there was no crime. Dr. Howard never stopped providing abortions and, according to his son, kept a large box of cash ready for bribes, paying at least $10,000 to police on two separate occasions.

Both Dr. Howard and Dr. Keemer continued their efforts to legalize abortion while providing care illegally. Dr. Howard trained providers in New York and other states as legalization caught on and supported efforts to challenge the ban in Illinois. He also used some of the profits from abortions to build Friendship Medical Center, a multifloor health center for Black people offering everything from ophthalmology to prenatal care—and, of course, abortions, once the procedure became legal in 1973. He envisioned "lunch hour abortions" early in the pregnancy with women able to get their abortions quickly and move on with their day. The clinic provided 60 to 100 abortions per day and upward of 20,000 in the first year, seeing half of Illinois's abortion patients. In 1973, two months after abortion was legalized, Dr. Howard was on the cover of *Jet* magazine with a photo spread of his clinic on the first day of legal operations, serving a few of the four hundred patients who had abortions that day. For his part, Dr. Keemer estimates he provided 30,000 abortions before legalization and 20,000 afterward. He joined the advocacy effort, serving as the Midwest vice president of the newly formed National Association for the Repeal of Abortion Laws (NARAL) and speaking to Black nationalists to dispel rumors that abortion was genocide.

LOOKING BACK ON THE FRUSTRATING ROAD TO LEGALIZATION

There were many discussions in the lead-up to *Roe v. Wade* about how to liberalize the abortion laws. Test cases sought to challenge the idea of what constituted a threat to a patient's health, while others were calling for full decriminalization. Many white doctors still believed that they were the ultimate authority on when an abortion should be performed. Dr. Alan Guttmacher, a prominent white physician, supported the efforts to legalize abortion but felt the entire repeal of abortion laws would be too radical, instead supporting efforts requiring patients and their providers to plead their case to a panel of doctors who would approve the circumstances, which usually included physical or mental health, health of the fetus, rape, or incest. Of course, you can imagine how this would work out for Black and Brown patients, if they even made it that far. Eventually Dr. Guttmacher changed his mind, but it was harder to change policies that fast, especially given the American Medical Association's long-standing position against abortion.

Then-governor of California Ronald Reagan legalized abortion under such a model in 1967, but it proved ineffective for the masses. Doctors referred patients to clinics in Mexico because few could meet the narrow restrictions, which allowed abortion in only certain medical instances. "La Casa de las Gringas" ("the White Girls' House") was a popular clinic in Mexico City that charged more than $1,000 for an abortion, according to Gutierrez-Romine. Those in Southern California, however, could take a quick day trip to Tijuana, receive their abortions for a few hundred dollars, and be home by evening. US emergency rooms saw the aftermath of the unsafe procedures and tried to save the lives of those who had had unsafe or incomplete procedures.

Dr. Leon Belous was an outspoken Russian-born gynecologist who kept his involvement in the efforts to send patients to illegal abortion providers a secret until his name surfaced during a 1966 investigation of a woman's death. Investigators, acting on a tip, raided a Chula Vista, California, apartment office and discovered that doctors such as Dr. Belous were sending dozens of patients there, which was illegal. Advocates used the case to push for a liberalized abortion law, arguing that it was better for a doctor in the US to provide the care rather than send the abortion seeker to Mexico. The provider in question, Dr. Karl Lairtus, a friend of Dr. Belous's, was a trained, competent abortion provider, but only licensed in Mexico, not the United States. Despite knowing Dr. Lairtus, Dr. Belous still spread the narrative of the "butchery" of the

Tijuana clinics. His argument played on racist fears and ignored the fact that Dr. Lairtus was licensed in Mexico, where he and Dr. Belous met. It seems that his argument was more xenophobic and nationalist in nature, relying on assumptions about Mexican health care rather than focusing on ensuring women had competent providers on both sides of the border. The case reached the California Supreme Court, which sided with Dr. Belous, agreeing that women in the United States were in danger of receiving substandard care in Mexico.

What's frustrating about this argument is how much it relies on xenophobia and US exceptionalism to prove its point. Dangerous abortions—as well as safe ones—were happening right here in the United States, yet the case needed to prey on racist assumptions about dirty clinics in Mexico in order to change the law. As Gutierrez-Romine points out, "While legislators in California grappled with their fears of Tijuana abortions, they failed to recognize that it was actually California's law that made women unsafe."

We can't help but notice the parallels with today. When abortion was recriminalized across the country, some pro-choice advocates warned of the dangers of back-alley abortions and people going to Mexico for what they considered "unsafe" care. We talked to reporters who were concerned with abortion pills coming across the border from Mexico or from India, questioning whether they were safe for people in the United States to take, ignoring the fact that most medications are manufactured overseas. It's the xenophobia, combined with abortion stigma and fueled by US exceptionalism, that creates the assumption that although the United States isn't offering widely accessible legal abortion care, the care abroad *must* be inferior *because* it is provided by Brown people. Some people never stopped crossing the southern or northern borders for abortion care.

USING ABLEISM TO ADVOCATE FOR ABORTION

The therapeutic abortion model was a workable one for a small population of women who needed abortions, particularly white women with financial means and those who could garner public sympathy. During the early twentieth century, the rubella (German measles) epidemic thrust abortion into the public conversation, changing the public's perception of the need for abortion due to health indications. Pregnant people who contracted rubella were more likely to deliver babies with disabilities. As historian Leslie Reagan explains in *Dangerous Pregnancies: Mothers, Disability, and Abortion in Modern America*, rubella was a threat both medically to those who contracted it and also to the idea of a perfect post–World War II nuclear family with healthy, nondisabled children. At the same time, many people—including Sherri Finkbine, a US children's television show host—were taking common medications containing thalidomide, which was found to cause fetal physical disabilities in pregnant people. Sherri's story made national headlines in 1962 when she sought an abortion but was refused by her provider's hospital and then traveled to Sweden for care. Finkbine and her family told their story in several magazines with family photos. Other national magazines highlighted white women's stories to garner support for specific reasons for abortion. People of color rarely entered the mainstream conversation.

In the 1971 *Bronze Thrills* cover story titled "I Performed an Abortion on My Sister," the Black publication details a woman named Marianne's story of fearing for her younger sister, Karen, who contracted rubella. Marianne explained that she would never have forgiven herself if Karen gave birth to a child with disabilities, writing, "I don't want to see you bring a handicapped child into the world." When doctors refused an abortion for Karen, Marianne took it upon herself to borrow instruments from the hospital where she worked and perform the abortion herself. Karen later hemorrhaged and died. Although Marianne's position on abortion shifted a bit, it was for ableist reasons. She did not believe abortion should be available for a young person or someone already parenting who "doesn't want to be bothered with another," but she did believe it was "a solution to an impossible situation where a child will be born with a handicap"; therefore, she argued, abortion should be legalized.

Marianne's concerns mirrored others: Abortions were granted in specific instances because young, married white women were considered sympathetic patients who shouldn't be "burdened" with children with disabilities. They were seen as "deserving" of a healthy baby. Although we support a person's decision to have an abortion for whatever reason, what is complicated is that rather than address the underlying issue of lack of social support for people with disabilities, ableism became a justification for abortion. Abortion's legitimacy became centered on the belief that healthy, nondisabled children were the preference. Sympathy for women who needed abortions relied on the legitimacy of their whiteness, marital status, class, and desire for a child to make a woman a worthy candidate for an abortion—a sympathy that low-income people and people of color could never obtain simply by who they are. Today, we still see this narrative used to justify abortions, especially later abortions, or to plead the need for exceptions within a restriction. In her paper "After *Roe*: Race, Reproduction, and Life at the Limit of Law," American University race scholar Sara Clarke Kaplan argues that in the wake of the *Dobbs* decision, despite public conversation about the impact banning abortion would have on low-income people and communities of color, the stories elevated focused on the plight of white, well-off, married cisgender women seeking abortions due to a medical indication. She knows this from her own experience as a Black woman who had a later abortion. These stories, she writes, served as "empathetic representatives of universal womanhood in crisis." Because these women's identity aspects are not discussed they can be a stand-in that everyone can sympathize with because they are not marred by bigoted views on their reproduction. Their whiteness symbolizes innocence and justification for their deserved desire for an abortion, as well as a healthy child. Often, the medical condition of the pregnancy or disabilities detected are the focus of the narrative, allowing a public discussion on the value of disabled people's lives and worthiness to spread unchecked. The focused conversation also erases the many barriers that impact a person's ability to obtain an abortion, creating delays leading them to have an abortion later in pregnancy. Of course, people of color are more likely to experience these delays. Thus, their need for an abortion, when a health condition is not disclosed, is viewed as less worthy than those who have medical indications, often symbolized in white women's stories. The racial divide in who is worthy of an abortion continues. The liberalization of abortion laws is critical, but it's important to recognize that it was advocated for using ableist tactics and left people of color who disproportionately needed care out of the conversation or facing criminalization.

* * *

As newspaper headlines continued to cover the stories of patients dying or being permanently injured by unsafe procedures, legislators began to take up the cause of legalization, believing that abortion would be safer if it were widely available and regulated. In *Unbought and Unbossed*, the late Congresswoman Shirley Chisholm detailed her connection to abortion, including why she chose to become the chairwoman of NARAL. She explained that data had shown that women were having abortions, whether or not abortion was a crime. "Abortions will not be stopped," she wrote, continuing, "the question becomes simply that of what kind of abortions society wants women to have—clean, competent ones performed by licensed physicians or septic, dangerous ones done by incompetent practitioners." Chisholm made the legalization of abortion the cornerstone of her political platform as part of access to safe pregnancy care for people of color across the country.

The conversation began changing publicly as women's liberation groups held speakouts where people who'd had abortions could share their stories in front of audiences, essentially admitting to committing crimes as they sought health care, bringing the private to the public. In *Abortion Rap*, Diane Schulder and Florynce Kennedy detail the March 1969 abortion speakout of the Redstockings, a New York City–based group that wanted to help people who'd had abortions let go of the guilt and shame associated with the procedure. The stories, or "abortion raps" as they called them, were central to forcing politicians to understand the unequal system the therapeutic model created for Black and Brown people who needed abortions. Their testimonies shifted the conversation in states such as New York, leading to legalization.

Legalization nationwide, however, came through a case out of Texas, involving Jane Roe, later identified as Norma McCorvey, a white woman who alleged she'd been raped and wanted an abortion but was unable to obtain one because it was illegal. She was connected with two young lawyers who took her case to the Supreme Court. Norma was unable to receive her abortion both because it was illegal and she was unsure of where to receive care, and because if she had received an abortion, she would no longer be pregnant, which would have rendered her case moot. She later contended this was frustrating to her. The irony is that one of her lawyers, a white woman named Sarah Weddington, had previously had an abortion in Mexico and knew how to have one. The case was huge, and "Roe" garnered sympathy because her pregnancy was a result of rape, an allegation that McCorvey later declared was not true. But the fact remains that the conversation about legal abortion hinged on the health, safety, security, and virtues of white women. They were meant to be protected, both from criminalization and dangerous providers.

The *Roe v. Wade* decision itself legalized abortion nationwide, creating the pregnancy trimester framework, but allowed states to restrict abortion once viability occurred, based on quickening. *Roe* didn't decriminalize all abortions, however. It legalized abortions within a certain set of rules and regulations, putting the procedure squarely under the authority of physicians and the state, not the people who sought them. This meant that the vision of community health care dreamed up by Jane and other community providers would still be considered illegal.

In the decades after legalization, the antiabortion movement sought to chip away at access, beginning with state laws restricting the procedures and the clinics they were performed in. Antiabortion activists had several wins at the Supreme Court including *Planned Parenthood v. Casey,* which allowed states to restrict abortion so long as it did not cause an "undue burden" on the patient, and *Gonzales v. Carhart,* which restricted later abortion procedures. *Harris v. McRae* solidified the class break in access when the Supreme Court ruled that the US government did not have to financially provide access to abortion for people enrolled in Medicaid for their health care. We'll talk about this more in the next chapter. But the biggest win on the path to abortion recriminalization was created through voter suppression.

* * *

The backlash to President Barack Obama's 2008 election saw the rise of the Tea Party, a white nationalist movement that fueled the Republican Party's efforts to grab control of state legislative houses and redraw congressional and state legislative districts, ensuring that they could maintain political control of legislative seats through a process called gerrymandering. Tea Party activists pushed through hundreds of anti-abortion restrictions and voter suppression laws. The voter suppression laws meant that Black and Brown communities had little recourse to counter the bad policies being enacted. And restricting abortion meant that the activists could eventually undermine *Roe*, a landmark case that set the precedent for other constitutional rights such as health care access, privacy protections, and same sex marriage. The Tea Party, and later Trump's Make America Great Again movement, stoked fears that Black and Brown people, immigrants, and trans people were corrupting the country, harming children, and would eventually outnumber white people in the United States—an idea called the great replacement theory. White people in the United States could endorse the growing number of abortion restrictions that accompanied the racist policies because they seemed to criminalize people of color, and white people felt they could still receive abortions without much hassle.

With this new power, legislatures increased state surveillance of communities of color and moved untold sums of money into local police departments. With support from both Republicans and Democrats in office, local police now have some of the largest budgets when it comes to city services, sometimes outpacing schools, hospitals, libraries, childcare, and food and housing programs. This investment in policing is not just to the disservice of communities—it's dangerous for abortion access.

Although some states have criminalized abortions, people are still having them. They are self-managing their abortions safely, and few are experiencing unsafe abortions, because of medical inventions such as medication abortion. What has not changed is the criminalization risk.

While *Roe* was the law of the land for decades, people were still criminalized for self-managing abortions, as well as accused of endangering their pregnancies by drinking alcohol, using drugs, or simply refusing medical treatments, as legal scholar Michele Goodwin documented in her book *Policing the Womb: Invisible Women and the Criminalization of Motherhood*. When abortion was legal nationwide, the desire of the state to control if, when, and how someone had a pregnancy was a priority, and those who did not follow societal rules or outright defied them could be punished.

As we have seen historically, the government uses police as the mechanism to raid abortion clinics and arrest providers. In the years preceding and following the overturning of *Roe v. Wade*, police have investigated people suspected of assisting and having abortions by reviewing social media and text messages, website browser history, and coerced confessions. Social workers, nurses, and family friends are among those most likely to turn over someone alleged to have self-managed an abortion to the police; in some cases, the motivation was malice, but others thought it was what they were supposed to do.

It is impossible to support both abortion access and the police. Abortion cannot be liberated so long as the police have a presence. As history has shown us, when abortion is a crime, criminalization and policing are the go-to answer.

"Criminalization is how we enact stigma," lawyer and advocate Farah Diaz-Tello told us. So long as abortion stigma exists, society will have the urge to punish people of color by criminalizing the means. Although abortion advocates today are resisting allowing policing to have an acceptable place in the movement, we're still missing the mark, explained Ash Williams, a trans abortion storyteller, doula, and abolitionist. He said that we're turning toward carceral systems because we don't understand how the system we live within and our reactions to it tend toward taking a carceral approach—for example, calling the police on a patient who needs help after self-managing an abortion rather than offering them health care and sending them home safely. But what's scariest is that this carceral system does not solely impact people seeking illegal abortions; while many abortion bans tout exceptions for people who are survivors of rape or incest, many of those laws require that survivors file a report with the police and the state in order to receive an abortion. This opens them up to state surveillance, potential violence by police, and potential criminalization of their identities. Compliance with the carceral system becomes a requirement for access and a barrier for marginalized communities. We believe that when we learn our history and how systematic treatment of us has been enacted, we'll be able to change the path going forward. It's not enough to legalize abortion (or sex work or trans bodies); it must be decriminalized so no one can be punished for seeking care.

"We are trying to resist this carceral turn that we all have because our society is so steeped in white supremacy culture, control, and domination," Williams said. "Abolitionists, movement attorneys, abortion doulas, clinic workers, and reproductive justice organizers continue to experiment by working with one another and outside of carceral modes of care and abortion access. We are learning from our mistakes as well as increasing choices for pregnant people beyond what the courts and what the medical-industrial complex says is possible or achievable." It is not possible to liberate abortion until we thoughtfully invest in and pursue an abolitionist vision, where no one fears police or criminalization for their pregnancies, the ways they use their bodies, and how the build their families. Until we do, we're doomed to repeat history.

What's Race & Class Got to Do with It?

By all accounts, Rosaura Jimenez was deeply loved by all who knew her. Rosie, as she was known to her family and friends, was outgoing, loved to dance, and enjoyed dressing up and wearing wigs that signaled her unique style and vibrant presence. Rosie grew up in a large Mexican American family in 1950s McAllen, Texas. Her parents were migrant farmworkers, traveling to work on agricultural fields, later opening a Mexican restaurant, while raising twelve children. Like her family, Rosie was ambitious. The twenty-seven-year-old mother wanted more for her young daughter, Monique, than what she had growing up. Receiving a meager $86 a month in social service benefits, Rosie worked hourly wage jobs to make ends meet, including cleaning houses over the weekends to provide for herself and her daughter. After passing her GED (General Educational Development) test and enrolling in a government-sponsored program for secretarial school, Rosie enrolled at Pan Am University in 1974. Shortly before her death, she received a $700 financial aid check. But she refused to use that check on anything other than her education. "She was going to college to have a better life, that was her goal," her daughter, Monique, said in a 2015 *Texas Observer* interview. "I know that she saw my grandparents struggle, and she wanted to provide me with a better life." Rosie would do anything for Monique.

In 1979, Ellen Frankfort, a white journalist, published *Rosie: The Investigation of a Wrongful Death*, a book investigating Rosie's untimely death. As part of her investigation, Frankfort spoke to a few of Rosie's close friends, who, Frankfort said, were not initially interviewed by the Centers for Disease Control and Prevention (CDC), which looked into Rosie's passing as the first known death after Congress passed the Hyde Amendment. Over the years, academics and scholars have criticized the book for, among other things, its portrayal of Rosie as a "feminist martyr," whose tragic and preventable death would be politicized to spur action against abortion funding restrictions, and the role it plays in perpetuating carceral feminism that sees justice as the criminalization of the immigrant midwife who provided the abortion rather than structural change.

Rosie's story has become an iconic and dire warning within the reproductive justice movement. For nearly fifty years, her death has served as a symbol for activists advocating for an end to the Hyde Amendment, a budget amendment that bars the use of federal funds for abortion coverage for Medicaid and Medicare enrollees in many states; residents of Washington, DC; federal employees; Peace Corps volunteers; and others. Although the Hyde Amendment certainly played a major role in Rosie's death, it was not the only player. But because Rosie's story had become larger than life in the movement, the full story and systemic failures—including those by people within the abortion care field—were overshadowed or erased. When we fail to tell a more complete version of her story and the stories of the countless others who have been affected by systemic injustices, we are destined to never learn from them.

During our research for this book, we were surprised to learn that Rosie had three abortions after her daughter was born: one in 1975 and two in 1977. This shouldn't have been a surprise, because most people who have abortions already have children and nearly half have more than one abortion. However, we were surprised that this fact had been omitted when her story was retold. There is a tendency to flatten abortion experiences in the media or for advocacy causes—to tell tidied-up versions of our lives—to garner more sympathy and understanding. But all of us are much more complicated. For us, this fact changes the story a bit; rather than the narrative we'd seen portrayed of a scared young woman who died with her financial aid check in her hand, we see Rosie as a confident mother who knew that abortion was an option for her each and every time she needed it.

Because they took place before the Hyde Amendment went into effect, Rosie's first two abortions were covered by her Medicaid insurance and performed at reputable clinics in McAllen and Harlingen. However, in September 1977, two months before she sought her third abortion, the state of Texas changed abortion coverage based on the new rules of the Hyde Amendment.

Rosie didn't know what to do. "She already had one child," Rosie's friend Diana told Frankfort. Diana Rivera and Rosie attended Pan Am University together and bonded as mothers of young children. "She really loved [her daughter], but it was hard."

Rosie was confident that she did not want to continue the pregnancy, but without Medicaid coverage she couldn't afford the price of an abortion at her local clinic. Abortion funds—community-based organizations that raise money to help people afford their abortions—didn't exist at the time, and she was turned away from the clinic because she couldn't pay.

Rosie knew that some women crossed the border to Reynosa, Mexico, for an injection that they believed would terminate a pregnancy. Some women received an injection of Depo-Provera. Rosie became desperate after she received an injection of an unknown medication in Reynosa that didn't end her pregnancy.

Another of Rosie's friends, "Evangelina" in Frankfort's book, suggested Maria Pineda, a *partera* (or midwife); her mother had heard of Pineda and knew someone who had visited her for an injection. Pineda was licensed to assist women in labor but was not legally permitted to perform abortions, so she charged Rosie $100, less than the $230 fee at legal clinics. Evangelina accompanied Rosie to her appointment in Pineda's home in McAllen.

After the procedure was complete, Evangelina recalled Pineda saying,

"I extracted blood from [Rosie]" before holding up what Evangelina said looked like an old rag with blood on it and a rubber tube. Evangelina said Rosie felt weak following the procedure, but relieved.

The next day, Rosie attended class at Pan Am but did not feel well and returned home shortly after. "Margie," her next-door neighbor and another good friend, stopped by that afternoon to use Rosie's phone and recalled seeing her lying on the bed asleep. Hearing her moaning, Margie asked whether she was okay, and Rosie mumbled that she was having trouble with her period. A few hours later, Margie was back home after picking up her son. That's when Rosie's boss, who had stopped by to see Rosie, knocked on her door to tell her that Rosie was not okay. Rosie had called out of work and had her mother take Monique. "See, she had it all arranged so [her daughter] wouldn't see her sick," Margie said.

Margie and Rosie's boss then recruited another neighbor to help carry her to Margie's car, because by that point Rosie said she couldn't feel her legs. Dr. Daniel Chester, an abortion provider called to McAllen General Hospital to treat Rosie, said that by the time Rosie arrived at the hospital, her skin was yellowish green, there was purple behind her eyes, and she was shaking. Dr. Chester said they diagnosed her with *Clostridium perfringens*, an infection that spread throughout her body and caused her organs to shut down. To try to keep her alive, the doctors performed a tracheotomy and then did a hysterectomy to try to identify the source of a severe pelvic infection. She continued to decline after the hysterectomy, and she died on October 3, 1977, eight days after she was admitted to the hospital, from kidney and heart failure, leaving her four-year-old daughter in the care of family members. The tracheotomy in Rosie's throat made it difficult for her to communicate, Rosie's friend Pauline told Frankfort, but she managed to communicate by writing on pieces of paper. One message was clear: "Let me die in peace." The other, Monique told CNN in 2021, was Monique's name. "They said 'Don't worry about it, Rosie. We're going to take care of Monique.'"

* * *

In 1969, the CDC created an abortion surveillance program to document the impact abortions were having on women's health, studying the different methods and complications arising from clandestine procedures. The research produced through this program played a pivotal role in the Supreme Court's *Roe v. Wade* decision, as it clearly showed the safety of first- and second-trimester abortions. But following the *Roe* decision, the CDC wasn't as effective as it was during those early years. In its initial report on Rosie Jimenez's death, the CDC only mentioned Rosie's first abortion, falsely stating she obtained it in Mexico, when she had received both of her abortions in Texas. Eventually the CDC corrected its report with Frankfort's assistance. But Pineda was still assisting women out of her home in Texas. The local health department didn't take any action. "Maria Pineda's clientele [Latinx women] posed no threat to the McAllen medical establishment," wrote Frances Kissling, a former executive director of the National Abortion Federation, who is white and contributed to Frankfort's book. Pineda's patients did not garner sympathy or attention, unlike the white patients of other providers who had been investigated and charged for their roles in unsafe abortions or births. It was up to the community to address the situation themselves.

In June 1978, Diana Rivera, Frankfort, and Kissling set out to stop Pineda through a sting operation while reporters listened in down the street.

When Diana and a friend entered Pineda's home with the $125 she requested for the abortion, they noticed a jar of dirty water with medical instruments in the room that Pineda used to treat patients. In an affidavit, the woman pretending to get the procedure recalled that Pineda explained how she would "put a small red rubber hose in me and that . . . bleeding [would start] tomorrow." Diana told the *Texas Observer* in 2015 that she still remembers the red rubber hose: "It was filthy." Pineda continued to instruct Diana and her friend on what to do, including not going to a doctor. She said "not to go to any doctors because they would ask questions, that if [there were] any complications to go to her and she would [provide] medicine for pain and infection."

As a result of the sting, Pineda was arrested. The women had reservations about getting the police involved, but stopping Pineda from practicing was their ultimate goal. Because the medical system didn't take any steps to hold Pineda accountable, the women took matters into their own hands. Four months after the incident, Pineda was sentenced to three days in jail and fined $100, the cost of the abortion that killed Rosie.

What we find tragic about Rosie's story—a part of the story that has been erased over the years since Frankfort's investigation—is that she was turned away from a clinic where she had received care previously simply because she couldn't pay. It's devastating, to say the least, to recognize that Rosie's lack of cash on hand meant she could not receive safe care and played a role in her death. Fundamentally, the story shows how class and race determine whether or not someone receives an abortion.

It's undeniable that Rosie became a national figure shortly after her death. Following national news coverage, activists across the country held candlelight vigils, propping her up as an example of what happens when abortion is made inaccessible. Rosie's death has been turned into a lesson about antiabortion policies—and it is a lesson. But by doing so, abortion activists have placed the blame for Rosie's death on one policy in particular rather than the entire capitalist health care system, rife with policies and stigma fueled by racism, that keeps people from being able to receive the care they need. The fact is that money—or the lack of it—kept Rosie from receiving competent medical care—an issue that impacts communities today. Rosie was denied an abortion at a reputable clinic because she did not have the money to pay for her abortion up front, and like so many others at the time and since then, that is part of the tragedy of her death. The Hyde Amendment led to her death, but so did a system that values payment and profits over people. Unfortunately, this hasn't changed. In her book *No Real Choice: How Culture and Politics Matter for Reproductive Autonomy*, sociologist Katrina Kimport writes about a young woman of color who was turned away from an abortion appointment because she didn't have cash to pay for her appointment and the clinic didn't accept credit cards or health insurance. By the time she realized this, the banks were closed and she wasn't able to get the money she needed or time off work for a subsequent appointment. She didn't choose to continue her pregnancy; capitalism chose for her. Clinics, of course, need to be paid for their services so they can pay their workers, afford medical supplies, and keep the clinics open. Most barely make ends meet as it is. Everyone is making difficult decisions in an impossible situation set up to privilege the profits of health insurance companies and to serve only those who have money and the access to health care that comes with money.

But it's not solely capitalism; it's how we consume these tragic stories without indicting the system. In the time since *Roe* was overturned, we have seen writers and journalists clamoring to cover a story about someone who has died from an unsafe abortion. They have opined about why those stories are not plastered all over the front pages of every newspaper. For us, the situation is complicated. Those who died deserve not to have their death—their stories—exploited and mangled for political gain. They deserve to have their memories live on with those who loved them, not flattened to make a point about the barriers to abortion that we already know about. It's frustrating to witness reporters salivate over the potential story of a dead person, rather than elevate the stories of those who are living and indicting the injustice of our system with their voices. But, most important, we have seen people die from unsafe abortions simply because of who they were and where they lived, and those stories have been mangled and misrepresented. The lessons were not learned the first time, so why are reporters begging for more stories of martyrs murdered by the system rather than illuminating and advocating for changes to a flawed system that has been in place for decades?

Whiteness is one reason. As we mentioned, Sara Clarke Kaplan argues that, although for years there was public discussion about the recriminalization of abortion and how it would harm communities of color and low-income people, after the *Dobbs* decision, reporting focused mainly on medical implications and ignored race, making the stories synonymous with whiteness. She also pointed out that the narrative painted these cases and the criminalization of abortion as unprecedented reproductive coercion, despite the centuries-long history of the United States applying that same coercion to communities of color. It is painful that people's allegiance to whiteness does not allow them to empathize with people of color experiencing systemic barriers leading to their death. We shouldn't have to lose another Rosie to act; Rosie's death should have been enough.

If we were ever going to learn anything from Rosie's death, it should have been that the racist, classist systems, rooted in capitalism, that make it possible for abortions to be denied in the first place need to be dismantled. That includes the health insurance system that grants corporations and governments the authority over what health care is and isn't covered, and the medical system that gives doctors the power to turn patients in desperate need away because of how much money isn't in their bank account. It's the Medicaid system that plays Russian roulette with lives, determining who receives care based on legislators' whims and budgets. Until those systems are completely rebuilt with the people who need abortions at the center, they will never, ever meet the needs of Black and Brown folks in this country.

THE CREATION OF MEDICAID

The effort to create a federal health insurance program for all began in the 1930s but lost steam after World War II, when President Harry S. Truman asked Congress for legislation to establish public insurance. President Truman had to abandon the idea after he faced fierce opposition to his plan, which included fearmongering about the idea of "socialized medicine." But advocates continued to retool the idea in response to growing needs among people age sixty-five and older in the United States and reintroduced it in the 1960s. (The population swiftly rose from 3 million in 1900 to 12 million in 1950 and was in need of increased health care services, but many had a hard time affording health care due to rising costs.) Congress invited testimony from key advocacy groups; their testimony highlighted how the private insurance industry was leaving behind this older population, whom insurers considered a "bad risk" for their financial investment.

Medicaid is a means-tested federal health insurance program for low-income families. The Medicaid program's structure was based on a previous program, Medical Assistance for the Aged, established by the Kerr-Mills Act of 1960. The program provided federal funds to states that participated voluntarily to expand health care coverage available to elderly people in the United States who had too much money to qualify for public assistance but not enough to cover their medical expenses. But the program had limited success in enrolling people due to the social stigma of being poor and needing government assistance, and states with large populations of Black people rejected participation because it might better those people's lives. This stigma would impact the Medicaid program as well.

After much debate, two programs were created: Medicare and Medicaid. President Lyndon B. Johnson signed the law creating these programs as part of the Social Security Amendments of 1965, one week prior to signing the Voting Rights Act. Both were monumental pieces of legislation that were products of the civil rights movement's attempt to right the status of Black people. Medicare became the federal health insurance program for elderly people and eventually some disabled people, while Medicaid insured low-income people in the United States. Because the structure of the public insurance program provides states with flexibility over how they comply with the federal standards to administer the program, state Medicaid programs vary significantly. Ultimately, states get to decide who is covered, what services are covered beyond some basic care, the models for health care delivery, and the reimbursement structure for doctors and hospitals. Reimbursement is slow and rates are notoriously low, sometimes not even covering the cost of the procedure; thus some providers won't even accept Medicaid insurance, which limits where low-income people can receive health care.

The rot in the Medicaid program is due to its original structure. The program's setup allowed politicians to control the health care access of low-income people in the United States, whom they chastised for their family size, poor health outcomes, and low incomes based on racist assumptions, and therefore the program perpetuated the very issues it was created to eradicate. Even though white people are enrolled in Medicaid, the overwhelming image of Medicaid enrollees conjured by politicians and media is of people of color—in particular, Black women. This is similar for welfare benefits; Black women are the controlling image, yet white people are overwhelmingly the beneficiaries. That's by design. Using anti-Blackness and racism—along with fatphobia, classism, ableism, and xenophobia—politicians have been able to denigrate Medicaid as an "entitlement program," casting those who are enrolled in it as nontaxpaying and undeserving people and thus experiencing less pushback when legislators enact cuts to the programs. The overt racism allowed politicians to create a system that decides who is and is not worthy of "free" health care from the government.

Racist pro-poverty lawmakers are then able to use Medicaid funding as a weapon to wield against populations they do not like or who do not support these politicians at their own discretion, particularly in states with large concentrations of low-income people and people of color. Herein lies the problem: states with large populations of Black folks tended to not participate in the program, making the public benefits program inaccessible to the people who needed it most. The idea of Black and Brown people receiving any sort of support or compensation from the government was portrayed with disdain, and lawmakers knew that the Medicaid program was a specific vehicle they could weaponize.

This was a tried-and-true tactic. In her 2020 book *Taking Children: A History of American Terror*, Laura Briggs, gender studies scholar at the University of Massachusetts Amherst, writes that states sought "to punish the most impoverished Black households for the NAACP's desegregation work" in the 1950s and 1960s, including the 1954 *Brown v. Board of Education* decision. Immediately after that decision, southern states such as Mississippi used "suitable home" requirements to cut Black women and children off welfare rolls. Mississippi also used common-law marriages, which were more prevalent among Black and low-income communities, as a tool to cut welfare rolls, by decrying these marriages as "an illicit relationship or promiscuity." This effectively cut Black children from welfare programs because they were considered illegitimate in the state's eyes. For example, Mississippi cut nearly 8,400 mostly Black children off welfare rolls "because they or a sibling were illegitimate."

In the 1960s, the image of welfare recipients underwent a transformation. Prior to this period, white widows were the larger share of welfare recipients, in part due to the intentional exclusion of Black mothers. Therefore the conjured image of a public assistance recipient was of a deserving white widow who was a single parent due to loss, emphasizing her white womanhood as a badge of innocence. Similarly, the New Deal's Aid to Families with Dependent Children program excluded Black mothers, on the grounds that "blacks needed less to live on than whites." Black parents were shut out of support. Already unable to earn the same wage as white people or men, Black women were further financially disadvantaged because they could not receive welfare benefits on account of their race. Following successful organizing by the National Welfare Rights Organization, more Black families enrolled in social service programs after previously being excluded. Benefits increased to women-led households, and the image of welfare recipients was transformed to one of a dishonorable and immoral single Black mother. Black women's reproduction and caregiving were weaponized against them and expanded to women of color overall, building on systems of discrimination. These women were blamed for having children but were also locked out of services when they tried to plan and space their pregnancies. Segregation was a feature of the US health care system.

CODIFYING ABORTION STIGMA

Lawmakers introduced and passed Title X in 1970 at a time of inequitable access to contraception, with women reporting that they were having more children than they wanted. Title X (read "Title 10"—it's a Roman numeral) grants are federal funds directed to health clinics for them to provide affordable reproductive health services for low-income patients. To this day, Title X funds contraception and other preventive health care services, including cancer screenings and treatment for sexually transmitted infections. However, lawmakers included in the legislation a ban on abortion, which prevents the health clinics receiving Title X funds from using those moneys to provide abortions. To add to the confusion, presidential administrations control how Title X is regulated, so the program's rules have vacillated based on who is sitting in the White House. Under the Trump administration, for example, Title X clinics could not refer their patients for abortions or even provide abortions in the same building as they provided Title X services, which contributed to a decline in the number of providers in the network, further marginalizing people with low incomes for being poor. The Kaiser Family Foundation reported that these regulations "led to a withdrawal of almost a third of the sites from the Title X network."

Although Title X marked the first time in history that congressional lawmakers would legislatively separate abortion from other health care services, it was far from the last. In many ways, Title X set a precedent for how lawmakers would go on to prevent people from accessing abortion care, even beyond the United States' borders, without enacting a total abortion ban. Conservatives would follow this same strategy again shortly after the *Roe v. Wade* ruling by passing the Helms Amendment to the Foreign Assistance Act in December 1973. The Helms Amendment prevented US funding that goes to other countries for a broad range of health care programs and services, such as HIV and AIDS prevention and treatment, from being used for abortions. Specifically, this policy prohibits US funds from being used for the "performance of abortion as a method of family planning" or to "motivate or coerce any person to practice abortions." Despite protests from the Nixon administration's US Agency for International Development (USAID) that the Helms Amendment "was at odds with the fundamental philosophy of US population assistance policy, because of its seemingly imperialistic and hypocritical overtones," the president signed the policy into law on December 17, 1973. In essence, the wealthiest nation in the world was telling other countries that it would help expand access to reproductive health care, but only if they adopted its antiabortion ideology, despite mounting evidence that abortion bans are deadly. But as we would come to see with the Hyde Amendment, the harm inflicted on the most marginalized in our society didn't matter to those seeking to maintain their power and ability to control the lives of others through capitalist systems and structures.

Congresswoman Barbara Lee's Abortions

In the early 1960s, fifteen-year-old Barbara Jean Tutt discovered she was pregnant. She knew little about how her own body worked and had previously become pregnant by her boyfriend, Carl, whom she immediately married, she wrote in her 2008 memoir Renegade for Peace and Justice: Congresswoman Barbara Lee Speaks for Me; *however, the first pregnancy had ended in a miscarriage. "Whatever your decision is, it's nobody's business," her mother told Barbara. With this second pregnancy, Barbara decided to have an abortion. Given that abortion was illegal nationwide, she had to find connections to a clinic. Her mother's friend and former co-worker suggested a reputable clinic for a safe abortion in Juárez, Mexico, just across the border from El Paso, Texas, where Barbara was raised. The family had recently moved to the San Fernando Valley, so Barbara got on a plane and flew to El Paso for care. Her mother's friend, who was Latina, took Barbara to a doctor the friend knew to get the procedure. In her memoir, Barbara wrote that the woman had all sorts of connections and that if it weren't for her, Barbara would not have known how to get a safe abortion. When Barbara and her mother's friend arrived, it was late in the evening. Barbara wrote that the "relatively clean and safe" clinic was not one that she would have any other medical procedure in but was better than the unsafe options others had gone to. In a 2022 NBC News interview, she described the room where the abortion was performed as dark, with the only lights shining down onto the bed. She wrote in her memoir about her vague memories of the Mexican abortion provider giving her an "unbearably painful procedure" that allowed her to finish high school and graduate from college. "I could have been put in jail and criminalized just like now," she told us in a phone interview. She also could have died before becoming a congresswoman, because as she explained, septic abortions, like Rosie's, were a leading cause of death among Black women before Roe. Barbara's own abortion experiences led her to become a tireless advocate for abortion policies supporting Black and Brown women.*

She has also found a renewed passion in her advocacy with sharing her abortion stories. Although she wrote about her abortion in her memoir, she didn't share the story much until it became clear that the Supreme Court was going to overturn Roe. In September 2021, days after Texas's Senate Bill 8 (SB8)—a

law that banned abortion after six weeks but also allowed private citizens to en-
force the law and collect a $10,000 reward for doing so—went into effect, Con-
gresswoman Lee joined fellow members of Congress, Representatives Cori Bush
and Pramila Jayapal, in a House committee hearing to share their own abortion
stories. It was a historic first for the legislative body and a critical hearing for
all to see. "Women around the country need to understand their members of
Congress who see them and who have been in this fight a long time," she told
us. "I felt like it was the time to talk about it so other people would understand
that they are not alone . . . and that there are those of us who look like them
who are fighting for reproductive justice and the right for them to make our own
decisions about our own bodies."

A decade later, President Ronald Reagan would bolster the Helms Amendment by implementing the notorious Mexico City Policy. Named after the location where the policy was announced at the 1984 United Nations International Conference on Population, the Mexico City Policy blocked overseas groups receiving US funds from using their grant funding, including non-US funds, for abortion services or referrals. The policy has been revoked by every Democratic president and reenacted by every Republican one, causing chaos for nongovernmental organizations seeking to provide the world's poorest communities with family planning services and reproductive health care.

These two policies have contributed to a rise in unsafe abortions in developing countries. Unsafe abortions result in 13 percent of global maternal deaths and account for one of every four cases of pregnancy-related death. In countries in Africa and Central and South America, the majority of abortions pose great risk. Although this is very much a US problem, it's become a global tragedy as antiabortion lawmakers in the US seek to control the reproductive lives of anyone who is poor or of color, and definitely those who are both. The United States continues to export its segregated health care system to other countries through policies rife with abortion stigma, causing countless deaths and unsafe pregnancy conditions for millions of people. Anti-Blackness and abortion stigma are always at the core.

Protesters holding placards reading "Legal abortion si yes" and "Free legal abortion" during a mass demonstration against New York State abortion laws, in the Manhattan borough of New York City, March 28, 1970. *Photo by Graphic House/Hulton Archive/Getty Images.*

HOW HYDE HAPPENED

Among other things, the Hyde Amendment was retaliation for the 1973 *Roe v. Wade* Supreme Court decision legalizing abortion nationwide. The antiabortion congressman representing Illinois who introduced the measure, Henry J. Hyde, made no secret of his desire to end access to abortion, but he knew that with *Roe* in place his only option was to restrict it through the national budget. The congressman was vehemently anti-abortion, once stating that "birth is no substantial change, it is merely a change of address."

Representative Hyde worked hard to find a way to cut off access to abortion, and while he could not legally restrict the procedure, he knew he could cut off financial access for all who depended on the government's support for their health insurance. Pro-choice lawmakers organized in response to the bill and debated about the impact it would have on low-income people seeking abortions. Tensions were high, as abortion had only been legal for a few years and many legislators knew people who had been harmed by unsafe procedures before legalization. But Representative Hyde was callous and crude in his August 10, 1976, response:

> *Mr. Speaker, let the poor women of America make a list of those things that society denies them and which are enjoyed by rich women. Decent housing, decent education, decent food, decent income, and then say to them, "Now, those will take second place. But we will encourage you to kill your unborn young children. Besides, there are too many of you anyway." If rich women want to enjoy their high-priced vices, that is their responsibility. They can get the finest heroin in the world that is not available on the street. They can get a face lift. They can fly to Las Vegas and gamble. That is fine, but not at the taxpayers' expense.*

During later debate on the House floor about the budget rider, Representative Hyde added, "I certainly would like to prevent, if I could legally, anybody having an abortion, a rich woman, a middle-class woman, or a poor woman. Unfortunately, the only vehicle available is the Medicaid bill."

Congressman Hyde never hid his racism and disdain for people of color seeking abortions. It was baked into every word he uttered. At the time, Representative Barbara Lee worked as a congressional staffer for Representative Ron Dellums and, she told us, she was furious from day one. To her, the racist and discriminatory nature of Hyde's amendment was clear, as were his words. Representative Lee correctly recalled that in 1977 floor remarks Representative Hyde claimed his policy would affect only "little ghetto kids," stating that "the life of a little ghetto kid is just as important as the life of a rich person." Stay classy, Henry.

Hyde believed that it was the government's role to intervene in the pregnancy decisions of all, explaining, "When the mother, who should be the natural protector of her unborn child, becomes its adversary, then the legislature has a duty to intervene." That intervention came in the form of a two-tiered medical system, one for the poor and one for the rich. After all, some people with money would continue to access abortions, as they could travel for care.

At first, the Hyde Amendment struggled to get through Congress. The measure failed to get enough votes in the Senate after Democratic Congress members argued that the purpose of the Medicaid program was to fund health care services for the poor, and the failure to cover abortion care would drive these women to "ugly, brutal options" if they could not access abortions through legal means. But antiabortion lawmakers defended Hyde, claiming that although *Roe* legalized abortion, that ruling "does not translate . . . into an affirmative duty on the part of the federal government to use public funds to finance the termination of human life." After failing to pass the amendment twice in the Senate, in fall 1976, Congress members agreed on a modified version that would provide exceptions for Medicaid-funded abortion "where the life of the mother would be endangered if the fetus were carried to term." Former Planned Parenthood president Faye Wattleton observed in her memoir, *Life on the Line*, that the forthcoming election was what drove the lawmakers to go from not backing the Hyde Amendment to passing an amended version, explaining that they didn't want to be seen as "disrupting government services over the single issue of abortion for poor women." They also assumed that the Supreme Court would rule against it, as "everybody knew" the bill was unconstitutional, Wattleton wrote. Indeed, President Gerald Ford vetoed the bill, only for Congress to override his veto. The bill became law on September 30, 1976. A lawsuit prevented it from taking effect for nearly a year until the Supreme Court ruled, allowing the restrictions. That's when Rosie encountered it.

Today, the Hyde Amendment prevents not only people with low incomes from accessing abortion, but also government employees, people in the military, veterans, and Indigenous people receiving care through the Indian Health Service—basically everyone who receives insurance through a government program. This rule has been one of the most effective ways of restricting access for millions of people in the United States. And since Rosie's death, many other pregnant people have been forced to seek care outside of a clinic setting or have been forced to continue pregnancies when they would otherwise have had an abortion.

Poster advertising a 1970 demonstration to repeal abortion laws by the Massachusetts Organization for Repeal of Abortion Laws. *Courtesy of the Valley Women's Center Papers, Sophia Smith Collection, Smith College, Northampton, Massachusetts.*

THE LEGACY OF HYDE LIVES ON

Perhaps one of the most important legacies of the Hyde Amendment is how it rolled back gains civil rights activists had made in integrating a segregated health care system. Under President Johnson's Medicare program, hospitals had to provide services to both Black and white patients in order to qualify for federal funding. The Hyde Amendment created an avenue for doctors to deny Medicaid patients services, in this case abortions, and many of those patients were people of color. After all, folks with money, often white people, would continue to access abortions, as their insurance covered it. Dr. Curtis Boyd, a white abortion provider who provided care in Dallas and Santa Fe before *Roe* through referrals from the Clergy Consultation Service on Abortion, told us that prior to 1973, most of the patients he saw were white women, middle- or upper-class, and predominantly university students referred by white clergy. It wasn't until the end of the 1970s that he noticed a shift in the race of his patients, from white women to predominantly Latinx and Black women, who previously were likely still getting care from community midwives or across the border. "I can't prove this, but these [white] women all had private doctors; they had money, insurance, access, and they went to their doctor to deal with this problem they had."

At the same time that Medicaid recipients were denied their abortions, the Medicaid program fully covered prenatal and postnatal care, including labor and delivery. So, in essence, the government has been forcing people to be pregnant, by making it easier for them to receive coverage to stay pregnant than to end their pregnancies. Make no mistake about it: nothing about the Hyde Amendment is normal or okay. People should not be forced into a life-changing situation based solely on the type of insurance coverage that they have.

We also want to note that although racist policies in welfare programs were designed to harm Black communities, other groups have been directly affected. Latinx people have been diverted away from applying for the meager welfare benefits or other social programs available in their communities when they were eligible for them or channeled into low-wage, unstable jobs. Immigrants who qualify for benefits have been discouraged from applying for fear of impacting their ability to live and work in the United States.

As part of its efforts to improve health insurance coverage for children, pregnant women, older people, and people with disabilities, Congress began uncoupling eligibility for Medicaid from welfare programs. Rather than relying on a person's ability to qualify for public cash assistance, the government measured the person's income against the federal poverty level. But since that had the inevitable effect of increasing the number of people eligible for Medicaid, in 1996, Congress banned immigrants from receiving coverage. Immigrants now had to wait five years after they entered the United States to qualify. President Bill Clinton signed the law as part of a slew of social welfare reforms that added work requirements and

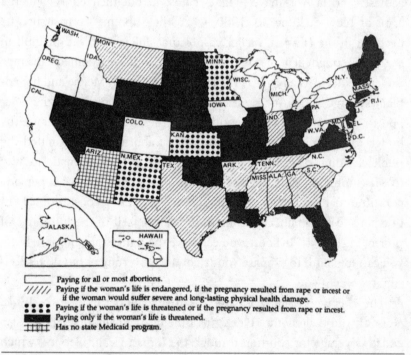

☐ Paying for all or most abortions.
///// Paying if the woman's life is endangered, if the pregnancy resulted from rape or incest or if the woman would suffer severe and long-lasting physical health damage.
⦂⦂⦂ Paying if the woman's life is threatened or if the pregnancy resulted from rape or incest.
■ Paying only if the woman's life is threatened.
⊞ Has no state Medicaid program.

Map of state policies on public funding of abortion as of March 31, 1978, published by the Committee for Abortion Rights and Against Sterilization Abuse, in *CARASA News* II, no. 5 (June 1, 1978). *Courtesy of the Karen Stamm collection of Committee for Abortion Rights and Against Sterilization Abuse in CARASA records, Sophia Smith Collection, Smith College, Northampton, Massachusetts.*

time limits for recipients. There was little challenge from the reproductive rights movement against the pro-choice president's decision at the time, even though the move was clearly antifamily and antireproduction. This policy impact is very real for undocumented immigrants, who have to go to great lengths to avoid the ever-increasing border patrols and local police who are given the power to question their immigration status as they cross an immigration checkpoint on the way to a clinic. The fear of detention and deportation is added to the list of barriers created by our inequitable health care system.

THE FIGHT TO END HYDE

Since the Hyde Amendment went into effect, some reproductive health activists and lawyers have fought against it, but their efforts suffered a major blow on June 30, 1980, when the Supreme Court issued its decision in the *Harris v. McRae* case. Cora McRae, the lead plaintiff in the case, sought a first-trimester abortion but was denied coverage under Medicaid as a result of the Hyde Amendment. McRae and her co-plaintiffs argued that the Hyde Amendment was a violation of the First, Fourth, Fifth, and Ninth Amendments to the Constitution, because the budget rider limited the public funding of abortion but permitted the public funding of childbirth costs. The case eventually made its way to the Supreme Court, which ruled in a 5–4 decision that a person's constitutional right to an abortion did not include "a constitutional entitlement to the financial resources to avail herself of the full range of protected choices." In short, you can have the right to an abortion, but if you cannot afford to exercise your right, the government has no responsibility to help you.

The *Harris v. McRae* case was the first to undermine *Roe v. Wade*. Not only did it allow the Hyde Amendment to remain intact, but it also ended coverage for abortion through the Indian Health Service, which had been covering abortion care until that point. The decision meant that the right to an abortion existed only on paper and for those who could afford it. As a result of the decision, for those who could not afford an abortion on their own, the government had the ability to financially coerce Medicaid recipients into continuing their pregnancies by solely covering care related to childbirth, thus ensuring there would always be a broken system of access to abortion. In his dissent in the case, Justice Thurgood Marshall underscored this point, writing, "By thus injecting coercive financial incentives favoring childbirth into a decision that is constitutionally guaranteed to be free from government intrusion, the Hyde Amendment deprives the indigent woman of her freedom to choose abortion over maternity, thereby impinging on the due process liberty right recognized in *Roe v. Wade*." Justice Marshall also noted that the Hyde Amendment was "designed to deprive poor and minority women of their constitutional right to choose abortion."

The outcome of this decision is further complicated by the lack of investment in pregnancy care across the United States, leaving low-income patients with no real options. A study published in 1996 examining the decade following the *Harris v. McRae* decision noted that financial barriers were the most important factor contributing to pregnant patients receiving inadequate health care.

And yet at the time, the Supreme Court argued that poor people's options for terminating their pregnancies wouldn't be any different had the Hyde Amendment not blocked their access to abortion. But they would have been different, as Rosie Jimenez's case clearly shows: she had had two previous abortions that were covered under Medicaid. It was only after Representative Hyde dismantled a lifeline for Medicaid recipients that Rosie sought an unsafe abortion.

The link between abortion bans and poor maternal health outcomes could not be clearer. Immediately following the *Roe* ruling, maternal mortality rates steeply declined, falling by 30 to 40 percent for people of color. As abortion became more widely available, maternal health care improved, because patients had legal options for termination rather than the dangerous methods or back-alley providers that were prevalent during the era immediately preceding *Roe*. Today, the states with the most extreme abortion restrictions also have the highest maternal death rates. A May 2023 *New Yorker* article documented that in Texas doctors were seeing more incidents of maternal sepsis after the notorious SB8 went into effect. One Houston doctor told the magazine, "We are seeing more frequent first-trimester complications, and my colleagues and I sense that it's leading to more death."

Clinicians are reporting that the patients arriving with first-trimester complications have experienced incomplete abortions, when fetal tissue remains in the uterus following a medication abortion or the use of another abortion method. Prior to the 2021 Texas law, most patients would seek follow-up care after their abortions without fear. But the criminal environment has led to fewer people seeking follow-up care. Doctors have also noted an increase in second-trimester deaths from sepsis, which they believe will likely be the leading cause of pregnancy-related deaths in Texas. But the problem isn't just in Texas, or even just in conservative states. As more hospitals are owned by Catholic churches or operated under Catholic doctrines, we are seeing an increase in patients being turned away from care or being denied abortions until it is too late. Given the maternal morbidity rate for Black and Brown pregnant people, access to an abortion in a timely manner is a life-or-death situation. But politics and money stand in the way of a pregnant person's right to life.

Political cartoon published by the Committee for Abortion Rights and Against Sterilization Abuse in *CARASA News* II, no. 5 (June 1, 1978). *Courtesy of the Karen Stamm collection of Committee for Abortion Rights and Against Sterilization Abuse in CARASA records, Sophia Smith Collection, Smith College, Northampton, Massachusetts.*

* * *

With the Supreme Court's 1980 blessing, the Hyde Amendment has remained in place. Abortion rights activists have created abortion funds in communities across the country to fill the access gap. Abortion funds are local organizations that raise money to help people pay for their abortions. One of the first abortion funds was named in Rosie Jimenez's honor, and although it didn't have a lot of money to support people seeking abortions during its formative years, it has since transformed into the Lilith Fund, which still operates in Texas. Today, abortion funds work to meet the needs of people traveling across state lines to have their abortions, to cover their transportation, childcare, and other costs related to complying with severe restrictions such as forced waiting period laws or outright bans in their home states. The resources provided by each abortion fund varies depending on the community's need.

For Rachael Lorenzo (Mescalero Apache / Laguna Pueblo / Xicana), who founded Indigenous Women Rising (IWR) in 2014, it was imperative that the organization provide both financial support to Native people in the United States and Canada for their abortions and funding for perinatal care and other sexual health resources that are not offered in Native communities serviced by the federal Indian Health Service, which is subject to the Hyde Amendment. Rachael started developing the organization shortly after having a harrowing abortion experience of their own in 2013.

At twenty-three, Rachael found out they were pregnant and was excited about having a second child. But at a prenatal appointment, their doctor said that the pregnancy was not progressing properly and that they would have to wait for it to pass on its own. "Abortion wasn't even presented as an option for me," Rachael told us. So they waited two or three months, letting the pregnancy progress on its own. Meanwhile, they were working on the Respect ABQ Women campaign, a 2013 effort to defeat an antiabortion ballot measure in Albuquerque, New Mexico. In early December, on the heels of winning the campaign, Rachael began experiencing contractions and could barely stand up. Although Rachael was experiencing "the most pain I've ever felt in my life," they told us the emergency room staff refused to administer pain management due to their weight. Rachael waited for hours and began bleeding on the hospital bedsheets. They felt dehumanized. Once the doctor arrived, Rachael was finally offered a procedural abortion and opioids for pain management (they subsequently developed an addiction). "After that experience, I really wanted to talk to other people about abortion." Rachael began asking about Indigenous people's experiences with abortion, such as whether they partook in any traditions or ceremonies following their procedure. "I just wanted to meet other Native people. We have to be able to tell our stories, because I can't be the only one who had such a painful experience."

As part of their effort to connect with others, Rachael launched IWR's abortion fund in 2018. They found the reproductive justice framework and learned about connecting oppressions, such as how fatphobia and racism impact the full spectrum of pregnancy care and all health care. "I started making all of these connections, and then I started realizing like, holy shit, not only was my abortion a dehumanizing experience, but basically my entire life experience with doctors, who commented on my body or different aspects of my body, and how that was actually really sexual harassment." This became an awakening for Rachael—not only to ways people experience abortion care but also to how we advocate for safety, sexuality, and pleasure. "It's about creating the life that you want, and that we don't have to subscribe to colonizer ideals of beauty."

Since its founding, IWR has assisted many people who rely on the Indian Health Service for care but are denied access to needed reproductive health care services. Although IHS is required to carry emergency contraception, tribally run clinics do not always carry it. A 2023 Medill News Service investigation found that around half of the Native health care clinics in Oklahoma don't offer emergency contraception, even though the state has one of the largest Native populations in the country.

Indigenous Women Rising strives to assist everyone who comes to IWR for financial support, but the ever-increasing need means not everyone can be helped. Abortion funds like IWR are regularly hitting or exceeding their monthly budget weeks before the month ends, forcing them to turn away clients in need of support or to refer them to other abortion funds. It's a never-ending cycle that cannot succeed without structural and policy changes. Seeing this impasse, abortion funds have had to shift from solely supporting people seeking abortions to advocating for political change.

In several states and municipalities, abortion funds have secured state or local government funding to cover abortion care for people living in and traveling to their areas for abortions. These smaller local campaigns to use taxpayer dollars to fund abortions (and other practical support services abortion funds offer) have jump-started community conversations to end the Hyde Amendment nationally.

Even in states such as Texas, lawmakers have introduced policies to repeal the state Medicaid coverage bans. First introduced in 2019 in the Texas state house of representatives, Rosie's Law, named for Rosie Jimenez, would end the state ban on Texans using their Medicaid benefits to cover their abortion costs and overturn a 2017 ban on private insurance coverage of abortion. Although the bill has yet to gain traction, it is model legislation that other states can replicate and advocates can rally supporters around.

Federally, the campaign to end the Hyde Amendment continues to reach new heights. In 2015, Congresswoman Barbara Lee introduced the Equal Access to Abortion Coverage in Health Insurance (EACH) Act in the House of Representatives, which would lift the Medicaid coverage ban, ending Hyde's reign once and for all. In its current iteration, the EACH Act would guarantee coverage for abortion in public health insurance programs, such as Medicaid, as well as ensure access to abortion care at government-run facilities, such as those operated by the Indian Health Service or Veterans Affairs, and include abortion coverage as part of insurance plans offered to government employees. Originally, the bill was named the EACH Woman Act, but has since been renamed the EACH Act to be more inclusive of trans and nonbinary people who have abortions.

The effort hasn't been easy, but Representative Lee knew she had to make it her life's work. "I said, I'm gonna take this on and try to repeal it," she told us. "It took a while because Democrats said, 'Oh, no, no, no, don't even talk about that amendment.'" But Representative Lee knew that with a coalition of people of color, it could be done. She told us that's when she saw a difference between the reproductive rights movement and the reproductive justice movement, with women of color at the helm. This movement is different, she told us. No longer are very few Black women at the marches; now the movement is full of women of color and trans people, and young people are involved. She believes that's what makes the movement to end the Hyde Amendment stronger. "We have to fight, sometimes everyone, for what's right," Representative Lee said. "It's an issue that women of color have had to deal with historically and [we] haven't been seen in these fights."

* * *

When we think about the stories of Rosie, Representative Barbara Lee, and Rachael, it's easy to focus on the antiabortion policies and stigma that made their experiences difficult and even downright deadly. It's easy to say, *This would all be better if abortion were widely available to everyone.* But the truth is, their stories tell us much more: their stories illuminate how inhumane and segregated our medical system is.

From the very beginning, each and every policy governing abortion was designed to hurt and hinder as many people as possible. Representative Henry Hyde never hid his racist intentions—and he didn't have to, because anti-Blackness and racism have been fused into abortion bans for centuries. He simply exploited and expanded the racism to make low-income people suffer the most. And for too long, pro-choice politicians allowed Hyde and his ilk to get away with it, leaning into abortion stigma and refusing to acknowledge the barriers race and class play in health care. They turned women like Rosie into icons of a moment in the past, ignoring how the policies and capitalist health care systems that led to her death are still harming people today.

But we are lucky that we have people who survived and have dedicated their lives to ensuring no one receives the dehumanizing care they experienced. Representative Lee is the antidote to Hyde, using her abortion story to change the conversation and inspiring a new generation of leaders along the way. Rachael is ensuring that Indigenous people across the nation and around the world are heard, that they receive funding for their care, and that their traditions are nurtured. They've been through it, and they are leading the way to liberate abortion.

Although we believe that equitable policies such as Rosie's Law and the EACH Act are imperative to achieving abortion justice, we also believe that to truly liberate abortion we have to fundamentally change our system, to one that rejects the notion that only those who can afford health care are entitled to it. For us, the key to liberating health care for all of us is in recognizing the way abortion stigma, anti-Blackness, and poverty played roles in the creation of our health care system and centering those issues within any and all solutions. Liberating health care also means keeping alive the full stories of those we lost along the way and recognizing all the factors at play, not just the ones that can be used to stick it to our opposition. Being reflective is the only way forward, and it's the best way to honor the memory of people like Rosie.

Abortionsplaining

Abortionsplain /ə'bôrSH(ə)nsplān/ verb (**INFORMAL**)

For a person who doesn't know anything about abortion or has not had an abortion to explain something about abortion to someone, typically a person who has had an abortion or who supports abortion, in a manner regarded as degrading, racist, or ahistorical.

Example: The congressman abortionsplained to me for more than an hour after I shared my abortion story.

In May 2022, two weeks after *Politico* published a leaked draft of the Supreme Court's *Dobbs* decision, Renee sat in the first row of a congressional hearing room supporting Aimee Arrambide, a We Testify abortion storyteller who testified to the impact of a Texas law offering a $10,000 bounty for anyone who helped someone get an abortion after six weeks' gestation. Aimee spoke truths about how her first abortion allowed her to have the time and space to figure out her newly diagnosed bipolar disorder and become a parent when she was ready, and her second abortion allowed her to decide when her family was complete. After Aimee's testimony, antiabortion witnesses had an opportunity to speak; at that point, Renee started to tune out, as she often does and advises the dozens of storytellers she has coached to do. But an odd statement caught her attention.

Did you know that the streetlamps in Washington, DC, are powered by abortions? That's if you believe a witness who testified under oath before the House Judiciary Committee after Aimee's testimony, claiming that medical waste from abortion clinics creates electricity. "Bodies thrown in medical waste bins and in places like Washington, DC, burned to power the lights of the city's homes and streets," Catherine Glenn Foster explained. "Let that image sink in with you for a moment. The next time you turn on the light, think of the incinerators."

How about instead you let it sink in that the president of Americans United for Life stated, under oath, that abortions create electricity—yes, the head of an organization that drafts most of the model legislation for states banning abortion. In their crusade against abortion, antiabortion activists will try to turn any lie into a law.

You've probably figured this out by now, but abortion is one of the most lied-about issues in our society. Misinformation about abortion is designed to make people who have, provide, and support abortions feel bad about themselves and stigmatized for being associated with abortion. The people who spread the lies often do it to shut down dissenting opinions or insist to people who have, provide, and are otherwise knowledgeable about abortion that they don't really know what they're talking about. We call that *abortionsplaining*. They believe that if they spread their lies far and wide enough, it will eventually become the truth or they can win a conversation by talking over us loud and long enough:

> Abortion is worse for Black people than slavery was. Abortion is worse than the Holocaust. Abortion is like killing puppies. Abortion destroys the economy because it kills a generation of workers. Abortion was not prevalent among Black women during the 1960s and 1970s until white feminists gave it to them. Abortion causes depression and infertility.

Those are all things we've heard abortionsplained in Congress. Myths and misinformation are spread not only by "expert witnesses" at congressional hearings but also on television shows, among politicians, and in families. You've probably been abortionsplained before. Have you ever been told that too many abortions will harm your fertility? Or maybe that Margaret Sanger created the procedure to spread eugenics? Did you know that abortions cause droughts—but also hurricanes? It's as if Mother Nature can't make up her mind.

Many of the myths are laughable, but some sound as though they might be true, especially when they're presented as facts by people in positions of power. Or the myth is so common that it must be true, right? The spread of disinformation and rumors is intentional. It's designed to make us question the safety of abortion, creating doubt in our minds and sowing division over support for abortion. And because of the questions swirling around abortion's legitimacy, we are discouraged from asking questions about such an impolite topic and don't know which sources we can trust.

The ballooning reach of abortionsplaining is troubling as politicians are staking their careers on limiting access to education and libraries and prohibiting critical thinking and challenges to fascist authority. What once were oddball ideas spouted by fanatics in random corners of the internet or outside of clinics are now the talking points of politicians and podcasters, spread to millions who trust what they're being told. Abortionsplaining spreads quickly and has dangerous implications, like misinterpreting or rewriting history. It's literally why we wrote this book. There's lots of abortionsplaining and only so much time, so we picked some of the wildest and most prevalent myths we've heard to explain where they came from, why they persist, and what the truth is.

ABORTIONSPLAINING MYTH: Abortions Power Your Lights and the Electrical Grid

A month before the congressional testimony claiming that abortions power the electricity of street lamps and homes in Washington, DC, a different antiabortion activist claimed abortions were powering the lights in Baltimore. Of course, the insinuation is ridiculous, but where did it come from?

Early in 2022, Washington, DC, police raided the home of an antiabortion activist, where they found the stolen remains of five fetuses. After the raid, prominent antiabortion advocates held a small press conference in response to the raids and used it as an attempt to change the subject back to the supposed horrors of abortion itself. They attempted to give context to how the stolen fetuses came to be in the activist's home; supposedly, a group of activists were outside an abortion clinic when they asked the driver of the alleged medical waste transportation and incineration company if they could have the fetuses and bury them. The company—which does collect medical waste such as pills, needles, and tissue—denied the allegations. At the press conference, one antiabortion advocate declared, "This means, tragically, that they receive, transfer, and burn the corpses of aborted babies to make electricity for the households and businesses of the Baltimore area. If you live in the Baltimore area, you must know that aborted babies have been burned to keep your lights on and your house warm."

It's a pretty hyperbolic allegation that evokes violent images. Yes, there are waste companies, including medical waste companies, that dispose of trash and materials in an ecologically safe way using incinerators instead of putting the trash in landfills that pollute the land and waterways. The trash is dumped into an incinerator, and the combustion heats up a separate water chamber, creating steam that turns a turbine, creating electricity. Obviously, explaining all of that is not as shocking as saying abortions are powering the lights in your home. Abortionsplainers are not decrying the liposuctions that are keeping our televisions on.

A headline claiming that your home's electricity is being powered by fetuses may make you cringe, because it's supposed to. The real question is, Why are they trying to show us fetuses anyway?

Quite simply, abortion involves a lot of things that make us uncomfortable or squeamish—sex, bodily fluids, pregnancy, death, life, and the in-between, as well as lots of medical things, as researcher

Carole Joffe notes, such as "confrontation with blood, vomit, and in some instances, discernible fetal parts." The point of depicting what an abortion *looks like* is to create disgust, which is a feeling of morality and judgment, alongside discomfort and stigma. If you're grossed out by an image of what happens during an abortion, the antiabortion movement is hoping that you'll be less likely to defend it. Meanwhile, not only is childbirth more life-threatening than abortion, but have you ever seen a video of a vaginal delivery (of both the child and the placenta) or a C-section? It's not pretty, as Regina can confirm from firsthand experience. But because those forms of labor and delivery are accepted in our society, the antiabortion movement is not going to show you what they look like at rallies or outside of an abortion clinic. There's no morality there.

Showing fetal parts to argue that abortion is disgusting has long been a tactic of the antiabortion movement. Antiabortion protesters gather outside abortion clinics with huge signs featuring images of bloody embryos and fetuses. Generally, it doesn't work. People still go to the clinic, past the protesters, and get their abortions because they need to not be pregnant anymore. States force a provider to show a patient an ultrasound, describe the procedure in biased terms, or make the patient listen to fetal cardiac activity (also known as a "heartbeat") before a heart has even formed. If given the choice, most patients don't want to view their ultrasound, but several studies found that of those who viewed the ultrasound, more than 98 percent of patients continued with their abortions. Since the antiabortion movement can't sway people seeking abortions, they try to sway the general public.

It's easy to be disgusted by what we don't encounter on a daily basis. Stigma, combined with our imagination, takes over. That's why horror movies are so gory. You're supposed to be disgusted by the blood, internal organs, and death on-screen. But we know abortion—like any medical procedure—is so much more than the blood. Abortionsplainers are counting on society's moral judgment and discomfort combined with disgust to sway political opinions into calling for abortion to be criminalized harshly. That's what has always been intended.

ABORTIONSPLAINING MYTH: Abortion Pill Particles and Fetal Parts
Are Floating in Our Drinking Water

If you drink tap water, it's probably time to stop. The FDA hasn't done an environmental impact study in twenty years about the abortion pill poisoning America's water. Turns out, the abortion pill, which is actually two different pills, contains three active metabolites that once it passes through the body of a woman don't actually become inactive. So after you've gone to the bathroom and flushed everything down the toilet, which is what you're told to do with your baby, by the way, is flush him or her down the toilet after they have been delivered through a chemical abortion. Those active metabolites stay active in our wastewater and go on to poison our water, our soil, our plant life, and our animal life. Plus medical waste of human tissue and human remains are being flushed down our toilets and through our bathtub drains into our wastewater systems, rather than being disposed of through a medical waste review process. We have absolutely no idea what the grand-scale impact on our environment from chemical abortion actually is because our government refuses to research that information. I don't care what your opinion on abortion actually is. If you care about the environment, like at all, it's time to tell the FDA, "do the study and remove these drugs from the market." It is up to us to conserve our nation's beautiful places, and that includes our wastewater, our drinking water, our soil, our plant life, our animal life, and of course the lives of all of us.

—Students for Life TikTok video, May 9, 2023

In 2015, Renee participated in a series of investigations into anti-abortion crisis pregnancy centers by posing as someone who was pregnant, desiring an abortion, and in need of help. While she wasn't pregnant at the time, everything she presented to the two Maryland center volunteers was true to her real-life abortion experience ten years earlier. She asked questions about the safety of abortion, what kinds of birth control the centers recommended, and whether she could get an abortion. Renee was unfazed by most of what the volunteers at the clinics said to her, which consisted of run-of-the-mill antiabortion talking points, but one so-called danger of abortion stuck out to her. The volunteers told her that because people take medication abortion and pass their pregnancies at home in the toilet, the embryos and fetuses—along with the remnants of the abortion pills—are in our drinking water. Trying not to break character, Renee engaged with curiosity. She held up her water bottle and asked, "So there are aborted babies in this water I'm drinking?" The volunteers eagerly nodded yes.

This myth has only gotten bigger over the past decade. In 2023, the antiabortion organization Students for Life published a TikTok video claiming that the government hasn't investigated the prevalence of abortion pills in our nation's wastewater system in twenty years, conveniently the exact amount of time since abortion pills were first approved for prescription in the United States. The video claims that medication abortions are causing people to flush human bodies down the toilet, destroying our environment, and that this should be investigated by the FDA and disposal should be via a medical waste process—you know, the one that powers the electricity in Baltimore and Washington, DC. We can't make it make sense. (If the TikToker had done her homework, she would have known she meant the Environmental Protection Agency, the agency that oversees the safety of drinking water.)

We probably don't have to go deep into explaining this one to you, but, no, there are no abortions in your drinking water. Renee won a science fair in kindergarten explaining where the water goes after we use it, so we'll reexplain her posterboard presentation thesis for you. In homes that aren't connected to a septic system, when you flush the toilet or empty any drain, the water flows through your pipes down to the sewer and is combined with the wastewater from your neighbors, local businesses, street drains, and more. Then the water travels to your local water treatment plant, where it goes through a series of processes to remove pollutants and large particle matter. During subsequent processes, bacteria, chlorine, and other mineral compounds are added to cleanse the water. That's why your drinking water doesn't contain feces or urine or vomit or period clots or your first pet goldfish or anything else we flush. Finally, the water is fresh to return to your communities, farms, and pools.

The entire point of these abortionsplaining myths is to move away from the topic of systemic inequality and health care, and move people to be disgusted by the prevalence of abortion itself. *If you think drinking water with blood and embryos in it is gross, you must think abortion is gross.*

ABORTIONSPLAINING MYTH: Abortions Cause Tornadoes, Droughts, and Hurricanes—Oh My!

These hurricanes are not the result of global warming; they are the Judgment of God because of the innocent blood crying to Him for vengeance. In America, the blood of nearly 60 million babies murdered by abortion ascends as a howling chorus to God from landfills and sewers, where these innocent little boys and girls have been discarded. These hurricanes are not "natural disasters"; they are super-natural chastisements.

—Randall Terry, antiabortion domestic terrorist, September 8, 2017

Apparently, abortion can change the climate. In 2011, an antiabortion activist claimed that tornadoes in the South, flooding in Mississippi, and wildfires in Texas and Oklahoma were caused by abortion. In 2012, another antiabortion activist claimed that a tornado destroyed a town in Missouri because of abortion but stopped in Texas because of an antiabortion march. In 2005, racist and everything-phobic evangelical leader Pat Robertson, the king of blaming abortion for everything that isn't abortion, blamed abortion for Hurricane Katrina, the September 11 attacks, and the United States not being "blessed." Whenever a natural disaster occurs, a myriad of things are blamed—queer people, feminists, immigrants, Muslims, fatherless homes, the American Civil Liberties Union; the list goes on—but the one constant is abortion. This pattern reminds us how prevalent abortion stigma is, even as the myth that abortion can manifest natural disasters is pure abortionsplaining.

In 2015, California was experiencing one of its many droughts. As *Rewire News Group* reported, at an antiabortion legislative banquet, California State Assemblymember Shannon Grove claimed that solving the drought in the state could be achieved by banning abortion. "Texas was in a long period of drought until Governor Perry signed the fetal pain bill," she told banquet guests. "It rained that night. Now God has His hold on California."

The wrath caused by abortion dries up the land creating droughts, while also causing hurricanes?

For decades, politicians, presidential candidates, and white evangelical Christian leaders have blamed abortion for disastrous hurricanes. It's offensive, to say the least. Combined, Hurricanes Katrina, Rita, Harvey, Irma, and Florence killed more than 2,200 people and destroyed the lives of thousands of families.

People tell me that Houston, Texas, is one of the darkest cities in America. Isn't it amazing, Katrina slammed New Orleans—we know about voodoo and the darkness in New Orleans. Then it moved right down the coast to Houston, Texas. . . . Boom, here it comes, now it's underwater. Water is a sign of judgment and cleansing. Is now not the time for the voice of the church to rise up and declare, "Let's stop killing the babies!"

—Dave Daubenmire, an evangelical minister and far-right activist, August 29, 2017

Abortion, obviously, doesn't cause tornadoes, hurricanes, droughts, or rain. Natural weather patterns and changes in air pressure and temperature exacerbated by climate change do. But what strikes us is how coded with anti-Blackness these comments are. Voodoo tends to be practiced by Black people. Black people were left for dead after Hurricane Katrina. Antiabortion ideology is rooted in anti-Blackness; thus, it's unsurprising that far-right activists would cite signifiers of Blackness, alongside abortion, as the reason for the disasters. They're preaching that communities full of Black people (and queer people, immigrants, and other people of color) and those who have abortions are in need of cleansing. The "cleansing" is a way to blame abortion, instead of lack of investment in infrastructure, for the preventable deaths of low-income Black and Brown communities who cannot evacuate the disaster regions—and subsequently to blame those who died by painting them as sinners and collateral damage.

Although abortions don't cause natural disasters, accessing abortion care is significantly more difficult in the midst of them. Quite literally, people can't travel for days or weeks, but a pregnancy continues on, pushing pregnant people up against their states' gestational limits. Evacuations and damage make interstate travel nonexistent. Clinic workers can't get to work through impassable roads, and in some cases clinics are inoperable. Connecting abortion to natural disasters serves to distract from our nation's severe disinvestment in communities, homes, and buildings—and from meaningfully addressing climate change.

ABORTIONSPLAINING MYTH: God Hates Abortion

By abortion, the mother does not learn to love, but kills even her own child to solve her problems. And, by abortion, that father is told that he does not have to take any responsibility at all for the child he has brought into the world. That father is likely to put other women into the same trouble. So abortion just leads to more abortion. Any country that accepts abortion is not teaching its people to love, but to use any violence to get what they want. This is why the greatest destroyer of love and peace is abortion.

—*Mother Teresa, National Prayer Breakfast, February 3, 1994*

At some point in your life, you've likely been led to believe that religion and abortion don't mix. Christian antiabortion advocates have weaponized their faith to undermine and gut abortion access (as well as some access to contraception). Although most people who have abortions are people of faith, the myth persists.

As we've already covered, abortion is older than most religions. Religious texts of all kinds have a lot to say about when life begins. Few have much to say about abortion, and some are clear that it is acceptable. Others may disapprove of it or call for the limitation of abortions after ensoulment or quickening. People of color and those who practiced pagan religions or old traditions often had ceremonies for birth, death, and abortion, and they knew that abortion was part of a life cycle. But those traditions died out as larger religions dominated them. Let's address a few of the biggest organized religions.

People in ancient Muslim societies frequently used oral contraceptives and abortion to regulate their pregnancies. In Islam, an embryo gains a soul at the end of 120 days. According to the Prophet Muhammad, "Each of you is constituted in your mother's womb for forty days as a semen, then it becomes a bloodlike clot for an equal period, then a lump of flesh for another equal period, then the angel is sent, and he breathes the soul into it."

Most Muslim scholars agree that abortion is permissible according to sacred texts, but, of course, different traditions within Islam have debated the interpretations. For instance, jurists of the Hanbali and Shafi'i schools believed in a shorter threshold, such as 40 or 120 days. Hanafi jurists believed that women could have an abortion without the permission of their husbands but regulated their reasons; for other schools of Islam, both partners must agree, and after a certain time period, reasons must be related to critical health indications of the fetus or the pregnant person. Scholar Zahra Ayubi, PhD, has explained that Quranic verses and hadith support abortion when a person becomes pregnant while nursing a child, because the living child's nutritional needs take priority over the embryo.

One thing we find interesting about the Prophet Muhammad's quote is the language that is used—in particular, "a bloodlike clot." This phrasing is something antiabortion activists say pro-abortion activists use to render the pregnancy irrelevant and inhuman. Given that the antiabortion movement is so deeply fueled by the white Christian supremacist movement and that they believe their efforts are part of a holy war, it's interesting to see how Muslim religious phrasing is assumed to be derogatory.

Most Hindu theologians agree that abortion is considered sinful and that the Mahanarayana Upanishad, an ancient Sanskrit text, considers abortion as a break with chastity, causing a woman to lose her status, or is equal to killing her husband. However, there's debate and interpretation about what stage is considered beyond ensoulment and the situation surrounding the abortion itself. The Suśrutasaṃhitā, an ancient Sanskrit medical text, calls for abortion when the health of the pregnancy is at risk. Overall, Hindu ethics prioritize the health of the pregnant person over the fetus.

In Buddhist religions, the acceptability has shifted over time and depends on the location. But there is not one specific Buddhist belief on abortion. Classical texts do not address abortion. Abortion is widely practiced in Asian countries and among Buddhists, even if it is considered sinful. In Japan, Buddhists practice *mizuko kuyō*, a traditional water-child memorial service for children who have died before their parents, such as by stillbirth, illness, accidents, and spontaneous or induced abortions. Those who have abortions can be encouraged to take part in the services to ask forgiveness for their abortion. Similarly, in Korea, the remembrance of aborted pregnancies—for those who choose to participate—is during the Festival of Hungry Ghosts, when a memorial tablet is dedicated to the "water baby" spirit. Because there isn't clear guidance, the beliefs are open to Buddhists themselves.

According to Hebrew religious law, a person is not considered pregnant until forty days after the sperm and egg meet. The Mishnah, an ancient Jewish written text documenting oral traditions circa the second century, clearly states that abortion is acceptable—necessary even—because the life of the pregnant person supersedes that of the fetus. One translation of the Mishnah reads, "If a woman is having trouble giving birth, they cut up the child in her womb and brings it forth limb by limb, because her life comes before the life of [the child]. But if the greater part has come out, one may not touch it, for one may not set aside one person's life for that of another" (Ohalot 7:6). The priority is the health of the pregnant person; however, if the fetus's head has begun to emerge during labor and the pregnant person is losing their life, it is because they are being pursued "from Heaven" or it's "an act of God." Similarly, the Mishnah says, "if the abortion was a foetus filled with water or filled with blood or filled with variegated matter, she need not take thought for it as for [human] young; but if its [human] parts were fashioned, she must continue [unclean the number of days prescribed] both for a male and for a female." Essentially, rituals performed after a later abortion to set a body back to normal differ from those performed after an early abortion, indicating that abortions were provided throughout pregnancy. Although the language can be a bit jarring for some, the Mishnah directly testifies to the ancient existence of and support for abortion for a period of time during and throughout the pregnancy. Today, polls have found that more than 80 percent of Jews support access to abortion. Organizations such as the National Council of Jewish Women set up some of the first birth control clinics. Ensuring the health and well-being of pregnant people is an important tenet of Jewish faith.

Christianity is the organized religion posited as most in opposition to abortion, but as in every other religion, members of different sects believe different things. Catholics, Evangelicals, and other Christian fundamentalists hold an outsize voice in the abortion conversation due to their growing political power within the United States. Examinations of the Bible and Jesus's teachings have not found mentions or condemnation of abortion; however, one Exodus passage in the Hebrew Bible does state that if a fetus were to be harmed by outside violence, damages would be imposed. Herbal abortion methods were certainly present during his preaching days. We assume that Saint Mary Magdalene—who, depending on your interpretation, was some combination of sex worker, wife, and partner to Jesus—knew a bit about abortion and potentially taught him a thing or two, given that he spent a lot of time with her.

Frequently cited scripture such as Jeremiah 1:5—"Before I formed you in the womb I knew you, before you were born I dedicated you, a prophet to the nations I appointed you"—are debated heavily, with some textualists claiming that Jeremiah was referring only to himself, while other interpretations see the text as antiabortion. Luke 1:15, referring to John the Baptist's mother—"For he shall be great before the Lord; and shall drink no wine nor strong drink: and he shall be filled with the Holy Ghost, even from his mother's womb"—is the subject of a similar debate. Again, textualists believe that this passage was likely referring to later abortions. Nevertheless, the debate continues, and Christians have abortions at the same rate as everyone else.

Although some sects of Christianity openly teach antiabortion political views now, that wasn't always the case. Some religions, including Christianity, opposed abortion but did not seek to make it illegal or punishable. It was simply immoral—a thing to disapprove of. It was during the Middle Ages that Church and secular law began to fuse to-gether into one, imposing punishments for abortion. In the late thir-teenth century, English law equated abortion (that is, giving a woman poison or striking by force to terminate a pregnancy) with homicide. It was rare for secular law to merge with Church law, and abortions, at that time, were only considered as such if they occurred after quickening. Not everyone followed these rules, either. Catholic priests offered juni-per to "old witches and prostitutes" to get them to attend mass and also provided it to sex workers who needed abortions. In fact, until the mid-nineteenth century, the Catholic Church did not take a stance condemn-ing abortion and tacitly allowed abortions prior to ensoulment. It was around 1869, when abortion became politicized and criminalized in the US, that the Catholic Church first condemned abortion as a concept, later specifically condemning therapeutic abortion in 1895. Meanwhile, Protestant churches still accepted abortion as necessary when a patient's life was endangered.

But when did abortion become the religious lightning rod that it is today? That was manufactured in the mid-twentieth century, as Black people began organizing for civil rights and the sexual revolution gained power. In particular, conservatives lost a trifecta of issues at the Supreme Court—the desegregation of schools, the elimination of Christian prayer in public schools, and the integration of public schools via busing—and began organizing white people around religion to regain control. Leaders of the white Christian movements sought an issue that could be exploited to maintain the benefits of the Jim Crow segregation voting bloc, and the legalization of abortion fit the bill.

As Jennifer L. Holland notes in *Tiny You: A Western History of the Anti-Abortion Movement*, Catholics spent much of the late 1960s and much of the 1970s railing against abortion, organizing communities to protest, and preaching fetal politics from the pulpits. Soon, Mormon and Protes-tant churches joined in the effort, and then the engagement of Mexican Catholics was targeted; but the effort ballooned when Evangelicals took up the mantle in the 1980s, culminating in the election of President Ronald Reagan. (Yes, the same Reagan who had legalized abortion in California in 1967.) Not only was abortion a perceived measure of values, but it became a political vessel for white supremacy. You were either pro-life or pro-death. If you were pro-life, it was a signifier of where you stood overall politically—in particular, it showed your preference for a white way of life.

Across the nation, abortion laws have been crafted not only to make abortion inaccessible but also to solidify a Christian way of practicing traditions. Laws requiring burial after the abortion are often associated with the Christian faith and force people to practice this ritual even though many religions acknowledge the transitions of life in a different way. Abortion laws are a deep violation of the separation of church and state, yet they persist. Some Jewish leaders have brought lawsuits to try to dismantle abortion laws based on their religious freedom, but their success has yet to be seen.

Abortion and religion aren't inherently at odds. It's only we mere mortals who are.

ABORTIONSPLAINING MYTH: Abortion Causes [*Insert Unrelated Health Issue Here*]

Future Infertility: The further along you are in your pregnancy, the greater the chance of serious complications that can cause you to be infertile and the greater the risk of dying from the abortion procedure. Some complications associated with an abortion, such as an infection, a cut or a torn cervix, may make it difficult or impossible to become pregnant in the future or to carry a pregnancy to term.

Breast Cancer Risk: Your pregnancy history affects your chances of getting breast cancer. If you give birth to your baby, you are less likely to develop breast cancer in the future. Research indicates that having an abortion will not provide you this increased protection against breast cancer. In addition, doctors and scientists are actively studying the complex biology of breast cancer to understand whether abortion may affect the risk of breast cancer. If you have a family history of breast cancer or breast disease, ask your doctor how your pregnancy will affect your risk of breast cancer.

—"A Woman's Right to Know" brochure, Texas Department of State Health Services, 2019

When Regina started trying to become pregnant with her husband she wondered, *Will I be unable to get pregnant because I had an abortion?* During the first few months of trying, she was filled with worry and doubt. She was thirty-five years old and would be having a "geriatric pregnancy," according to the medical community. Regina blamed herself with every negative pregnancy test—and even more when she had a miscarriage. It didn't matter that she had felt more confident about her abortion than she had about any other decision she had ever made. It didn't matter that she knew there was no link between abortion and her fertility and that she understood miscarriages were incredibly common, particularly in the first few weeks of pregnancy. The abortionsplaining she'd heard for years crept in and created self-doubt and shame at a time when she was most vulnerable.

Worries about the safety of abortion procedures and the impact it will have on a person's health are common. In her book *No Real Choice*, sociologist Katrina Kimport illustrates how women who wanted abortions ultimately couldn't make the decision to have one because of their beliefs that abortion would damage their reproductive organs. "I know that abortion can be really damaging to the body," a woman named Kara said, explaining that the procedure can "affect the vaginal walls of some women [so] they're no longer fertile like they used to be." Another woman, Khadijah, believed that an abortion clinic wouldn't care for patients who had more than one abortion because abortions caused a lot of scar tissue. These concerns about the safety of abortion, although completely untrue, made abortion unchoosable for these women.

It's normal to be concerned about your health before you undergo any medical procedure. But fears about unsafe and adverse outcomes from an abortion are significantly more prevalent because they're coupled with the morality issues surrounding abortion. With so much disinformation, it's hard to know what is the truth.

This is one part of a decades-long calculated strategy by the anti-abortion movement to make abortion unthinkable. When abortion was criminalized, some people experienced unsafe and downright scary procedures. They were blindfolded, robbed, or abused by people who promised to give them an abortion. They were experimented on. Some were unable to have subsequent pregnancies because of ill-trained providers or because they used dangerous and unsafe methods such as douching with bleach or using coat hangers or knitting needles. That is absolutely part of abortion history, and these issues remain very real today.

At the same time, the antiabortion movement began investing in crisis pregnancy centers, fake clinics designed to persuade people not to have abortions. Their volunteers met with people who were seeking and who had had abortions and listened to the horror stories of unsafe abortions. These volunteers assigned negative psychological symptoms to people's behaviors and created "post-abortion syndrome," a totally made-up form of post-traumatic stress disorder. The list of symptoms is varied and long but includes avoidance of people involved with the abortion, suicide, avoidance of sex, sexually promiscuity, obsession with having children, inability to bond with children, overly intense involvement with pro-choice or "pro-life" activism, anniversary syndrome (we call them "abortionaversaries"), guilt, moodiness, relationship issues, and more. Even though this is not a medically recognized diagnosis, that hasn't stopped antiabortion activists from forcing it into the public lexicon.

It's pretty normal to feel depressed and upset when you're going through one of the biggest decisions of your life. You might not have anyone to turn to or fear that if you tell someone, they'll reject you. That's going to bring up a lot of feelings. This is the reason that it's so critical to talk openly about abortion and to show up with love and support for people who are having abortions.

Legislators have passed laws requiring abortion providers to tell their patients about the risks, despite a lack of evidence. But nearly half of the statements made about first trimester abortions in brochures are inaccurate. The booklet "A Woman's Right to Know" has over six pages listing negative health outcomes caused by abortion, but only two pages about the dangers of pregnancy, childbirth, and postpartum symptoms, which, according to a 2012 study, are fourteen times more dangerous—and that's before race and class are factored in!

Former Supreme Court justice Anthony Kennedy opined that this "regret" phenomenon must be real, even though there's no evidence for it. In his 2007 opinion in *Gonzales v. Carhart*, a case that limited the use of later abortion procedures, Justice Kennedy wrote, "While we find no reliable data to measure the phenomenon, it seems unexceptionable to conclude some women come to regret their choice to abort the infant life they once created and sustained. Severe depression and loss of esteem can follow."

As a result of Justice Kennedy's opinion, a team of researchers at Advancing New Standards in Reproductive Health, housed at the University of California San Francisco, sought out reliable data to evaluate the outcomes of abortion. In landmark research known as the Turnaway Study, demographer and MacArthur "Genius" Fellow Diana Greene Foster and her team of researchers followed almost a thousand women for ten years and looked at the impact abortion had on their lives economically, physically, and mentally, as well as their future childbearing and support for their other children. The study found that, no, abortion does not have a negative impact on a person's mental or physical well-being or one's fertility. In fact, 97 percent of women did not regret their abortions and believed they had made the right decision three years later, and that figure rose to 99 percent after five years. The most common feeling after an abortion was *relief*. When people are seeking an abortion, they are often in a crisis moment, with many of life's challenges converging all at once. For those who did experience mental health issues, substance abuse, or suicidal ideations, these were present before the abortion. (We'd also like to quickly note that there's little public conversation about people who regret parenthood, and to admit as much is incredibly shameful and ostracizing, but could go a long way in helping people to recognize the toll parenthood takes and normalizing their feelings and experiences. Unfortunately, the burden of reproductive regret is placed solely on abortion decisions.)

And, no, abortion does not cause breast cancer. How do we know? The American Cancer Society says so. Susan G. Komen says so. The American College of Obstetricians and Gynecologists says so. This abortionsplaining comes from a random study in the 1980s that basically saw a correlation between women who had given birth and lower rates of breast cancer as compared with women who had never had a birth or who had had abortions. The authors of the study decided that pregnancy therefore protects against breast cancer. No one has been able to find a link since. Sounds to us like some abortionsplaining to promote procreation! Abortion, when provided by someone with medical training, is one of the safest medical procedures we have. It has a complication rate of 2 percent overall (additional cramping, bleeding, and other things that are painful but do not need hospitalization) and a serious complication rate of 0.05 percent, which is extremely low. Most complications do not require admission to an emergency department. Medication abortion is safer than Tylenol—safe enough to be sold over the counter next to Tylenol. But it's not available at your local pharmacy because of politicians, stigma, and a whole lot of abortionsplaining.

ABORTIONSPLAINING MYTH: Adoption Is a Solution to Abortion

So let us work together to reduce the number of women seeking abortions, let's reduce unintended pregnancies. Let's make adoption more available.

—President Barack Obama, Notre Dame University Commencement Address, 2009

Outside any abortion clinic with protesters, you'll hear a common refrain: *Give us your baby! There's a couple waiting to care for your baby!* They're talking about the other *a*-word: adoption. It's common to see billboards, bus ads, and brochures touting adoption as the brave, loving choice. It's the bipartisan option! The choice everyone can agree on! Right? Not really.

Adoption is manufactured as the solution to abortion but in reality, it's not. When you're pregnant, you have two options: continue or terminate the pregnancy. If you'd like to terminate, you seek an abortion. If you continue the pregnancy, you then can decide whether you want to parent or relinquish for adoption. The binary here is actually between adoption and parenting.

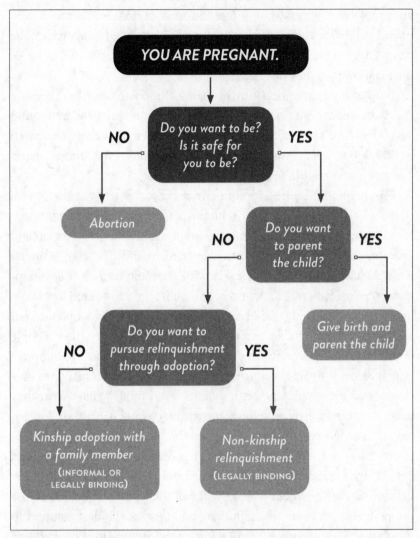

Logic model adapted from research by Dr. Gretchen Sisson, author of *Relinquished: The Politics of Adoption and the Privilege of American Motherhood*

In her book *Relinquished: The Politics of Adoption and the Privilege of American Motherhood*, sociologist Gretchen Sisson expands on her research into the decision-making of women who sought abortions and those who relinquished their children through adoption. Women having abortions were generally uninterested in adoption, and women who placed babies for adoption were generally uninterested in abortion. The latter group were considering parenting but didn't have the social or financial support they needed.

Furthermore, adoption can't be the solution to abortion, because the math doesn't add up. The best estimates are that there are around 18,000 to 20,000 private domestic adoptions per year. That's compared to 800,000 to over 1 million abortions each year in the United States. The math ain't mathin'! People want abortions.

The politicization of adoption is not based on real experiences of those who have abortions or relinquish their children for adoption. It's a convenient abortionsplaining narrative to stigmatize abortion and promote birth. As the antiabortion movement and Christian Evangelicals align themselves more closely with adoption as *their issue,* adoption becomes even more about whose families are considered legitimate and who are deemed "good parents." Queer and trans people are not recognized as acceptable parents. Single parents aren't either. People with money are preferred, as governments give tax breaks to adoptive parents and compensation to foster parents, all while refusing to give "handouts" to low-income birth parents, even though that's what they needed in the first place. Educated, wealthy, white, Christian, heterosexual, married parents are considered the ideal guardians of children of color in the United States and from around the world. Money and conservative ideals become the most important factors in state-law determinations of whom a child will call their parents. People across the political spectrum are identifying adoption as the best solution to the abortion "problem" without taking into account who is harmed and who holds all the power.

Adoption was never the solution to abortion. Abortion is a solution to being pregnant when a person doesn't want to be. Adoption is a response to our nation's disinvestment in social safety net programs that would make it easier for low-income people to parent and raise their children, and it's an outcome of the social stigma surrounding young, single, and/or low-income parents of color.

ABORTIONSPLAINING MYTH: Abortion Is Black Genocide

Eight decades after Sanger's "Negro Project," abortion in the United States is also marked by a considerable racial disparity. The reported nationwide abortion ratio—the number of abortions per 1,000 live births—among black women is nearly 3.5 times the ratio for white women. And there are areas of New York City in which black children are more likely to be aborted than they are to be born alive—and are up to eight times more likely to be aborted than white children in the same area. Whatever the reasons for these disparities, they suggest that, insofar as abortion is viewed as a method of "family planning," black people do indeed "tak[e] the brunt of the "planning."

—Justice Clarence Thomas's concurring opinion in Box v. Planned
Parenthood of Indiana and Kentucky, Inc., *2019*

A few years after Renee's abortion, while in the car with her family on the South Side of Chicago, she passed a billboard featuring an illustration of President Barack Obama that read "Every 21 minutes, our next possible leader is aborted." In other major cities, billboards featuring stock images of Black children read "The most dangerous place for an African American is in the womb." Although they were mostly present in Black neighborhoods, Spanish versions of the billboards, targeting Latinx communities, appeared in Los Angeles as well. The billboards were part of a 2011 national campaign targeting low-income Black and Latinx neighborhoods. Black women, the message asserted, were a danger to Black children. Abortion was the ultimate Black-on-Black crime.

When Justice Clarence Thomas issued his concurring opinion in the case *Box v. Planned Parenthood of Indiana and Kentucky, Inc.*, he wrote twenty pages of abortionsplaining about abortion, eugenics, and the impact they have on Black communities in particular. For decades as the lone Black justice on the Court, Justice Thomas has taken it upon himself to abortionsplain Black women's experiences to the nation, ignoring basic context about why communities of color have reproductive health disparities. Abortion isn't Black genocide. He's using a complicated history to distract from the blatantly antidemocratic policies he is allowing to flourish.

In the United States and globally, colonizers and white supremacists have employed eugenics, violence, and torture to wipe out entire populations of Black people and Indigenous communities. That is a basic fact. But, as we've already explained, abortion predates colonization. Nonetheless, the antiabortion advocates have recast themselves as the saviors in the tale.

Antiabortion leaders aren't concerned with the nation's history of sterilizing Black people and genocide. They are simply constructing a message that can be used to place embryos and fetuses alongside the historical plight of Black people (and Jews—but more on that in a minute). Antiabortion leaders can feign that they care for imaginary Black children without doing anything in the real world to help actual Black children who are in need of food, housing, education, and the right to a police-free life. Becoming a crusader against Black genocide is the perfect position for white saviors who don't want to engage with actual Black people, Black culture, or Black history.

The "abortion is Black genocide" narrative is so pervasive that white people aren't the only ones abortionsplaining about the Black birth rate. Hoteps, some Black nationalists, and members of the Nation of Islam, among others, have opposed abortion as a tool of mass genocide due to white violence and efforts to extinguish Black populations. During the height of the Black nationalist movement, men decried abortion, causing a rift and general distrust with the abortion liberation and reproductive freedom movement organizing at the same time. This caused a struggle between Black men who wanted to grow political power through reproduction and Black women who were concerned for their health during pregnancy and the welfare of their children. Leaders within the Black Power movement believed that the newly available birth control pill and abortion were being deliberately released in Black communities to eradicate Black populations. At the 1967 Black Power Conference, a resolution was passed denouncing contraception as Black genocide; a group of Black people shouted "Genocide!" as a birth control clinic burned in Ohio later that year.

In her book *Abortion Rap: Testimony by Women Who Have Suffered the Consequences of Restrictive Abortion Laws*, Black feminist and organizer Florynce Kennedy and her coauthor Diane Schulder tussle with the salient points that Black nationalists made about abortion's potential to cause Black genocide. Although most of the champions of the cause were Black men, Black women were also among their ranks. Kennedy quoted Black Panther leader Brenda Hyson, who wrote in a 1970 issue of *The Black Panther*, "Eliminating ourselves is not the solution to the hunger problem in America nor any other problem that could exist from a so-called unwanted pregnancy in the context of this capitalistic society." Kennedy appreciated Hyson's argument that abortion "hides behind the guise of helping women, when in reality it will attempt to destroy our people." Kennedy believed it was understandable for Black and Puerto Rican people to be distrustful of the government providing "long-denied" reproductive health services while also offering "dire predictions about 'population explosions.'" However, she was clear that Black women's role in the revolution wasn't to breed babies: "Breeding revolutionaries is not too far removed from a cultural past where Black women were encouraged to be breeding machines for their slave masters."

Congresswoman Shirley Chisholm, the first Black woman to run for president, also opposed the idea of Black genocide from the House floor in 1969. "One hears talk about 'genocide' from Black militants," she told Congress. "I think the principal things in operation here are the feeling of Blacks that they want to control their lives and of the Black man's pride and ego. Most of those who raise the genocide issue are Black men, not Black women." In her book *Unbought and Unbossed*, she explained how for her it was a "serious step" to lead NARAL's campaign, given the "deep and angry suspicion among many Blacks" that reproductive health care was a "plot by the white power structure to keep down the numbers of Blacks." But she again addressed the gender gap in the rhetoric: "But I do not know any black or Puerto Rican *women* who feel that way." She called the argument "male rhetoric, for male ears," pointing out that "it falls flat to female listeners, and to thoughtful male ones."

Image of Florynce Kennedy circa 1970. *Gloria Steinem Papers, Sophia Smith Collection, Smith College, Special Collections, Northampton, Massachusetts.*

Radical Puerto Rican groups dealt with similar tensions stemming from the birth control experimentations that pharmaceutical companies did on Puerto Rican women because they lived in a colonized land and were low-income, illiterate, and without recourse. When a thirty-one-year-old woman, Carmen Rodríguez, died from an abortion eighteen days after New York legalized it in 1970, the militant Puerto Rican nationalist group the Young Lords Party occupied Lincoln Hospital, alleging that it was "only [a] butcher shop that kills patients" and that doctors did not take adequate precautions to care for Rodríguez's health. They took this position because the hospital had a history of neglecting Puerto Rican patients, and they believed the new abortion law was "a plan for the limitation of our population." While some in the Young Lords Party believed that abortion was another form of genocide, they eventually, with the persuasion of feminist members, changed their position to include abortion and reproductive freedom as core beliefs. "End All Genocide. Abortions Under Community Control!" became their slogan, highlighting the need for reproductive health care to be protected in the Puerto Rican community.

Similarly, the American Indian Movement of the 1960s and 1970s was against the use of birth control because activists believed that reproduction was a critical way to replenish tribes and counter the genocidal policies of the US government. "We felt there were not enough Indians left to suit us," Mary Brave Bird, a Lakota activist, said.

Still, civil rights leaders, such as Fannie Lou Hamer, were vehemently opposed to abortion and birth control in Black communities. As the youngest child of twenty children, she deeply believed that if her mother had had access to birth control, she would not be alive. Moreover, because of her own experience of being forcibly and unknowingly sterilized during her efforts to become pregnant, she became extremely outspoken. According to biographers, in 1961, Hamer had experienced a few miscarriages and at least two stillbirths, but in her forties, when she went to see a doctor about "a knot on [her] stomach," the white doctor removed her entire uterus. She later found out about her sterilization when the white wife of the owner of the plantation where Hamer worked—a cousin of the doctor—was gossiping about it. Hamer later confronted the doctor, but knew she had no recourse or power as a Black woman in the South. Although her experiences charged her activism, she continued to work side by side with feminist icons including Gloria Steinem. When we asked Steinem to reflect on their working relationship and the complicated abortion views Hamer held as a feminist, Steinem told us, "I had the distinct impression that she came to see reproductive freedom as the power of the individual woman to decide."

Hamer was far from alone in her experience. As part of a campaign to improve the genetics of various populations, scientists engaged in eugenic practices and ideas at the start of the twentieth century. Although the concept of selective breeding is nothing new, this specific effort employed sterilization and other methods to keep people who were disabled, low-income, Black, Indigenous, Brown, or some combination of these identities from reproducing, often without their knowledge. When the government forced Native Americans into reservation hospitals, white doctors engaged in eugenics by sterilizing generations of women without their consent. This created fear about giving birth at a hospital, because white doctors could potentially sterilize Indigenous patients while they were seeking care.

One case in particular allowed the practice to skyrocket. Carrie Buck, a young white girl whose mother was accused of sex work while living with syphilis, was placed in the home of foster parents. Carrie was raped by her foster mother's nephew and became pregnant at seventeen. With big accusations of "moral delinquency" and disabilities despite little to no evidence, she was placed in an institution, where the doctors sterilized her, gave her daughter away to her foster parents, and then released her. She never had any remedy for the reproductive injustice she endured. In 1927, the Supreme Court ruled in the *Buck v. Bell* case that compulsory sterilization of disabled people was constitutional, writing, "Three generations of imbeciles are enough." Although we have protections in place through the Americans with Disabilities Act and states such as North Carolina have paid reparations to sterilization survivors, the ruling in *Buck v. Bell* still holds.

The thing is, when you hear "abortion is Black genocide," usually one name pops to the forefront: Margaret Sanger, a white nurse, feminist, socialist, and birth control advocate who founded the American Birth Control League, which would later become the global corporate nonprofit Planned Parenthood.

Sanger's mother was pregnant eighteen times and had eleven live births. Sanger saw how her mother's inability to control her fertility impacted what she could and couldn't do, as well as her health. Sanger believed that without the ability to refuse sex or avoid pregnancy, women could never truly enjoy heterosexual intercourse. Birth control became her crusade. She operated a clinic in Harlem open to people of all races, and she expected her staff to be respectful to Black and white patients alike, later firing a white nurse who complained in a report that Black people didn't arrive to appointments on time because of "irresponsibility and laziness."

As part of her work, Sanger partnered with Black civil rights leaders such as W. E. B. Du Bois, Mary McLeod Bethune, and later Dr. Martin Luther King Jr., who believed that access to contraception should be available to Black communities. Sanger toured clinics in the South in 1938 and saw that they were segregated, neglecting the needs of Black women. So, Sanger wrote to Du Bois pitching "The Negro Project," which would offer birth control to Black communities specifically because they were being denied it elsewhere.

But this is where words have been mangled and abortionsplained. In the Negro Project proposal, Sanger writes,

The mass of Negroes, particularly in the South still breed carelessly and disastrously, with the result that the increase among Negroes, even more than among whites, is from that portion of the population least intelligent and fit, and least able to rear children properly.

Sounds pretty racist, huh? It absolutely is. The problem is that this quote of Sanger's is actually a direct quote of Du Bois from his article in the June 1932 edition of *Birth Control Review*. But Sanger did agree with him. At the time, Du Bois and other Black leaders believed that poor Black people were a blight on racial uplift. For his part, Charles S. Johnson, the first Black president of Fisk University, wrote that "eugenic discrimination" was necessary for Black people. Unfortunately, the anti-Blackness in these statements is still common today, although the phrasing has changed. There are loads of examples of politicians, internet talking heads, a particular Supreme Court justice, or even your own family members who whine about how Black people—as well as other people of color—could be more upstanding citizens if they'd stop having babies as teens, dress right, get educated and obtain better employment, and behave like the rest of society (aka white people). Du Bois's words are sadly still sentiments that we hear today. Anti-Blackness, ableism, and slut-shaming have been universal through time and space.

Telephone call to
Tucson - Nov.7.1939.

Comments made by M. S. re. Negro project

I'm absolutely against xxxx our turning this work over to any other group or organization
for direction.   If we can't do it then we should close our doors.   To ask others
to decide for us sounds weak.   From my experience with medical politicans and state
officials they are going to go "soft-pedal" every step of the way and I'm not going to ask
them how we should do this job. We have outlined the plan and know what should be
done and how.   It is up to us to set up the plan and let them O.K. it and hold the
reins in our own hands.

I do not feel that others should decide but they should be asked to cooperate.   But we
should xxxx pick both Minister and doctor, and be clear as to what we want to do, and
then at Atlanta submit same to Seibaa or anyone else for their ixa O.K.   I am still
disturbed about that idea of three medicos to interview ix poor women to see mfxxhxx
if they are worthy of B.C. It makes me cold and doubtful of trusting that kind of
thinking to lead or decide.

Mrs. Moorehead visited Hampton or Tuskegee on the way down and they were anxious to
help us secure the kinn kind of men and to assist in every way. (copy enclosed)

I do feel that it is asking mf a lot of Dr. Morris crowded as he is to take on any
more things to worry about now, and that perhaps Dr. Gamble can help with the
initial interviewing , and then the rest of it can follow the same routine as any
other field work, but I would like to see you giving part of your time to helping on
this project and I hope that some plan can be worked out to permit this. Consult
some of our good Negro friends in Harlem as to possible candidates - that kind of
suggestion can be helpful, but be careful not to be led off into some side project to
advance someone else's plans rather than our own. This is a rare opportunity, and
I think that if we can locate a good pair - a Negro doctor and a Negro physician, they
could cover several states, rather than pushing everything into South Carolina where
so much has already been done - -   minister

If we consult white people too much they will be xxxxfxkxxmixxkxxkxix cautious about
doing too much. IT IS THE NEGRO GROUPS WE SHOULD BE CONSULTING. I do not understand
why a Negro doctor working among Negro groups and negro agencies could not - as
presented in the plan submitted - do a fine piece of educational work.

I do not want to disturb whatever thinking you are all doing in New York and I realize
from this distance it is hard to understand all the details that govern your thinking
there - but and for that reason I do not want these thoughts to block your plans,
or confuse them, but that is how I see the situation.

"I think that if we can locate a good pair—a Negro minister and a Negro physician, they could
cover several states, rather than pushing everything into South Carolina where so much has
already been done. If we consult white people too much they will be cautious about doing too
much. IT IS THE NEGRO GROUPS WE SHOULD BE CONSULTING. I do not understand
why a Negro doctor working among Negro groups and negro agencies could not—as presented
in the plan submitted—do a fine piece of educational work." —Comments by Margaret Sanger
to her secretary, Florence Rose, via telephone call on November 7, 1939. *Courtesy of the
Florence Rose Papers, Sophia Smith Collection, Smith College, Northampton, Massachusetts.*

Sanger began setting up the project by seeking funders, including Dr. Clarence Gamble, a nepo baby heir to the pharmaceutical company Procter & Gamble. She wrote that she "[did] not believe that this project should be directed or run by white medical men" and that it should be run with Black leaders. That's when she recruited Dr. Martin Luther King Jr. and Reverend Adam Clayton Powell Jr., along with Black doctors, to help spread the word. In 1939, she wrote a letter to Dr. Gamble explaining that she knew Black people were concerned about receiving contraception from white doctors, so it would be best if Black doctors were engaged to do the work within their own community so that Black people wouldn't get the wrong idea. The quote is probably her most famous:

> It seems to me from my experience where I have been in North Carolina, Georgia, Tennessee and Texas, that while the colored Negroes have great respect for white doctors they can get closer to their own members and more or less lay their cards on the table which means their ignorance, superstitions and doubts. They do not do this with the white people and if we can train the Negro doctor at the Clinic he can go among them with enthusiasm and with knowledge, which, I believe, will have far-reaching results among the colored people. His work in my opinion should be entirely with the Negro profession and the nurses, hospital, social workers, as well as the County's white doctors. His success will depend upon his personality and his training by us. The minister's work is also important and also he should be trained, perhaps by the Federation as to our ideals and the goal that we hope to reach. We do not want word to go out that we want to exterminate the Negro population and the minister is the man who can straighten out that idea if it ever occurs to any of their more rebellious members.

An edited portion of the final sentence is the one that gets passed around in antiabortion memes, but the irony is that in full context she was saying the exact opposite of what she's accused of. Alas, the entire plan fell apart anyway when the funders refused to hire Black doctors.

Overall, Sanger did have some awful thoughts about reproduction, believing that intellectually disabled people shouldn't be allowed to reproduce or vote. Sadly, she was one of many who felt this way. During the early twentieth century, many contraception advocates engaged in what's called "negative eugenics," meaning populations are culled through sterilization procedures that do not allow people from certain communities to reproduce. The opposite, "positive eugenics" (eye roll, we know), is enacted through so-called preventive measures, such as focusing on the health outcomes of a population and encouraging reproduction with genetically similar people or lighter-skinned people to lighten a population. At the time, it was the science du jour, but that doesn't make it right.

The irony is that Sanger was actually quite antiabortion. In fact, she held the same views about abortion as many antiabortion politicians today: it should be available only in cases of health indications, rape, or incest. "Although abortion may be resorted to in order to save the life of the mother," she once wrote, "the practice of it merely for limitation of offspring is dangerous and vicious." She denounced the idea that abortion would be conflated with birth control, once instructing her private secretary to write to a Colorado physician legislator who did conflate the two in his bill to legalize abortion in 1939. Like many of the white feminists and suffragettes of her day, she was sympathetic to those who self-managed their abortions, but she believed that with enough access to birth control, abortion could be avoided altogether.

Sanger's legacy is a divisive one. What's even more painful is the way Sanger's work is used today to denigrate Black women who want abortions and who may have never heard of her work from a century ago. Sanger was a lot of things. At worst, she was an overzealous white nurse who gave a pass to racism and really believed in the promise of birth control to the point that she would engage with anyone who would fund her work—eugenicists and Black elites alike. At best, she was a problematic, racist, white feminist who thought she knew better than the women of color she served.

But if Sanger hated abortion, why are Black people being made to answer for her? Because it's a convenient narrative and easy misogynoir. Attacking Black women is a go-to tactic; they've been maligned as bad parents or welfare queens and slut-shamed for centuries. As Malcolm X once said, Black women are the most disrespected, unprotected, and neglected people in the United States. The message imputed to Sanger reviles Black people who have and support abortions, Planned Parenthood, and history all at the same time—and it allows antiabortion activists to fight for Black fetal rights to birth without advocating for Black children's right to life.

During the Black Lives Matter movement, instead of joining the calls to curb police brutality, antiabortion activists perverted the slogan to say that more important than the deaths of Black children at the hands of police were the deaths of Black unborn babies at the hands of abortion providers and the unborn babies' own mothers. *Black unborn lives matter*, antiabortionist activists cried. Much like "blue lives matter," this became a retort to the "Black lives matter" call. But, if Black unborn lives matter so much to you, shouldn't they be included among the collective Black lives that we're saying matter?

For abortion, the problem is not the method—it's who is wielding or denying the power behind it.

ABORTIONSPLAINING MYTH: Abortion Is a Silent Holocaust

It is fashionable, or at least usual, that when in the first few months of a pregnancy doctors do studies to see if the child is healthy or has something, the first idea is: "Let's send it away." We do the same as the Nazis to maintain the purity of the race, but with white gloves on.

—Pope Francis, June 16, 2018

The Holocaust was a violent state-sponsored mass execution and genocide between 1933 and 1945. The Nazis murdered six million Jewish people, as well as millions of Slavic, Roma (Gypsy), and queer people; people with disabilities; Jehovah's Witnesses; communists; and socialists. Entire communities in Europe were rounded up and forced into concentration camps, where they were experimented on, tortured, abused, forced to labor, and slaughtered. To compare abortion to the Holocaust belittles the heinousness of the Holocaust, is deeply offensive to the people who survived it and the memories of those who were murdered, and is a gross misrepresentation of what abortion is.

Nevertheless, comparing abortion to the Holocaust is a predictable abortionsplaining refrain during congressional hearings, political campaign ads, papal comments, and antiabortion rallies.

* * *

While visiting a friend in Berlin, Renee stopped by a museum exhibit featuring political propaganda in the lead-up to and during World War II. She saw a poster with a gaunt-faced pregnant mother holding the hand of a small child while cradling a baby. It was a 1924 print by German socialist and pacifist artist Käthe Kollwitz that read "Nieder mit den Abtreibungs Paragraphen!," which translates to "Down with the abortion paragraph!," referring to § 218, a paragraph in the German criminal code that made abortion illegal at any point during the pregnancy.

Shortly after World War I, German feminists, socialists, and low-income women organized for a liberalization of the country's abortion laws. In 1926, it was decriminalized for women to perform their own abortions or receive help from others. By 1931, the Nazi Party began introducing legislation calling for the banning of abortion and contraception, writing that "anyone who attempts to curb artificially the natural fertility of the German people" would be jailed for "racial treason." After the Nazi Party took power in 1933, one of the Nazis' first actions was to recriminalize abortion, so that both people who had abortions and abortion providers would be committing a crime against the Volk (the people). In 1935, a German herbalist noted that the savin tree was still used as an abortifacient; Nazis forbade its cultivation in public and fenced off the tree in botanic gardens, but people still broke in. The Nazis' goal was to return white German women to domesticity, end marriages between Jewish people and Christian Germans, and create an Aryan, pure white race of people through genocide and reproductive control.

Through legislation, the Nazi Party enacted severe penalties for anyone who provided abortions, including death in some cases, and criminalized white Christian German women who sought them. Nazis saw abortion as a threat to the growth of the Aryan race and empire. They did not, however, oppose abortions, death, and sterilization as a method of eugenics for disabled Germans and all non-Germans. The Nazis solidified this stance again in 1938 by legalizing abortion for Jews, but the Nazis still surveilled pregnant women who appeared to be German and could further their eugenic goals. In 2022, Germany repealed the Nazi-era law banning providers from offering information about abortion.

Does the use of abortion for genocide make the Nazis pro-abortion? The simplest answer is no. They did not see abortion as an essential reproductive freedom like the German feminists of the time; Holocaust survivors such as Simone Veil, who went on to campaign for the legalization of abortion globally; and those of us who fight for access today. Abortion was critical to Jewish women's traditions and liberation. Nazis didn't believe in reproductive freedom. They took a common medical procedure and twisted it for nefarious eugenic reasons. Abortion restrictions were used as a tactic of reproductive coercion to force people to either have children or not have children in an effort to create a white supremacist society.

However, the comparisons to the Holocaust made their way into the US lexicon beginning in the 1970s with the Value Life Committee, the precursor to Americans United for Life, which compared "anti-life" efforts to the Nazi propaganda created by Joseph Goebbels. Antiabortion campaigns began to use high estimations of unborn babies that had died in a "holocaust" due to abortion, often directly comparing these abortions to the Nazis' murders. While serving as US president, Reagan published *Abortion and the Conscience of the Nation,* a book arguing against the morality of abortion. In it, he republished a 1977 speech by his surgeon general, C. Everett Koop, titled "The Slide to Auschwitz," and another chapter titled "The Humane Holocaust." This narrative had become mainstream.

Koop, a Christian fundamentalist, was staunchly antiabortion and spent much of his early career using his credentials as a pediatric surgeon to push the idea that abortion was infanticide and akin to the atrocities of the Holocaust. Koop routinely misappropriated the violence of the Third Reich by comparing abortion providers, including Jewish providers, to Nazi soldiers.

The comparison between abortion and the Holocaust has stuck. Antiabortion activists who claim to have "survived" an abortion procedure as a fetus have branded themselves "abortion survivors," mirroring the language of Holocaust survivors. Signs decrying the "abortion holocaust" are a staple at antiabortion rallies. At the same time, the term "life" itself is understood to be shorthand for "white life." The white supremacist dog whistle is a siren.

Antiabortion rallies are fertile recruiting grounds for activists' efforts to spread their great replacement theory, a conspiracy theory that claims the white population in the United States is being intentionally "replaced" by nonwhite people, immigrants, and anyone who isn't white. It's the same excuse that was used to criminalize abortion shortly after Black enslaved people were emancipated. The idea has been spread widely by Fox News and high-ranking Republican politicians and is usually coupled with concerns about the flattening or declining birth rates of white people.

What is getting scarier about the analogy is the use of abortion to minimize the Holocaust. More Republican politicians are praising Nazis openly while antiabortion activists are outing themselves as white nationalists. One Illinois gubernatorial candidate claimed that the extermination of Jews during the Holocaust "doesn't even compare on a shadow of the life that has been lost with abortion since its legalization." In 2022, Renee and Abortion Access Front founder Lizz Winstead wrote for NBC News about the increasing presence of white nationalist groups at March for Life rallies. "Lots of our people join [the antiabortion movement]," a leader of Aryan Nations said. "It's part of our Holy War for the pure Aryan race." It would seem, then, that white supremacists and US Nazis see their vision as inextricably linked with the antiabortion movement.

The only comparison between abortion and the Holocaust is this: Nazis—then and now—see abortion liberation as a threat to their world domination.

ABORTIONSPLAINING MYTH: Abortion Is Worse than Slavery

Half of all black children are aborted. Far more of the African-American community is being devastated by the policies of today than were being devastated by policies of slavery. And I think, What does it take to get us to wake up?

—Ex-congressman Trent Franks, 2010

The first time Renee was thrown out of a congressional hearing was because of this abortionsplaining argument (and for calling ex-congressman Steve King a white supremacist, but we'll get to that). The hearing was on so-called race-selective and sex-selective abortions, an abortion restriction based on racist and xenophobic assumptions that Black people are having abortions because their fetuses are Black and East and South Asian people are having abortions because their fetus is female. In support of race-selective abortion bans, antiabortion politicians use slavery rhetoric to restrict access for Black people. (Of course, the argument makes zero sense because what Black person doesn't know their fetus is Black—the reality is that the only people who would be upset or surprised if their fetus was part Black would be racist white people.)

Abortion is worse than slavery. We've heard the argument ad nauseam. But, for Renee, there was something even more sinister about the claim being made during the remarks of a Black woman testifying in support of a bill that would ban abortion nationally after six weeks of pregnancy. "Slavery was, as abortion is, a crime against humanity," the antiabortion witness testified. "It is ironic," she went on, "that while the Fourteenth Amendment to the US Constitution in 1868 humanized slaves, the US Supreme Court of 1973 dehumanized the life of the being in utero—handing down a decision that reeked in ethnic cleansing, to once again allow a powerful few to determine exactly who had a right to humanity."

The testimony was unbearable to listen to, so Renee sighed audibly in her seat. "Are you going to let any Black women who've had abortions speak? Can we actually talk about what slavery is?" Renee kept saying to the entire room, but she was told to observe decorum or be removed by Capitol Police. During his remarks, Representative King, who is *not* an obstetrician, began to narrate a sonogram, equating the white fetus to President Lincoln and again comparing abortion to slavery. "I wonder if Lincoln is going to move his arm and show how active he can be," he cooed. "It's time to emancipate every little unborn baby." (In another hearing Renee was present for, the year before, Representative King had compared Black women having abortions to killing a litter of puppies.)

Enraging—especially coming from a white nationalist. At the end of the hearing, Renee yelled, "Representative King is a white supremacist!" (She was right—in 2019, he was ousted from the Republican Party for *openly* being one.) In response, a white male antiabortion activist mumbled that she was "a bitch." Never one to back down from a fight, Renee dared him to say that one more time, louder, to her face, at which point Capitol Police forcibly removed Renee from the hearing.

For descendants of enslaved Black people, likening abortion to slavery is a particularly painful form of abortionsplaining. If you have ever heard the testimony of formerly enslaved Black people and all that they endured, it's impossible to say that this medical procedure is comparable. To compare them is abhorrent.

Obviously, the comparison is reprehensible—no, abortion is not like slavery. Abortion is not like the hundreds of years of kidnapping, brutality, rape, forced birthing, torture, medical experimentation, and murder of millions of Africans and enslaved Black people across the Americas. To downplay the generational impact of slavery is revolting and ahistorical. But what's worse is that even *if* the comparison were apt, it posits Black people having abortions as the slave owners.

By drawing a comparison between slavery and abortion, antiabortion advocates seek to demonize Black people in a horrific way, using the horrors our ancestors lived through to threaten us for choosing the futures that best fit our families. The irony is that bodily autonomy was always at the core of slavery. Black people did not get to make decisions about any aspect of their lives or families.

The only times enslaved Black women received medical care was to ensure their reproductive health was maintained so that they could continue to produce enslaved children. Doctors such as Dr. James Marion

Sims, the inexperienced and incompetent "father of gynecology," did heinous experiments on enslaved Black women and babies he owned and "borrowed," refusing to use anesthesia and killing a number of them.

The rape and forced breeding of enslaved Black people was always part of slavery but picked up significantly after 1807, when slave owners were no longer allowed to import kidnapped Africans for their labor. Enslaved Black women in particular bore the brunt of chattel slavery, as they were bred to create more slaves while also laboring on the plantation. Slaver President Thomas Jefferson famously said, "I consider a slave woman who breeds once every two years as profitable as the best worker on the farm." Their fecundity and lack of ability to choose their pregnancy was a particular enslavement. Infertility and miscarriages were punishable as they devalued the women as property. In several instances, enslavers dug ditches in the ground for the enslaved Black women's bellies when they were beaten, believing that would protect the fetus.

More than a few enslaved Black women were accused and convicted of killing their children, including after birthing them, because they had few ways to save their children from the fate of slavery with all its horrors. Toni Morrison's *Beloved* is based on the story of Margaret Garner, a pregnant enslaved Black woman who had been raped and fled her plantation in the dead of winter with her four children, husband, and his parents. When slave catchers surrounded the home she was staying in, she killed one of her children with the intention of killing the others and herself. However, when Garner was arrested, Professor Michele Goodwin, author of *Policing the Womb: Invisible Women and the Criminalization of Motherhood*, told us, she wasn't charged with feticide; she was charged with destroying property, because that's what her children were to the state and her enslaver. Goodwin further explained that her defense team wanted to see her charged with a crime for having killed a child, because that would have proved her personhood, and the personhood of her child.

The painfully frustrating part of comparing abortion to slavery is that it's ahistorical. Enslaved people had abortions during slavery, using everything from the peacock flower to tools and anything else they could get their hands on. The use of cotton root bark was a particularly popular method as it was easy to gather from the very plant that enslaved people were being forced to pick and was mild and effective. Enslaved Black women used to chew the root so much that several former enslaved Black men said they were concerned the Black race "would have been depopulated." The ingenuity of using this particular cash crop to deny slavers the women's babies as property was a brilliant survival tactic. The women knew that, in part, slavery depended on their ability to reproduce. Abortion carried significant risks, because having an abortion without the permission of a slave owner meant that enslaved Black women were destroying property that wasn't theirs. But the stigma of abortion was different, as Marie Jenkins Schwartz writes in *Birthing a Slave*: "Black women—already degraded in the eyes of whites by class and race—could hardly be accused of debasing themselves morally in performing abortion."

Although, Dorothy Roberts, author of *Killing the Black Body: Race, Reproduction, and the Meaning of Liberty*, notes that we don't have evidence identifying whether enslaved Black people used abortion and infanticide to specifically terminate pregnancies as a result of rape or pregnancies in general; we do know that they had abortions and used contraception to prevent pregnancies. Roberts points out that Southern medical journals reported abortion practices of enslaved Black people. In 1849, a Georgia doctor noticed that enslaved Black women had more abortions and miscarriages than white women; although he attributed some to the stress of slave labor, he wrote that slavers complained "the Blacks are possessed of a secret by which they destroy the fetus at an early stage of gestation." Other doctors documented enslaved Black women's use of medicine, herbs, "violent exercise," and "external and internal manipulation," including stuffing hard rags inside of the vagina. Others used teas made from such herbs as pennyroyal, rue, and tansy.

Refusing to become pregnant or to birth children was a radical act among enslaved Black people throughout the Americas. Abortion was resistance to slavery, not slavery itself.

The antiabortion movement's legal argument comparing abortion to slavery focuses on comparing the *Roe v. Wade* decision to the *Dred Scott v. Sandford* decision as the two worst decisions of the US Supreme Court. In 1856, Dred Scott, an enslaved Black man, sued for the freedom of himself, his wife, and his two daughters after his enslaver took them to

Illinois, where slavery was illegal. The Supreme Court eventually ruled that Black people were not considered citizens and did not have rights. Of course, the antiabortion movement sees the fetus as its Dred Scott. Goodwin said that the cases don't relate because not being considered human—a real live person—as an enslaved person meant that in addition to not being compensated for labor, you had no rights to expression about the use of your time, body, mind, and hands; no ability to vote or engage as a member of society; and certainly no recourse if you were harmed. Goodwin added that this had a particular relevance for Dred Scott's wife and daughters because they were subjected to a pernicious type of human exploitation—sexual exploitation—anticipated and demanded from American slavery.

Beyond the antiabortion movement's dedication to calling abortion slavery, there's an insistence on comparing the images of whipped enslaved people to images of embryos. Outside of abortion clinics, we have seen protesters—sometimes calling themselves "abortion abolitionists"—with signs featuring images of "Whipped Peter," an infamous photo of an escaped enslaved Black man, whose name was actually Gordon, with whipping scars on his back, side by side with enlarged images of embryos and fetuses, proclaiming that both abortion and slavery were legal. In 2015, heavily doctored videos of abortions from a Planned Parenthood clinic were released to the public, creating a firestorm of attention around abortion. As part of their efforts, activists with the antiabortion group Live Action created a campaign, Call Him Emmett, naming the images of the aborted fetuses after Emmett Till, a fourteen-year-old Black boy who was kidnapped, tortured, and lynched by white men while visiting family in Mississippi. Borrowing from Till's mother's decision to have an open casket at his funeral to show the world the violence of his murder, Live Action named the various images of the fetus Emmett. "Our hope is that just as Emmett Till's murder awakened a nation to action, the video footage of Baby Emmett's broken little body would awaken the nation's conscience," the organization said. (This antiabortion campaign is beyond sickening and ignorant of the fact that abortion provider and civil rights leader Dr. T. R. M. Howard was instrumental in supporting Till's mother and bringing publicity to Emmett's murder.)

Goodwin said using the trope of enslavement of Black people is once again white people making Black people do their work for them: "Because you are ineffective at carrying out this kind of discourse, now what you want to do is drag Black folk out of the grave into your argument to try to help you." To the antiabortion movement, Black pain and death are only a tool to be exploited to further the antiabortion message, not history to learn from and avoid repeating.

We'll be honest: we also don't like it when white feminists equate being denied an abortion to slavery or compare the journeys people have to travel to access abortion to the Underground Railroad. Making these comparisons is unnecessary and plainly offensive. It is true that the antiabortion movement has proposed and enacted laws that are reminiscent of the slave catcher days. That's because anti-Blackness is at the core of the antiabortion movement's vision. It's possible to address the injustice of being forced to continue a pregnancy without comparing it to an entire four-hundred-year period in which Black people were brutalized and raped. It's possible to explain the special hell of having to travel across the country for an abortion without comparing it to hordes of people escaping plantations, hiding in homes, and facing torture or death when they were caught. Forcing someone into pregnancy is bad enough; we don't need white people exploiting Black people's enslavement to make a point.

ABORTIONSPLAINING MYTH: Abortion Disappeared a Generation of Workers

JEC [Joint Economic Committee] Republicans estimate that the economic cost of abortion in 2019 alone—due to the loss of nearly 630,000 unborn lives—was at least $6.9 trillion, or 32 percent of GDP. . . . Abortion imposes external costs on society not reflected in JEC Republicans' $6.9 trillion cost estimate. In the long run, abortion shrinks the labor force, stunts innovation, and limits economic growth. It also weakens the solvency of social insurance programs like Social Security and Medicare that rely on workers to support a growing elderly population.

—*"The Economic Cost of Abortion," Joint Economic Committee Republicans, June 15, 2022*

In preparation for the unpopular overturn of *Roe v. Wade*, antiabortion legislators began spreading a new argument: abortion is detrimental to the economy.

The reproductive justice movement has always argued that the ability to decide if, when, and how to grow a family is as much a bodily autonomy issue as it is an economic one. Half of people who have abortions have an income below the federal poverty level. More than 75 percent cannot afford their abortion or basic living expenses, which is part of the reason they're having an abortion to begin with. It's also pretty basic economics. If someone is forced to continue a pregnancy they weren't planning to because they couldn't access an abortion, the extra financial costs of another child will be difficult to overcome.

The Turnaway Study and every other economic analysis done on this topic has found that when women are denied a wanted abortion, they're three times more likely to be unemployed and four times more likely to live in poverty than women who were able to access their abortions.

The "missing baby capital" reasoning is an offshoot of the genocide argument. *Kids are missing siblings. Parents are missing children. Companies are missing workers.* This reasoning imagines missing people but fundamentally ignores the children people are able to have when they are ready to continue a pregnancy. It ignores the financial stability people are able to achieve by delaying parenthood or spacing their children.

The financial situation of people who have abortions is not what the antiabortion movement is worried about. Rather, it's the lost capital babies could have made for companies, their absence from the tax base, and their nonexistent Social Security and Medicare contributions. Antiabortion activists have made arguments ranging from claiming that 22 percent of the workforce has been lost to fretting that billions in federal tax revenues are missing, all because of abortion.

The truth is abortion is a threat to capitalism. Under a capitalist system, every action and moment must produce wealth. Forcing people to continue pregnancies in order to create more workers is as old as slavery. The only value people are perceived to have is as labor. The luxury of leisure is available only to those who can afford it. Abortion allows for leisurely, nonprocreative sex.

Feminist socialist scholar Silvia Federici explains that attacks on abortion will always go hand in hand with efforts to regulate a supply of labor. "The new leaders of mercantile capitalism agree that the number of citizens determines a nation's wealth," she explains in *Caliban and the Witch: Women, the Body and Primitive Accumulation*. "Infanticide becomes a capital offense," because it is considered the destruction of potential labor.

Similarly, in her book *Work Won't Love You Back: How Devotion to Our Jobs Keeps Us Exploited, Exhausted, and Alone*, labor journalist Sarah Jaffe writes about utopian socialist societies in the early twentieth century that made domestic caregiving work available to all through public schools, laundries, and cafeterias. Legalized abortion was critical to this utopia, so that women could participate in the labor force and their domestic and child-rearing work didn't subsidize men's labor achievements.

Capitalism does not value pregnant people. If it did, there would be a system of financial and physical support for them and no need to work while pregnant or to go back to work while still healing from pregnancy, and there would be adequate pay for caring for and raising children. Pregnant people work and exist to create more workers who will be socialized by the system to love nothing but work and create wealth for others while receiving little in return. This isn't a new concept; it's the idea behind chattel slavery. It's just been dressed up in new antiabortion rhetoric and economic analysis.

* * *

Abortion *is* powerful. It may not be able to power electricity or cause rain, but it can cause colossal shifts in our futures. It's a power that we have felt, collectively, for centuries. Our hope is that now you'll feel confident—armed with the simple truth of what abortion is and isn't—to stand up to whatever abortionsplaining comes your way.

Everybody Needs Reproductive Justice

Dr. Toni Bond had her first abortion at twelve years old. It was 1977 and the first time she'd heard about abortion. She didn't know anything about how her reproductive system worked; her family didn't talk about sex or abortion. Her family didn't talk about it, even after she became pregnant, because of how steeped in shame, religious stigma, and assumptions of sexual promiscuity it all was. Still, Dr. Bond's mother made her an appointment for care. Dr. Bond would later learn that her mother had also had an abortion, before it was legal. Her mother took her to Friendship Medical Center in Chicago, the clinic owned by civil rights leader Dr. T. R. M. Howard. Because of the Hyde Amendment their Medicaid insurance wouldn't cover the abortion, Dr. Bond told us in an interview, so her mother paid out of pocket, delaying paying the rent and other bills and borrowing additional money to afford the abortion. The experience, Dr. Bond said, was quite traumatic, and she nearly died from it. The clinic was focused on trying to do as many procedures a day as they could, so the patient care suffered, but there was little recourse or accountability at the time. (As you may remember from chapter 4, "The First Time Abortion Was a Crime," Dr. Howard was interested in pioneering the "lunch hour abortion," and his clinics provided between 60 and 100 abortions each day. Although that rate may have impacted the volume of people who needed abortions, it seems to not have translated to thoughtful care.) Dr. Bond remembers the lack of humanity and being "treated like cattle" at the clinic, which she said had a bad reputation. The nurses refused to allow Dr. Bond's mother inside the procedure room, and they held the young girl down. Dr. Bond says the doctors yelled at her. She was scared because she was a child; she didn't know what was going on. All she knew was that her period had stopped and that she was pregnant. She had little understanding of her body beyond that. A few months later, around 20 weeks gestation, Dr. Bond began to hemorrhage and was rushed to the emergency room where she learned that her abortion was incomplete. The providers at Friendship Medical Center left fetal tissue inside of her body. When we asked her about the contradictions between Dr. Howard's position as a civil rights leader and her own abortion experience at his clinic, she explained that it felt like the difference between providing care and connecting with community. "It wouldn't be out of the realm of reality that Black women and girls were treated differently at Friendship Medical Center," she explained. Her abortion, although traumatic and life threatening, became a source of inspiration for her work today. "I think it was because of that traumatic experience that it was important for me to do this work."

It wasn't until Dr. Bond was sixteen that she heard someone talking about abortion. As she walked by Daley Plaza, she heard a speaker sharing her abortion story at a rally for the Chicago National Organization for Women. "I just stopped and I listened," she told us. "And I remember saying that's what I wanted to do when I grew up. That's what I wanted to do one day."

Dr. Bond would have four abortions before she learned how her reproductive system worked at age twenty-nine, which is also when she came into reproductive rights work. She later cofounded the reproductive justice movement. In 1994, after working as a medical advocate at a rape crisis center, she was recruited to apply for the role of executive director of the Chicago Abortion Fund. The organization was committed to hiring not just its first woman of color executive director but also the first Black woman to run an abortion fund in the country. Dr. Bond was hesitant to take on the role without prior experience running an organization, but she did, and she went on to learn much more than she anticipated that year. At one point, when she went to the Chicago Women's Health Center for a pregnancy test, a health care worker asked her whether she was familiar with her menstrual cycle. Dr. Bond was not; she just knew that her period would come every month, and "usually when it came, it was damn inconvenient." The health care worker proceeded to explain Dr. Bond's reproductive system to her, helping her chart her cycle and teaching her how to do a cervical exam. "That was like my aha moment," said Dr. Bond, realizing that after four unintended pregnancies and four abortions, she—the executive director of the Chicago Abortion Fund—didn't know how *not* to become pregnant. "But once the health worker helped me learn about how to chart my menstrual cycle, it was like a fog had been lifted. I didn't know that I had that much power and control over my own body."

During Dr. Bond's second month on the job, she attended a conference sponsored by the Illinois Pro-Choice Alliance and the Ms. Foundation for Women. It brought reproductive health advocates together in Chicago to discuss a recent shift in policy by then-president Bill Clinton, who by that time was touting rhetoric that abortion should be "safe, legal, and rare." He also had campaigned for the presidency on a racially coded promise to "end welfare as we have come to know it," which would be detrimental to low-income Black and Brown families.

Dr. Bond and the other Black women in the room worked on the front lines for sexual and reproductive freedom; they all understood how these issues were deeply affected by systemic and institutional anti-Blackness and poverty. They instinctively knew that President Clinton's policy platforms were harmful, but they also knew that the narrow solutions—such as focusing solely on abortion—proposed by a pro-choice framework wouldn't be adequate to counter this proposal, nor would it serve the totality of Black and Brown people's lives. These women knew that the path toward liberation had to involve a vision cementing our fundamental rights as human beings, something Black women had never been afforded in this country without some sort of government surveillance or interference. Twelve of the Black women met in a hotel room to discuss another way, Dr. Bond explained. "We didn't understand the magnitude of what we were coming together to do in that hotel room."

* * *

The lore of the founding of reproductive justice, as it is told in the movement, is that twelve Black women created the reproductive justice framework in June 1994, during a Chicago convening. They were frustrated by President Clinton's 1993 health care initiative that stigmatized abortion while also failing to center the needs of women of color. That story is true, but the concept has its roots much further back in history.

Since before the days of the suffragettes, Black and Brown organizers have always challenged the systems and organizing that left their experiences on the margins. They've intimately experienced living at the intersections of race, class, and gender, knowing these issues must be addressed together. The reproductive rights movement was no different. As early as 1973, Black women were denouncing the reproductive rights organizing framework for leaving out the needs of their communities. In a 1973 editorial on the *Roe* decision published in *The Black Woman's Voice*, the National Council of Negro Women identified ways Black women were forced to accept sterilization in order to continue receiving welfare benefits, and other Black women and girls were sterilized without consenting to the procedure. In some cases, Black women were forced to have abortions as punishment for advocating for civil rights. The editorial issued this important warning: "We must be ever vigilant that what appears on the surface to be a step forward, does not in fact become yet another fetter or method of enslavement." Similarly, in 1977, the Combahee River Collective issued its defining statement identifying Black feminism as "the logical political movement to combat the manifold and simultaneous oppressions that all women of color face."

As Dr. Bond explains it, the modern reproductive justice movement stood on the shoulders of Black activists such as Byllye Avery and Lillie Pearl Allen. Avery is an iconic Black feminist health advocate who cofounded the Gainesville Women's Health Center, an abortion clinic and birthing center, shortly after abortion became legal. She worked in partnership with Allen, a medical educator who developed the "Black and Female: What Is the Reality?" workshop, in which participants were able to explore how racism and misogyny impacted their medical experiences. The work of Avery and Allen was essential in tying together the impacts of race, gender, and class on Black communities. In 1983, Spelman College held the first National Conference on Black Women's Health Issues, with nearly 2,000 attendees. The three-day event, the *New York Times* reported in November 2023, changed how Black women thought and talked about our health and racism's toll on us. Afterward, Avery and Allen knew they needed to continue organizing around Black women's health, creating the National Black Women's Health Project (now the Black Women's Health Imperative). The program centered on Black women's health and well-being and initially did not take a public stand on abortion. Avery and other women at the National Black Women's Health Project were dedicated to the issue; others considered abortion to be genocidal toward Black communities or a white woman's issue. But as legal attacks on abortion continued, national Black women's organizations, including the National Black Women's Health Project, joined with white-led mainstream abortion rights groups. In 1986, alongside the National Council of Negro Women, which was led by the legendary civil rights leader Dorothy Height, and more than one hundred organizations led by women of color, the National Black Women's Health Project endorsed that year's March for Women's Lives, marking a turning point for the issue of reproductive rights in the public sphere.

That same year, Missouri enacted a law establishing fetal personhood, meaning the state claimed "life" began at conception, giving legal protections historically reserved for living humans to embryos and imposing a number of restrictions on abortion, including prohibiting the use of public funds, employees, or facilities for "encouraging or counseling" a patient to have an abortion unless it was to save the person's life. Not only did this law extend beyond the boundaries established in the 1980 *Harris v. McRae* decision by applying restrictions on the use of public funds for abortion services to all pregnant people, not solely Medicaid recipients, but it also interfered in the practice of medicine.

In 1989, the case *Webster v. Reproductive Health Services* made its way to the US Supreme Court, with the state of Missouri asking the Court to review the law and reconsider *Roe*. Although the Court did not take up or reconsider *Roe*, it did uphold the provisions of the Missouri law, signaling what the future held for the constitutional right to abortion in the United States. Faye Wattleton, then president of Planned Parenthood, said that because the ruling denied access to abortion in all publicly funded facilities, "*Roe* as we knew it ceased to exist."

The court's *Webster* decision rattled activists, in particular Black women leaders who had been fighting to preserve and even expand abortion rights. Political strategist Donna Brazile organized a call with other leaders representing the most prominent Black women organizations at the time. Byllye Avery suggested they produce a pamphlet making it clear once and for all that abortion rights and the freedom to control our reproduction, or reproductive freedom, were issues essential to Black women. Written by *Ms. Magazine*'s Marcia Gillespie, the pamphlet, titled "We Remember," connected the efforts to control Black women's reproduction from chattel slavery to present-day restrictions and told everyday Black folks having abortions that this is our fight and we should not back down. The pamphlet gave "reproductive freedom" an expansive definition that included these rights: to be provided with comprehensive, age-appropriate information about sexuality and reproductive health; to choose to have and not have a child; to have good, affordable health care for safe pregnancies and deliveries; to easily access contraceptive, abortion, and infertility health care; and to make one's own informed, safe, and effective reproductive health choices. The pamphlet included this statement:

> *There have always been those who have stood in the way of our exercising our rights, who tried to restrict our choices. There probably always will be. But we who have been oppressed should not be swayed in our opposition to tyranny, of any kind, especially attempts to take away our reproductive freedom. You may believe abortion is wrong. We respect your belief and we will do all in our power to protect that choice for you. You may decide that abortion is not an option you would choose. Reproductive freedom guarantees your right not to.*

All that we ask is that no one deny another human being the right to make her own choice. That no one condemn her to exercising her choices in ways that endanger her health, her life. And that no one prevent others from creating safe, affordable, legal conditions to accommodate women, whatever the choices they make. Reproductive freedom gives each of us the right to make our own choices, and guarantees us a safe, legal, affordable support system. It's the right to choose.

In total, sixteen Black women signed the statement, including Avery and Wattleton. Planned Parenthood and NARAL sponsored the printing of more than 250,000 copies. At the time, there were few organizations and organization leaders willing to call out the racism and discrimination Black women faced; the statement connected the realities of Black women's lives in a way that would be modeled in the reproductive justice framework.

African American Women Organizing for Reproductive Freedom: "We Remember," 1989. *Courtesy of the Byllye Avery Papers, Sophia Smith Collection, Smith College, Northampton, Massachusetts.*

After the distribution of the "We Remember" pamphlet, the National Black Women's Health Project organizers began building widespread support for abortion access in Black communities. They sponsored a conference, Sisters in Session About Our Reproductive Health, in 1990, and four years later launched the Campaign for Abortion and Reproductive Equity (CARE), which laid the groundwork for future efforts by reproductive justice activists working to end the Hyde Amendment.

However, even though NARAL cosponsored the printing of the brochure, supporting the critique of a narrow lens, the organization was doubling down on its "choice" framework, which centered rights rather than access. In 1993, the organization changed its name from the National Association for the Repeal of Abortion Laws to the National Abortion Rights Action League and launched the "Real Choices" campaign to "highlight the goals of its expanded mission: preserve access to abortion while working to enact policies to make abortion less necessary." NARAL began engaging in efforts to stigmatize and minimize abortion's role, the remnants of which we still experience today. Despite offering public and financial support for the clarion call of the "We Remember" pamphlet and for organizations led by women of color, NARAL staked out a contrary position, choosing political pragmatism that maintained the status quo over the liberation of abortion that Black and Brown communities needed to survive. It is within that context that the founders of reproductive justice met in Chicago.

* * *

Back at the June 1994 meeting, Black advocates were unimpressed by the plan reproductive rights advocates were putting together to address the ways that President Clinton's Health Security Act fell short. As Dr. Bond explains in a chapter she wrote for *Radical Reproductive Justice: Foundation, Theory, Practice, Critique*, the plan, shepherded by First Lady Hillary Rodham Clinton ahead of the 1994 midterm elections, would further institutionalize the two-tiered system of health care that harmed so many communities of color. The founders of reproductive justice decided to write a statement in response with recommendations, particularly ones that included abortion and centered Black women's

Women hold signs and yell in support of abortion rights and the passage of the Freedom of Choice Act during a 1992 rally in Washington, DC.
Photo by Owen Franken/Getty Images.

needs. They felt that women's health advocates didn't fully grasp the impact Clinton's entire proposal would have on low-income and racially marginalized women. Dr. Bond wrote that "while abortion was a crucial resource for us, we also needed health care, education, jobs, day care, and the right to motherhood."

Dr. Bond told us that prior to that meeting in Chicago, there had been other efforts to create a national coalition for women of color leaders in sexual and reproductive health. "It's not to say that folks weren't already doing reproductive justice work prior to us coming together in '94," she said. "But I also think that it was just the right timing, and it was the right grouping of people in that particular moment."

After issuing the statement from the conference, the leaders wanted this vision to create a larger impact. They placed a full-page ad in both the *Washington Post* and *Roll Call*, a political newspaper, on August 16, 1994.

Titled "Black Women on Health Care Reform," the ad declared to Congress that they "will not endorse [any] health care reform system that does not cover the full range of reproductive services for all women—including abortion." They also noted that health care reform must include universal coverage that is accessible to all people, must be comprehensive in its nature, and must have explicit antidiscrimination provisions.

The Twelve Founding Mothers of Reproductive Justice

* Toni M. Bond (Chicago Abortion Fund)

* Rev. Alma Crawford (Religious Coalition for Reproductive Choice)

* Evelyn S. Field (National Council of Negro Women)

* Terri James (American Civil Liberties Union of Illinois)

* Bisola Marignay (National Black Women's Health Project, Chicago chapter)

* Cassandra McConnell (Planned Parenthood of Greater Cleveland)

* Cynthia Newbille (National Black Women's Health Project)

* Loretta J. Ross (Center for Democratic Renewal)

* Elizabeth Terry (National Abortion Rights Action League of Pennsylvania)

* "Able" Mabel Thomas (Pro-Choice Resource Center, Inc.)

* Winnette P. Willis (Chicago Abortion Fund)

* Kim Youngblood (National Black Women's Health Project)

The ad was signed by 836 Black women, including author Alice Walker and activist Angela Davis. "The response was amazing," Dr. Bond told us. "I mean, everybody wanted to be sure to get their name on it, I think because of what it said and because of how we brought it to the various communities that each of us worked in. . . . People wanted their names included because we took such a broad lens to what it meant for Black women and pregnant-capable persons to be reproductively and sexually healthy. That was the difference."

The women hadn't yet fleshed out their thinking on these connections, but they were in the process of doing so. They also needed a name. As they planned the ad, they began thinking about what they wanted to call this new framework: they settled on "reproductive justice" and called themselves Women of African Descent for Reproductive Justice. The term "reproductive justice" married "reproductive rights" and "social justice" to more accurately center the fuller scope of social justice needs of marginalized people than the concept of "reproductive choice." "Our thinking was headed in that direction that we were tying reproductive and sexual autonomy, self-determination, and liberation to the human right to be able to make decisions about our lives and our bodies as Black women, given our history, particularly in this country."

The day after the ad ran, Women of African Descent for Reproductive Justice hosted a press conference in Washington, DC, and distributed reprints of the "We Remember" pamphlet. The second issue of the pamphlet listed twenty-nine more signatures, including the twelve founding members of reproductive justice, as well as two statements: one in support of Surgeon General Dr. Joycelyn Elders, the first Black woman to hold the position, who was forced to resign by Republican pressure after she suggested in an HIV and AIDS forum that youth should be taught about masturbation in schools in the context of curbing transmission rates, called for the legalization of some drugs, and advocated for contraception distribution in schools. The second statement endorsed Dr. David Satcher as her replacement. Women of African Descent for Reproductive Justice understood the intersectional analysis and the lived experiences of Black women and how critical these were to reproductive health. They were determined to make sure legislators did, too.

A few months later, in September 1994, several of the reproductive justice founders attended the International Conference on Population and Development in Cairo, Egypt. There they learned from the international women's health community about using the global human rights framework as outlined by the United Nations' common standard of international laws. Building on the similar connections they saw between their lives and the lives of the global activists, they felt this framework was more expansive than the rights afforded in the US Constitution and the narrow privacy rights of *Roe*. The framework also demanded that policies recognize the historical context of Black women's forced reproduction during slavery, medical experimentation, and forced sterilization. The framework insisted that policies and health care efforts look at the totality of Black women's lives and the context in which their decisions are made.

The definition of reproductive justice was simple, yet visionary: the right to have children, to not have children, and to parent the children we have in safe and healthy environments.

The vision built on Black feminist theory and the "We Remember" pamphlet recognized the unique needs of Black and Brown families who have never been able to raise their families free from coercion and oppression. The vision sought to address the political reality for all who could not afford to choose the outcomes of their pregnancies, whether it was because of stagnant wages, policies such as the Hyde Amendment, the lack of reproductive services in their communities, immigration policies, or lack of information. The vision also was naturally inclusive of queer and trans people, including those who had abortions, because it centered those most unable in our society to access the sexual and reproductive care that they need, irrespective of their sexual orientation or gender identity and expression. When we talked to Cazembe Murphy Jackson, a southern Black queer trans man, for our podcast *The A Files: A Secret History of Abortion*, he told us that it was mostly southern Black women in the reproductive justice movement who held him and kept him engaged in the movement. Cazembe credits his abortion for saving his life. As a college student in Texas, he was raped by multiple assailants due to his gender presentation as a butch lesbian at the time. The experience of trying to get an abortion was even more challenging. He reported the rape to police, but he was met with skepticism and disregard. He took out a payday loan to cover the cost of the care and faced shouting antiabortion protesters both times that he went to the clinic because of the government-mandated multiple appointment law.

Cazembe now shares his story because he believes that if he had heard other Black trans voices at the time of his abortion, it would have affirmed his experience, particularly since the pro-choice movement has historically erased queer and trans people from the movement for reproductive rights. He's not alone either; the Guttmacher Institute estimates that at least 1 percent of abortion patients identify as nonbinary or trans men. "Everybody has organs to reproduce, so of course everybody needs reproductive justice," Cazembe explained.

This inclusivity is what makes reproductive justice essential for people of all genders. "[It] gives us the framework to apply an intersectional lens to the systems of oppression that could preclude Black women, Black pregnant-capable [people] from being able to be self-autonomous over their bodies and ultimately over their lives," as Dr. Bond told us.

For us, reproductive justice is a worldview; it demands that we examine every plan, system of care, and policy, as well as our treatment of one another, with a lens that recognizes the humanity of the person in front of us and supports them in receiving all of the rights, resources, and respect they need to make their own informed decisions about their bodies. Reproductive justice demands that we recognize how history, place, oppression, and access can limit the decisions that we make, and seeks ways to rectify it toward justice. Remember how Dr. Bond didn't learn about her menstrual cycle until the health care worker explained it to her? The worker didn't shame Dr. Bond for needing another pregnancy test after having had four abortions; instead the worker asked Dr. Bond questions and offered her education so that she could make her own informed decisions about her body.

But reproductive justice isn't solely about the personal level; it also seeks to mitigate and redress the harm caused by racist policies. Take, for example, a policy known as "family cap," in which states limit the cash aid and welfare benefits they offer to recipients should they become pregnant while receiving aid. If a person becomes pregnant, they may feel like they are forced to terminate a pregnancy they wanted to continue simply because they are poor and wouldn't receive additional support from the government to raise that child. But then their problems could snowball: they might not be able to afford the abortion and thus must continue a pregnancy with less financial aid to raise all of their children, or they could be coerced into relinquishing their parental rights through adoption because they cannot afford to raise another child. With less financial support and presumably a low-wage job, they may have a hard time affording childcare, food, and stable housing, which could cause them to run into the family-policing system that criminalizes parents for raising their children in poverty. Parents are punished not because they harmed their children but because they struggled to afford the basic necessities to raise children. These issues are further complicated based on race and location and for disabled, queer, trans, immigrant, young, and currently or formerly incarcerated people. Meanwhile, all of the funding our nation spends policing parents and monitoring the meager welfare benefits they receive vastly outweighs the money it would cost to financially support low-income parents so that they can feed and raise their children. The problem becomes even more complicated on a political level, because politicians will tout their commitment to protecting abortion and contraception rights while gutting Medicaid funding and welfare benefits, increasing policing and border patrol in our communities, and bombing people who also deserve the liberation of reproductive justice all around the world. The reality is that the reproductive rights framework and pro-choice slogans do not address this complicated reproductive journey that people are put on simply because they don't have enough money to provide for their families.

Dr. Bond does warn, however, about the "prevailing misperception" that Black women were trying to replace the pro-choice and reproductive rights frameworks. "Rather," she writes in *Radical Reproductive Justice*, "our focus was on centering Black women within the debate, moving our voices from the margins to the center of the discourse." She cites the intentionality of the framework that builds on their own personal experiences in their journey toward self-determination and liberation. Reproductive justice was not meant as a replacement, Dr. Bond writes. "This assumption promotes the myth that women of color are incapable of formulating theoretical analyses to successfully break the historical bonds over our embodied flesh." Reproductive justice was a vision to center the ways multiple oppressions were a threat to Black women's bodily autonomy and liberation. Reproductive justice was created as a concept to guide us as we dismantle sexual and reproductive oppression in our communities.

As visionary as the reproductive justice framework is, it wasn't immediately accepted. When Dr. Bond cofounded Black Women for Reproductive Justice in 1996 with Winnette P. Willis, she encountered philanthropic funders who wanted them to focus on policy change rather than comprehensive community education. But Dr. Bond rejected these calls; she was clear that she cocreated the organization and reproductive justice as a framework "so that women could liberate themselves through this process of self-actualization and gaining control and autonomy over their bodies."

At its core, the work of reproductive justice is much bigger than any one policy or federal program. Liberation cannot come from one billionaire philanthropist or policy, nor can it be achieved by any one individual candidate, organization, or political party. It is a recognition of an entire system of change in our families, communities, and world. The founders of reproductive justice developed this path for future reproductive justice advocates, activities, and allies to follow. As we are redesigning our communities to look like the world we want and deserve, we have to push ourselves to see how reproductive justice can be applied in our lives and organize without the constraints of white supremacy, capitalism, and anti-Blackness. It cannot be limited by the unimaginative whims of political parties or philanthropists. Yet in order to spread the gospel of reproductive justice, the founders of the framework needed to set up nonprofit organizations to continue to do the work and serve our communities, whether the funders saw the vision or not.

ORGANIZING THE MOVEMENT

One of Luz Marina Rodriguez's early reproductive health memories was learning about her uterus from a plastic model, how to insert a diaphragm, how IUDs worked, and other options of contraception. She even took what she learned and incorporated it into a video short she made about a young girl who needed an abortion as part of her work with a local nonprofit youth program when she was sixteen years old. Luz was born and raised on the Lower East Side in New York City, where her parents migrated to from Puerto Rico. Their move in the 1950s was the result of Operation Bootstrap, a coordinated effort by the US and Puerto Rican governments to address shortages of low-cost labor. Luz grew up in an eclectic neighborhood of "Puerto Rican hippies," as she put it, and was exposed to shared leadership and collective activism from an early age. "I didn't realize that the rest of the world [didn't also practice collective activism] until I left the neighborhood," Luz told us in an interview. She spent her formative years biking to different youth leadership programs focused on community organizing.

While a college senior at New York University, Luz researched the sterilization of Puerto Rican women on the island. Luz read about the partnership between doctors and US pharmaceutical companies that saw the island as "a perfect laboratory" for the research and development of the contraceptive pill, before it was considered safe enough to market to American women. She learned about their racist ideas about Puerto Rican women's fecundity and education levels, overpopulation, and the desire to control who could procreate. The sterilization campaign was supported by the governor of Puerto Rico because he saw overpopulation as the root of poverty and a threat to Operation Bootstrap's success with US companies. "As a young Puerto Rican woman I was infuriated and politicized around not just reproductive rights for the right to choose abortion, but the right to have a child," Luz told us. "That was my platform before the term 'reproductive justice' was coined." She served as the executive director of the New York City–based Latina Roundtable on Health and Reproductive Rights shortly thereafter. Founded in 1989, the Latina Roundtable was the only reproductive rights organization advocating for the health needs of Latinas in New York City amid an escalation of attacks on reproductive health care in the '80s and '90s.

Even as she found purpose in reproductive rights work, Luz always stopped short of seeing herself as part of a movement. "It was just what I did, the day-to-day struggle was what was ever-present on my mind," Luz said in a 2006 interview with Smith College's Voices of Feminism Oral History Project. "And one doesn't notice when one is part of a movement until you look back and you see there's been some movement," she said, laughing. She said that she ended up at the Latina Roundtable not because she was a reproductive rights activist but because she was a social justice activist. She worked with food pantries, youth programs, and women's shelters. "To me, it was all the same family," Luz said. "We were either dealing with the kids of that family or the mother of that family . . . it led me straight to reproductive justice."

One fortuitous day at the Latina Roundtable, Luz got a call from Reena Marcelo, a program officer at the Ford Foundation, who had heard Luz speak about the dire state of women's health during a funders' briefing. Marcelo, who has since passed, was from the Philippines and "had her own story about reproductive oppression [there]." She was interested in funding grassroots women of color organizations typically overlooked by the Ford Foundation that could focus on reproductive tract infections and culturally relevant solutions. Luz had the idea of funding a total of sixteen groups—four from each of the four communities of color considered under the "women of color" umbrella: African American, Asian American, Latina, and Indigenous women—securing a three-year, $4 million grant from the Ford Foundation that led to the creation of SisterSong.

During the lead-up to the launch, Luz organized a series of meetings open to women of color in the reproductive health field, with some key leaders identified to help spread the word. Many reproductive health leaders of color were skeptical of the effort and the meetings, and some even declined to attend. Others who did attend explained that this sort of foundation-led effort had been attempted before: the funders would take the information they learned to build a request for proposals for which nonprofits could apply, but the funding wouldn't necessarily go to the groups that participated in the convening. As a way to ease the concerns of women of color attendees, Luz and Marcelo opened up the first meeting by telling a story about the shared leadership of geese flying south for the winter. "By flying in V-formation, the whole flock adds at least 71 percent greater flying range than if each bird flew on its own," explained Luz, creating a comparison between the flock and what would be the collective of reproductive justice organizations. "People who share a common direction and sense of community can get where they are going more quickly and easily because they are traveling on the thrust of one another." The geese, she told the group, also look out for one another if one gets sick or wounded. Two geese would fall out of formation with the hurt goose and stay with it until it could fly or it died, and then launch out in their own new formation. "If we have the sense of a goose, we will stand by each other like that."

Luz talked about what brought her to reproductive justice: the experimentation on and sterilization of Puerto Rican women. Each of the groups in the room said the state did the same to their communities. "It was a powerful, defining moment," Luz told us. It highlighted how there was a long history of reproductive oppression that impacted every women of color group. But those common connections were rarely addressed or acknowledged until that meeting. "There was like this profound silence and heaviness that hit the room, where it was like a good thing that it connected us, but it was such a sad, sad, horrendous thing," said Luz.

In the end, the groups who regularly participated and showed up for these meetings were invited to apply to be part of SisterSong. The initial groups received capacity-building funding from the Ford Foundation to get their sexual and reproductive health programs off the ground. The $4 million grant was a boon for the organizations, but it was divided by the sixteen groups over three years. Once the initial grant funding ran out, everyone expected more to follow, but under a new program officer the Ford Foundation sought a new cohort of sixteen groups to receive funding using the SisterSong name. None of the original organizations would receive additional funding. "So Loretta Ross stormed into the Ford Foundation, and she said, 'If we're not going to get money that's fine, but you're not taking our name,'" Luz recalled. The Ford Foundation changed its position, and Ross, who would become SisterSong's first staff leader, brought together the original organizations and the new cohort to plan the first national conference.

"At that conference, SisterSong was born again," said Luz. In 2003, some six hundred women of color joined together in Atlanta to learn about the reproductive justice framework and how to make an impact at the local or national level, or both. "The questions explored at the conference came about because women of color were frustrated with the limitations of the privacy-based pro-choice movement that did not fully incorporate the experiences of women of color, and the failure of the pro-choice movement to understand the impact of white supremacist thinking on the lives of communities of color," Dr. Bond explains in *Radical Reproductive Justice*. For the groups and leaders involved in defining and developing the movement, envisioning what a society could be *with* reproductive justice became just as crucial, if not more so, than reacting to attacks on reproductive and sexual health care.

Following SisterSong's inaugural conference, several organizations within the collective rebranded to incorporate the framework of reproductive justice as well as adding the term itself to their names: Asian Communities for Reproductive Justice (formerly Asian Pacific Islanders for Reproductive Health), Black Women for Reproductive Justice (formerly African American Women Evolving), and SisterSong, which changed its name in 2010 to the SisterSong Women of Color Reproductive Justice Collective, named by founding board member Juanita Williams.

Reproductive justice was catching on, but the funding to do the work was not. Foundations still offered money, hand over fist, to white-led reproductive rights organizations focused on growing political power but made smaller, short-term investments in reproductive justice organizations. Once some foundations shifted to create new opportunities for reproductive justice funding, the gentrification of reproductive justice grew. Some white-led organizations claimed to shift the focus of their work toward women of color without hiring any women of color to work at their organizations, let alone in leadership positions. Large national organizations with more financial and political power overshadowed the small grassroots groups doing the work in their local communities, and some have taken credit for this work as the vision of reproductive justice appealed to more audiences. After Planned Parenthood was widely applauded in a glowing 2014 *New York Times* profile about its visionary new shift in strategy to move beyond the pro-choice organizing framework toward a more holistic approach that looked at all the factors in a person's life, and the organization failed to acknowledge or cite the then-twenty-year-old reproductive justice approach, reproductive justice leaders publicly addressed the organization. The erasure opened old wounds and was compounded by a long-standing funding gap between the amount of donations and grants issued to white-led national groups and reproductive justice organizations led by people of color, which continue to struggle to build the financial stability and sustainability that their larger counterparts have acquired over the years. "Black-led organizations working on reproductive justice issues have never been sufficiently funded. And the irony behind that is this movement was created by Black women. So why is it that the population that created the movement gets funded the least?" Dr. Bond asked rhetorically. "I think it's so deeply embedded in culture that Black women can't be trusted. We can't be trusted to control our bodies, our fertility, so of course we can't be trusted to manage the funds that come [from philanthropic organizations] to create change."

* * *

It is a precarious thing to build a reproductive justice world within the structures of nonprofit organizations. Nonprofits are funded, in large part, by corporations and wealthy families who place their money in their own foundations to avoid paying taxes. Those are the same tax dollars that are needed to fund health care programs such as Title X, libraries and hospitals, roads and bridges, Medicaid, and other public projects and services. However, philanthropists are only required by law to disburse 5 percent of their endowments to charitable organizations and can continue to grow their own foundation endowments. This means that not only do those who endowed the foundations get to keep more of the profits that they made using exploited labor, nonexistent worker benefits, and cheap goods, but the money is not reinvested in our communities to rectify the harm caused by companies overworking their employees. There's little money for community health centers where people can learn about their bodies or receive the contraception they need, because their employer's health insurance won't cover it or they simply can't afford it. All social justice nonprofits are inherently funded by the very systems that they are trying to dismantle. While some are trying to shift the systemic injustice in the world, others are limited in their approach because they benefit from the political power and clout of the status quo—and the funding they receive as a result. It's the same reason that making systemic political change is difficult: politicians are funded by the same wealthy individuals and corporations; therefore, they are incentivized to focus on their interests, not the interests of marginalized people. And all of this, as Dr. Bond pointed out, is coated in anti-Blackness. It's a vicious cycle.

Reproductive justice organizations are trying to build a different world with a fraction of the funds the larger, status quo reproductive rights organizations have. The vision of reproductive justice calls for a seismic shift in our political system. Reproductive justice as a framework is inherently anticapitalist, because it requires us to address the way economic coercion fuels anti-Blackness, racism, and reproductive oppression. The framework invites us to imagine a world in which everyone has the resources to decide if, when, and how to grow their families, but that is only possible if everyone is fairly compensated for their work, families have all that they need to thrive, and our bodies are not commodified based on what—and whom—we can produce. For reproductive justice to be real, capitalism must cease to exist. But as things stand, for nonprofit organizations that are building toward reproductive justice to exist, capitalism must thrive.

There are ways in which a reproductive justice world is possible. Our system already has the money it needs, but it's invested in the wrong places and takes the wrong approach. For example, many states make their tax funds available to crisis pregnancy centers—fake clinics that lie to pregnant people. Imagine if that money were instead given to clinics and organizations that use evidence-based and culturally competent care to support people and their sexual and reproductive lives. Or take the funds provided to state and local police forces, the military, and school and immigration police officers. Imagine if these funds went to providing condoms, contraceptives, IVF treatments, and hormone replacement therapies for people who cannot afford them. Rather than locking up families for crossing a border or arresting parents who "steal" food for their children, those officers' salaries could fund programs or cash aid to support those families.

To build a world with reproductive justice, we have to think toward liberation and abolition. Abolition works hand in glove with reproductive justice; when we defund the programs, agencies, and people that have only served to take away and criminalize our freedoms, we can adequately invest in reproductive and sexual freedom and in all families.

But liberation cannot be achieved if it relies on capitalist budget lines and political parties that seek to retain power. Reproductive justice requires us to challenge any system or political party that claims to support sexual and reproductive health care, including abortion, but trades on the humanity of communities of color to increase criminalization and maintain power. Reproductive justice organizations are a core part of achieving liberation, but the vision for liberation has to be owned and carried out by all of us. Those of us with the most to lose should be nearest to and centered in the decisions. Otherwise we're just re-creating a new version of the problem.

We believe there's much to learn from reproductive justice leaders who are building bridges with our communities and growing the number of people who see reproductive justice as their issue and calling. Many of their stories begin with trying to rectify the negative experiences they had or replicate the considerate care they received.

MAKING REPRODUCTIVE JUSTICE REAL FOR US

When Cherisse Scott was pregnant in 2002, the vocalist, songwriter, and actress went to a nearby clinic in Chicago expecting to receive an abortion. After the workers at the first clinic failed to talk her out of having the abortion she'd scheduled with them, they sent her to another clinic, on a different day, and assured her that the second clinic appointment would be for an abortion. The workers at the second clinic gave her an ultrasound and told her that if she had an abortion she would no longer be able to have children, and she believed them. "They changed my mind about having the abortion because I wanted to be a mother at some point. They used my ignorance about abortion, and their lie changed the trajectory of my life," Cherisse told us. Instead of being given fact-based information and the ability to think through all her options, Cherisse was manipulated and lied to by the crisis pregnancy center. In a 2022 interview with *The Tennessean*, Cherisse said about the experience, "I think I'm even more upset now than I was then because now I recognize the disingenuous nature of why abortion rights are at stake."

Several years later at a party, Cherisse met Dr. Toni Bond, who told Cherisse about her organization educating the community about reproductive health. Dr. Bond gave Cherisse her card. When Cherisse became pregnant again, she called the number on the card. Dr. Bond referred Cherisse to a local women's health clinic to access emergency contraception, and when that didn't work—because she was beyond the range of effectiveness—an abortion clinic's information. Dr. Bond later invited Cherisse to volunteer with her organization, then to serve on the board. And when an opportunity for employment became available, she offered Cherisse a job with the organization. "While working at African American Women Evolving, which was later renamed Black Women for Reproductive Justice [BWRJ], she taught me how to chart my fertility and understand when I was ovulating. She then assigned me to teach other women in the community," explained Cherisse. Dr. Bond showed Cherisse that reproductive justice was about empowering people to be self-determining and take control of their lives as Black women. "She poured into me so that I could be empowered and then empower others."

One of the skill sets Cherisse also brought to her position at BWRJ was being an ordained minister of eleven years, with deep relationships in the Black Christian church. Dr. Bond assigned Cherisse to organize Black religious communities and serve on an advocacy board of clergy to help inform what that approach should look like. This pivot was a needed addition to the collective organizing strategy of the Trust Black Women campaign, a partnership of Black reproductive justice organizations and advocates facilitated by SisterSong in 2010. The partnership was responding to a nationwide racist antiabortion billboard campaign denigrating Black women for having abortions. Dr. Bond's hope was that Cherisse's leadership in the Black church would be a way to build bridges with those who wanted to leverage their faith in order to advance liberation and reproductive justice.

Cherisse began organizing Christians as well as Jews, Muslims, and members of the Nation of Islam in Chicago, where billboards featured a picture of former president Barack Obama and stated that "Every 21 minutes, our next possible leader is aborted." Cherisse explained that the goal of the campaign was to stigmatize Black women while placing a wedge between Black women and men. "There were multiple billboards erected across the country with vilifying messages about Black women—our sexuality, our promiscuousness, our being irresponsible—but never about us loving our children. There was nothing that was affirming and loving or supportive and empowering." Not only that, said Cherisse, but the billboards' messages overlooked one important factor: why Black women choose to have abortions. "They intentionally left out the issues that inform why Black women have abortions, including by way of sexual assault or molestation as little girls. They didn't talk about the economic impact of low or no wages, poor access to education, racist governmental social support and policing, intimate partner violence, or in my case, heartbreak and the reality of bringing a child into the world who would only have one willing parent to love them," Cherisse told us. Cherisse wanted to see love and affirmation for Black women reflected out in the world, particularly from religious leaders in the movement for reproductive justice.

In 2011, Cherisse relocated back home to Tennessee, where her ministry began, after her ill mother requested her assistance. Cherisse quickly learned there were no reproductive justice organizations in Tennessee and, with her mother and grandmother's encouragement, founded the first such nonprofit in the state. And for the last twelve years, Sister-Reach—a reproductive and sexual justice organization that focuses on education, policy and advocacy, culture change, and harm reduction for Black women, youth, and other marginalized people in Tennessee—has trailblazed and shifted the repro advocacy movement in and around the region. Under Cherisse's leadership and by applying a reproductive justice analysis, SisterReach challenged Tennessee's Fetal Assault Law, which prosecuted pregnant women for drug use during their pregnancy and removed their parental rights. The 2014 law, which expired in 2016, was the first of its kind in the nation, and SisterReach used a reproductive justice–based messaging approach to combat it. "The law was putting mothers in jail for a health condition instead of expanding medical and behavioral health access to help mothers navigate substance use disorder, maintain custody of their children, and strengthen their families," Cherisse explained. "Comprehensive, patient-centered, and patient-led access to health care is what pregnant people with substance use disorder required to become well—not handcuffs and shaming. Incarceration for pregnancy outcomes is antithetical to reproductive justice; the framework calls for all of us to recognize the humanity of pregnant people, looking at what they're going through and offering resources, not locking them up over a health condition that is often uncontrollable without assisted medical care and compassion."

As Cherisse explained, in 2015, antiabortion groups erected billboards in Memphis, targeting Black fathers to turn them against Black women who have abortions. "Dad's princess #♥beat at 18 days" read the billboard next to the smiling face of a Black infant. "They are inflammatory and racist," Cherisse told Renee for an *EBONY Magazine* interview in 2015. "They were put up to make us invisible and dismiss why we have to have abortions." Cherisse applied the same strategy used during the Trust Black Women campaign, and SisterReach erected its own billboard campaign to reframe the shaming and divisive antiabortion language. SisterReach's billboard campaign featured an array of messages addressing what Black women, Black children, Black teens, and Black families in Memphis really needed: support and a chance to thrive. "I don't deserve to be shamed for my reproductive health decisions, even when it's an abortion. Trust me to make the best decisions for me, my family, and my community," one of the billboards read, ending with the declaration "Trust Black Women." "We don't need outsiders to tell us about our lives," she told Renee in 2015.

Cherisse embodies reproductive justice as her ministry calling. The organizing SisterReach does combines harm reduction models, legislator and voter education, comprehensive sexual health education for youth and adults, interfaith-based organizing, and training to liberate people who may not only need to choose an abortion but need to transform their lives. Cherisse stated that she "believes in organizing in lockstep with religious leaders to undo the harm religious communities have perpetuated, to help aid in healing the lives of the people harmed, and to bridge the disconnect that the reproductive justice, health, and rights movements have with religious communities to unify our collective agenda—for people to live abundant lives in every aspect of their human experiences." As Cherisse explained, "I'm in the buckle of the Bible Belt down here in Tennessee. There was no way for us to do our work and not include our Black Christian churches and other religious communities, because the majority of the people that we serve identify as Black women and men, queer community members, and youth of the Christian faith. This is righteous evangelism we are leading in this movement, and it is the type of organizing I truly believe will help us achieve liberation for our people."

Similarly, We Testify storyteller Shivana Jorawar heard religious anti-abortion messages that impacted how she felt about herself when she needed two abortions. Shivana, who is Indo-Caribbean and the daughter of immigrants from Guyana, grew up in the Bronx in New York. Although she was raised practicing Hinduism, she was part of her Catholic high school's Right to Life club because the club volunteered at homeless shelters and also gave out pizza every Friday. She was told by the club leaders that abortion was something bad girls did. Her Catholic education left her with little sexual health education, but her homeroom teacher took it upon herself to teach her students about STDs and how to use an external condom. "She was a young woman of color, and it was an all-girls school mainly made up of students of color from the Bronx, Brooklyn, and Spanish Harlem," Shivana told us in an interview. "I always thought she did this because she knew her students were having sex and wanted to protect them."

When Shivana became pregnant for the first time at fifteen years old by a twenty-four-year-old man, she didn't realize that the sex was actually sexual assault and the relationship was abusive. "I remember feeling like if I don't stay in the relationship with him it will mean that I am a slut, that I am dirty." Thanks to her high school Right to Life club, Shivana knew she could get an abortion at Planned Parenthood. She told her boyfriend, but he wasn't emotionally supportive. "I just remember feeling so scared and alone. This is a sterile medical environment with strangers who are adults. . . . Talking to adults was not something that was comfortable for me, especially white adults." Shivana had never been to the doctor without her mother, and traveling to downtown New York City from the Bronx alone was a big ordeal.

Shivana said the abortion wasn't a hard decision for her and she never doubted her decision, but she was afraid that if her parents found out she would be cast out of the family or be told that she would be sent back to their homeland, a common threat in immigrant communities. She was also afraid of her community finding out. As she explained on a 2020 episode of the podcast *Unholier Than Thou*, she was deeply involved in Indian classical and folk dancing and Hindi language classes, and the community was small. But once Shivana left temple life and found reproductive justice, she was able to reclaim her spirituality and religion in a way that felt aligned to her and her values. She read stories of fierce Hindu goddesses who rejected patriarchy and realized that she hadn't been taught those stories; rather, she was told ones that taught women "morality" and submissiveness. As she explained on the podcast, these stories are a product of who is doing the storytelling and writing the scriptures. There has to be a new story about sex, sexuality, pregnancy, and what support for all of those experiences looks like in all of our communities.

Additionally, epidemiology researcher and We Testify storyteller Sheila Desai points out that the myth of the Asian model minority spreads the lie that Asian communities don't experience such health issues as needing abortions and that those who need abortions are bad. Condemnation can be harsher when combined with racist and classist stereotypes. She felt that when she had her own abortion and was afraid of being perceived as irresponsible, as in the idea that "there's another Brown girl who doesn't know how to control herself," she told us.

Although abortion isn't widely discussed in Asian and South Asian communities, it is common. A 2021 study coauthored by Sheila found that Indian women had the highest rates of abortion among the Asian population in New York City. Other research has found that abortion attitudes among South Asians, including Muslims, Hindus, and Sikhs, are overwhelmingly supportive. Unfortunately for Sheila, she didn't necessarily feel that support when she had her abortion. But with her research, we are better able to understand how Asian communities—and all of us—experience abortion, so that we can change the conversation toward liberation. Our hope is that the key to that conversation is reproductive justice.

Today, Shivana is rewriting the story as the cofounder of Jahajee Sisters, an organization supporting Indo-Caribbean New Yorkers to end intimate partner and sexual violence and organize around reproductive justice and abortion liberation. Shivana sees sharing her abortion story not only as critical to humanizing people who have abortions but also essential to reducing the criminalization of Asian and South Asian people based on discriminatory laws such as sex-selective abortion bans. Several high-profile cases of women who were criminalized for the outcomes of their pregnancies pre-*Dobbs* involved Asian and South Asian women, and the cases against them were fueled by anti-immigrant misogyny. The US penchant for solving health crises with incarceration has dangerous implications for people living at these intersections, and language barriers, immigration status, and cultural stigmas can make it even harder to free them from the grip of the law. To liberate abortion, we must build a culture of reproductive justice not only in our communities but also in our policies and health care systems.

* * *

Shortly after graduating from high school, seventeen-year-old Cori Bush went on a church trip to Jackson, Mississippi. She dreamed of attending a historically Black college or university (HBCU) but became lost when her grades slipped as a result of bullying and she had no chance of securing financial aid. On the trip, she met a friend of a friend, a twenty-year-old man who made her laugh and later asked to stop by her hotel room. She obliged, thinking they would continue their conversation, but when he showed up late that night, he raped her without saying a word.

Shocked and frozen, Cori didn't know what to do. After the rape, he simply got up, dressed, and left her room. Later, when Cori discovered that she was nine weeks pregnant, she attempted to reach the man but never heard back. She felt alone but knew what she wanted to do. Cori found the number of her local clinic in the Yellow Pages and made an appointment at Planned Parenthood. The cost of the abortion was more than $300. Cori worked part-time for minimum wage, then a little over $5 per hour, and it took her a few weeks to save up the money.

In her historic 2021 congressional testimony alongside Congress-women Barbara Lee and Pramila Jayapal, Representative Bush recalled her rape and degrading experience at the clinic. She told us that the Planned Parenthood clinic has since "made huge, tremendous strides" in improving its patient care, but that wasn't the case in 1994. "What I faced was being treated like a burden—a subhuman, degenerate," she told us. "I was this young Black girl, and I was there alone." Representative Bush testified that while in the waiting room she overheard clinic staff making disparaging comments about another young Black patient, saying that she had ruined her life, and "That's what they [Black girls] do." During a counseling session, Representative Bush recalled she was told that her baby would be "jacked up" if she continued the pregnancy because her pregnancy was not healthy and she would end up on welfare. The degradation continued when she overheard white patients in the postprocedure room talking about how the counselors told them that their futures were bright and their options would be limitless.

Representative Bush told us that she had a second abortion while attending a local HBCU. This time she was more confident in her decision; becoming a parent at that time was not part of her plan. However, her abortion was delayed until she was twelve weeks pregnant because she took time to make her decision and it took a while to come up with the money for the procedure while a full-time student.

Representative Bush felt it was important for her to highlight the differences in care and treatment between white and nonwhite patients because these are the disparities that contribute to poor health outcomes for our communities. "You can't talk about abortion without talking about the barriers and limitations," she explained. She recognizes the hypocrisy of her colleagues who would rather that someone receive government assistance, give birth, and parent than have an abortion, while those same people, she said, work to defund government assistance and kick people off social safety net programs. She knows that's not reproductive justice; we have to support and invest in all decisions at the same time.

Representative Bush infuses her personal experiences and those of her constituents in all her policymaking. As a registered nurse and ordained pastor, a core part of Representative Bush's platform has always been health care for all, because everyone deserves access to health care regardless of their job or economic status. "As I approach this work," she told us, "it was me thinking back to those moments when I needed help. It was me thinking what is it that I needed during that time when I did not have a lot of information about my reproductive health and understanding what was going on with my own body." Representative Bush is proud to share her story to change the narrative and infuse reproductive justice into the policy conversation because, as they say, the personal is political. "We have nothing to be ashamed of," she testified in 2021. "We live in a society that has failed to legislate love and justice for us. We deserve better."

Dr. Ying Zhang is one of those abortion providers trying to make care better for her patients, and the patients of other providers she educates, using a reproductive justice lens and her own experience. Although Dr. Zhang's mother shared that she'd had abortions, and Dr. Zhang knew that abortion was normal and should be normalized, she still received the message from her Chinese American parents that sex outside of marriage was wrong. Growing up in the Carolinas, she did not have comprehensive sexual health education; the sexual education that was offered focused on images of sexually transmitted infections, designed to scare rather than educate. Even when Dr. Zhang was in medical school and an aspiring abortion provider, all of the education was about contraception as a method to prevent abortion and stigmatizing abortion as a procedure that should be safe, legal, and rare. This stigmatization of abortion in her medical training led her to feel stigmatized when she needed an abortion during her last year of residency, she told us.

She'd been married for a little more than a year when she had an unexpected positive pregnancy test. The timing wasn't right for her and her husband; he was supportive during the abortion, which she was able to receive due to the state's more liberal laws. But still, she felt the stigma; she didn't tell any of her colleagues she was having an abortion. "I felt ashamed that I wasn't able to prevent needing an abortion." When she found the reproductive justice framework, everything clicked. "I have come to understand that family planning desires are on a spectrum," she told us. "The only way to destigmatize abortion is to normalize it and to talk about it, not as this thing that needs to be prevented, but actually as part of comprehensive services for people who have the capability of getting pregnant."

Now Dr. Zhang is a family medicine doctor and an abortion provider who trains other doctors to provide abortion, contraception, and miscarriage care using a reproductive justice lens. She recognizes how racist and classist stereotypes impact the care patients receive, particularly for patients who do not use contraception. The perspective of some health care providers, she told us, is one of judgment and fixing a patient's immediate need, rather than a holistic approach of talking to them about their options and family planning goals.

For Dr. Zhang, abortion allowed her to plan for her family on her own terms when she and her husband were ready. When she became pregnant with her child, she enrolled in a program for early parent support, where she was paired up with other expectant parents with similar due dates in her neighborhood. Although she wished she had been able to connect with more Black and Brown families, the program helped her meet with other parents who supported one another through the experience. For us, this is the beauty of reproductive justice: Dr. Zhang was able to receive the care and support she needed for both of her pregnancies and is changing her part of the system so more patients have better, more caring reproductive health care experiences.

* * *

Reproductive justice is more than an organizing framework; it's a vision for a way of life. It forces us to look at the systems of power, privilege, and oppression that inform all of our daily decisions and pregnancy options in life. It asks us to show up differently for ourselves and our loved ones and to design different, more humane policies. It invites us to get curious about why someone may make a decision and offer them the resources and support to make the best one for themselves. It was easy for medical providers to dismiss Dr. Bond's and Cherisse's experiences, but their belief in reproductive justice encouraged them to connect over learning about their bodies and being able to decide if, when, and how to grow their families. How different would Representative Bush's and Shivana's abortion experiences have been if someone like Dr. Zhang was there caring for them, because she had been through the procedure herself and understood that reproductive justice is a key to unlocking better health care in a sterile, elitist environment?

What is possible when reproductive justice is realized? How can reproductive justice change our lives? The beauty of the framework is that it can be applied to everything in our world. We can build a better immigration system if we have a focus on keeping families together and ensuring undocumented people have the reproductive care they need. We can call for an end to our mass incarceration and immigration jails because they are inhumane, particularly for pregnant and parenting people. Our foreign policy looks different when we recognize the humanity of the families on the other end of our nation's bombs. They, too, deserve the ability to raise their children free from state-sanctioned violence.

Taking a reproductive justice approach shifts the way we view our domestic policies; rather than spending money on wars and prisons, we demand that the money be spent on feeding and housing families, educating our nation, and expanding Medicaid and Medicare for all—including fertility treatments, gender-affirming care, and abortion for everyone, not just those who can afford it. In this vision, everyone can choose if, when, and how to grow their families—including queer families, single-by-choice families, poly families, and disabled parents. Parents don't have to make pregnancy decisions constrained by how much money is available to them during their pregnancies, so that their bank accounts or the government make these decisions instead. With adequate funding for parents, it is possible that adoption would become irrelevant, because those who now relinquish their children would have the money they need to parent, which is what they would prefer to do.

For us, the reproductive justice vision is integral to liberating abortion. When all of us feel liberated to decide what to do with our pregnancies, including choosing abortion, without shame or stigma, the other stigmas fall as well. They're all interconnected, because they all come from the same racist beliefs about who is worthy and able to procreate and whose families are deserving of support and care. Reproductive justice encourages us to look at history and our nation's massive safety net failures and do right by all of us, whatever we decide. But first, we have to be willing to see what is possible with reproductive justice and be willing to be transformed by this new vision.

Our Right to Parent

For Taté Walker, the decision to have a kid was one they did not come to lightly. Living in a group home for part of high school, surviving abuse and a suicide attempt, and knowing the way the US government systematically denied Indigenous people the right to parent meant that they wanted to be intentional about their circumstances. Abortion allowed for them to do that.

Taté had the first of their two abortions when they were seventeen and living in a group home. Prior to becoming a ward of the state, Taté lived most of their youth with their dad—a "white, military guy"—who had primary care of Taté after divorcing their mom and what Taté described as an ugly, years-long custody battle. Taté is a citizen of the Cheyenne River Sioux Tribe and had minimal contact with their mom postdivorce. Taté came out as queer as a young teen; this, combined with traumatic experiences, unstable family dynamics, unrequited cultural longing, and religion-based expectations led to severe depression, cutting, and a suicide attempt on their seventeenth birthday.

Taté became pregnant while living in a group home. During a meeting to discuss the pregnancy with Taté's parents, a social worker, and group home staff, Taté recalled their mom saying, "I will take care of this kid for you. When the baby arrives, I will parent it." Taté was shocked. "I'm in a group home," they remembered replying. "What makes you think you can parent a kid of mine when you couldn't take care of me?" Taté dared to request an abortion and was given permission, so long as they independently arranged for that care. Taté said this still surprises them to this day, given their ward status at the time and the fact that they lived in a state governed by religious and political conservatism. Taté was transferred to another group home in a rural community that housed pregnant teens ages eleven to twenty. It was also a place Taté described as a queer conversion camp, as residents were subjected to educational lessons on so-called healthy sexual relationships between heterosexual cisgender men and women.

It wasn't all bad. Taté had a great therapist there who was vocal about bodily autonomy and directly addressed Taté's history of cutting in terms that they could understand, helping them to heal. The therapist helped Taté find a clinic and schedule their abortion before their high school graduation.

Taté was unsure of how far along they were in the pregnancy but assumed eight weeks—this was essential because the clinic stopped performing abortions past twelve weeks. Once the appointment was scheduled, the therapist called Taté's father to take Taté, because they needed a guardian to approve the abortion. Taté recalled the awkwardness of the drive with their father, stepmom, and elementary school–age siblings, who were singing during the three-hour trip to Fargo. On arriving at the clinic, Taté and their dad passed by a few protesters. The clinic worker at the front desk explained that the cost of the abortion would be $400. Taté's dad handed over a check, but the clinic accepted only cash. He walked through the protesters again to get the cash, and once he returned to the clinic, Taté was able to start the appointment. "I don't even remember being in the waiting room. I just remember going into the procedure room and the nurse was talking me through everything and I think my pain tolerance . . . and emotional capacity was super high. I don't remember it hurting at all."

The abortion procedure was quick. Taté lay back in a procedure bed looking at the ceiling, surrounded by images of teddy bears, rainbows, and a Devon Sawa poster. And then it was done. "I was like, 'This is amazing. That was it.'" Taté went into the recovery room and remembers being fully awake because they didn't have the sedation they saw other patients waking up from. They saw one woman bawling after the procedure. "I remember thinking, *Should I be like that? Is this a sad moment?* I remember smiling to myself, like I got away with something massive." Once Taté was cleared to leave the clinic, they drove back to Bismarck with their whole family and began preparing for their high school graduation the very next day.

"It was so weird, right?" Taté said. "It was a massive thing in my life that happened, and I was still going through this ward of the state bullshit. But here I am graduating, and I look back on the pictures and I just look so, I don't know, dark under the eyes and just unhappy, for all intents and purposes. But the abortion was great. And then right after graduation, like the same day, I have to go back to the pregnancy ranch." And that's where they stayed until Taté was free to return to their dad's home before moving away to college.

Taté had their second abortion a few years later under vastly different circumstances. They had just graduated from college and were living in Lincoln, Nebraska, and had a one-night stand, without a condom, with someone they had met at a bar. They did not want to have the child of a person they hardly knew, not to mention that they did not feel they had established job security or permanent housing—two main goals that would make them feel secure enough to continue a pregnancy—so they made an appointment at the nearest abortion clinic. This time there were no protesters at the Planned Parenthood clinic, and the procedure was uneventful. What they remember the most from the experience wasn't the abortion but the taxi driver who waited for them outside of the clinic and who didn't charge them for the round-trip ride. Taté didn't have anyone who could go to the clinic with them, so they had called a taxi at six o'clock in the morning. A few hours later, after their procedure, when Taté spotted the driver outside the facility, they asked if he had dropped someone else off at the clinic. "No, I just waited," he replied. "I'd want my kid to have help if they were [ever] in this situation." Taté recalled how good it felt knowing that there were people like him out in the world.

At twenty-five years old, Taté became pregnant for a third time when their contraception, Depo-Provera, failed. This time, though, the pregnancy was with their partner, and they made a conscious choice to continue that pregnancy. They felt ready because they were in a committed relationship with someone they knew they could rely on during this big life change. Taté and their partner examined their health insurance coverage, housing situation, and financial readiness, and they concluded together that they could do it. Taté's many years of therapy also contributed to their belief that they could become an attentive and devoted parent, without burdening their child with their past trauma and experiences.

"I knew I had to be the best of myself," Taté told us. Taté said they felt, after spending time in therapy, they had "developed the best mental space for raising a human being and living with another human in a partnership." They were adamant that their traumatic experiences weren't ones they wanted to repeat or project onto those they loved. All of their pregnancy experiences informed how they wanted to become a parent. Abortion made it possible for them to become pregnant under the circumstances they desired.

* * *

Late in their pregnancy, Taté switched jobs for a better, more supportive work environment, but that meant they would have to wait six weeks before becoming eligible for their employer's health insurance plan. Taté and their partner had significant reservations about marriage as an institution, but they agreed to marry so that Taté could have health insurance under their partner's plan when they went into labor. Three weeks after they married, their child was born.

In preparation for childbirth, Taté chose a midwife at their local hospital in South Dakota. The midwife helped Taté to feel supported throughout their pregnancy. When the midwife asked if Taté had had any prior pregnancies, they shared that they had two abortions without any complications. The midwife moved on, and their lack of worry "immediately put me at ease," Taté said. The midwife was encouraging of Taté's birth plan. Taté wanted a birth process that aligned as closely as possible with their Lakota beliefs and practices, such as taking home the placenta to bury it and root their child's existence to the land, uplifted and supported. Even though the midwife had been affirming, the hospital's practices seemed to question Taté's suitability as a parent. Taté explained to us that although they have white privilege in certain circles because their dad is white, in places like South Dakota they are recognized as Native.

After giving birth, Taté asked for their placenta as part of their Lakota practice. Instead of recognizing as such, staff began asking about their home life and whether it was a safe space for their baby. "They were like, 'Where's your kid going to sleep? Do you have a bed?' And I was like, 'Yeah, we do.' But hospital staff continued to ask, 'Well, what if we sent somebody with you just to make sure?'"

Although Taté's midwife made them feel safe, hospital staff did the opposite, whether it was for breastfeeding support or other services. Even Taté's mention of attending therapy sessions was referenced in questioning their fitness to parent. "There were just so many questions about suitability as a parent that we got then."

In spite of these issues, Taté said the overall experience was positive, and they were able to execute their birth plan, had support, and generally felt in control. But, without access to paid parental leave, Taté had to return to their new job immediately after giving birth. "That was traumatizing," Taté said. "You hear now about [new moms taking] maternity leave for months, and I'm like, 'It would have been really cool to have as much [uninterrupted bonding] time with my kid as possible.'" Where Taté worked, they were able to bring their newborn with them for a couple of months to breastfeed. "That was really nice. But it would have been even nicer just to give me that time off." In Taté's office, they had a space under the desk, "and that's where the kid went when they slept. I was able to close the door to breastfeed, and the women I worked with were super supportive and would hold the baby if they weren't doing anything." It wasn't all bad, Taté said, "but overall, I really wish I just had time off." Even in having control over when and how they wanted to parent, Taté's decisions were still questioned and constricted.

Black Women and The Motherhood Myth

by Bev Cole

The abortion issue must be faced by each and every woman, especially Black and Third World women. The Black woman throughout history has been a breeder--breeder of slaves and breeder of slave owners' bastards. Then today, Black men tell Black women ' to continue to breed, so that We shall outnumber the White men and seize control. On July 4th, 1970, the Black Panthers came out with the most absurd statement, "Black women love children and like large families." While the Panthers hopscotch on the subject of the Black woman's innate love for children, and declare that the quantity (not mentioning quality) of forces must be overwhelming to insure victory, they also say that the Black man and Black woman must stand and fight together against the enemy. How can we have this togetherness on the front if women are busy being balled by night and coping with the results, children everywhere, during each and every day. The gun in the hand of every Black man seems also to mean diaper swinging females following close behind.

That the Black woman's only dream is to reproduce is a false myth, as shown by the fact that 70% of the abortions performed in this country are done on Black and Third World women. The economics of this racist society makes it impossible for many of these women to afford safe abortions, thus illegal, unsafe abortions occur. The poor woman's fate is usually injury or death from having flushed detergents and soaps into herself, or having tried to sever the uterine wall to cut away the multiplying cells.

These futile abortive attempts have caused a high death rate among Black and Third World women, so that the Black brother's argument against legal, safe abortion is, in itself, genocidal, killing off Black women in the name of the fetus. A Black brother told one of my girl friends that "if any woman of his got pregnant (note that the fault lies solely with the female) and hurt or killed anything of his inside her, he'd kill her." That's a brother's concern for his sister.

There are women who decide to have and keep their children, and to many of these Black women pregnancy is the admission stub to the nearest welfare office. But many a welfare mother finds herself pregnant for the second third, fourth time and wants to avoid sacrificing the lives of her previous children with one more mouth to feed. Some women seek help, but many times Welfare Agencies step in beforehand, promising an abortion only if one will submit to sterilization. In my hometown, any welfare recipient expecting either her 10th or 11th child is sterilized by court action. Some women do not even have these legal procedures taken against them; they find themselves awakening in the recovery room where they are told, "You don't have to worry no more." In cases such as these, it seems that the government has taken it into its own hands to punish the welfare recipient for having another pregnancy by forcing sterilization. This method totally takes away the women's right to choose and control her body. A Black woman, and every woman, is entitled to the right of abortion. At the same time, forced sterilization must come to an end.

I want safe, legal abortive practices provided, especially in Black community hospitals, run by the Black community to assist Black women, and I want all this NOW!

"Black Women and the Motherhood Myth" by Bev Cole, in *The Right to Choose Abortion*, published by Female Liberation. *Sophia Smith Collection, Smith College, Northampton, Massachusetts.*

* * *

When we talk about a future in which reproductive justice is realized, we mean that everyone who wishes to become a parent has the freedom to exercise that right: they can freely choose whether or not to continue their pregnancies based on their own desires, and not how much is in their bank account, whether they can seek the care they need, or how much support they're lacking. As simple as this may sound, it's quite radical. It requires that we reimagine our entire society and how it functions to center the needs of people who are making pregnancy decisions as well as those who are parenting. It also forces us to reckon with our nation's insidious history of using coercive tactics to deny Black and Brown people the right to parent, from forced sterilization to family separation during slavery, at immigration borders, through family policing, and as a genocidal tactic for centuries.

Using a reproductive justice lens with Taté's story, we can see all of the historic and current systems at play: the removal of Native American children from their families, systematic denial of access to abortion care for young people within the child welfare system, and the questioning of every aspect of their lives in relation to their fitness to parent. This isn't an isolated case; it's history. As Brianna Theobald explains in *Reproduction on the Reservation*, some Indigenous tribes' traditions of communal child-rearing were destroyed by the US government's insistence on removing Native American children from their homes and placing them in boarding schools while also separating families as the government forced them onto reservations or outright stole their children and placed them with white families. This destruction of traditions continues today through coercive adoption tactics and family policing. The Indian Child Welfare Act, a law that seeks to keep Native American children with their families and culture and to right the wrong of the removal of children to boarding schools, was challenged by white conservatives at the Supreme Court as unconstitutional in hopes of not only reactivating the tactics to separate families but also undermining Indigenous tribal sovereignty over land for resources and other capitalist ventures. The Supreme Court's 2023 decision affirmed the constitutionality of the law, reaffirming the rights of tribal nations over the welfare of their citizens and families, but it's a reminder that white supremacy and capitalist governments will always use the right to parent and reproduction as ways to separate communities from their land and humanity. Rachael Lorenzo said that advancing reproductive justice is essential to tribal sovereignty, because tribes don't prioritize the nuclear family that the United States pushes, and creating the families that Native Americans want is part of sovereignty. "Reproductive justice helps keep our communities together," they told us. "We can't have tribes without our people."

Government coercion is also used to separate immigrant families. During the Trump administration, people marched in the streets against the policy separating migrant children and parents in immigration detention centers. Many of the children were placed in the care of Christian, anti-abortion adoption agencies and were adopted out without any record-keeping. Rather than children being reunited with their parents, they were separated forever, and we will see the implications of that for decades to come. At the same time, Trump administration officials were openly denying constitutionally protected abortion access to unaccompanied migrant minors in an attempt to coerce them into continuing their pregnancies. The coercion is the point.

For We Testify storyteller Layidua Salazar, her immigration status impacted her pregnancy decision in choosing an abortion. When she was twenty-eight, married, and in the process of an immigration status adjustment, she received startling news: first, a deportation letter, and then, a positive pregnancy confirmation a few days later. Layidua, who is Mexican American, said to us that when the nurse told her she was pregnant, she felt overwhelmed and began sobbing, thinking of the deportation letter. "It felt real in that moment because I had to make a decision about what I wanted my life and family to look like with all of the possibilities of potentially having to be in a country that I had not been to since I was five," she told us in an interview. "I would be in a whole different country while potentially being pregnant or with an infant." Her choice was removed from the decision, she said, because it did not make sense to be pregnant during a deportation proceeding. Layidua chose not to inform her then-spouse until after she decided what she wanted to do.

He was upset and unsupportive, and he went on a weekend trip with his friends as she had the abortion, giving her all of the information she needed about the future of that marriage, she told us. About a year later, her deportation case was administratively closed, and the marriage came to an end. At the same time, Layidua found reproductive justice, giving her a space to have the conversations to process everything that had happened. "In many ways, as much as I felt like choice was removed from the process, because it simply didn't make sense for me to be pregnant in the middle of a deportation proceeding, it also allowed me to not have these conflicting feelings around what I should do," she told us. "What I needed to do felt very clear to me in that moment." Our immigration system forces decisions about our reproduction.

Similarly, We Testify storyteller Kay Winston's (a pseudonym) pregnancy decision was made for her while she spent time in jail. During the intake process at an Ohio jail for a minor nonviolent crime, a nurse yelled from another room that Kay was pregnant. She was moved into a cell for pregnant incarcerated women and wasn't able to see a provider for two weeks. She didn't receive prenatal vitamins or medication for her bipolar disorder. Kay thought about her options; because she had had an abortion before, she knew what it entailed. At her appointment, she asked for an abortion, which she was constitutionally entitled to, but the providers told her she wouldn't be able to get one until she was released two months later. As she slept on the hard mattress poked by sharp springs, she realized that she would be too far along to receive an abortion when she was released and that the decision about her parenthood had been made for her. "I love being a mother, and I wish the decision wasn't made for me by a jail nurse whose name I don't know," she wrote for *Rewire News Group* in 2021.

The right to parent is a radical demand. It's a struggle for so many that has never been fully realized and influences how many people view their reproductive health decisions, even abortion. Fears of genocide and the denial of the ability to reproduce and parent, founded in history, have led some in communities of color to think that abortion is antithetical to the right to parent and a thriving community. We disagree. Abortion itself is not the problem; white supremacy is. Liberating abortion is essential to achieving reproductive justice. If people are not able to freely decide to *not have* a child, then they are not actually able to freely decide to *have* a child on their own terms. Their parenting is inherently dictated by someone else, even if they are going along with the desired outcome of continuing a pregnancy. The rest of their pregnancy and parenting decisions are questioned, just as Taté was questioned at every step. No society that restricts abortion also makes parenting easier. That's why the same people who are banning abortion are also making parenthood difficult for queer parents and criminalizing parents who want to be supportive of their queer and trans children. The government would rather put parents in jail for parenting in poverty than set up a universal basic income to support all families. It's all about reproductive control, no matter what you decide.

When we talked to Cazembe Murphy Jackson, a We Testify abortion storyteller and community organizer on our podcast, *The A Files: A Secret History of Abortion*, he told us that creating families is harder for queer, trans, and nonbinary people, but it's essential to bodily autonomy and self-determination. He said queer folks have had to get creative in building their families in spite of the lack of financial support, insurance coverage, or medical investment. "I don't think that it's just to get pregnant and have babies. Obviously, trans people are hot and they fall in love with each other, so that happens," he told us. "But also it's a creative way to beat back at the system to be able to make our own families when that's what we want."

In our society—and even in pro-choice talking points—we stress that someone should become a parent when they are ready, whatever "ready" means for them. Readiness is framed as an individualistic measure, and the conversation invisibilizes the systemic failures that leave people to fend for themselves. Taté felt *ready* to parent with their third unintended pregnancy and still faced barrier after barrier. Layidua's readiness was irrelevant because of her immigration status. It is a struggle to obtain health insurance that covers prenatal and postpartum care, to receive paid parental leave that allows new parents to bond with their child, and to access ongoing childcare that makes it possible for us to provide for our families.

Then there are the people who may not feel ready to parent but who have to begin their parenting journey anyway, because they lack resources to choose any other option. Researcher Katrina Kimport's book *No Real Choice* is full of stories of people who felt they couldn't choose abortion because of stigma and barriers but didn't actually choose to continue their pregnancies either. Once they become parents, they are punished (both emotionally and literally by the state) for not having the money, housing, time, education, and other resources necessary to meet an unattainable standard of parenting set by an adherence to whiteness and capitalism. These are the very same factors that make adoption coercive to birth parents, as noted in Gretchen Sisson's *Relinquished*. Most birth parents wanted to parent, but they didn't have the resources or support to do so and thus felt forced to relinquish their parental rights and place their children with families who had more material resources. We have normalized that parenting must require struggle and sacrifice, and we punish those who do not have the money to parent "the right way." Just like abortion, the right to parent is real only if you have the money for it.

Teens who become pregnant are shamed and then legally locked out of having an abortion if their parent isn't notified or doesn't consent to the procedure in at least thirty-five states. Teens' only recourse in those situations is to prove to a judge that they are mature enough to have an abortion through a judicial bypass process. If they are denied the abortion or would like to continue the pregnancy and parent of their own volition, they may be kicked out of their homes and school and be unable to receive any support to care for themselves and their baby. Low- or no-income parents are forced to prove they are suitable to raise the children they do have, potentially even having to fight the state in court for parental rights, which are far too often taken away for dubious reasons. All the while, if they ask for more financial support from the government to raise their children, they are chided and derided and are denied coverage for abortions if that's what they choose. It's a never-ending cycle. At the same time, some people who waited to have children, after jumping through a lot of hoops in their careers to get to a point where they feel *ready*, may be stigmatized for their advanced maternal age, body size, or inability to become pregnant. They may never be able to exercise their right to parent simply because the cost of reproductive technologies puts parenthood out of reach.

Our nation doesn't make parenting easy. Without national paid leave, universal childcare, or real supports for families raising children with disabilities, parents—particularly mothers—bear the brunt of the labor. These same systemic failures made it difficult for us to finish this book. When people don't have the resources they need to exercise the right to parent, families are broken, and potential is lost. We live in a society that is rooting for parents of color to fail. For some people, parenthood costs them personal projects or relationships. For others, the cost is their entire livelihood.

* * *

Of all the things Regina's abortion taught her, what resonated the most was that she wanted to become a mother on her own terms. She hadn't given parenting serious thought before becoming pregnant, but after her abortion she knew that it wasn't a matter of whether she would become a mother but when—and when would depend on however long it would take for her to feel ready.

After her abortion, at twenty-nine, Regina got an IUD and began to think through what being "ready" really meant. Thinking it through forced her and her then-boyfriend to discuss what they each wanted to change or make happen to support the family they wanted to start. In their conversations, they began to unpack their perceptions of the toll of parenthood and their fears about having children. Regina feared becoming a single parent because of the stigma around it for Black women and knowing how hard this would be given the lack of a social safety net for parents in the US. To guard against that, she wanted to make enough money to cover all of the household expenses in the event that she had only herself to rely on. Her boyfriend feared the financial aspect of parenting as well. They lived in New York, where, according to the Economic Policy Institute, the average annual cost of infant care is more than $15,000. For reference, someone making $15 an hour would earn $31,200 before taxes; thus infant care would be roughly half of that person's yearly salary.

By the time Regina and her now-husband felt ready to start their family, they were in their midthirties, and Regina had a salary that she felt would cover her family's expenses in the event she became the sole provider. They moved out of New York City to reduce their monthly living costs and the future cost of childcare. Regina had the benefit of twenty weeks of parental leave with full salary thanks to her company's union. But barely three months after her son was born, the World Health Organization declared the COVID-19 outbreak a global pandemic, and the family watched in slow motion as the frail systems that parents rely on to survive in the United States unraveled.

During shutdown, many families were completely overwhelmed by the inadequate childcare system. Because Regina and her husband worked from home, which was not an option for everyone, they could take turns working and caring for their baby. But as the pandemic dragged on and her husband's work dried up, he took on the bulk of the childcare. Still, to make it work, they again had to move into a more affordable city in New York to keep their monthly expenses low. The setup definitely added substantial pressure to their relationship, both financially and emotionally, as they navigated a childcare system that was ill-equipped to handle the needs of families and day care staff during a public health crisis.

It was unsustainable. There is no other way to describe the challenges of parenting a young infant during a pandemic. Many parents were already nearing their breaking point before the pandemic started due to the stresses of child-rearing without a social safety net, but the isolation that people experienced when the entire country shut down was on a whole new level. Still, they had no choice and just powered through, because that's what is expected of parents.

Eventually, childcare centers reopened, and many parents breathed a sigh of relief. Regina and her husband were excited to enroll their son so he could experience socialization with other people and babies. However, after only two months, the facility informed them that because their son wasn't yet walking due to low muscle tone and a developmental delay, he wouldn't be able to stay after he turned twenty-one months, because of a state regulation limiting the maximum number of months a child who is not developmentally ready to advance to the next age group can remain among the younger age group. Unable to find other day care options nearby, they would have to keep him home until he was walking or they could make another arrangement. The lack of childcare delayed the work Regina could do on a book about these very issues. Regina and her partner decided to move, again, to New Jersey, to be closer to family and receive support. They also hoped the childcare system could bring them some relief. But on the day that they went to tour a facility near their new home, they didn't make it past the front office before the staff member told them that they would not be able to enroll their son if he wasn't walking, due to a state regulation similar to New York's.

Regina cried harder than she had in months, sitting in the parked car outside of the day care center with her partner. As Regina and her partner were going through the process of navigating an unequal day care system, they struggled with the idea of having another child. Where they lived, it was easier to have an abortion than it was to get the resources they needed to raise their child.

Support was not coming. She would have to continue putting off book interviews and other writing deadlines to get through the week. This put more work on Renee to take over whatever tasks Regina could not follow through on. But this didn't work, and tension between us grew. For Regina, she wanted to take on more work but was limited in her capacity and schedule, and three years later when she was going through a second pregnancy that she decided to continue, her body simply wouldn't let her. For Renee, she wanted Regina to have the space and time to focus on her children, and she needed a collaborator she could rely on. Regina didn't realize she had bought into the *moms can do it all if they just work hard enough* mentality, which so many of us feel forced to accept in order to make ends meet, instead of challenging all of the systems that put us in that position. But in buying into that narrative, Regina wasn't honest with herself and Renee about what she could realistically take on. Neither of us was happy, and our deadline was only getting closer and closer. We were able to finish the book because of our resolve and sheer force of will, and thanks to our amazing editor and book doula. But there was no tidy ending to this problem. We had to continue having honest and hard conversations about what we each needed. We realized that what made us struggle felt like individual challenges, but actually it was the runoff of systemic failures denying us the right to parent.

All of this is what we are talking about when we say "the right to parent." It's also why we argue that abortion liberation is crucial to achieving reproductive justice. Abortion access brings freedom to parents who are at their limit—mentally, physically, or financially. Representative Pramila Jayapal, the first Indian American woman to serve in the US House of Representatives, shared her abortion story in June 2019. She had an abortion years after she had given birth to her child and after learning of the "tremendous risks" she would face continuing a pregnancy. Her child arrived unexpectedly at 26.5 weeks while Representative Jayapal was in India and required multiple blood transfusions and expensive, rare medications that she and her child's father had to procure because the hospital did not have them. Once Representative Jayapal and her family returned to the United States, her child continued to face health care challenges due to weak lungs and pneumonia.

In seeking to ban abortion, people overlook how difficult pregnancy *and* parenting can be. "People forget what the physical experience is," she told us. "They also forget what it's like to go through a really difficult birth and also to have a child that has a lot of [health] issues. Her child was still having seizures at the time, and they were just so fragile for so long." This weighed on her mind heavily as she considered whether to have an abortion. "The experience of birth and parenting has so many complex dimensions to it, and physical and mental, emotional, and also the future."

As an Indian American woman, Representative Jayapal grew up in an environment where not having children wasn't even considered an option and having an abortion carried a lot of stigma. "Abortion was never discussed," Representative Jayapal told us. "You're supposed to get married and you're supposed to have kids. My mother always talked about how having kids was the most important thing for her, and the more kids the better."

This idea isn't unique to South Asian communities; it is the prevailing narrative about cis women's bodies and families. But the problem with our society is that it's just a narrative, with no real policies or resources to support it. What's particularly painful is knowing that it doesn't have to be this way at all.

* * *

The biggest threat to achieving the universal right to parent is criminalization and poverty. US Congresswoman Gwen Moore knows this firsthand. When she had her abortions, she already knew what it was to struggle as a young parent in a world that shames low-income and teen parents. "I was gonna be treated with contempt and disdain by anybody that I asked for any help for, if I needed SNAP, Medicaid, child support, or anything else," she said, recalling her thoughts as she contemplated ending the pregnancy. "It was very clear to me that whatever hardship I would face, it was going to be double or triple" whatever challenges nonteen parents already face. When she had her daughter in 1970 at age eighteen, she received a lot of support from her community, but she also felt their admonishment to not have another child until she was financially stable.

When Representative Moore became pregnant in 1972, she was able to connect with a local organization that arranged a flight for her from Wisconsin to New York for an abortion. She first shared her story publicly fifty years later when a draft of the Supreme Court's decision to overturn *Roe* leaked. When we spoke with Representative Moore for this book, she told us about her second abortion, which she had never spoken publicly about.

When her daughter was five years old, Representative Moore missed taking her birth control pills and got pregnant. She did not tell her partner because he was violent toward her and her daughter. But, she explained, when he found out, he almost beat her to death. She was able to get away from him with the support of friends. "[Back then] there really was no hotline to call to really escape that relationship," she told us. "I had to put my own little posse together—a Jamaican woman, a white woman, [and another woman who helped develop a plan]—to hide me and help me escape."

Since then, Representative Moore has dedicated her life to helping others going through similar situations, whether through her support for expanded access to reproductive health care or protections for survivors of domestic violence. She recognizes the difficulty of parenting within these contexts and the importance of resources for survival. Parenting in poverty made it difficult for Representative Moore to leave.

* * *

Our society puts obstacles in our way at every turn, not only when having abortions but also when trying to parent our children in safe and sustainable communities. It's exacerbated by lack of money and fear of criminalization for not having the money to be a "good parent." These experiences facing Black parents and other parents of color today are not new but are a continuation of the centuries-old struggle to exercise control over our bodies and care for our families. As Dorothy Roberts lays out in *Torn Apart: How the Child Welfare System Destroys Black Families—and How Abolition Can Build a Safer World*, the current broken government systems are extensions of the brutal founding of the nation, including the violent rupturing of families of color during settler colonialism and slavery that has continued in the present-day family-policing system.

These systems both remove children and also dictate the methods of parenting and penalize parents who don't adhere to the expectations. In 2023, Dallas Child Protective Services (CPS) took a newborn from her family after their pediatrician reported the parents because he didn't agree with the family's decision to care for their child in their own home. The mother, Temecia Jackson, and her husband, Rodney, had a home birth with a midwife. At their pediatrician appointment, the doctor diagnosed the newborn with jaundice, a common condition that causes yellowing of the eyes and skin and typically goes away without any treatment. The pediatrician felt their child's condition was severe enough that it necessitated phototherapy treatment at a hospital, but the parents opted for providing the therapy for their child under their midwife's care at home. Although the doctor wrote to CPS that the parents were "loving" and "care dearly about their baby," he also noted that "their distrust for medical care and guidance has led them to make a decision for the baby to refuse a simple treatment that can prevent brain damage." This is reminiscent of the same providers who tried to insert themselves during Taté's labor and delivery.

Dallas Child Protective Services and police officers traumatized the family with multiple visits, ultimately removing the two-week-old newborn from the home and placing her in foster care. It took nearly a month before the Jackson family's little girl was returned to them, thanks in large part to public pressure. Roberts told us this occurred due to family policing—the belief that "Black families do not have loving bonds, and therefore. . . . Black children are better off away from their families." The family's disagreement with a medical provider led to the child welfare police being called on them and their right to parent removed, causing significant trauma and harm to the parents and the child.

We want to imagine another way. What if instead of calling the police to have the child removed, the doctor had listened to the family's concerns and they had worked together to find a treatment that treated the child and her parents humanely? But right now that's not possible, because family policing, foster care, and mass incarceration are big businesses. There are billions of dollars on the line for "a conglomerate of CPS agencies, government bureaucracies, hired professionals, and business contractors" that make money off every child stolen from their family, Roberts explains in *Torn Apart*. The local, state, and federal family-policing system accounted for $29.9 billion in 2016—the bulk of which was spent separating children from their parents. To recover some of these expenses, some states take over the children's assets (without notifying the children about it), including Supplemental Security Income survivor benefits or Veterans Affairs (VA) benefits (which children receive after losing a parent who served in the military), Medicaid funds, or child support payments. Providers are using their biases and working in lockstep with the family-policing system to deny the right to parent.

Doctors who do not believe people are worthy of parenting quietly take that right away from patients with coerced sterilization. In the 2010s, Erica Davis-Crump, twenty-six, was receiving Medicaid benefits while living in Kansas when a doctor told her that she should get a hysterectomy. She made an appointment with a doctor because of her discomfort from heavy, painful periods. "You have kids?" he asked. She did; Erica has one boy and one girl, and had an abortion at age nineteen after she had her son. "Okay, well, let's get you a hysterectomy," the doctor declared. Erica had a lot of questions, but this doctor insisted removing her uterus would "fix everything," and she didn't need to worry about the details because he did them all the time, Erica recalled.

Erica asked whether she could get a second opinion, and he told her that because she had Medicaid benefits, she'd have to pay out of pocket. "I felt really coerced," she told us. "Next thing I knew, Wednesday morning at seven, I was on the table. And that was it."

Erica, who is Black, equates her experience to the Mississippi appendectomies and sterilization of Black, low-income, and disabled people over decades. "I've had a lot of healing to do around that," Erica told us. "I remember going to get my abortions and [protesters were] calling me 'a fucking murderer' and 'you bitch,' everything short of spitting at you. But nobody called that doctor a murderer, right? They're snatching legacies out of us on purpose and for funsies."

We Testify storyteller and Chicago-based activist Brittany Mostiller told us that as she was in labor with her third child, she remembers the doctors handing her papers for a tubal ligation. "I was afraid to say something," Brittany said, emphasizing that she was just twenty-two and not sure whether she was finished having kids. "So I'm like, 'I'll think about it, just leave the papers.'" But she remembers thinking, "How dare y'all come in and slide that in here. I didn't tell you I wanted that." Because she was a young Black unwed mother on Medicaid, she felt she had been targeted.

Brittany has had seven abortions, all of which were after she became a mom. She was sixteen at the time of her first pregnancy. She recalled that her best friend at the time was pregnant, and another friend already had a child. "And I was like, well, being a parent can't be that bad," Brittany said, adding that it was "foolishness," because she feels like she never thought through any of her pregnancies that she carried to term. "It was just like, *I'm having a baby, and I know what I gotta do. I gotta work.* It was just like that because I saw my mother just, like, do what she needed to do." Brittany doesn't remember wanting an abortion. She was aware that it was a procedure people had when they didn't want to be pregnant, but she was indifferent about abortion and confident in her decision that she didn't want one for this pregnancy. Having already graduated from high school and attended a semester of college, Brittany also didn't feel that the stigma commonly associated with being a teen mom applied to her, though people in her family, at the clinic she visited for prenatal care, and in society at large made her feel shame or embarrassment about her decision to parent. Her daughter was almost two years old at the time of her first abortion. Brittany told us that she made that decision in the same calm, uncomplicated way that she decided to keep her first pregnancy. There was no crying or long, drawn-out process, she said. She just knew she didn't want a baby by the person who got her pregnant, so she made her appointment, found out what it cost, came up with the money from her grocery store job, and got the abortion.

When Brittany became pregnant again, she had two daughters under the age of five and knew she wanted an abortion, but because it was not covered by Medicaid and she didn't have the money to pay for an abortion out of pocket, the decision was made for her. Although Medicaid covered the cost of her prenatal care and labor and delivery, she had a rough pregnancy. At the time, she lived in a two-bedroom apartment that she shared with her sister and both of their children, and she had been laid off from her job. Brittany explained that the shame, stigma, and challenges of being a young parent were beginning to take a toll on her mentally and physically; she became depressed, and her water broke at thirty-two weeks, forcing her to be induced into labor a week later. Without a job, she struggled to care for her growing family and buy all of the necessities. Unfortunately, this is a common experience for those who are denied abortions, according to the Turnaway Study. Over a decade, researchers studied the impact of abortion denial on women's lives when compared to women who were able to receive their desired abortion. As we mentioned earlier, those who were unable to receive their abortions were four times more likely to be living in poverty and to have other negative health outcomes.

A few months after her third child, Brittany was pregnant once more, and she knew without a doubt that she could not handle another baby. "Shit was rough," Brittany told us. "I remember walking to work one day and telling my friend, *Girl, there's gotta be something else for me. This can't be it.*" This time, she connected with the Chicago Abortion Fund (CAF), which covered a third of the cost, but she still had to come up with about $600. She borrowed the money from her sister and great-grandmother, whom she told the money was for rent. Her Medicaid benefits in Illinois gave her a $50 or $75 "discount," she told us, but otherwise it did not cover the cost of the procedure. She was able to have her abortion with the money she received from CAF and the money she borrowed from family members.

The experience was empowering for Brittany because she had control over her decision this time. She wanted to build a better life for her children, and she knew that she would not be able to do so if she had another child at that time. Quite simply, money made that possible. "They deserve more," Brittany recalled thinking, "and I ain't giving them away, so I have to figure my shit out, so they can get something that I didn't have."

Abortion access made it possible for Brittany to live the life she desired and restore her positive outlook and drive for success. Her experience was again reflected in the Turnaway Study, which found that people who had the abortions they wanted were more likely to set and achieve one-year aspirational goals, compared to those in the longitudinal study who were denied an abortion. At the end of the day, many experiences are similar to Brittany's: parents are struggling to make the best decisions they can for themselves and their families, but their decisions are constrained by stigma, money, and restrictions. Abortion access was liberating for Brittany, but so too was the ability to have the resources she needed to parent without shame.

* * *

Parents make up the majority of people who have abortions, but only rarely is their expertise on these matters centered in conversations about abortion liberation and what that would look like or mean for families. The solutions that would bring us closer to achieving reproductive justice must involve undoing all of the pro-poverty policy measures and stigmas that lead to parents, and all people, being unable to make their own reproductive decisions free from coercion.

As human rights lawyer and writer Derecka Purnell suggests in her book *Becoming Abolitionists: Police, Protests, and the Pursuit of Freedom*, we could design a world that addresses the needs of families rather than one that punishes them for existing. But to do so, we'd first need to dismantle systems of white supremacy and anti-Blackness that fail to see families of color and economically exploited people as human and worthy of dignity. Until we do, reproductive justice will be impossible to achieve.

We can start by looking at where we do and do not invest our money and focus. There's never enough money for universal childcare or a basic income for all families but always enough for more police officers and bombs. These policy funding decisions are directly tied to reproduction. For example, the water pipes in Flint, Michigan, where more than half of the population is Black, are contaminated with lead, creating unsafe drinking water. A 2017 study found that fertility rates of women in Flint had decreased by 12 percent and fetal death rates increased by 58 percent since the contamination began. Other women have experienced multiple miscarriages and attribute it to the water. The right to parent is inherently connected to every other policy issue that our nation makes. Yet, rather than making parenting easier, legislators focus their time and energy on restricting abortion and criminalizing pregnancy outcomes.

Parents know how many children they can handle and when they have reached their limit. But of course one of the greatest ironies of the antiabortion movement is complete ignorance of and allergy to policies that would support families and save lives. For all of the shouting that antiabortion protesters do outside of abortion clinics, claiming to protect life, neither they nor any of the judges or legislators advancing the movement's ideology are anywhere to be found when the real policy work of child-rearing begins. Rather than engage with the framework of reproductive justice, white antiabortion activists are seeking to pervert the definition, removing abortion as a core value and claiming that banning abortion is protecting people from state-sanctioned violence. These activists advocate for more adoption, for example, without making available the resources and systems that birth parents need so they can parent their own children. Antiabortion activists do not advocate for reproductive technologies or gender-affirming care so that queer, non-binary, and trans parents are able to create their families on their own terms. No matter how the words of the founding mothers are twisted, encouraging the criminalization of people for their pregnancy choices is the antithesis of reproductive justice.

But, if we're being honest, it's not just antiabortion lawmakers. Pro-choice politicians make it hard to parent as well, with policies that prioritize parents who already have money and refusing to fully fund programs that could make raising children easier for everyone. Where is our national paid leave policy? Where is our fully funded Medicaid insurance and welfare program? Why are programs that help low-income families the first that get cut when it's time to trim the national budget? These policies coerce people into making parenting decisions that they may not have chosen otherwise. If we are truly serious about ensuring people can have children, we have to make it possible for them to do so.

Forcing anyone to make a pregnancy decision they do not want to make is exactly what the founders of reproductive justice sought to end. That is why the framework is not solely about abortion but also about our bodies, the right to parent, and the ability to make these decisions free from state-sanctioned violence and coercion.

* * *

The calls for justice of the Black Lives Matter movement and reproductive justice are intertwined. Antiabortion politicians, joined by some pro-choice politicians, have given untold sums of money to police departments that harm pregnant people of color, from spraying Black Lives Matter activists with tear gas, which can increase the risk of miscarriage, to violently confronting pregnant people and killing them and their children. This was the case for twenty-one-year-old Ta'Kiya Young and so many others. The pregnant Black mother of two was shot in the heart by police after being accused of shoplifting in August 2023. She was in her third trimester. She lost her right to life and right to parent. Families trying to piece a life together are just another scapegoat for the nation's woefully inadequate systems that render all of their choices irrelevant.

As Israel began another bombing campaign of Palestinians in Gaza and the West Bank after the attack by Hamas in October 2023, many reproductive justice groups took a stance calling for a ceasefire and an end to the occupation. Some pro-choice leaders refused to take a stand, even as the death toll in the genocide rose to nearly forty thousand dead Palestinians, as of publishing, a majority of them children and women— citing that it was neither a domestic issue or a reproductive rights issue. At the time, an estimated fifty thousand pregnant people were trapped in Gaza without prenatal care due to the intense bombing of nearly all hospitals and family planning clinics, which led to a 300 percent increase in miscarriages and reports of people using tent materials for menstrual pads. Prior to the start of the 2023 genocide, Palestinians had lived under a seventy-five-year military occupation with reports of children being stolen, and of people having to cross occupation border patrols to give birth and having miscarriages in unsafe conditions, or being unable to obtain abortions due to checkpoint delays and denials. The Biden administration bypassed Congress multiple times to sell more weapons to Israel, using US taxpayer money, while hinging President Joe Biden's reelection campaign on reproductive freedom, barely saying the word "abortion," and issuing a vague call to restore *Roe*. Using our reproductive justice worldview, our position is clear: This is state-sanctioned violence that denies people the right to decide if, when, and how to grow their families and that kills families by the thousands, leaving young children with no parents or living kin. There is no reproductive freedom or justice in that.

Killing people—destroying their ability to be alive, be a parent, or parent their children—is denying them their right to parent and their rights to life and the pursuit of reproductive justice. Ta'Kiya Young should be alive. We should be asking ourselves what supports Ta'Kiya might have needed. On a larger scale, we need to ask how we can excuse a genocidal bombing campaign to maintain the discriminatory reproductive rights policies we have in place. Why is it we can separate ourselves from the struggle of Black mamas like Ta'Kiya and those in Palestine and around the world? As outraged as people feel when a married white woman with a "wanted pregnancy" is denied her right to a safe abortion or access to in vitro fertilization and thus her right to parent, we need to be just as outraged, if not more, when Black and Brown parents are denied the same things. Applying the inherent right to parent aspect of the reproductive justice framework allows us to see that parenting in poverty and war serves only white people who want to maintain power and does nothing to improve the lives of Black and Brown parents trying to get through the day. A hierarchy of whose parenthood is worthy of attention and investment is created. We need to apply a reproductive justice lens to every aspect of our policies and include the right to parent.

Abortion liberation cannot exist without reproductive agency for people who have children, no matter their income, age, sexuality, gender identity, or ability. But so much of our system is built on the idea that there is a right way to parent; this idea is used to criminalize parents who do not adhere and to remove their right to parent their children or potential children.

Abolition is crucial for parents of color. An abolitionist framework would allow us to forge a present and future "that eliminates the possibility of policing and family punishment for children," writes Purnell in *Becoming Abolitionists*. Such a vision would allow us to put the resources families actually need in their communities, which as Purnell explains could include a community council that makes decisions about quality-of-life needs in a neighborhood and that actually treats everyone equally; free twenty-four-hour childcare; art, meditation, and conflict-resolution centers that eliminate the need for a police presence when violence happens; a free health clinic; and a green team, which would handle trash pickup and sorting as well as oversee community landscaping and greenery. We want this for our communities. Every parent and "rich auntie," "fun uncle," and nonbinary loved one deserves access to the resources that liberate us from the white supremacy and patriarchal norms that have for centuries caused devastation and trauma.

We would add to Purnell's list full-spectrum reproductive health care in every community, including doulas for people seeking abortions as well as those seeking to continue their pregnancies. The country's maternal health crisis has only worsened under extreme antiabortion laws. The way to right these wrongs is a complete overhaul of the health care system and related systems that negatively contribute to maternal and infant health outcomes, including food systems, transportation, housing, and environmental policies that pose a threat to our bodies and physical health.

Scholar Dorothy Roberts reminds us it's important to center joy, too: "Abolition is not just about tearing down oppressive systems, it's about building a society where we can joyfully raise our children." Roberts, who has four children, mentioned that she's often asked how she maintains joy amid all of the injustices she studies against Black women. "I think it's because I've been able to be blessed by connecting the joys I have in the movement for reproductive justice with my intimate relationships and my relationships with my children." Roberts was clear that she knows that raising children isn't for everyone. "But I can say that my greatest joy is caring for my children and the relationship that I have with them."

Regina, who didn't realize until her abortion that she wanted to become a mom, feels that she found liberation in taking control of her reproduction by not having a child before she was ready, acknowledging the changes she and her partner wanted to make to become ready, making those changes to the best of their ability, and starting their parent journey with a clear understanding that there would be things within their control and things completely out of their control. And rather than getting too caught up in the struggle of trying to counterbalance expectations put on her as a Black mother, although that's sometimes unavoidable, she focuses on taking time every day to connect with her partner and make her children laugh real belly laughs. If that's all she can do in a given day, it's enough. As has been true for millions of others, her abortion allowed her that liberation.

Feelin' Ourselves:
Sexuality & Pleasure

Regina did not immediately want to have sex with her partner after her abortion. It was the first time in her life that she understood the consequences of sex beyond having an orgasm, and it scared her how little she knew about how her reproductive system worked. Up to that point, she thought she understood how to avoid pregnancy. She was nearly thirty and figured if she had not gotten pregnant by then, she must have been doing something right. The unintended pregnancy shifted her center. Some *thing*, a potential person, had taken up residence in her body. She had felt, or imagined feeling, a flutter in her body as the early pregnancy progressed. And then she aborted the *thing*. She was relieved to have her body back, but it felt like her body 2.0. She also realized that she wanted to become a mom, and she didn't know how to reconcile those feelings with also being a sexual person. Our culture impresses on women and girls that mothers are sexless, that their priority is their children, and that satisfying their sexual partner is an obligation and not an opportunity to explore their own desires or find sexual freedom. Regina didn't understand what any of that meant, for her, for her future self, or for her partner. But for a brief time, anyway, she felt that she needed to abstain from sexual activities as she rediscovered herself and her libido, which did return after numerous conversations with her partner about what she was feeling and why she was feeling that way.

However, after Renee's abortion, she couldn't wait to get back to having sex. She felt that the abortion allowed her to feel free and in control of her body and what happened to it. It allowed her to leave a toxic relationship and begin having sex with people she respected and who respected her body. She trusted that her contraception would work for her, and if it failed, she knew abortion would be there for her, too. The abortion allowed her to explore her sexuality in a way she hadn't before.

"There is no playbook around resuming sexual activity," explained Dr. Jamila Perritt, president and CEO of Physicians for Reproductive Health and an ob-gyn and abortion provider in the Washington, DC, area, making clear that timing should be up to the formerly pregnant person. Everyone assumes that there is a playbook—that there has to be one—because our society uses every other excuse to tell women and girls what to do with their bodies. But from a medical perspective, Dr. Perritt told us, that is just not the case. These myths don't arise in a vacuum, of course. They are reinforced in all levels of a society that maintains old-fashioned ideas and expectations around sex and a woman's role in sex through a heteronormative lens. But the health care providers we visit for reproductive and sexual health information aren't doing us any favors by leaving our sex lives unexamined. Dr. Perritt told us that ob-gyns often do not talk to their patients about sex as a part of regular check-in conversations—whether it's painful or enjoyable, or whether they have concerns about being forced into sexual activities. "I'm a provider who, when folks come in, if they come back for a follow-up or I've seen them after their abortion, I ask them, 'Are you having sex again? How is it going? Are you enjoying it? And did you before?' Because if you're not now, but you never did, then that's a different kind of conversation," Dr. Perritt said. "But doctors often don't unpack any of that with their patients." Although providers have a lot of work to do in initiating those conversations, we as patients can, and must, advocate for ourselves and for fact-based sexual health information.

It's no surprise, though, that we often don't. Like abortion, sexuality and pleasure are difficult topics for many, whether we are in a clinic's office, a classroom, or our own households. A lot can be blamed on our childhoods, during which few of us were taught at home or in schools about how to have healthy and satisfying sexual lives. Even the parents who have the best intentions for initiating conversations with their children are not always providing comprehensive or sex-positive information, because maybe they didn't get any from the adults or peers in their own lives.

Growing up, Regina's three older sisters were six or more years her senior and started having children while she was still an adolescent. As a family, they didn't really talk in great detail about sexuality or pleasure, or whether any of her sisters had considered abortions when they became pregnant unexpectedly. And despite being surrounded by pregnant and parenting siblings, the biology behind pregnancy remained a mystery to her: it seemed to just happen. She had used some form of contraception, including the pill, since she started having sex, but it wasn't until she became pregnant that she learned how to track her menstrual cycle to prevent another pregnancy or to try to get pregnant. And it wasn't until years later, shortly after she and Renee began working on this book, that she started talking to her sisters about their experiences with pregnancy and abortion. She wishes they had had those conversations earlier on and often wonders how doing so might have changed her abortion experience, or not. Would she have felt less shame, guilt, or sadness about what had happened if she had known just how common it really was? Probably. Knowing what she knows now has motivated her to become the Abortion Auntie for her nieces and nephews, so that they know she is there to talk to them whenever they need her to support them in their decisions, no matter what they decide. This role has made her feel the relief and liberation she wanted to feel when having an abortion more than a decade ago.

Similarly, no one in Dr. Toni Bond's family talked about safe sex or reproductive health. Her mom took her for her first abortion at twelve, and it was only when Dr. Bond started working at the Chicago Abortion Fund that her mother told her that she had also had an abortion. Dr. Bond's family was African Methodist Episcopal and she said that at the time of her first abortion, "I was way too young to be having conversations with anybody about abortion. So I didn't have a conversation or know anybody who had had an abortion besides me." Although no one in her family spoke to her directly about her experience, it changed the way she was seen and treated by family members. She recalled going to church every Sunday with her paternal grandmother up until her abortion, when her grandmother stopped taking her to church. Dr. Bond, who is the co-founder and CEO of Interfaith Voices for Reproductive Justice, said she believes the Black community has evolved some since the 1970s when it comes to talking about sex and abortion, but some Black religious denominations still preach that "you have to be a virtuous woman, that you have to be good," meaning not being sexually promiscuous, not engaging in sex before marriage, and even dressing in a certain way to avoid revealing too much of your body. This concept of a "virtuous" Black woman or girl is steeped in patriarchal and misogynistic norms and respectability, when in fact we should just be treated with dignity and respect for being who we are. Dr. Bond explained that the patriarchal arms of the Black church "are all about keeping Black women, girls, and pregnant-capable people in their place to the benefit and convenience of Black men in leadership at these religious institutions." For example, there continues to be a common practice prior to the start of church service of offering Black women, especially those in the first two rows, a cover for their laps if their skirt comes above the knees when sitting down. "That practice is not to protect you," Dr. Bond explained. "That practice is to protect the rolling and wandering eye of the men in the pulpit. Because for some reason your kneecaps will interrupt their ability to give a sermon."

There are myriad reasons people of color often feel they have to hide their thoughts and questions about sexuality and pleasure, and the church is one major factor. Some might feel compelled to keep these feelings to themselves for fear of being ostracized, particularly if they identify as queer or trans, or for fear of being labeled "fast." Women and girls are uniquely impacted by these patriarchal norms that demand they be "good" and "virtuous," but the silence around sexual and reproductive health negatively affects everyone.

In some Asian and Pacific Islander (AAPI) cultures, the church and other philosophical belief systems have influenced different positions concerning sexuality and gender roles. For East Asian communities, gender inequality has its origins in Confucianism, the ancient Chinese belief system, in which women are subjugated to household roles. Consequently, some Asian American women with traditional parents or grandparents are expected to live with their family until their marriages are arranged for them. At the same time, sex is a taboo subject in Asian American households, leaving young folks unprepared for sexual activities and the marriages their parents seek to arrange for them, unless their school provides some of this information. Former California state assemblymember Mary Chung Hayashi, founder of the National Asian Women's Health Organization, wrote in her 2003 autobiography, *Far From Home: Shattering the Myth of the Model Minority*, that Korean culture puts an emphasis on women not getting jobs. "The be all and end all was meeting the right man and having his children," wrote Chung Hayashi about the ideas that were prominent as she was coming into adulthood. Her parents attempted to arrange a husband for her, but she resisted their efforts.

At the same time, Asian women and girls are hypersexualized in American culture, thanks to racist and sexist stereotypes about AAPI women originating in the nineteenth and twentieth centuries. As a result of these myths, the sexual and reproductive health care needs of Asian American women and girls are often overlooked, including the need for information and resources about intimate partner violence, building healthy relationships, and HIV and AIDS prevention and treatment. When it comes to intimate partner violence among Asian Americans, research suggests the rates are lower than for other communities of color; however, those numbers are likely due to underreporting. The Urban Institute attributes such underreporting to social stigma surrounding being a victim of violence; entrenched gender roles, leading some to believe the violence they experienced is justified; and the notion that reporting the violence would bring shame to their family. Chung Hayashi noted, "Asian American women in particular make their own health and well-being less of a priority, as most Asian cultural norms dictate that they put the lives of their family members first." She added that shame and scant access to information about sexual health have contributed to a belief among many Asian American women that they were also at low risk for different health conditions, including breast and cervical cancers. But if you examine breast cancer research, for example, the CDC has found that the incidence among non-Hispanic Asian or Pacific Islander women increased 1.4 percent per year between 2005 and 2018. The federal agency cited a 2011 study that found that AAPI women under forty-five born in California had a higher risk of breast cancer than their white counterparts.

This is why reproductive justice organizations, such as the groups founded by Chung Hayashi and Dr. Bond, have been advocating for comprehensive sexual and reproductive health education since the 1990s. Yet, a growing number of parents and religious organizations, funded by the same groups that fought to overturn *Roe v. Wade,* are advancing campaigns to stop this curriculum at the local and state levels due to misguided fears of kids being oversexualized and the puritanical idea—rooted in capitalism—that sex is purely for procreation and not to be enjoyed.

THE ORIGINS OF SEX ED

Comprehensive sexuality education, or CSE, is an LGBTQ-inclusive, consent-centered, sex-positive approach to teaching schoolchildren about sexual health and development that doesn't shame or stigmatize them about their bodies or sexual development. It empowers them to foster healthy relationships and communication strategies and encourages them to take a responsible approach to sexual and reproductive health. Here's the thing, though: like everything else in the United States, sex ed didn't start out as a program aimed at supporting the development of young people—and it was very much rooted in white supremacy and eugenics.

Sex education in the early twentieth century was a response to concerns about prostitution and human trafficking, venereal diseases, and preserving the sanctity of marriage between a (white) man and a (white) woman. The early sex education movement—called the social hygiene movement—was also a response to a decline in the birth rate of white babies and the growing number of nonwhite people in the United States. World War I intensified concerns about sexually transmitted infections, which skyrocketed, with rates about 50 percent higher for younger soldiers. Government programs geared toward soldiers emphasized abstinence as a sacrifice military personnel could make for their country, not to mention improving their social status and class.

Sex is often associated with vice and utilitarianism. The US government furthered these narratives, particularly for the benefit of capitalism and reinforcing a social order that put white men at the top. But it didn't stop there: the government built on its legacy of brutalizing enslaved people and conducted medical research on thousands of vulnerable people of color in disturbing ways, including intentionally not treating Black men who were gravely suffering from syphilis and other medical conditions due to scant access to health care. Doctors carrying out these experiments for the US government in the early and mid-1900s believed that Black people were hypersexual and irresponsible and that was why they had chronic venereal disease infections—not because they may have experienced sexual violence or were denied access to health clinics or doctors for adequate treatment. In the 1940s, the US government expanded its racist and unethical medical research to Guatemala, where doctors infected more than five thousand Guatemalan people with sexually transmitted diseases, including syphilis and gonorrhea, and ten years later to Puerto Rico, where researchers targeted poor women, some of whom were illiterate, for a trial of high-dose oral contraception. These actions contributed to lasting distrust of the medical system among people of color as well as to negative ideas about sex within (and about) the communities—stigma that has also outlasted the medical trials.

In 1918, the government began to approve funding sex ed in high schools, and the focus expanded beyond STIs to include lessons on building a successful (heterosexual) marriage and family life, while stigmatizing relationships between different races, ethnicities, and religions. The lessons also emphasized the importance of abstinence until marriage and did not address biology or sex really at all. It was in the 1960s, as the antiwar movement, the civil rights movement, and the women's liberation movement were all gaining momentum, that calls for a more sex-centered approach to sexual health education began to grow. The medical director of the Planned Parenthood Federation of America, Dr. Mary Calderone, established the Sexuality Information and Education Council of the United States (SIECUS) in 1964. Even as SIECUS made progress toward developing the first standards for comprehensive sexuality education, in 1981, Congress passed the Adolescent Family Life Act (AFLA) to advance its Christian puritanical principles about adolescent sex. AFLA provided funding for programs that counseled youth on abstaining from sex until they were married. And in 1996, President Clinton's welfare law included a five-year, $250 million abstinence-only program fund. These two diverging approaches to sex education—abstinence-only education and comprehensive sexuality education—persist today, with states offering varying levels of information to people in hopes that they, we don't know . . . figure it out? Needless to say, the approach of hoping for the best is definitely not working.

SIECUS estimates that the federal government awarded more than $2.2 billion from 1982 to 2019 to abstinence-only-until-marriage programs, which do a disservice to young people, particularly those most at risk of violence or abuse, STIs, or unintended pregnancy. Numerous research studies have shown that "abstinence-only education programs don't succeed in reducing rates of teen pregnancies or STDs. Moreover, public health data indicate that such programs 'have little demonstrated efficacy in helping adolescents to delay intercourse,'" wrote authors of a September 2017 report. Laura Lindberg, coauthor of the report, went so far as to say that teaching abstinence-only-until-marriage "violates medical ethics and harms young people." Professor Michele Goodwin, who wrote an article for the *New York Times* in November 2021 about her experience having an abortion at twelve years old after being raped by her father for more than two years, echoed Lindberg's conclusion, saying that the parents and religious groups pushing against comprehensive sexual health education or insisting on abstinence-until-marriage-based education are undermining children's safety. "When we ban books, we ban conversations. We become hostile about what it is that [school-children] can learn," Goodwin told us, adding that these parents and organizations may think that they are acting in the best interest of children, but in actuality they are leaving children "open to be harmed and suffering years upon years of psychological trauma." The parents are also showing their kids that they are not available for these conversations, which might give the kids the impression that talking to any other adult about sexual health and development is not an option; it's off-limits. And when cases of sexual violence come up, the kids are left completely vulnerable and alone.

Goodwin chose to start talking to her daughter at age three about bodily autonomy and agency. "Kids pee. Kids poop. Kids throw up. They pick their noses, they have mucus," she told us. "All of these things are happening, so to pretend that kids are naturally alienated from their bodies, that their bodies are just blobs where nothing happens, is not accurate." She explained that she was motivated to begin the discussion at an early age after speaking with a close friend, who had been sexually abused at age six. "It dawned on me that waiting to have a conversation with your kids until they're mature enough, when they know enough, when they're like 12 or 13 or 14—that's way too late. You've got 6-year-olds, 5-year-olds, kids who don't have a language, because we're not giving them a language that they can use to tell us about what has happened to them."

Numerous peer-reviewed research studies back up the importance of age-appropriate comprehensive sexual health education. A 2021 report analyzing three decades of data on comprehensive sexuality education found "strong evidence for the effectiveness of child sex abuse prevention efforts in elementary school." The report explained that such programs, which can start in preschool, will involve role-play and encourage parents to participate, so that young children can gain a better understanding of their agency and right to control their bodies and how to protect themselves and communicate concerning these issues. The report looked at data on CSE across multiple outcomes beyond child sex abuse prevention, including LGBTQ-inclusive curricula, dating, intimate partner violence prevention, consent and healthy relationships, and sexual health. The report concluded that there is substantial evidence demonstrating the effectiveness "of approaches that address a broad definition of sexual health and well-being and take positive, affirming, and inclusive approaches to human sexuality, across multiple grade levels." Still, the US government has provided billions of dollars on ineffective abstinence-only programs: Why?

As we have noted in just about every chapter, the reasons are about maintaining power and control among largely white, male leaders and organizations in the country at the expense of everyone else. These folks do not believe that people of color, young people, and poor people should be having sex on their own terms. And they have worked tirelessly to try to control who, when, and where sex takes place. When they lose that control, they throw fits and pass legislation that bans basic conversations about our bodies. Furthermore, SIECUS explains that abstinence-only education "has been sold as a way to prevent disease, end unintended pregnancy, preserve marriage, and ensure wealth and prosperity." When connected to values like that, any lawmaker (Republican or Democratic) who sees themselves as a supporter of those values *and* capitalism must also fund abstinence-only education, which is led by and financially benefits conservative religious organizations. And when public health officials have attempted to steer the nation toward sexual and reproductive health liberation, they've gotten fired, even by Democratic administrations.

* * *

The AIDS epidemic really forced the country to confront so-called bedroom issues as public health concerns. At the 1994 UN conference on AIDS, psychologist Dr. Rob Clark said as much when he asked Dr. Joycelyn Elders, then US surgeon general, to talk about what the prospects were for more discussion of masturbation as a method for reducing the transmission of AIDS. Dr. Elders said in response that masturbation "is something that is a part of human sexuality and . . . something that perhaps should be taught" to schoolchildren. Conservatives had already targeted the doctor, a pediatric endocrinologist from Arkansas and the first Black woman surgeon general, for her support of widespread distribution of condoms and the legalization of drugs to reduce crime rates. She had said of her haters to the *New York Times* months earlier, "You've got to get people's attention before you can achieve change. As surgeon general, you have to take a stand. People are either going to love you or hate you." Still, she was forced to resign by President Clinton after her comment about masturbation was weaponized by conservatives. Her firing deeply angered Black reproductive justice activists, who in their 1994 reissue of the "We Remember" brochure solidifying support among Black women for abortion rights included a letter defending Dr. Elders. Up to and including that conference, she had always sought to educate children in healthy and positive ways about their bodies. Her firing also prompted a group of San Francisco–based sexual health activists to designate May as National Masturbation Month, starting in 1995.

In a 2005 interview, Dr. Elders said that "it made no sense" that people disagreed with her on comprehensive sexual health education, particularly during the AIDS epidemic. She said conservative groups argued that giving teens sex ed meant that we were giving them permission to have sex. "Well, as far as I'm concerned, when you've got the highest teenage pregnancy rate in the industrialized world, nobody needs to give them permission. They are already doing it," Dr. Elders said.

It's as true today as it was in the 1990s that teens are having sex, and a number of factors contribute to teen sexual behaviors. That is why renowned relationship therapist Dr. Laura Berman has for decades encouraged parents to start the conversation with their children at a young age so that by the time they are making sexual decisions, they have the information they need. Waiting until they are in their teens is too late, she has warned. They need to know before then that "it's okay to ask questions about their body." But when Dr. Berman walked a mother through how to talk to her ten-year-old daughter about sex, including masturbation, on a 2009 episode of *The Oprah Winfrey Show*, viewers complained. The young girl approached her mom with questions about sex, and after their conversation with Dr. Berman, the daughter was happy and relieved to have answers to her questions. But it was when Dr. Berman told the young girl that she could touch around her clitoris to see whether it felt good that some of these viewers filed complaints with a broadcasting complaints commission. They said they were "disgusted" by the "explicit" content, meaning the diagrams of the female and male sexual organs shown to the ten-year-old. Renee remembers the episode as a pivotal moment for her. It was the first time she heard people talking about masturbation among women at all, let alone in a way that wasn't the brunt of a joke. It was incredibly powerful to see a young girl get educated about her own sexual organs and to be encouraged to discover what feels good, independent of any partner, particularly given the troubling history of female stimulation in a medical setting. The commission seemed to agree, because it rejected these viewers' complaints. For Renee, this became a learning moment and an early foundation of her reproductive justice education. Her sexuality and pleasure were in her hands and didn't need to come at the whims of her partners. That level of confidence and power was life-changing.

Masturbation for those of us with vaginas has a complicated history. As documented in the 2011 film *Hysteria*, doctors in the late nineteenth century diagnosed women with "hysteria" for everything from sleep deprivation to depression. Doctors treated this made-up condition— that they argued, without evidence, affected only women—with "pelvic massages" that stimulated them to the point of orgasm. A doctor who ended up with very tired hands after giving out a lot of these "pelvic massages" developed the first vibrator to make it easier for providers to treat their patients diagnosed with "hysteria." So basically cisgender men were violating women, but they were calling it "medicine." Once vibrators became more widely available and became associated with sexuality and sexual pleasure, cisgender men still controlled access to them. Only cisgender men could buy them in sex stores, and even women's magazines wouldn't advertise them to their readers. Thanks to the proliferation of feminist sex toy shops and feminist porn, many people are unlearning the notion that cisgender men control our sexual organs and sexuality. But it's still an uphill battle, as religious beliefs and anxious, sexually uninformed parents continue to influence what they believe sexual education should look like and instill shame in people who take charge of their own sexuality and health.

We believe that masturbation, owning your sexuality, and having sex for pleasure rather than procreation is anticapitalist. Those who are anti-sex are usually deeply racist, antiabortion, and antilabor. They believe that all of us—but particularly Black and Brown people—should not be having sex for anything but procreation of children we can afford. It's common to hear people ask, "Why were you having sex if you can't afford birth control or children?" There's the idea that people who are poor should be focused on working and making money at every waking moment. They must work harder so they can afford leisure, but if they're overworked and underpaid for their labor, they will never be able to afford joy or relaxation, or have time and energy for sex. Abortion and nonprocreative sex allow for sex without consequences, making it possible for people to decide if, when, and how to grow their families and not create baby workers for the future. Both allow us to explore our sexuality and freedom without being locked into partnership with another person who could bring us harm or economic instability. Having free time to masturbate and orgasm means having nonworking time—aka time when you're not making money for someone else. Abortion and masturbation, at their core, are rejections of capitalism and patriarchy.

Parents should be giving their children as much information as possible about their sexuality and sexual health, which serves to counter these early problematic notions about female health. As that *Oprah* segment showed when the mother said she learned something during the conversation with Dr. Berman, too, this information helps us all to build healthy relationships with ourselves and to find partners who will want to practice consensual and safe sex. It's exactly the information Dr. Elders, who had worked as a pediatric resident and saw the worst of the worst cases of sexual violence, was advocating for.

Thankfully, groups such as Advocates for Youth are working in coordination with young people to develop programs that meet teens where they are at—quite literally. One such project is the Condom Collective, a partnership between Advocates for Youth and Trojan that sends select college students a box of condoms to distribute on their school's campus. Numerous studies have shown the effectiveness of peer-led education when it comes to sexual health, and this program is one of many in which Advocates for Youth is leading the way, not only on the issue of safe sex but also concerning sexual and dating violence (through the Know Your IX project), HIV stigma and criminalization (through the Engaging Communities around HIV Organizing, or ECHO, program), and abortion rights advocacy and storytelling (through the Youth Testify program with Renee's organization, We Testify). South Asians for Abortion (SOAR), an organization building a survivor-centered movement to end gender-based violence, too, initiated a powerful guide demystifying abortion for the South Asian communities in the United States, as the Supreme Court was rolling back federal abortion rights. Sarah Michal Hamid, a We Testify abortion storyteller and full-spectrum doula based in Southern California, played a pivotal role in the guide while serving as a reproductive justice fellow there in 2022.

SOAR's Abortion Care Guide offers basic information about abortion methods and support services in twenty South Asian languages, helping to break the silence around abortion among gender-based violence organizations and in the broader South Asian community. Sarah said that when she showed her dad the guide, and in particular one of the beautiful illustrations in it of an older man hugging a young woman and telling her, "I am proud of you," the next day her dad went to Walgreens and asked to move his prescription to a different pharmacy because he knew that the company was one of the giant chains that initially said it would not distribute mifepristone by prescription in states where abortion is illegal, despite the FDA permitting pharmacies to dispense the medication. "That image [in the guide] made my dad, a sixty-something Pakistani man, stand in solidarity with people who have abortions like that," Sarah told us.

* * *

The work of groups such as SOAR and Advocates for Youth stands in stark contrast to the government-funded efforts and messages at the onset of the AIDS epidemic, when AIDS was treated as a joke by the Reagan administration, and when the response from state officials was to increase stigma against gay men, trans women, and other queer people, as well as anyone with HIV/AIDS. Rather than respond with fact-based information and resources for the most impacted communities, which over the years has included Black women—who are fifteen times more likely than white women to be diagnosed with AIDS—the local, state, and federal response only added to the shame and fear many feel about sex both inside and outside of marriage.

It was in this context that Dr. Elders was asked a provocative but legitimate question about how we talk to young people about sexual pleasure. She defended her position in the 2005 interview, saying, "Masturbation never made anybody go crazy. Hair won't grow on your hands. It's never given anybody a disease. It's never gotten anybody pregnant. And you know you're having sex with somebody you love." But the religious critics who pushed for her resignation felt that she was saying sexual health educators should teach children how to masturbate. She maintained that it's a lie to think anyone needs to learn how to masturbate. "God taught you how to masturbate," Dr. Elders countered in that interview. "Think about it: 80 percent of women masturbate, 95 percent of men masturbate, and the rest lie."

We couldn't agree more. If you're not masturbating, you should interrogate why. It's completely natural and safe to do. And it's fun! But it's also true that people of color have never been afforded the luxury of exploring our sexuality and pleasure centers free of stigma and shame. Leaders such as Dr. Elders may have been speaking out in defense of reproductive and sexual freedom their entire careers, but not everyone who needed to hear their voices was exposed to them. Part of that responsibility falls on the abortion rights movement, which—like the doctors Dr. Perritt spoke of who fail to engage patients about their sex lives—fails to connect the dots for advocates and people who have abortions.

* * *

Latina artist and activist Favianna Rodriguez, who created the "It's My Body. It's My Pussy. Get Over It You Patriarchal Fuck Head Woman Hater" posters in 2012, noticed early on that abortion activists weren't talking about sex. She told us in an interview that she feels the movement is barely connecting those dots today between "how we choose to build our families and our romantic relationship and the implications of the choices we make without comprehensive sex education." Favianna said that she got pregnant and had her first abortion because she didn't have CSE nor the language or practice to communicate what she needed in order to protect herself from getting pregnant during sex. "And that was always the thing: you can't talk about abortion without talking about sex and sex education." Through her art, she said that she's been making those connections, "and the space of reproductive justice is the space to do that."

Favianna said her high school emphasized abstinence while talking about some menstruation topics and anatomy, without mentioning consent, sexual assault, or sex. "The messages in high school and in my family, and the way I was sheltered, didn't give me the tools to build healthy relationships," she said. Favianna sought out that information at a community clinic for immigrants, where she learned some essential information such as how to put a condom on a cucumber. But when she was in college, she didn't know how to set safe boundaries when engaging in sexual activities. "I honestly didn't have the skills to identify how to create standards for the people I was allowing inside my pussy." So when her sexual partner, "who was older than me and more established" as an artist, didn't put on a condom, she did not have the language to tell him otherwise. "It came down to negotiating sex with protection, and I just didn't have practice in that," she said. Favianna got pregnant and was abandoned by this person. It was a traumatic experience, one in which she experienced shame because the first provider she visited for an abortion tried to dissuade her from seeking that care. She was in the middle of a prestigious art internship and knew that she did not want to have a baby. She had to ask a friend to lend her the money to pay for the abortion and a different friend to drive her to the appointment at a Planned Parenthood clinic.

Favianna later had two other abortions, and she connects her experiences with unintended pregnancies with larger cultural shortcomings: the lack of sexual health education and the failure for us as humans to be taught about or provided with representations of healthy relationships. Favianna reflected on the fact that throughout her life, she's been given so much support in developing as a leader, growing into the successful artist she is today, and becoming a truth-telling public speaker—but "I didn't actually get support around how to build healthy romantic relationships, or how to have a healthy sexuality where I can be fully expressed and sexually fulfilled." Over the years, she has had to backtrack and figure out what information and resources she needs to build healthy relationships. This happened after entering adulthood and after she started having sexual partners—much like most of the other people who've had abortions whom we interviewed for our book. She explained that the need for connection and to feel the full spectrum of emotions are related to sex, and that it's critical that we learn how to love ourselves "enough to know when something isn't right for us"—because, she added, "at the core, if I would have had more tools, more cultural examples of that, I would not have needed to have more abortions."

Currently only three states—California, Oregon, and Washington—require CSE to be taught in schools, although a bill introduced by Representative Barbara Lee seeks to change that. Not only would the Real Education and Access for Healthy Youth Act (REAHYA) require all states to provide comprehensive sex education, it would emphasize the importance of equitable access to sex education and sexual health services, which historically kids of color have not had. But until this legislation becomes law, cultural institutions and households have an important role to play in building the foundation Favianna referenced. Unfortunately, for too many of us, no one is talking about sexuality and pleasure in these terms.

PERIOD CULTURE

In many ways, the 2022 *Dobbs* decision overturning *Roe v. Wade* and the national right to abortion opened up the floodgates to restrictions beyond abortion bans that seek to control not only the decisions people make about their bodies but also the information they receive, starting at a young age. Conservative lawmakers introduce and pass these bills because they know that when people do get this knowledge, they seek more control over their lives, not less (which is how these lawmakers would prefer it). Look no further than Florida's "Don't Say Period" law, which took effect in July 2023, shortly after Representative Lee introduced her federal bill seeking to expand access to sexual health information. The Florida law deepens the state's discrimination against queer and trans youth by mandating that students be referred to by the sex they were assigned at birth, regardless of their preferred pronoun or gender identity. The law also prohibits students from receiving information about menstruation and puberty at the age when they would be undergoing these changes. State Representative Stan McClain, who introduced the legislation, said in no uncertain terms that it would prohibit young people from discussing their periods.

Young people already feel a lot of shame or embarrassment about their periods, particularly when they are teased for bleeding through their clothes by their peers. We also don't think it was an accident the discrimination toward queer and trans youth was combined with the menstrual silencing; it's about maintaining gender binaries and not allowing young people to talk about how their bodies are changing. It also exacerbates dysphoria for trans kids who menstruate but are forbidden from talking about it with their classmates or trusted adults. Policies such as Florida's law add to that stigma and may prevent young people from seeing their menstruation as an issue they can form bonds or community around. That paralysis is the point, because as we've seen, when bonds are formed, young people will start organizations and advocate for ending stigma and advancing solutions to "period poverty," such as demanding period supplies in school bathrooms. Indeed, nearly a quarter of all students lack access to period hygiene products, such as tampons or pads, according to a 2023 study by reusable period underwear brand Thinx and PERIOD, a global nonprofit founded by two high school students fighting for menstrual equity. Rather than see menstruation as an isolated experience, many students today are fighting for the resources they and their peers need. Any attempt to ban discussions or education around puberty and menstrual health must be seen as a gag on students' rights.

The ban on puberty and menstruation discussions is particularly damaging for young people facing reproductive health conditions such as endometriosis, a condition in which tissue typically grown inside of the uterus grows outside of it, resulting in severe pelvic pain. Despite the fact that about 1 in 10 women and girls experience endometriosis, many are unaware it exists, because of the lack of education about reproductive systems and the health conditions that can begin at the onset of menstruation. The pain many are forced to endure because of the silence on these issues is the point; lawmakers opposed to CSE would rather students suffer than advocate for their rights and freedom from injustice. From a young age, we are taught to endure this pain, and really any pain, because it is the cost of having a uterus. It is only when we unlearn these common beliefs and behaviors that we can truly liberate ourselves and begin to find power and satisfaction in our bodies and sexual lives.

Sarah Michal Hamid's abortion put her on the path to liberation and wellness in treating her endometriosis. She told us that she was put on birth control at a young age to help with her pain, but it didn't help. "I was taught to ignore what I was feeling," Sarah said. Sarah also felt that because of her condition and the way her parents and doctors responded to it, without explaining what was happening, why it was happening, and how birth control might (or might not) help, she felt that her reproductive agency had been taken from her and that she didn't have control over her own body—an experience compounded by physical abuse and sexual assault. It was her abortion experience at sixteen that allowed her to take back her body. "When I found out I was pregnant, I was so fucking proud of myself," Sarah said. "Because that day I told my shitty abortion baby daddy I thought I was pregnant, and he was like, 'No, you're on birth control. There's no way . . .,' but I knew I just felt different. I trusted myself, and that was a pivotal moment." Sarah found out she was pregnant shortly after her junior year of high school concluded. She was scared and worried about what her parents would think. "But part of me was really excited that I could get pregnant because I had been on birth control from such a young age," Sarah said. "The decision for me to be on birth control and those kinds of reproductive health decisions were really always made with doctors and my parents, and I had never felt like, *Oh, this is my body*. But with the pregnancy, I knew that whatever I wanted to happen in this scenario is what would happen."

Sarah said she hadn't known other South Asian people who had had abortions at that time, which contributed to her feeling alone and overwhelmed. "But I went to Planned Parenthood, and I got my abortion care and medication abortion from a nurse practitioner who treated me with dignity and kindness and respect and held my hands. And I went home and was able to have my abortion at home and bleed and pass tissue in a way that I needed and felt dignified doing, and in a way that also resonated with me, culturally and religiously." Sarah was able to access care without being forced to notify her parents or get their consent, using California's Medicaid program, Medi-Cal, which covers abortion care because it is considered basic health care. Because she was able to get the care she needed and wanted on her own terms, she could also tell her parents about the abortion when she was ready, which further empowered her. When she finally told them, she said, "it yielded beautiful, fruitful conversations about the broader context of abortion in our communities—specifically in Muslim Islamic law and Jewish law, too."

* * *

Conservative lawmakers are hell-bent on banning sexual health information in the United States, but a number of cultures and communities around the world mark what is seen as a girl's entrance into womanhood with a traditional ceremony. In the northeast Indian state of Assam, the Hindu menstruation ceremony, called Tuloni Biya, includes a big symbolic wedding, during which the young girl learns about the significance of her cycle and fertility from older women in her family and community. During the multiday celebration, her diet is altered so that she eats certain foods that are associated with healthy eating and digestion in Assam, including dried fruits and boiled vegetables. Her movement is also restricted to her room, where she is told to stay and rest, and she is not able to have any male visitors, including relatives. On the day of her mock wedding ceremony, the girl is married to a banana tree as a symbol of her entrance into womanhood and in recognition that she can now get pregnant. The banana tree in Assam culture represents fertility. A March 2023 study on the practice, which included interviews with adolescent girls from the communities where this tradition takes place, explained that its main purpose "among the Assamese Hindu community is to announce when a girl reaches puberty because the celebration of the power of fertility gives girls and women the social status of being fertile, which the community regards as worthy of respect." Nevertheless, this study concluded that the tradition itself hasn't equated to a positive impact on overall menstrual health in Assam and makes the case for better integration of education and resources in the Tuloni Biya ritual to improve its impact on the community. Some have also criticized the practice for reinforcing gender stereotypes about how females are *supposed* to live and present themselves in contrast to males in their society.

Here in the United States, different Indigenous communities have their own menstruation rituals to mark the occasion. In 2019, Mary Annette Pember wrote a beautiful essay for *Rewire News Group*, pushing back against the idea that all traditional menstruation practices are backward and a threat to women's and girls' health and well-being. Pember pointed out how some Indigenous women are revitalizing their own community ceremonies: "To an outsider, these practices may cast menstruation as evil and threatening. But for Ojibwe women, their moon can be a healthy time of rest, regeneration, and recognition of their important roles as life givers and community leaders."

Rachael Lorenzo (Mescalero Apache / Laguna Pueblo / Xicana) participated in a yearlong puberty ceremony at fifteen in Mescalero, New Mexico, during which participants were guided by a medicine woman, participated in spiritual outings, and harvested traditional foods, plants, and clay. Rachael told us that you're not supposed to have had any sex before the ceremony, and the purpose of the ceremony is a recognition of your new ability to have children as well as certain spiritual duties you acquire once you're able to bear a child. During the year, Rachael could not shave their legs and had to dress modestly. "I had to go through this process and it was a lesson to let go of, I guess, vanity, because our bodies are supposed to do certain things." They did a lot of manual labor, chopping down trees, using a chainsaw, and learning how to shave teepee poles using a big razor. They also learned how to harvest traditional tobacco and how to identify different plants and other natural resources. "I had to learn a lot of physically intensive skills because our mother, White Painted Woman, did all of these things for her children, and if we are becoming this deity over time, we have to [acquire] those same skills because that's what is expected of us as mothers." The ceremony itself lasted four days. It was open to the public. Called a "maiden" during this process, Rachael had to wear a leather dress that felt as though it weighed twenty-five pounds and was made of buckskin and dangling metal cones, typically known as jingles. Rachael and the four other maidens slept all day and danced all through the four nights.

Families shoulder the costs of the ceremonies, which *New Mexico Magazine* reported in 2019 can be as much as $20,000. But Mescalero council member Pascal Enjady said that the ceremonies need not be as elaborate as some families make them, giving away trunk-loads of food, candy, and other local treats. Enjady told the magazine, "My grandmother said that you can do a ceremony like this with coffee and fry bread. It's all about respect to the young lady." The aspect of the ceremony Rachael remembered most was at the end, when they had to run as far as they could, wearing moccasins and the very heavy leather dress. It was the fourth run of the ceremony and the longest of them all. "They say that the farther you run and the amount of effort you put into that is the amount of effort and the success that you're gonna have in your life. And I was like, *I just want to be a good mom. I just want to be a good student, and I don't want to be fighting with my family anymore.*" Rachael and their mom, who was a teen parent, had had a strained relationship since Rachael hit puberty between 10 and 12, because of their mom's concerns about them becoming boy crazy. Their mom had threatened to throw them out of the house if they became a teen parent just like her. Rachael's first sex education was very much rooted in trying to scare them away from sex instead of teaching them about their body and how to prevent pregnancy. Despite these early fear and shame tactics, Rachael's family also put them through this puberty ceremony, which helped with their self-actualization in many ways. As Rachael explained, in the final stretch of the run, instead of running to their aunt or mom, as girls typically do, so they could all run together, Rachael's family couldn't keep up. "They ended up having to turn around, and

I just kept going. I don't know how far I ran, but I know I was alone." After they finally turned back, Rachael recalls people asking, "Where did you go?" But Rachael remembers feeling "so proud of myself. I will always cherish that I did that for me." The experience set a precedent for how Rachael addresses parenting. They work hard every day, "just to be a good parent," Rachael said. "I'm so grateful for that."

With all of the bans and stigma concerning periods, sexual health, and sexuality, it's easy to feel discouraged about the current political climate, but there are so many people, like Rachael, reclaiming ancestral practices on their own terms that remind us of all we are capable of. The same is true of the youth-led nonprofit organizations that are fighting for liberation and growing support in communities nationwide and across the globe. A future where sexual and reproductive health is widely accepted and encouraged by parents, schools, and community institutions (like churches) is within reach. But to get there, we all have a role to play in normalizing this information and putting any attempt at restricting conversations about our bodies in the proper context. These restrictive efforts will not protect children, as conservative lawmakers claim. Restrictions will cause more harm in children's lives and prevent them from being able to protect themselves and build safe and healthy relationships—not only with others but also with themselves. What could the future look like when comprehensive sexual education is not only normalized but universally available? What would our conversations and experiences be like if our government invested in sexual and reproductive health and wellness at the level that is needed to ensure every person has equal access to information, resources, and health care? That is the world we are fighting for—and it includes radical healing and great sex.

HEALING OURSELVES AND HAVING THE BEST SEX OF OUR LIVES

For Favianna, who is Latina with Afro-Peruvian roots, it was important to decolonize her third abortion experience because her first two abortions did not make her feel good or allow her to reconnect to her body and the Earth. "I know the history of Planned Parenthood. I know the history of how all these white doctors became ob-gyns. And I also know that when I wake up in a fucking place with these lights on top of me and people in all these surgical outfits and no one there to offer me the kind of soothing that I want, it's not it," she told us.

As we noted in chapter 3 ("'We Took the Tea': Abortion Methods Throughout History"), Favianna used a combination of medication and herbs for her abortion. She also decided to bury Karmila, her "creature," as she calls the living-yet-not-human being that she carried and passed, in the garden her father helped her build. "It was just so meaningful to do that because it helped me understand the full process of what my body is capable of," Favianna said. "And it helped me grieve in a way that I had never grieved before [by] putting it into a place of new life [where plants grow]."

This experience also allowed her to embrace the mothering energy she felt by creating a chosen family that calls in children whom she didn't need to give birth to in order for them to be in her life. "We have this very narrow view of what birthing is, but for me having an abortion birthed the new me. It opened the door to motherhood in a way that I would have never thought possible."

This is such a great way of looking at one's abortion, particularly the potential it has for experiencing a new version of oneself. And it counters one of the many lies antiabortion folks love to tell us about our abortions. Another one of those lies, as we mentioned in chapter 6 ("Abortionsplaining"), is that if you have an abortion, you'll never enjoy sex again. That's exactly what Taté Walker was told at the pregnancy farm (also conversion camp). But Taté thought, "That wasn't the flex that I think they wanted it to be." That's because Taté was far from interested in having coitus at that moment. "I was like, great. I don't even want to have a penis inside me. Like it hasn't been a great thing so far." Looking back, Taté said their abortion experiences reinforced their desire for femme folks and also affirmed their sexual desires in a way that didn't feed into heteronormative notions of how we've been told to live our lives. The abortion didn't change their attraction to both femmes and men; rather, in their healing journey, they sought pleasure that would ease their mind as well as satisfy their sexual desires. "I hate gyneco-logical visits in general. The two abortions I had were not painful; they were super quick. I remember feeling super relieved afterward . . . but I didn't want to have another abortion." Taté had taken birth control to prevent pregnancy, but it didn't always work for them, and Taté was also very aware of the potential risks of taking medication of any kind to alter their biological makeup and their body's natural rhythms.

Similarly, because the antiabortion movement would like us to believe that abortion somehow ruins our sex lives, we feel it's important to be clear about how, for many of us, our abortions marked only the begin-ning of an even better, more liberated sexual life than the one we lived prior to them. By giving herself the time she needed to rebound phys-ically and emotionally from an unexpected pregnancy, Regina had the space and mental capacity to begin to unlearn ideas she had absorbed as a teen about the transactional nature of sex. In many ways, her abortion gave her permission to question other notions about her body and sex itself that she had just accepted as true—for example, the idea that the sexual experience should center around a male partner's orgasm if you're in a heterosexual relationship. This is a fucked-up idea that's reinforced in sexist pop culture and misogynistic porn. Healthy relationships involve the people within them, no matter their gender or sexual orientation, connecting in a consensual and mutually beneficial way, on whatever level feels right and satisfying. And because she got an IUD after her abor-tion, she finally began to shed any shame she felt about enjoying sex. She now knew more about how and at what point during her cycle a preg-nancy could happen, and she had foolproof contraception. So while she and her partner were working on getting "ready" for parenthood, finan-cially and otherwise, they grew into lovers who explored one another's bodies with the eagerness of newly horny teens and the sophistication of confident and skilled bodywork professionals. They made love every-where, including in friends' bathrooms at parties, trying new techniques and positions. It was a sublime period. After Regina gave birth to their first child, their sex life regressed, as Regina was touched-out and her libido took a hit while she was pumping breast milk around the clock to feed their son. It's not at all surprising, she learned, because breastfeeding (whether chestfeeding, pumping, or exclusively nursing without bottles) can affect your hormones and drain the desire right out of you, not to mention cause vaginal dryness and discomfort during penetrative sex. (Lube helps!) But waiting until you're ready to resume sexual activities is most important, whether that readiness is immediate or takes months (or years). Once Regina was ready, she picked up some adult toys to take their sex to a new level. She figured out that becoming a parent didn't have to mean the end of their sex life. In fact, when she was ready, their parenthood marked the beginning of a new adventure in their sexual lives, because when you have a limited amount of time, you might as well make the most of it. And these sexual explorations helped Regina to feel like herself again, particularly because her partner frequently showed her how much he craved her, by caressing her hips or back or elsewhere as often as she permitted him to. Creating room for their sexual desires to blossom before they became parents allowed their behaviors to return once they both agreed they were ready.

Other people we interviewed who had abortions expressed that their sexual lives got better after their abortions. "I was horny immediately. I started fucking as soon as I could," Jack Qu'emi Gutiérrez, a nonbinary We Testify abortion storyteller who had their abortion at nineteen, told us. Jack and their high school sweetheart had sex for the first time with one another, dated on and off for five years, and lived together for a year after high school. But it wasn't a particularly empowering sexual experience. "If he wanted to have sex, I was just like, 'I guess we're doing that,'" they explained. After having a painful medication abortion, Jack wanted to have sex again. "I was like, 'Oh I feel so good. Now I want to fuck,'" they told us. Jack attributes that feeling to having full control of their body after exercising their right to not have a child. When they started having sex again with a new partner, they felt like they were finally having the experience they deserved, one that felt pleasurable and good. "It was awesome," Jack said. "I was like, 'Oh my God, this is what it's like to want sex.'" And ten years after their abortion, in 2023, Jack told us they were experiencing a new sexual revolution. "I've been gay as hell. I only got gayer in my thirties, if that's possible," Jack said. "And now I almost—and this is not intentional—almost exclusively fuck other kinky trans people. It's awesome. I'm having the best sex of my life."

Although it is often overlooked or underaddressed, sexual freedom is a core part of abortion liberation. That is exactly why the people who are fighting against abortion access also want to ban contraception and resources for queer and trans people. Our bodies are a threat because they threaten capitalism, the status quo, and the political order that keeps power in the hands of wealthy white, cisgender men at the expense of everyone else. But when we reclaim our bodies, which are a source of great power and deep satisfaction, we taste freedom. A world with abortion liberation frees our libidos from shame and stigma. When we see our sexuality as ours for the taking, rather than something to be ashamed or embarrassed about—when instead of shrinking our desires when we feel that all-familiar tingle or ache in our genitals, we follow the yearning where it takes us with our partners—we are releasing ourselves from the shackles of colonialism and white supremacy. We are reclaiming what was stolen from our ancestors and setting their legacies free. And we are creating a sex-positive, stigma-free path for future generations to follow, in making their reproductive and sexual health the foundation to freedom in a just society.

There are also practical, health-related reasons for engaging in consensual sexual pleasure, whether showing yourself some love or inviting a partner or partners: pleasure can boost your immune system and reduce the number of days that you'll need to recover from a common cold or virus; it can lower your blood pressure (though some research suggests this doesn't apply to masturbation—hey, we're just the messengers); it's good for your heart; it can help with sleep, stress, and pain relief; it counts as exercise; and it can strengthen menstrual health. And as we noted, on the cultural side, well, life is just too damn hard not to find ways to make the most of it, and consensual sex of all types, with or without toys, really does make life worth living. Until the person feels ready physically for touch of any kind, however, we very much support the notion of seeking "mental pleasure" or other forms of pleasure. This is particularly true for survivors of gender-based violence.

Sarah explained that while doing this work, she's also struggled with her own healing as a survivor of sexual violence and reproductive health violence, as well as navigating what comes after. But being able to recognize that opportunity for growth has only motivated her to seek out information and resources to heal. "My greatest pride in my work in this movement is that I decided I couldn't be silent about wanting to experience joy and pleasure in my body. And I knew that I really couldn't have those conversations with my parents. So I was able to find people in my community who I could talk to and ask questions."

For Sarah, one of the most alarming experiences was feeling scared in her body, because although she felt safe in the moment of a consensual physical encounter, "my body was reacting as though I was afraid and so it almost made me feel like, whoa, what are you doing?" After having surgery to treat her endometriosis and starting therapy, including pelvic floor physical therapy, Sarah has been able to physically release a lot of the tension and trauma that had built up in her body. "When I went to therapy I realized that I haven't centered my pleasure in my life and in my body, and a lot of that has to do with the role I've been relegated to play in my family, which is specifically because I'm South Asian and we have structures of kinship and family networks that, at times, can delegate restrictive social roles," Sarah said. But she has shed that: "I rejected those ideas and decided to be unmarried and to control my reproductive health care decisions." She feels better positioned to care not only for herself but also for her parents and her community. "I think it's in our fullness, just accepting our full selves without expectations of what we are supposed to produce, that's when we get to have pleasure. It's when we get to do things because it feels right—and we know what's good for ourselves, for our family, for our community."

Seeing Ourselves: Abortion On-Screen

In May 2020, Emma Hernández was determined not to let her abortion take over her day. She had a lot to do; her sister, Lyn, was not available to help set up for the evening's extravagant drag king show at the Los Angeles bar they inherited from their late mother. Emma was focused. As a Type A Chicana queer eldest sister, she knew what she needed to do to get through, and nothing—not even an unexpected pregnancy resulting from a quick romp in her office with her bar's contractor and a breakup with her partner and bartender Nico—was going to slow her down. Her body was the one thing she could control.

The morning of the drag king show, she went to the clinic early to pick up her abortion pills. Although the white nurse explained to her that Emma needed to take the mifepristone pill first, then the four misoprostol pills a day or two later, and what the side effects would be, she comically popped all five pills in her mouth, handed over her credit card, and went on her way. Later, while raiding Emma's closet, Lyn suggested that Emma should wait until after the event to take the pills because of the toll the medication would take on her body. Emma, barely looking up from her phone, told Lyn she had already taken them.

"What? This is you on the pill?" Lyn asked, surprised. "OMG, I'd be totally green by now if I were you. The one time I took it, I got so sick. I literally had to curl up in bed with caldo for two days, almost three." But Emma dismissed her sister's abortion wisdom. She had "a rock for a stomach."

Between Lyn not showing up to help set up for the event and Nico putting in their two-week notice, Emma's day fell apart as the cramping and nausea took control. When she succumbed to the pain, she finally admitted she had to accept support. "Today I really needed you," she tearfully told Lyn. The penultimate episode of the STARZ series *Vida* closes with Emma vomiting in a toilet and Nico caressing her hair.

In early 2022 the real Emma Hernández was living in San Antonio when she realized she was pregnant. Texas's SB8 law had recently gone into effect, which meant that anyone who helped her get an abortion could be sued by any random stranger for up to $10,000. She knew immediately she wanted an abortion and sought out abortion pills in her community. Real Emma knew what to expect because she had been through it before. She was in a different place in her life, one that mirrored Character Emma in *Vida*.

When Real Emma had her first abortion, she was distraught about everything going on in her life. She was a twenty-one-year-old trying to finish college while in a toxic relationship, economically unstable, and navigating her father's deportation to Mexico a month before. By the time Character Emma in *Vida*, portrayed by Mishel Prada, had her abortion, Real Emma's life had changed drastically; also different was her second abortion experience, which was surrounded by love and support from her partner, despite the precarious political situation. But, like Character Emma, Real Emma didn't want to turn to her sister, who had worked at a clinic, for advice. She felt that telling her sister would make it all real and that she couldn't let anyone know about her failure because, she said, she was the one who was "supposed to have [her] shit together." The depiction of Character Emma was critical in normalizing Real Emma's own acceptance of her abortions. "To see a portrayal of someone certain, just like, let's move this process along, was great to see," she told us. "I think it's important that abortion and Latinidad be on-screen together. For me, both of those things living within the same universe is really important."

Character Emma's abortion experience on *Vida* and Real Emma's connection with the portrayal was the goal of the show's creator, Tanya Saracho. She wanted to create a show about the experiences of Mexican American millennial women and their own exploration of their identities, family, and place in their community. The characters' journeys were based on the lives of the show writers, half of whom were queer and almost half of whom had also had abortions. "So many things, not just the abortion, but the way we dealt with stuff was dealt with because of who was in the room." When the writers found out the third season would be their last, Tanya told us that she wanted to make sure abortion was a topic they tackled. Drawing on her own two abortions, Tanya wanted her character to be clear-eyed about her abortion. "I never doubted it or myself or had moralistic qualms with it. It was a logistical thing. It was never like a spiritual thing." Having Character Emma break away from the stereotype of Latinas having a crisis of conscience about their abortions due to Catholicism allowed the character to break the mold, separating abortion from religion; the complex Character Emma helps the audience understand why she needed an abortion to be able to move forward in her life, just as Real Emma did.

It was important for Tanya to show a decisive Latina going into her abortion alone thinking she didn't need help but then receiving nonjudgmental care from her queer lover as she had to submit to the softening of her own body. (The depiction is the first plotline with a queer Latina character having an abortion.) Seeing that support felt like a model for Real Emma and others who have seen the *Vida* depiction and may not know how to show up for someone needing an abortion or how to ask for the support they need. "I know maybe people support me in theory, but I don't know what that looks like in practice," Real Emma told us. "I know everyone in theory is having the cool stickers on their notebook and is gonna say your body your choice and is always down for the cause, but I don't know what that actually looks like in practice. I have no reference point for how to go about this in the community that I'm in, in the body that I inhabit, in the language that I speak."

Seeing ourselves reflected on television and film is critical to an individual's self-esteem and understanding of their own value and place in society. Pop culture has always been a tool of education and communication. When our stories are told accurately, it allows people to know that whatever they're going through is not shameful or uncommon, even as it might be an isolating experience. A study published in 2012 examined the long-term effects of children's programming on Black and white children and found that the only group whose self-esteem was not negatively impacted by the way they saw themselves on television were white boys. All other groups experienced lower self-esteem, and Black girls were more likely to see Black female characters portrayed as exotic and sexually available. That impact on self-esteem is deeply harmful at young ages, as we're developing our own understanding of who we are, and continues throughout our lives as we watch television to unwind. For Real Emma, this impacted her understanding of her own body and sexuality. "I remember the first time I saw brown nipples, and that like rocked my world because literally for years of my life I thought there was something wrong with me," Emma told us through tears. "Why does everyone on TV have pink nipples? What the fuck? And how anxiety-producing it is to a person when you think that you're the only one going through it?"

Additionally, the lessons we learn about how we are supposed to behave and what "normal" experiences are is skewed based on what is reflected back to us about our communities, our lives, and the morality of decisions. We aren't the only audience. These negative messages are also communicated to people who do not have extensive contact with cultures different from their own and legitimize stereotypes as well as messages about how others can and should treat us. The belief that people can build across differences through meeting one another is the basis of Intergroup Contact Theory, developed in the 1950s by psychologist Gordon Allport. The idea behind Allport's hypothesis is that people, under appropriate social circumstances, can build a connection and understanding to reduce prejudice. For Real Emma, the connections with Character Emma extended way beyond their shared name and abortion story. Seeing a character with a father who had been deported for criminal charges—a conversation that is stigmatized and counter to the model immigrant narrative—was pivotal for her as someone with a parent who had been deported under similar circumstances. In a show such as *Vida*, the expansiveness of Emma's world and everyone she is in a relationship with can help audiences connect with the experiences of US Latinas, and those women themselves feel more confident in their lives.

Television and film can also further this understanding and connection on a mass scale. We all have a favorite show and that one character whose life we're invested in and follow from episode to episode. When that beloved character chooses to have an abortion, we're taken on that journey with them, empathizing with their decision-making process and in some cases seeing our own stories reflected. This is also the basis for Renee's coined phrase, "everyone loves someone who had an abortion." By reminding people of the commonality of the procedure, we're asking those who may judge people who have abortions to recognize that someone they care deeply about has made this decision and that we should pause to build understanding and center love. All of this is possible only if thoughtful abortion narratives are actually portrayed on television and in film.

* * *

Abortion has been featured on US television programs and in films for more than a century, nearly as long as film has been around. But most of the depictions then and now center on the experiences of white women of wealth. The first abortion narrative was featured in the 1916 dramatic silent film *Where Are My Children?*, about a white district attorney prosecuting a doctor who had performed illegal abortions on many in the community, including his wife. The film contained clear antiabortion themes, portraying the white women characters as flippant in their abortion decisions and abortion as unilaterally dangerous to mental and physical health and to future reproduction.

After a series of Hollywood scandals involving rape, queerness, and drug overdoses, political pressure threatened the censorship of film in the 1920s. In response, producers created a governing code of conduct, the Motion Picture Production Code, commonly known as the Hays

Code. This self-imposed censorship went into effect in the 1930s and banned depictions of sex and sexuality, sexually transmitted infections, passion, mixed-race relationships, and scenes of childbirth, among other things. Although it wasn't specifically spelled out in the Hays Code that abortion was immoral, it was implied. Films that were adapted from novels replaced abortion plots with stillbirths; other films couldn't be made because they contained illegal operations, illegitimate pregnancies, and sex. Of course, given that the code was technically voluntary, some films were released to challenge the Hays Code, but most large studios complied because they wanted their films shown in theaters, which created a long silence about abortion even as the public and political conversation was liberalizing throughout the century.

While Hollywood was stifling depictions of abortion on-screen, they certainly knew their starlets and leading men were having abortions off-screen. White actresses of the golden era have told stories about the abortions they had to preserve their careers, bodies, and relationships, both by choice and at the behest of studio executives who put pregnancy clauses in their contracts. Pregnant bombshells and mothers could not sell films or fantasies to men with money. The arranged abortions of white actresses such as Joan Crawford, Bette Davis, Ava Gardner, Lana Turner, and Judy Garland have all been detailed in their memoirs, bi- ographies, and interviews. Tallulah Bankhead had "abortions like other women got permanent waves," according to her biographer. We know this was true for the few actresses of color of the time as well. For de- cades, Rita Moreno has detailed the abortion she had while dating Marlon Brando. In her 2011 book, *Rita Moreno: A Memoir*, the Oscar-winning actress wrote that Brando found a doctor through friends who could per- form the illegal procedure for $500. Rita recalls in her memoir that the doctor didn't know how to provide abortions, thus he only "interrupted [her] pregnancy," and she began to bleed out and was rushed to the hos- pital by Brando. Although many actresses of the time didn't share their stories for fear of the stigma, Moreno still shares her story to emphasize the importance of safe access to abortion for all today.

Studio executives clearly weren't opposed to abortion when it per- sonally and financially benefited their companies but were unwilling to influence the national conversation or tell, in their films, the real stories of why people, including their actors, needed abortions or the risks they took to have illegal abortions.

Studios and well-known white actors began to challenge the Hays Code in the late 1950s, which eventually led to the Code falling out of favor by the late 1960s. Eventually, abortion was shown to audiences and posited a political perspective, but that didn't mean audiences—and more important, advertisers—were ready, as was the case for *The Defenders* and *Maude*. In 1962, *The Defenders*, a series about father and son attorneys debating current-era legal issues, aired an episode featuring a white abortion provider on trial. The episode elevated the case for legalizing abortion and the reasons white women of the era had abortions. In response, the original three sponsors of the show pulled their support, while a Catholic magazine encouraged readers to oppose new sponsors. Similarly, in 1972, the comedy *Maude* aired its infamous two-part abortion episode, "Maude's Dilemma," about Maude (Bea Arthur), an independent, liberal, forty-seven-year-old white grandmother choosing to have an abortion with her fourth husband, who did not want to have a child. The episode clearly depicted Maude's decision process, but after the show aired conservative groups condemned the depiction as a "convenience abortion" and organized campaigns against it. Nearly forty CBS stations canceled or moved the episodes, and advertisers fled, although the show's creator, Norman Lear, remained steadfast behind the series and continued to insert nuanced narratives in its scripts. The reaction to the *Maude* episodes taught studios that not only are abortion episodes subject to sustained backlash, but they also lose revenue. To this day, studio executives—who, according to a University of California, Los Angeles Hollywood Diversity Report, tend to be more than 90 percent white and 60 percent male—allow their drive for profits and conservative perceptions to override the creative decisions of writers, showrunners, and actors, and suppress narratives that could correct misinformation on-screen and in policy.

As US abortion laws became liberalized, television and film responded by including the abortion conversation sparingly but focusing on narratives that depicted abortion as a dangerous and immoral decision, a debate between pro-choice and antiabortion factions, an issue to be investigated by police, or a choice a white character considers before experiencing a miscarriage or choosing to continue the pregnancy. The stories perpetuated the idea that abortion is dangerous and something that should be secret or subject to prosecution, whether warranted or not. Although the public overwhelmingly supported abortion as a legal right, on-screen depictions elevated the debate over the morality of abortion in an outsize way. Police procedurals featured clinic bombings and gave way to characters discussing their perspectives on abortion. Since its inception in the 1990s, for example, *Law & Order* and all of its spin-offs have used abortion as a plot device to demonstrate the moral differences between detectives such as Benson and Stabler on *Law & Order: SVU*, as a justification for the victims' murders, and to signal the guilt of suspects. Overall, abortion depictions were generally reductive, stigmatizing, and inaccurate, and, most important, they underrepresented the majority of people who have abortions: people of color.

* * *

Do you remember the first time you saw a character having an abortion on television? What about a character of color? Although it's becoming more commonplace today, thinking about the first depiction you saw might be kind of challenging. Most of the people we interviewed for this book could not recall the first time they saw a character of color having an abortion, and more than half couldn't remember seeing any depiction with a character of color. Like most of the people we asked, Regina remembers Penny, Johnny's white dance partner in *Dirty Dancing* (1987), who nearly died from an unsafe illegal abortion.

The first depiction Renee remembers was in *For Colored Girls* (2010), Tyler Perry's film adaptation of Ntozake Shange's 1976 choreopoem. In the film, Tessa Thompson plays Nyla Adrose / Lady in Purple, a teen who becomes pregnant, and in keeping it a secret from her mother (Whoopi Goldberg), turns to her jealous sister Tangie Adrose / Lady in Orange (Thandiwe Newton) who sends her to Rose / Lady in Pink (Macy Gray), a known unsafe provider in their neighborhood. Nyla ends up in the hospital with complications but is supported by her caseworker Kelly (Kerry Washington). The depiction is . . . complicated. Although Renee identified with the pressures Nyla was facing and her desire to attend college, the portrayal of Rose as a mean, cigarette-smoking drunk using dirty tools is enough to make anyone's skin crawl. The procedure is dangerous, and Nyla becomes sick and recovers in the hospital. What is shown was a true abortion experience for some women of color, particularly before legalization, but it was a far stretch from the story the Lady in Blue tells in Shange's poem "abortion cycle #1." We recognize that the story needed to be expanded for a feature film, but the needless violence of the film narrative traded on antiabortion tropes punishing Black women for their pregnancy decisions. Rather than focusing on the shame and isolation that's featured in Shange's original choreopoem, the seediness of Rose's behavior and despicable home clinic took precedence, which was particularly inaccurate and stigmatizing for the modern setting of the adaptation. Although Renee knew this wasn't an accurate representation of her own abortion, she questioned whether this was what other Black women were experiencing. She thought maybe that was the norm. Still, she felt less alone to see someone on television who looked and sounded like her having an abortion. At the time, seeing that was rare. But the messages Regina and Renee both received from the first depictions they saw were the same: abortion is dangerous and done in secret.

According to the Abortion Onscreen project at Advancing New Standards in Reproductive Health at the University of California, San Francisco, which studies depictions of abortion on US television and film throughout the last century, there have been more than six hundred depictions of abortion, with most of them airing after the dissipation of the Hays Code. That number may surprise you as high, and it is quite a few, but the reality is that most of them weren't great. Quite a lot were harmful and full of misinformation.

By our own calculations, there have been over one hundred depictions that include a character of color obtaining or disclosing an abortion. That's a lot—especially if it's hard to think of any that you've seen—but it's barely 20 percent of the depictions thus far. Pretty shabby when you realize that nearly 70 percent of abortion patients are people of color.

In two studies examining the demographics of characters having abortions on US television from 2005 to 2014, and from 2015 to 2019, researchers found that the characters considering and having abortions were mostly white, young, wealthy, in committed relationships, and not parenting any children—characteristics that are almost exactly opposite to those of people who have abortions.

ONSCREEN CHARACTERS WHO HAVE ABORTIONS (2005–2014)	ONSCREEN CHARACTERS WHO HAVE ABORTIONS (2015–2019)	REAL-LIFE PEOPLE WHO HAVE ABORTIONS (GUTTMACHER, 2016, 2023)
88% white	66% white	30.2% white More than 60% people of color: 33.4% Black 26.1% Latinx 3.6% Asian, Pacific Islander 6.7% other races and ethnicities
33% are teens	22% are teens	60% are in their 20s
83% are not parenting	87% are parenting	59% are already parenting
80% are depicted as upper- or middle-class	59% are depicted as upper- or middle-class	73% are living under 200% of the federal poverty level
58% did not experience a barrier	67% did not experience a barrier	A majority experienced one or more financial, logistical, and/or legal barriers to care
Most are in-clinic procedural depictions	Most are in-clinic procedural depictions	63% of abortions are via medication

The majority of people who have abortions in real life are in their twenties (60.4 percent) and parenting at least one child—but a third are parenting two or more children. Most are living around or below the federal poverty level; thus, they're struggling to afford their abortions, as well as basic needs such as housing, food, clothing, and more. The financial, logistical, legal, and cultural barriers that are commonplace for those of us having abortions in the real world are virtually nonexistent on-screen.

Of course, much of the minutiae of life is left off the silver screen, especially when it comes to daily tasks such as paying for things. Pick any medical show on television: How often do the patients get a call from their insurance company denying the expensive tests the doctors order? Do we ever see someone settling a co-pay in the doctor's office? Nope. It (arguably) would be boring television, wouldn't further the plot in a substantive way, and would critique the profit-based insurance system that thrives on refusing coverage and saddling patients with uncurable medical debt, thus encouraging audiences to question the role of capitalism in health care. *Whew.*

But we also believe the lack of these depictions robs us of the reality of life. When characters aren't experiencing the challenges of everyday life, there's no depiction of the trade-offs people have to make to survive. There's no depiction of what it's like for an undocumented person to cross the country on a bus or train because the person seeking an abortion doesn't have an ID to board a plane. There's no depiction of the chaos at the hotel front desk because the $250 hold fee is $200 more than the abortion traveler has in their bank account until the next payday. And with all of those challenges, there are few depictions of the hijinks that take place during the journey. Most important, there's no depiction of how friends show up for one another when they're in need, whether by paying for a friend's abortion, working together to distract the pharmacist as one friend steals the box of pregnancy tests, or selling plates of food to pay for the procedure itself. The lack of depiction of class in general, but particularly in abortion narratives, leaves us without beautiful stories about how we show up for one another in a pinch.

As it stands, it's rare to see low-income people's lives on television. Generally, most television shows illustrate poverty as a destitute circumstance of an individual's own making in depictions of background characters, such as houseless people, to advance a main or recurring character's narrative. That poverty is often coded: the characters may be Black, Brown, or white and southern; or a character's weight or hygiene or the cleanliness of their home may be used to denote poverty. It's rarer to see the reality of poverty, in families whose access to food, income, or housing fluctuates week to week and who have to use creative solutions to navigate any situation—such as having an abortion—that could be rendered logistically simpler just by having health insurance or enough money in their bank account.

But those aspects of our lives are not considered interesting enough for audience consumption. In a 2022 interview with *Rolling Stone*, the creator of the hit series *Abbott Elementary*, Quinta Brunson, shared that she received pushback on an earlier project from a CBS executive when she wanted a character to ride the bus. "They thought that looked too poor to be enjoyable," she explained. The executives who green-light the shows we watch generally want to see solidly middle-class or wealthier people who are happy and have all the money they need to live their lives, not the "not rich" people struggling in the lives created by systemic inequality. It's assumed that every aspect of daily life for low-income people is boring, hard, and void of joy—thus, not entertaining.

Similarly, a critique we hear of abortion stories is that storytellers "celebrate" their abortions because they talk about aspects of their abortions beyond the oppressive experience. Abortion storytellers often say they feel pressure to leave out the joyful parts of their abortion experiences for fear of being judged for not taking the decision seriously. But censorship keeps our stories from being realistic. All aspects of our lives have a mix of the good, the bad, the ugly, and the downright ridiculous. All of it must be shown, because it's our human experience.

A 2023 report by New America's Better Life Lab and the Abortion Onscreen project found that only 4.8 percent of television shows and 5.5 percent of movies with abortion plotlines included a portrayal of financial circumstances, childcare or family responsibilities, workplace concerns, or health issues as part of the abortion decision. Meanwhile, in the real world, a person's bank account and need to care for their own children or other family members are among the top issues factoring in an abortion decision.

Dirty Dancing is usually the first film that comes to mind when thinking of abortion on-screen; Penny, a white resort entertainment dancer, receives an unsafe abortion from a low-cost provider in 1963. Over the past decade, US audiences have started to see more depictions of characters without steady access to money navigating financial abortion barriers: Sage in *Grandma* (2015), Fiona in *Shameless* (2016), Deb in *Little Woods* (2019), Autumn in *Never Rarely Sometimes Always* (2020), Veronica in *Unpregnant* (2020), and Ofwarren/Janine in *Handmaid's Tale* (2021). In *Grandma*, *Little Woods*, *Never Rarely Sometimes Always*, and *Unpregnant*, the characters—mostly family members—embark on a road trip to the nearest abortion clinic that can care for them. Money, distance, and even age are critical barriers along the journey. The depictions sometimes show how characters access abortions through government systems. During the five-episode abortion arc, *Shameless* shows its characters visiting the welfare office to receive financial support for their pregnancies, discussing how poverty forces abortion decisions, and considering what it would mean to parent in poverty. In *Little Woods*, two adopted sisters, one who is white and pregnant while raising a young child and another who is biracial and facing foreclosure, travel from rural North Dakota to Canada to obtain an abortion with a fake national health card, making the procedure cost-free. These depictions are significant and were game-changing when they debuted; they aired the truth that we already knew: just because abortion is legal doesn't mean it is literally or physically accessible to those who need it. *Little Woods* director Nia DaCosta, who is Black, told Renee in an interview for a 2019 *Washington Post* article, "I am much more interested in the reality that, no matter what laws are in place, abortions will happen. Once someone decides and realizes that there are so many barriers to access, what will they do?"

Besides the lack of money as a barrier to abortion, these depictions, like most abortion story arcs, all have one thing in common: all the characters are white. And largely, the depictions don't explore how the characters' experiences of poverty or lack of access to cash are impacted by their whiteness. In fact, when Renee and her colleagues looked at how race intersected with abortion stories on-screen, within the data set, no white characters' race factored into their abortion experience. Whiteness was so much the default that it did not exist.

Given that stories about the majority of people who have abortions—

people of color—are few and far between, the pressure is on the depictions that do exist to do all and be all, thus creating little space for the details of our lives that make depictions feel real. They start to resemble a caricature or stereotype rather than a picture of a real person's experience. That's what *For Colored Girls* felt like for us. Although it was a breath of fresh air to see a Black woman have an abortion, the overemphasis on danger and unsanitary conditions conveyed a message of immorality and isolation, rather than the familial commonality the story could have highlighted.

The first film depiction of white women having abortions debuted in 1916, but it wasn't until the late 1980s that the first characters of color were shown considering abortion as an option, although as background characters their narratives and perspectives were secondary and supplemental to the main characters' discussions. In "The Clinic," a 1985 episode of *Cagney & Lacey*, an abortion clinic is firebombed, killing a pregnant patient and igniting a debate over whether the fetal death is an additional murder. Throughout the episode, New York City detectives Christine Cagney and a five-months-pregnant Mary Beth Lacey debate with other characters their own opinions about abortion, including their moral limits as pro-choice women. At one point, they are approached by Mrs. Herrera, a Latina woman outside of the clinic who is seeking an abortion but is scared of the protesters and requests a police escort to her appointment.

Although the audience doesn't see Mrs. Herrera receive an abortion, during her ride with the detectives they listen to her reasons for the abortion: her husband is on disability, she fears being unable to work and wants to attend business school, and her desire is not to be on welfare, like her (presumably Latina) friends who "watch TV all day." Like the characters of color that would come after Mrs. Herrera, this character holds the responsibility of not just giving the audience a glimpse into the lives of Latinas who have abortions but also representing a respectable depiction of her people, all in a few script lines. Her character justifies the economic hardship of raising a child and financial challenges facing disabled people in the United States, but rather than addressing the systemic issues at play, like few humane social safety nets for low-income families and people with disabilities, her narrative points to her desire to work and not use public assistance. As Celeste Michelle Condit argues in *Decoding Abortion Rhetoric*, Mrs. Herrera demonstrates to the audience that white people and police are a moral authority by pleading her case to the detectives, and their position on the issue is the correct moral authority. After dropping Mrs. Herrera off, the detectives continue their abortion discussion, with both agreeing that Mrs. Herrera has the right to an abortion but with Cagney citing her Catholic upbringing as the source of her discomfort with abortions that aren't a result of rape or "severely damaged children." Aside from her name and accented tongue, the audience isn't invited to learn anything about Mrs. Herrera's life as a Latina American and her life decisions become fodder for debate by the white characters. She's a surface-level character but sets the tone for how women of color would be depicted for another two decades.

Similarly, in the 1988 "Whose Choice Is It Anyway" episode of *21 Jump Street*, Officer Judy Hoffs, portrayed by a young Holly Robinson Peete, goes undercover as an undecided pregnant teen at a high school while she investigates protests and vandalism at the campus birth control clinic, which offers abortion counseling. Judy befriends Rebecca, a white student who is pregnant and considering her options. Together they attend group counseling at the clinic and an adoption agency, where the agency makes it clear that adoptive parents want to meet only with Rebecca, not Judy, because she's Black. Much of the episode focuses on the moral debate of abortion, centering the white antiabortion activists' views and violence, the rising anger of Rebecca's boyfriend, and Rebecca's angst about her decision. While in the police station, a crying Judy discloses to Officer Harry Truman Ioki, who is Asian, that she became pregnant in high school and had an abortion. After Rebecca's boyfriend bombs the clinic, causing her to have a miscarriage, Judy visits Rebecca in the hospital, and the two talk about the lost pregnancy and Judy's "decision." "Do you regret the abortion?" Rebecca asks Judy, who pauses for a moment. "I regret getting pregnant. And boy, do I regret not sharing it with my mom," Judy tells her. "I can't say that I did the wrong thing. I can't say that. Because I love my life. I'm happy. And I'm really proud of what I've been able to accomplish." The episode ends with Judy calling her mother and beginning to tell her about the abortion.

Although the episode is very dated and spends more time focusing on antiabortion violence and the morality of abortion rather than the characters' decisions, it was the first depiction of a Black woman disclosing an abortion and talking to other characters of color about it, and it was one of few depictions showing characters who are considering or are having an abortion discussing their decisions with other people who have had abortions; this remains rare in depictions today. The depiction focuses on support and showing up for someone, no matter what their decision is. But it falls into the same traps that have plagued abortion on-screen depictions for decades: the waffling about the decision takes center stage; the debate is framed as "both sides have good points," even though one side is depicted as overtly violent; and whiteness is centered. Even though Judy is a main character disclosing her abortion, she is not shown having the abortion, and her story serves to elevate Rebecca's narrative. It isn't until the very end of the episode that Judy's feelings about her abortion are explored, and then they are explored only for a few moments, when she is talking with Officer Ioki, who has begun sympathizing with the antiabortion terrorists, and when she is helping Rebecca come to terms with her loss of agency. Additionally, throughout the episode, when Judy's Blackness is raised in connection with her pregnancy, it's thrown at her by white characters who reference stereotypes of single Black women raising fatherless children or insinuate that she is a negative influence on Rebecca because Judy is also pregnant, rather than exploring how she as a pregnant person—or a police officer pretending to be pregnant—might feel. Judy is the focus of the rage of several white male characters, including an antiabortion organizer who chases after her, shouting and tripping her, but the visible racial dynamics are never explored.

For the next two decades, abortion depictions featuring characters of color were sparse. Black or Latina characters had or disclosed abortions on shows such as *All My Children* (1995), *The Practice* (1997), *The L Word* (2007), and *South Park* (2008) and films including *Swing Vote* (1999), *Baby Boy* (2001), and *Coach Carter* (2005). The story arcs generally focus on the morality of the procedure, uncertainty about abortion decisions, and legal arguments and abortion clinic violence. Characters having abortions and those they spoke to are used to spread stigma about abortion and as reminders of what the pregnant person should have done—for example, use a condom or abstain from sex. These characters are pressured into considering parenting by partners and are shown navigating the mental and emotional challenges of their experiences in isolation. It was during this time that the first depictions of Asian characters having abortions appeared, in the 2004 horror film *Dumplings*, the Canadian teen television show *Degrassi: The Next Generation* (2004), and *Boston Legal* (2008).

In a double episode of *Degrassi: The Next Generation*, fourteen-year-old Manny Santos has a bout of morning sickness and realizes she's missed her period. Manny visits Spike, the white mother of Manny's friend Emma who became pregnant with Emma at fourteen years old and continued her pregnancy during an earlier iteration of the show from the late 1980s. Manny, who is Filipina, worries to Spike that her parents will send her to a convent in the Philippines, like her cousin when she became pregnant. At first, Manny and her boyfriend, Craig, who is white, consider the idea of parenting—especially after their pregnancy is outed to the entire school—but after babysitting Spike's infant with Emma, Manny realizes she is not ready for parenthood. She musters the courage to tell her mother that she wants an abortion. "I don't care what you say. I don't care what Dad says. And I am not going away like Mary had to," Manny says defiantly. "I've thought about it, I can't go away. I can't be pregnant. I can't be a mom yet." Her mother is concerned, but they cry together and she holds Manny. In a later scene, Manny tells Emma that her mother was supportive of her decision to have an abortion, but Emma becomes furious, drawing parallels between her own life and Manny's pregnancy. As in the *21 Jump Street* episode, Manny defends her abortion decision from an angry boyfriend, again highlighting white male violence in opposition to her decision, and she needs to be rescued from his anger by Emma, who changes her mind about Manny's choice. The episode ends with Manny and her mother at the clinic discussing the safety of the procedure and common after-abortion feelings.

As in other episodes featuring characters of color, Manny's race is raised only as a problem in the context of her pregnancy, rather than a source of support or part of her experience. The negative reactions of her white boyfriend and friends are belabored, while the physical and emotional support from her Filipina mother is underexplored and even cut away from in one scene. This leaves viewers with little opportunity to reflect on what it could look like to care for someone who wants an abortion, showing few models of support within families or a girl of color experiencing unconditional love at a time when she is feeling rejected by peers. What is centered instead is the anger, rejection, and isolation from white characters and society.

Similarly, in a 2008 episode of the legal dramedy *Boston Legal*, fifteen-year-old Chinese immigrant Kim Wang Shu asks the lawyers to represent her in obtaining a judicial bypass because her father is dead and her mother won't consent to the abortion. Almost immediately, the conversation moves from Kim talking about her desire for an abortion to the two white male lawyers debating whether Kim would "burn in Hell" for the abortion and who would watch a show about abortion. "I can hear them changing the channel," one lawyer quips. He proceeds to make snide comments about traveling for abortions because "God doesn't care about what happens in Mexico because it's kind of a pre-Hell." While one lawyer worries about how restrictive abortion laws in Massachusetts are becoming despite the "almost always granted" judicial bypasses, the other characters debate their personal feelings about abortion, with lawyers and Kim's mother all stressing what Justice Kennedy opined in the *Gonzales v. Carhart* Supreme Court decision: everyone comes to regret their abortion decision. Later, two white lawyers argue about Kim's motivations for her abortion: one opines that Kim's life seems "too struggle-free," while another says her decision might be based on sex selection, due to China's one-child policy and preference for male children, and later interrogates her about this possibility. In court, Kim's own lawyer opines about sex-selective abortions in China and India and the "holocaust of women," while Kim is portrayed as a conniving teen. Although Kim is granted the judicial bypass, the audience never finds out whether she has her abortion. Very little screen time is focused on Kim's actual perspective, her procedure, or her relationship with her mother; in fact, Kim and her mother barely exchange two sentences. Everyone talks around Kim about the legality and morality of abortion and Chinese culture as viewed through a white perspective, while Kim herself is reduced to spreading talking points against teen pregnancy, parenthood while on welfare, and the dead-end future of continuing an unplanned pregnancy.

These depictions constitute narratives of the time: characters using "my body, my choice" tropes and parroting movement language of the time to defend the right to an abortion; overdramatized conflicts between men wanting fatherhood, even violently, and women wanting to end the pregnancy and the relationship; and characters navigating barriers to their abortions in the form of interpersonal relationships, rather than the actual financial, logistical, and legal barriers that existed when the episodes or films aired. The depictions use racism to further the morality of white people's antiabortion positions, spreading propaganda and xenophobic oversimplifications of cultures to position the lives of white people in the United States as superior, all while shaming people of color for wanting abortions.

Audiences see that abortion decisions are always met with opposition, even from characters who may later be supportive. Although depicting that journey is important, the overall message is that rejecting people who want and have abortions is the norm. This is even more challenging for characters of color, who have few or no conversations with other people of color and thus are not shown as deserving of love and care. They have to wade through the anger of unsupportive white antiabortion characters with little recognition that race is part of the experience.

The complicated part of the depiction of characters of color on-screen, particularly those that exist in predominantly white fictional communities, is that their race is either hyperemphasized through stereotypes or deemphasized, creating a regressive color-blind world. Both approaches are unrealistic portrayals of our lives, making the abortion depictions fall flat. The stereotypes may spotlight negative attributes about a community of color, such as the use of welfare benefits, the prevalence of fatherless homes, and sending pregnant teens to another country, which serves to build on what scholar Patricia Hill Collins calls "controlling images." It's why a certain type of person comes to mind when someone says "welfare queen" or "jezebel"; those ideas are spread throughout media so that they become the dominant images, coded by race, and people become resistant to the facts and figures of who actually obtains welfare benefits or what a sexually liberated person looks like in the real world. When those messages come from characters of color themselves, they become more legitimized, despite the reality that they may be racist concepts from the imaginations of white creators.

On the flip side, the shows can also deemphasize a character's race to the point that it is not a factor in the narrative. As researchers Stephanie Gomez and Megan McFarlane wrote, the concept is called "refraction." It's when a character's race and gender are depoliticized, but the depiction also conceals the depoliticization, which allows the audience to forget there's an entire system that impacts a character's race or gender identity in real life. The characters simply aren't burdened by anti-Blackness, racism, sexism, or even economic inequities. They just exist. As Renee and her colleagues wrote in a 2020 paper for *Feminist Media Studies*, this "results in alternatingly progressive and regressive narratives that 'refract' characters' abortion stories through ongoing negotiation with familiar tropes around race."

We think that might be one reason few people can recall the first time they saw a character of color on television having an abortion: the character's experience as a person of color was refracted during her abortion. It's as if the writers of the depictions could only imagine the characters experiencing one aspect of their identity at a time, and their conflict with other characters who are opposed to abortion took precedence over their own thoughts, feelings, and beliefs as women of color having abortions.

Renee experienced this firsthand when she was sought after by a television streaming service to participate in a documentary episode discussing the importance of depictions of characters of color having abortions on television and film. The show had previously aired an episode featuring an iconic white feminist activist paired with a white abortion activist working toward legalization in her European country. For months, Renee worked on her script, and she spent several days filming the scenes complete with sets and hired extras. But a few months after filming, she was informed that her segment wouldn't make the final cut because the topic of abortion wasn't suited for a global audience (and, according to the showrunner, Renee said the word "abortion" too many times.) It seemed to Renee that her point in the episode was being proved before her very eyes: even when the conversation about abortion representation was approved for television, the inclusion of race and class rendered the conversation unairable.

When we interviewed Hollywood writers who worked on scripts with characters of color who had abortions, few could tell us about a depiction they'd seen with a character of color. We wondered whether this was because many depictions avoid using the word "abortion," so they hadn't recognized an abortion in a depiction they had seen. But we also think it might be due to the scarcity of depictions and fleeting disclosures and the downplaying of the characters' race in relation to their abortions—not to mention that the depictions weren't great. It's unlikely that people would commit a milquetoast representation to memory.

But when did we start to see more characters of color making "the decision" on our screens? One could argue it was once Shonda Rhimes arrived on set.

* * *

In 2005, Dr. Cristina Yang (Sandra Oh) sat with Dr. Meredith Grey (Ellen Pompeo) at their favorite bar. Cristina explained to Meredith, a fellow surgical resident, that the abortion clinic paperwork required her to declare an emergency contact person. "You're my person," Cristina says, solidifying the iconic phrase every *Grey's Anatomy* fan mimics to declare their love for their best friend. Despite the popularity of the statement, few people remember that it stems from an abortion arc that was never completed during the show's second season. Cristina, a Korean American doctor, became pregnant by Dr. Preston Burke, her Black boyfriend and fellow doctor; however, the wanted abortion ended in an ectopic pregnancy during the episode. Why was the abortion storyline aborted? The reason was fear of how the audience would react, Shonda Rhimes told *HuffPost* in a 2022 interview. ABC executives did not object, she explained, but "they shared data and told me what they fear the audience reaction would be. . . . I felt insecure about making that controversial choice for my character when I was so new to the game." Once Rhimes had more episodes of *Grey's Anatomy*—and a whole slew of other shows—under her belt, she was able to redo Cristina's abortion arc for real in 2011.

At the end of the seventh season, Cristina realizes she's pregnant by her then-husband Dr. Owen Hunt, who is white and initially won't give his full support for the decision. Recognizing that Cristina needs Owen to give consent before she can go through with the procedure, in season 8, Meredith steps in to convince Owen to put his narcissism aside and be Cristina's person. "By Season 8, I was sure of myself as a showrunner," Rhimes told *HuffPost*. "I was sure of my place in the TV landscape. I'd told complex stories about women's health through Addison on both *Grey's* and *Private Practice*. . . . Both Cristina and I had grown. I was sure that abortion was the right choice for Cristina and for the show at that point. After all, we were a medical show and this is a medical procedure." Later in the show, as Cristina and Owen's marriage falls apart, they argue over a surgical decision, and Owen throws the abortion back in her face, shouting at a child's birthday party, "You killed our baby! You don't ever forget that!" Thankfully, Cristina left his ass.

Rhimes's other iconic abortion depiction came during the 2015 midseason finale of *Scandal*. In the previous season, audiences watched political fixer Olivia Pope (Kerry Washington) hold the hand of a naval officer and rape survivor as she obtained an abortion, so audiences already knew she was empathetic toward people who have abortions. The fifth season episode featured Senator Mellie Grant, the white ex-wife of President Fitzgerald Grant, holding a filibuster in support of funding for Planned Parenthood, as Olivia runs around the Capitol handling things per usual. The audience didn't know Olivia was pregnant until the doctor was shown providing her with a D&C in a large operating room, avoiding the common waffling decision-making arc and taking the audience straight to her pregnancy notification and abortion decision all in the same moment. Because the show was so beloved, audiences knew immediately why Olivia was having an abortion, so no explanation was needed; however, the political talking points were filled throughout the episode by Senator Grant's monologue on the importance of the government funding reproductive health care.

As iconic as these representations were, scholars and television critics have critiqued the shows for their choice to "reinforc[e] a colorblind, post-race society" through color-blind casting and not writing race into the script. Race is not an explicit part of Cristina's and Olivia's abortions, nor is race mentioned in the case of the naval officer Olivia supports. (Similarly, in the animated comedy BoJack Horseman, the Asian character having an abortion, Diana Nguyen, is actually voiced by a white actress, and race is not part of her abortion arc.) Although some argue that it is a progressive move to increase the diversity of actors of color on-screen— and it certainly is—what can be lost is the narratives that come with living as a person of color in the real world.

Yes, there is the subtle racism that we experience on a day-to-day basis—but there are also the joys, traditions, and celebrations from our cultures that feel like home and comfort and that make our families unique. The loss of these narratives becomes heightened during abortion depictions because, historically, depictions of characters of color tend to shed their racialized experiences so that their abortion experience can come to the forefront—but that's not the reality of our lives. Intersectionality, legal scholar Kimberlé Crenshaw's theory that describes how our identities overlap and intersect with multiple systems of oppression, recognizes that we can experience all of these identities at the same time; we long for an exploration of all of them at once in every depiction.

Even though race was overlooked, Cristina's and Olivia's procedures were cultural resets for abortion on television. With Cristina as the first Asian American character to have an abortion on US television and Olivia's abortion as the first procedure depicted on-screen, and with both characters portrayed as having clarity about their abortion decisions, the episodes were welcome representations for women of color who longed to see themselves shown with agency over their futures. Besides, their certainty matched the high level of certainty experienced by real-life people who have abortions. Most characters choosing abortion—whether they were of color or white—were not the main characters, so audiences couldn't always connect with a character's decision-making process over multiple episodes, or even seasons, before, during, and after "The Abortion Episode." That's the experience that TV writers Renee has worked with have expressed wanting to portray; more screen time allows them to make the abortion decision true to the character so the audience can see and understand the decision as it's coming, rather than it being a shocking moment that makes the audience uncomfortable or confused. We think this is helpful for changes in the cultural conversation about abortion over time, too. Think about it this way: you're more likely to shift your opinion if you know a close friend involved in a situation such as needing an abortion, because you know the person and their situation, and you're willing to empathize with what they're going through. Comedian, actress, and writer Sarah Jones, who identifies as both Black and multiracial and had an abortion in her twenties but didn't feel able to talk about it publicly until her thirties, remembers the *Being Mary Jane* abortion disclosures as a moment that "sent these shockwaves" through the Black community. The show gave people a starting point for a conversation that was different from what she'd seen before. "Having conversations about abortion in a way that wasn't about a tragedy or a problem or a misstep and now needed to repent. It was just never a choice of self-determination about what's good for me in my life." But, as Sarah rightfully points out, few white audiences watched the "Black" show, so the conversation was not as widely discussed outside of the community. We've seen this happen repeatedly; abortion depictions with white characters get heralded as "firsts," such as *Shrill* (2019) being labeled the first to depict a fat character having an abortion, when *Empire*'s Becky (Gabourey Sidibe) had an abortion in 2018. Of course these depictions are not nearly enough, but the overlooking of Black and Brown shows as conduits for cultural conversation change on abortion is a problem.

No matter what shows we watch, we love our TV shows, and our main characters are like our friends, so we're willing to extend empathy to better understand why they might choose an abortion, even if we might initially think they should make a different decision. The complexity and well-written characters speak to our lived experiences and allow us to connect with the screen and the abortion experience.

* * *

We wrote this book as writers and actors were both on strike for much of 2023. Some of their biggest demands centered around the use of artificial intelligence on scripts and the use of actors' likenesses, as well as a lack of residual pay with streaming services, but another was the size and diversity of writers' rooms, the advancement of writers, and the ability for writers to be part of the production process to ensure their creativity on the page makes it to the screen. (Personally, we're not confident that artificial intelligence could write a good abortion script.) When we spoke with several Hollywood writers during this time, they shared that despite abortion being a political winner in every election, networks were still nervous about including abortion in shows. What's critical to the ability to air these abortion stories is the desire of those in power to use their power to tell our stories.

According to a study by the Center for the Study of Women in Television and Film at San Diego State University, only 14 percent of the top 100 films in 2023 had female filmmakers making decisions, and that was an increase over 11 percent in 2022. The study also found that women made up only a quarter of producers and 17 percent of film writers. In television, things are not much better. Although women make up 45 percent of television series writers, women of color are only 21 percent, queer writers make up 12 percent, and disabled writers are only 2 percent, according to a 2022 equity and inclusion report by the Writers Guild of America. When it comes to the role of showrunner (the top boss of each show), nearly 60 percent are white men. Not only are these groups of writers, showrunners, and creatives underrepresented in the field, but they aren't in positions of power to choose which scripts get picked up, green-lighted, put into production, and aired—and which shows will be aired long enough to make it to the "Very Special Abortion

Episode™." One 2023 journal article interviewing television creators found their efforts to include an abortion storyline would be immediately shut down for being too political and because of a fear of boycotts and loss of advertisers, as well as general ignorance about the topic on the part of a show's leadership. Despite abortion's popularity and prevalence in the United States and globally, the prevailing belief is that it doesn't make good television—especially among characters of color. Industry executives are still remembering advertisers' reaction to *Maude* rather than focusing on re-creating the audience's reception of Olivia Pope's abortion. As a writer, Sarah said she has been afraid to include abortion because of the reaction. "I'm mixed race. I have Latine family, Jewish family. I'm talking about all of these identities and it feels like if I put the abortion on it's a hat on a hat on a sombrero, and a lot of that [shame] was in me. I had so much internalized shame around my abortion."

Erika Green Swafford sought to portray complicated family dynamics in a similar way with her 2019 abortion plotline on the medical drama *New Amsterdam*. After a van accident, a young Black woman with Down syndrome, Chante, presents at a hospital ER with her church members and learns she is nine weeks pregnant. Although Chante is clear that she wants an abortion, her aunt who is her guardian refuses to consent and is concerned that the white doctors might be pressuring Chante, despite Chante's clear desire for an abortion. Erika wanted to show a disabled Black character who is sexually liberated and autonomous making a decision for herself that was solely about her autonomy rather than her economic ability to raise a child. Erika was able to do that with the support of NBC, she said, but the biggest challenge was finding an actor to portray the character and maintain the intersectionality they wanted to highlight. And the thoughtfulness to identity shows in the episode.

The truth is, abortion episodes do make good television; in fact, abortion makes for great television, allowing characters to connect in a way that highlights their values, vulnerabilities, and care for one another as they make a huge decision that may or may not add another "character" to the show.

Although writers' rooms are still very white, they are changing. We believe that is why in the past decade, abortion stories have become more realistic and part of a character's backstory, in addition to the pregnancy decision the character is making on-screen. Shows like *Being Mary Jane* (2015) and *Insecure* (2018, 2020) give characters the space to disclose their past abortions, allowing the audience to imagine what they've been through and how it is impacting their current pregnancy decisions, just as in real life. Another common thread we found from our interviews was that the shows with the more realistic depictions tended to have writers of color who had had abortions in the writers' room, drawing from their own experiences for the characters, as in the *Vida* writers' room. Njeri Brown, a writer on the show *Dear White People*, told us that the abortion plotline came from the writers' own experiences. "The idea birthed itself because we were talking about kids in college," she told us. "There were some people in the room who either had their own experience or knew people who made an abortion decision in college, so those two moments met."

The *Dear White People* sliding-doors style depiction in season 2 is one we appreciate because of its complexity and centering of Blackness, unconditional support, pleasure, and the exploration of Coco's options. Coco Conners is a Black college student at the fictional Ivy League college Winchester University and has high ambitions for herself. She becomes pregnant as a result of hot sex and considers her options. "We crafted her as the character who had the most to lose," Brown explained. "She came from very humble beginnings, aspiring for more, very ambitious, but who also lacked a safety net. She was the best embodiment of what was true for a number of Black women in this country, and that is, life doesn't afford us a lot of room for error in our lives." The episode explores what Coco's life could be like raising her daughter, juxtaposing awkward conversations with her own mother, who is working hard to make ends meet and raise her children, with Coco's vision of joy while dropping a teenage Penelope off at Winchester to begin her own college life. Suddenly, Coco is snapped out of her dream sequence when she hears a voice calling her name. "What do you want to do?" Kelsey asks. They're in the clinic waiting on her appointment. "Right here," Coco says defiantly to the clinic worker, then walks back to the exam room with a confident, determined look on her face.

Choosing the sliding-doors style of storytelling was intentional, as the writers' room had different opinions on abortion, and that format allowed them to explore the range of Coco's emotions—a visual representation of her list of pros and cons and "the what if of it all," Brown told us. Watching the episode feels like watching people who are considering abortion, or any big decision, think about what the future would hold if they made one decision or another. In both scenarios, Coco could be happy, but in the abortion scenario, she chose herself and her future.

The depiction is also set apart from others in portraying how friends who might not fully agree with a decision can still be supportive. Kelsey, Coco's lesbian, Trinidadian roommate, whom Coco turns to for support, isn't exactly keen on the idea of the abortion but pampers Coco anyway with traditional Caribbean pregnancy rituals, including tea and a foot massage. Despite her slight preference for continuing the pregnancy—which was a purposeful inclusion, Brown told us—Kelsey's support for her friend is clear. "Well, no matter what you decide, I'm the girl who will be there for you every step of the way. No matter what." Then, while toying with Coco's wig, she asks, "Is this new?" "No, I just washed it," Coco replies, normalizing the entire conversation—abortion, wig, and all.

Of course *Dear White People* is a show about Black college students, and their Blackness is core to the show's motivations, but what is refreshing is that it coexists alongside the abortion plotline, rather than taking a back seat. "Seeing Coco being cared for by another Black woman in a space where she navigated her Blackness very differently than other Black people on the show was really heartwarming and necessary," Brown said. "In this country, women's health care is serviced and regarded without enough concern for the actual woman. Our voices are silenced, our pain is ignored, and our emotions are inconvenient. We wanted Black women through Coco to have the space to articulate their concerns, fears, and complaints without being silenced or ignored, and for Coco to show that vulnerability and to be met with support from Kelsey."

Similarly, in the comedy *Jane the Virgin*, about a twenty-three-year-old devout Latina who is accidentally artificially inseminated, Jane's mother, Xiomara, realizes she is pregnant again. Xiomara had her daughter at a young age and did not want to be pregnant again as a grandmother. The 2016 depiction alludes to the abortion happening between episodes, and instead focuses on Jane supporting her mother after her abortion, and Xiomara telling her disappointed and devout Catholic mother about the abortion. As in many depictions of Latinx characters having abortions, the conflict between abortion and Catholicism takes center stage (despite Latinx folks practicing lots of different faiths!), but in this show, the story rested on family showing unconditional love for one another across generations. The audience watches Xiomara's mother come to terms with the abortion and opens up a dialogue about what it means to put your own personal feelings aside for the people you love. It's refreshing when more depictions take a nuanced, holistic, and intersectional approach, allowing characters to exist as multidimensional beings.

This style of abortion storytelling without committing to a full procedure arc is something Lena Waithe chose for *The Chi*'s 2020 disclosure episode. Kiesha Williams, a Black teen, was pregnant as a result of being raped during a kidnapping. Her lesbian mothers encouraged her to seek an abortion and supported her in talking through her options with Black women in her life who made different decisions. "I think in society we have this idea that particularly when Black girls get pregnant, they have [the baby]. Period. There's no other choice," Waithe told us. "And I just really wanted to introduce something new to the narrative where this was an option if so chosen, and also wanted to lean into that choice." Waithe said she wanted to show Kiesha making an educated decision while talking to the people in her community with healthy communication, not antiabortion rhetoric, which wasn't true to the character's world. "[*The Chi* is] a part of culture, and we're in conversation with the culture."

The audience becomes a fly on the wall for Kiesha's conversations with her mother, an ex-boyfriend's mother who had her son as a teen, and a friend, Tiffany, who had both a child and an abortion. Viewers have seen Tiffany raise her child on-screen; through the conversation with Kiesha, they learn that Tiffany had an abortion off-camera. "Me and Emmett found ourselves in a situation last year, and I didn't know what I wanted to do, but ultimately I had to look at my life and decide if I wanted to bring another child into this world," Tiffany tells Kiesha. "And, uh, after a lot of soul searching, I realized that the one I got is all I could handle right now." Tiffany, Waithe said, offers Kiesha the most help in making her own pregnancy decision. "We make it very throwaway, not in a way that's like, *Oh, she doesn't care*, but she's very practical about it. Tiffany was really the one who really ultimately gave Kiesha the most clarity of a person who experienced both." Although Kiesha chooses adoption, a decision she regrets and reverses in later episodes, audiences see that she is able to consider abortion as an option while being met with love and support, and that Tiffany is a parent who chose abortion and is at peace with both of her decisions as well. "I'm not trying to preach what I believe, but rather speak to the humanity in all of us in terms of having autonomy over our lives and the kind of lives we want to lead," Waithe explained.

We told Waithe that *The Chi*'s depiction was reminiscent of the iconic abortion episodes on *Claws* (2018) and *P-Valley* (2022), and it made sense because all of the writers know each other and, like their art, are in conversation. On *Claws*, Virginia (Karrueche Tran), a biracial Black and Asian nail tech, becomes pregnant by her boyfriend, Dean, an autistic Black man. Although Dean's sister's first outburst on learning about the pregnancy—"I can't believe your mixed ass wasn't on the pill!"—focuses on Virgina's being biracial, the episode centers the anti-Blackness Virginia experiences as a result of antiabortion rhetoric. Outside of the clinic, Virginia, accompanied by her colleague Quiet Ann, wades through antiabortion protesters shouting "Unborn lives matter!" while inside the clinic she ponders whether her embryo might be the next Barack Obama or Martin Luther King Jr. At a panel on abortion on television, Renee asked Janine Sherman Barrois, the show's executive producer and writer of the episode, about that inclusion and learned that it was a nod to the real billboards Renee saw in Chicago that were placed in Black communities that read "Every 21 minutes, our next possible leader is aborted." The audience also learns that Quiet Ann's support is rooted in her own pregnancy experience; she was pregnant and forced to relinquish the baby.

On *P-Valley*, a drama about Black workers at a Mississippi strip club, one of the top dancers, Mercedes, learns that her fourteen-year-old daughter, Terricka, is fourteen weeks pregnant and fantasizing about continuing the pregnancy. It's clear to the viewer that Mercedes doesn't think Terricka should continue the pregnancy but wants her to make the decision on her own, so Mercedes drives her daughter ninety minutes to the only and nearest clinic, in Jackson. Although the show's creator, Katori Hall, said that she wanted to include the abortion storyline to reflect the *Dobbs v. Jackson Women's Health Organization* case that was making its way to the Supreme Court, by the time the episode aired, it was already a relic; the actual clinic in Jackson, Mississippi, had closed due to the overturning of *Roe v. Wade*. Much of the episode takes place in the car, with the estranged mother and daughter discussing what it takes to raise a child, talking about the reality and dangers of Black maternal health in the South, and working through their own relationship. Later, at the hotel, Mercedes is confronted by her own pregnancy experience: as a fifteen-year-old, she was pressured into carrying Terricka to term, and shortly afterward, her daughter was taken from her. Eventually Terricka decides to have an abortion, but what's beautiful about the writing in the episode is how the characters work through their own relationships and model what it looks like to listen and support someone through open communication and healing. "Mercedes, as a character, was thinking about all of the statistical things, and she was coming from a place of having been that little Brown girl before," Hall explained. "[Mercedes was] really wanting to hold space and be the mother that her mother could not be for her."

Orange Is the New Black writer Merritt Tierce felt that showing all aspects of pregnancy and parenting decisions at once was imperative for the show's 2019 self-managed abortion episode. The show depicted Daya trying to self-manage an abortion in 2013 but revisited the issue with the characters in a private immigration prison facility. Santos, an undocumented Guatemalan immigrant who speaks only K'iche, became pregnant as a result of rape by a coyote while crossing the border, and she receives abortion pills from Natalie, the warden, who is going through fertility treatments. The plot is in the backdrop of characters appearing before an immigration court, with one mother sentenced to deportation while her kids are allowed to remain in the United States. "You walk in and it's all right there," Tierce told us of visiting a California immigration prison and then writing the episode. "You just have to tell the story of what's happening. If you're a human, you can see." The complexity of a character spending her salary, earned from detaining families, on trying to have a family, while the detention center denies undocumented women both access to abortion and access to their children, highlights the inhumanity of the system.

Although early depictions showed a character choosing abortion with other options being posited as better alternatives, more modern abortion storylines position abortion alongside a variety of options that characters choose at different points in their lives for different reasons, leading to lots of different outcomes and a spectrum of emotional aftermath. These stories give the characters—and all of us—space to breathe and linger in our decisions. "The dreams of Black women are very fragile," Hall said. "We have to water Black women and we have to hold space for them to make the best decisions they can for their lives." *Ashé.*

* * *

Still, we have a long way to go. The first and so far only disclosure of a Native American character's abortion didn't appear until Tanis's abortion in *Letterkenny* (2017); the abortion happens off-screen and is conveyed in a quick exchange. It's rare to see someone pay for abortion, let alone navigate the Medicaid, Indian Health Service, Medicare, and private insurance barriers and delays. Medication abortion makes up more than half of abortions nationwide but still accounts for only a small percentage of depictions on-screen. It's rare for two characters who've had abortions to talk to each other. We haven't seen trans characters obtain abortions, and there are too few disabled or fat characters appearing on-screen at all, let alone having abortions. Few genres include abortions, and almost none include characters of color having abortions. While horror as a genre loves to use pregnancy and abortion as a plot device to debilitate or haunt a character, few horror shows or films include characters of color having abortions. Tropes about characters of color and their reasons for abortions are finally dissipating, but that doesn't necessarily mean that good depictions will erase the "controlling images" in place.

Television is still the most dangerous place to have an abortion, with overrepresentation of complications and death resulting from the procedure—or from just considering the procedure! A 2017 study of abortion depictions between 2005 and 2016 found that nearly 40 percent of characters who obtained an abortion had a complication, intervention, or negative health consequence such as hemorrhaging or a hysterectomy; this figure is astronomical compared with the 2.1 percent who experience complications in real life, with the majority of those complications being minor. On-screen characters are seven thousand times more likely to die from an abortion than in real life, where the likelihood is close to zero.

You may be thinking, *Yeah, because television and film is full of drama! Besides, it's not real, so who cares?* That might be true, but consider this: television is one of the primary ways people in the United States receive information, and it shapes how we think about ourselves and our beliefs. That's why Black psychiatrists created *Sesame Street* in the wake of the civil rights movement. In particular, television can have a significant impact on our understanding of medical knowledge. A 2018 study in the *International Journal of Adolescent Medical Health* found that increased viewing of medical television shows was associated with greater medical knowledge. Viewers assume the medical information coming from the sexy doctors is accurate, so it's important that it *is* accurate. Even a short abortion scene can be a teachable moment. In a 2021 study, researchers found that after watching an episode of *Grey's Anatomy* featuring a white mother who unsuccessfully self-manages her abortion and then receives the correct medications from a medical provider, audience knowledge of medication abortion was significantly improved. Another study, published in 2024, found that audiences who saw safe portrayals of medication abortion use had more awareness of the pills than those who hadn't seen the portrayals, and the audiences who saw depictions of safe uses of medication abortion and self-managed abortion were more likely to understand that it is safe. Accurate depictions of options such as self-managed abortion are essential to counteract the collective historical memory of dangerous pre-*Roe* abortions and the dangerous or incomplete depictions on shows such as *Orange Is the New Black, Mercy*

Street (2016), *Underground* (2017), and *Bridgerton* (2020), which give the impression that abortion is still dangerous.

Medical accuracy is also critical for people who are considering or having an abortion; watching an episode can help them prepare for their procedure or show them what safe methods they can use. In her book *No Real Choice*, sociologist Katrina Kimport found that some patients who desired abortions were ultimately unable to choose an abortion solely because they were concerned about the complications, pain, potential infertility, and adverse outcomes that could result from an abortion. Generally, the risk of such issues is very low, but with family members, television, and politicians reinforcing the stigma we see on television, the patients felt abortion simply was unchoosable.

As state and local governments ban books, prohibit the discussion of abortion in sexual education classes, and criminalize the spread of abortion methods, television becomes an increasingly essential educational medium. For decades, the absence of real abortion stories allowed fictional ones to take up space, and they created the myths that we believe. Gretchen Sisson, a scholar of abortion on television, explains it this way: When people see a massive car accident or truck explosion in a movie, they know how unlikely that scale of damage is in the real world, because they or someone they know have been in a car accident before. But when it comes to abortion, they have fewer real-life examples to compare a particular portrayal of abortion to; maybe they haven't heard an abortion story or don't know what happens during the procedure. So they take what is depicted as reality—that is, until they hear more everyday abortion stories and those become the norm, allowing people to recognize that the wildly exceptional depiction they saw is just that, an exception. The more realistic on-screen abortion stories become, the more people are educated about what abortion is and is not.

You know what it feels like to see a character on-screen who mirrors your life, from your insecurities to your joys. That feeling of seeing your experience—especially as a person of color, disabled person, immigrant, or queer person—is immeasurable. The isolation that we may feel dissolves when we find our crew in real life, and our confidence grows when we see our people and cultures celebrated on-screen.

At We Testify, We Rate Abortion Depictions Based on a Few Simple Measures

* The character having an abortion does not experience fatal outcomes as a result of the abortion.

* The abortion portrayed is medically accurate.

* The depiction uses the word "abortion."

* The storyline's tension is focused on elements other than the "will they or won't they" of the abortion decision.

* The character having the abortion reflects a minimum of two significant demographic profiles of those who have abortions and the reasons behind their decisions.

* The character having an abortion speaks with at least one other person who has had an abortion about their abortion.

Of course, depictions don't have to include every point to be thoughtful and nuanced. There are fantastic depictions that include only a handful of the criteria or even just one. But that's because they're done with care and thoughtfulness. The goal is for the abortion stories we see on-screen to reflect a myriad of aspects related to abortion experiences and to be true to reality.

Of course, on-screen representation is only an oasis in a drought of stigma, but it certainly helps when you're sitting on the couch recovering from an abortion and you know that you're not alone. For *Rewire News Group*, first cohort We Testify abortion storyteller MJ Flores, who identifies as a Mexican Iranian American woman, wrote about what it meant to her that the late *Glee* actress Naya Rivera wrote in her memoir *Sorry Not Sorry* about the abortion she had while filming the show. While recovering from her own abortion procedure, MJ binge-watched *Glee*. "During my own abortion, I didn't know anyone who had had an abortion, celebrity or otherwise," MJ wrote. "The profound stigma I felt and the resulting feelings of isolation may have been mitigated if I had known the story of even one person in my network." At the time, Naya Rivera responded that the article was "beautifully written."

Celebrities sharing abortion stories in their memoirs isn't new, but there has been a resurgence of sorts in the past decade as the national conversation has become more supportive and more everyday people are sharing their stories. When *The Choices We Made: Twenty-Five Women and Men Speak Out About Abortion* debuted in 1991, few celebrities of color who'd had abortions had shared their stories. "I talked to nobody. I panicked. I sat in hot baths. I drank these strange concoctions girls told me about—something like Johnny Walker Red with a little bit of Clorox, alcohol, baking soda (which probably saved my stomach) and some sort of cream. You mixed it all up. I got violently ill," actress Whoopi Goldberg wrote of her abortion at age fourteen. "At that moment I was more afraid of having to explain to anybody what was wrong than of going to the park with a hanger, which is what I did." Since then Goldberg has gone on to speak at numerous abortion rallies, including the 2004 March for Women's Lives.

A growing number of celebrities of color have shared their abortion stories. Vanessa Williams, Viola Davis, and Leslie Jones wrote about their abortions in their memoirs, and others, including Jameela Jamil and Nicki Minaj, have shared their stories in interviews or on social media. Renee was watching live at an intimate event when Chrissy Teigen shared the story of realizing that the highly publicized pregnancy loss she had at twenty weeks was indeed an abortion. "I told the world we had a miscarriage, the world agreed we had a miscarriage, all the headlines said it was a miscarriage," she explained. "And I became really frustrated that I didn't, in the first place, say what it was, and I felt silly that it had taken me over a year to actually understand that we had had an abortion." Her delayed realization was not uncommon, given the way abortion is stigmatized; she faced backlash for admitting the realization but also helped others recognize their experiences, too, and has since become an even more outspoken advocate for abortion.

Similarly, actress Dawn-Lyen Gardner didn't see herself as part of the abortion conversation until after she heard Renee speak about how the medication worked and about attacks on abortion during a private presentation. Despite being engaged in social justice issues, she had been unaware of the growing erosion of abortion rights or medication abortion; but as she listened, she realized how familiar all of it sounded. A few years earlier, following a nonviable pregnancy loss, she took the abortion pills that her doctor had recommended and they were a "lifesaver." But hearing Renee speak had thrown her experience into question. "I remember feeling like, wait a minute. Wait, wait, wait a minute. Have I had an abortion? I know these things. I have this experience." That questioning completely transformed her relationship with and advocacy for the issue.

In her 2023 memoir *Thicker Than Water*, actress Kerry Washington details having an abortion in her late twenties using a fake name at the clinic so she wouldn't be recognized. During the procedure, however, the provider mentioned that she looked like the actress Kerry Washington. In the years afterward, she would hold the hands of two other characters having abortions, in *For Colored Girls* and *Scandal*, and of course portray Olivia Pope, the first woman to be shown undergoing an abortion procedure on network television. She produced the television adaptation of the book *Little Fires Everywhere* and bought the screen adaptation rights to *The Mothers*, two novels that include abortions alongside a myriad of pregnancy options. By our count, Washington is the actress attached to the most abortion stories on-screen. She has made her personal her political, and she channels that with every character she plays and project she produces. With her story, she is changing the narrative in massive ways.

As part of changing the narrative on abortion, comedians have shared their stories with jokes and levity, giving audiences the opportunity to feel more comfortable with the subject, recognizing that it doesn't always have to be a tragic topic. But it wasn't an easy task, and comedians who've had abortions have worked at it for years. Comedian and actress Kathy Najimy, who is Lebanese American, also shared the story of her college abortion in *The Choices We Made*. Her abortion experience, which she had at a Planned Parenthood in the 1970s, inspired her to later work with teens at Planned Parenthood to create sketches and monologues about their lives, including their abortions. Years later, Kathy incorporated her abortion story into her comedy show, *The Kathy & Mo Show*, focusing on how she didn't feel sadness or guilt over wanting an abortion even as the doctor who confirmed her pregnancy expected her to. When we talked to her about her experience performing this material before audiences, she said that it was not easy, because it was the only three minutes of seriousness in the show, and the audience took a minute to catch up.

Decades later, Margaret Cho included her multiple abortions in her stand-up sets, although no matter how progressive the audiences were, they became uncomfortable with the topic. She recalled pressure to portray an apologetic sentimentality concerning how hard the decision was. "It's not okay if you don't care. It's not if you treat it as a form of birth control, which I did. It's the best form of birth control," she told us. In one of her jokes, she tells the real experience of her male abortion provider critiquing her comedy show during her abortion, telling her that she needed to have more creative control on it in the future; Margaret retorted, "That's fine, but could you just kill my baby?" Sometimes the audience doesn't laugh and gets upset.

She felt that her nonchalant attitude could make an audience shut down, but she decided that she would continue to share her experiences in that way anyway, to challenge the notions of femininity and reverence for fertility that are forced on us. "It's finding the right combination of your own way of talking about it."

Still, Margaret knows how important it is for her to talk about her abortions as a Korean American woman. "It's so rare to even hear us talk about abortion in any capacity," she told us, recognizing that thus far she is the only Asian American woman to talk about her abortions in a stand-up special. "When I talk about it in a primarily Asian audience it's very challenging, because you come up against a puritanical nature around sexuality, even though we're all people of color, and we're all on the progressive side, in general, but they don't want to hear that level of nonchalance or somehow disrespecting this ability to give life."

Thankfully, times have changed, and audiences are laughing more at abortion jokes on television shows and stand-up sets. Part of that is due to the work of organizations such as Abortion Access Front, led by Lizz Winstead, co-creator of *The Daily Show*, which uses pop culture to expose antiabortion propaganda and works with comedians to talk about abortion and volunteer with local abortion clinics. The more people tell their own abortion stories with humor, the more others will follow.

Joyelle Nicole Johnson, an alum of Abortion Access Front, included jokes about her abortion in her 2021 Peacock comedy special *Love Joy*. When we asked her why she decided to include the jokes midway through the set, she was clear that it was because of how important the experience was for her and the reaction she got from the audience. "People who've had abortions were telling me they feel seen and they felt it's okay for them. Just knowing that as part of my story, I want others to feel that it's okay and that they made the right decision." Joyelle, who is Black, said she never felt any pushback from producers on her decision to include her jokes about needing an abortion after having sex on the floor of an Amtrak bathroom and about her deadbeat father, who was an abortion provider. For her, the key to getting the audience to laugh hysterically is getting the audience comfortable with her and the fact that she is going to talk about race and politics, so abortion talk isn't a surprise. The other factor is the confidence with which she talks about abortion; the audience feels her exude that confidence, trusts her, and stays with her throughout the jokes. "I love my abortion jokes and humor because of the fact that people tell us it's not funny and it should be very serious and we should be mourning for the rest of our lives," she said. "I actually found some humor in it, and you should find humor in most things in life." It's a liberating feeling to be able to feel all of the emotions of an experience to the fullest, without judgment.

As more audiences hear more abortion stories, we believe they're less likely to assume that all abortion experiences are the same; they're not all heartbreaking or tragic. In some cases, we can laugh with the storytellers; in others, we can cry with them; and sometimes, we can do both at once. Audiences can empathize. They can share their own stories. They can be more prepared for their own abortions. That's the beauty of a breadth of stories—real and fictional—on our screens.

Accompanying your favorite character during their abortion might be the best advice you have access to if you have no one in your life you can ask for support. You see that it is okay to choose an abortion, celebrate your decision, and honor your experience because your favorite on-screen character did, too. It's the same when you know that your favorite celebrity had an abortion; it's the next best thing to having a trusted friend or family member to talk to.

Will we see every character represent every aspect of our abortions? No. There are lots of us and an infinite number of experiences. But it does matter when more of the characters reflect what we go through. Television is a black mirror, and we deserve to see a thoughtful reflection resembling ourselves in it. There's a different feeling as you watch something and the foods, mannerisms, and other details are done just right, making that world on-screen real and relatable because it feels like an extension of your own world. The closer that alignment of the character and their world is to reality, the more viewers will see themselves, and other audiences will have a glimpse into our communities in an understanding way, rather than a voyeuristic or whitewashed way or from the viewpoint of a "savior."

Remember the real Emma Hernández, who reflected on the *Vida* character Emma Hernandez and her abortion? *Vida* is about a specific Mexican American community in Los Angeles with specific issues impacting their lives, and Real Emma found it refreshing to see a character intentionally written to depict all of these conflicts and experiences at once. "To have a depiction of a person who is similar to me as first-generation, coming out of an unstable family of a similar socioeconomic status, mixed-status immigration situation, and sexual and gender identity who doesn't have a stereotypical Chicana Latina accent . . . like even that level of nuance; we all speak in different ways."

It's the same thing when it comes to the abortion depiction. "I want to see abortion and Latinidad portrayed in the same universe and within the same realm of possibility," she told us. "I can be a flawed Latina, who is managing different traumas, who's not portraying a model minority myth. And all of those imperfections don't have to be connected to why I had an abortion." Similarly, Margaret Cho told us she wanted to see more Asian characters having abortions, putting their needs first rather than their Asian family's aspirations, and more people having abortions and celebrating their decisions, emotionally and literally, with a party.

"Somebody who is more interested in managing their own life? That's what I would love to see."

The world of possibility opens, including around pregnancy decisions and abortion, when the stories change. Liberating abortion on television will help us liberate it in real life, and liberating it in real life leads to it being shown as liberated on-screen. It's a cycle.

Abortion is part of our lives, and on-screen it doesn't need to be the entire source of our conflicts, challenges, or moral failings. It's just one more thing that we're dealing with on a daily basis. Hopefully, as we explore more of our history, share our stories, and write our own reflections, the narratives we read and watch about us will paint us in a more beautiful, nuanced, and joyful light.

What to Expect When You're Expecting an Abortion

The morning of Renee's abortion, the thing she fretted about the most was what to wear to her procedure. *Should I wear comfy clothes that are easy to remove? But what if I look messy—will they think I am not taking this seriously? If I get too dressed up, am I going to be out of place? Will what I'm wearing be too much to remove? Do I have to take off all my clothes, the way I would for surgery, or just the bottoms, like at a gyno exam?*

At first, getting in this much of a tizzy over what to wear to an abortion might seem silly or frivolous. But as Renee talked to more people about their abortion experiences, she found that worrying about what to wear was quite common. It is the manifestation of uncertainty that stems from near-constant abortion stigma and lack of knowledge and expectations. For Renee, it was a fear that people would judge her for being a teen who had sex, got pregnant, and wanted an abortion, as well as the uncertainty about what was going to happen during her procedure. All of a sudden, what she wore to a medical appointment seemed as though it could become an indictment of her entire life and all her choices.

Often we hear from people having abortions that they didn't think it would ever happen to them, so when it does, everything is so rushed and secretive that they don't have the space or time to gather information or advice from people who've been in the same situation. It can be a stressful moment, so even the advice people receive goes in one ear and out the other, because it's all too much at once.

"I wish I had known" is a common refrain.

Despite abortion being such a universal experience, it can be hard to find advice that resonates. Maybe, as you read this book, you're reflecting on your own abortions, or you're about to have your first, or you're about to have another, or even if you yourself never have an abortion, you're supporting someone you love who is having one. No matter the situation, we believe that a critical part of sharing our abortion stories and changing the narrative is sharing abortion wisdom.

Renee's friend, somatics coach, artist, and abortion storyteller Nik Zaleski first taught her about abortion wisdom—the advice that those of us who've had abortions impart to one another to try to make the path forward a little easier for those coming after us. These are the little tips and tricks we've learned from experience or that someone passed along to us—the little touches of care that we know to provide when showing up for one another, because we've been there, too.

Throughout the writing of this book, we asked abortion storytellers for their best wisdom for someone who is about to have an abortion, because abortion wisdom should be shared. We deserve to know what to expect and how to handle everything as best we can. You may not be able (or even want) to take all of our suggestions. Unfortunately, classism, racism, xenophobia, unsafe communities and homes, stigma, ageism, and just plain shitty situationships mean that we're often making whatever decisions we can with a limited amount of resources and support. And incarceration and government surveillance mean that some people's abortion experiences are wholly left up to the state, if they happen at all. Your circumstances may vary. We hope you can create an abortion experience that's meaningful for you based on the advice of those of us who've been there. Although we can't pick out your appointment outfit for you, we hope that after reading this chapter, you'll have the confidence to pick out clothes you feel confident in as you begin this next chapter of life. (And we do have a few suggestions to help you along the way.)

CONFIRM WHAT YOU'VE SUSPECTED

There are a lot of reproductive conditions that mimic pregnancy symptoms, so first and foremost, the best thing to do is confirm your pregnancy with a test. (After reading chapter 3, you may be tempted to try the old peeing-on-barley-and-wheat method the ancient Egyptians documented on papyrus. Still, we'd suggest a more modern test.) Pregnancies can be confirmed through a blood test at a clinic or hospital or using a urine sample with an over-the-counter pregnancy test at least one week after missing an anticipated period. Before that time, there may not be enough of the pregnancy hormone in your system for it to be detectable. Also, despite what the marketing suggests, you should know that the cheap pregnancy tests from the dollar store work just as well as the expensive ones at the pharmacy or grocery store, so grab whatever feels right for you and your budget. You may want to pick up more than one in case you don't believe the positive result of the first one, which is quite common, or in case you take the test too early after your missed period and you need to test again in a few days. We suggest picking up at least two—one to confirm the pregnancy now and another to confirm that you are no longer pregnant a month or so after your abortion. But if you don't believe the first positive test, get as many as you want. They'll all say the same thing: it might be time to schedule an abortion.

What you should be wary of is free pregnancy tests. Antiabortion crisis pregnancy centers love to advertise free pregnancy tests to entice you to stop in, only to use the opportunity to proselytize, slut-shame, and misinform you about your options. A lot of really wonderful community organizations, clinics, and abortion funds give out free pregnancy tests because they know the tests are expensive—so free isn't always bad. But if you're looking for a free test, be thoughtful about who is giving it out.

ABORTION WISDOM: *Peeing on the pregnancy test stick can be kind of awkward, positioning-wise. If it's easier for you, just pee in a cup and then dip your pregnancy test into the urine sample, just as you would at a clinic—less mess and awkward reaching.*

COVER YOUR TRACKS

Depending on whom you live with, where you live, and a whole host of other factors, you should be careful about whom you text with, what you search on the internet, and what information about your condition and decision you share with someone else. The sad truth is that we can't always trust everyone, even those closest to us. As Texas-based organizer and We Testify storyteller Nancy Cárdenas Peña explained, it's often the people who are closest to us who put us at deeper risk. She knows this from experience: "I wish I could have had more time to disclose my abortion story in the manner I felt comfortable with just as anyone should be able to share their story on their own terms." (You'll hear more about Nancy's experience in chapter 12.)

Surveillance is a reality of life now and can lead to criminalization for people seeking abortions. Even if you end up not having an abortion, you should be careful about your digital footprint throughout your process. There has been a steady stream of stories about people who sought abortions with the help of loved ones and other friends, medical providers, or search engines. Social media companies turned over their private communications, which aided in their arrest, prosecution, and conviction for seeking an abortion.

* * *

Be very careful about what you write in texts or messages and share with others. Talk to people on the phone or in person rather than in writing. Try to use messaging apps with encrypted or disappearing messages or those that don't allow screenshots. Delete your call log history. Clear the browser history of the search engine you use or use a private browser that doesn't save or track your history. Use a lock on your phone and computer so that others can't look at your messages or browser history when you're not watching. Nothing is perfect, but being prepared can help.

THINK THROUGH YOUR OPTIONS

The path of options when you're pregnant can be as straightforward as a logic model. Check out the logic model in chapter 6 ("Abortionsplaining") for a refresher and some questions you can ask yourself to help you think through your decision.

The reality is that deciding which path to take might not be so simple and may not be fully in your control. You may want to be pregnant, but not right now. You may want an abortion, but support and access to care aren't something you have in your community. You may want to parent, but you're already holding so much. These choices aren't much of a choice once our actual lives, bank accounts, families, and emotions are factored in.

You deserve the time to think through what you'd like to do with whomever you feel safest with. Unfortunately, the never-ending abortion restrictions and bans, and increasing costs of the procedure, can make it difficult, expensive, and logistically challenging to take an extended period of time to pause and think. We suggest you take the time you need to think about what you want before you talk through your thoughts with others, when they might influence your thinking. Esmarie, a We Testify abortion storyteller, agreed: "I would say don't talk about it with someone until you find out how you really feel, because some people will try to put their feelings onto you and you shouldn't let it change how you feel."

ABORTION WISDOM: *Journal about your feelings. Make a list of pros and cons for all of your options. Whom can you lean on for support? What are the factors you're weighing? Hold space for all of your feelings.*

For some people, making the decision is something they'd like to do alone, whereas others want the input of people in their lives such as friends, family members, partners, therapists, medical caregivers, religious leaders, or internet forums. People who have already had abortions are often good sources of support and information, because they've already been there.

Paula Ávila-Guillén, a global abortion activist and storyteller, said that she is a better mom because of her abortion, which allowed her to become a parent when she chose to be. "Becoming a parent can be hard, especially if you don't feel this is right for you or if you don't feel this is the right moment," she explained. "Just follow your gut. You know yourself better than anybody else. Follow the instinct that's telling you what might be right for you or might not be at the right moment for you."

If the people you confide in ask you questions, they should ask you open-ended questions that allow you to think through your decision on your own rather than leading you to what they think you should do. We Testify abortion storyteller Layidua Salazar's abortion wisdom is to surround yourself with people who are going to love on you and support you through your decisions—people who won't need an explanation and who won't question whether you have the capacity to make this decision for yourself. You don't owe others an explanation. "If you, unfortunately, don't have those people in your life, seek us out online," she said. "We are out there—people who are ready to love on you for making decisions that feel good for your life and your body."

WE THINK DR. YING ZHANG, AN ABORTION PROVIDER AND WE TESTIFY ABORTION STORYTELLER, PUT IT BEST:

Listen to your heart and that voice inside of you because that voice and heart know best what you need. Everyone else will have their opinions, but they don't live in your body or in your head. You are and will continue to be loved. For those who don't like it, fuck 'em.

We also recommend calling one of our favorite organizations, All-Options, which runs a talkline that provides emotional support to people experiencing all pregnancy options. Their trained volunteer counselors provide an unbiased, supportive, listening ear. Sometimes it's easier to talk things out with a stranger than with someone you know, who might convince you to do what they would do.

FIND CARE

When it's time to find abortion care, you should think about whether you'd like to have your abortion on your own at home or in another safe place outside of a medical setting or at a clinic with medical providers. Sometimes you may not have this freedom of choice depending on how far along you are in the pregnancy, where the nearest clinic is, and whether you're at risk for being criminalized.

CLINIC-BASED CARE

If you want care at an abortion clinic, you can search for the nearest one at INeedAnA.com, by searching for accredited abortion clinics nearby, or by calling another local reproductive health clinic for a referral. Confirm that they provide abortions on the phone or on their website. A real clinic will be up-front with you about all of your options and schedule an appointment for you. Most abortions are provided at independent abortion clinics. It's common for people to have only heard of Planned Parenthood and think that there isn't an abortion clinic nearby because there isn't a Planned Parenthood that provides abortions they can get to. Call around. Ask for referrals. Look for local abortion clinics, too.

You may not be able to get an appointment for a few weeks, because clinics are trying to see as many patients as they can. This is caused by the forced closure of clinics and people having to travel hundreds or even thousands of miles for care.

TELEMEDICINE ABORTIONS

Some states allow the use of telemedicine for an abortion. With a telemedicine appointment, you wouldn't need to visit a health care center;

instead, you log on to a protected website and talk to a medical provider or enter your information into an online form to see if you're eligible for an abortion. The provider will prescribe abortion pills to you that you can pick up at a pharmacy or have mailed to you. If you have the pills mailed to you, be sure you can catch the mail before others in your building or home do, especially if they're less than supportive of your decision.

A few states allow abortion providers to prescribe abortion pills from their state, where abortion is legal, to patients in states where abortion is restricted or criminalized. Look to see if there is a provider who can support you in your own community without having to travel. Be sure to know the abortion restrictions in your own state as prosecutors may criminalize people who are reported for self-managing their abortions. More on that next!

SELF-MANAGED ABORTION

Whether it's personal preference or the circumstance of barriers, some people decide to have their abortions at home on their own terms. This can be done using abortion pills ordered online or sourced within a community, with herbs sourced through a knowledgeable herbalist, or through a procedure with a midwife or trained doula.

Local organizations may be able to point you to places where you can access abortion pills in your community, or you can find them online. Although they are the same pills that you would receive from an abortion provider at a clinic, you still must follow all of the instructions and make preparations to have your abortion at home or in another safe place. Keep reading for ideas on how to set up your own comfortable abortion space.

Although self-managing an abortion with pills or with a trained support person is medically safe, it may or may not be legally risky. In some states, choosing to do an abortion on your own can be criminalized, whereas in others it's decriminalized or not specified. Take all precautions to protect yourself legally and minimize your digital footprint and risk. If/When/How's Repro Legal Helpline is a great resource if you have specific questions about your legal rights when it comes to self-managed abortion and digital security. Call them at (844) 868-2812. You can also call their Repro Legal Defense Fund at (866) 463-7533 if you find yourself or someone you love facing criminalization and you need bail or money for other costs related to your case. Both the Helpline and Legal Defense Fund are there to support you if your issues are related to abortion, miscarriage, stillbirth, or pregnancy.

BE WARY OF CRISIS PREGNANCY CENTERS

When Renee searched for an abortion clinic, she wasn't totally sure how to find one, but she did know she needed to ask directly whether the clinic provided abortions. That's because fake clinics, called antiabortion crisis pregnancy centers, set up next door to abortion clinics or in place of abortion clinics that have closed in hopes of confusing people looking for abortion care. These centers often have names that make them sound as though they might be an abortion clinic, and they frequently have vague information about abortion on their websites. Antiabortion centers will avoid answering your questions about scheduling an appointment in hopes that you'll come in and waste your time thinking that you can receive an abortion when they have no intention of giving you one. Their entire goal is to abortionsplain you until you're no longer "abortion-minded," meaning that you are no longer considering an abortion.

GET YOUR MONEY RIGHT

One of the most challenging aspects of obtaining an abortion is paying for it. The cost of an abortion (depending on how far along you are and the method) can range from $150 to well over $15,000. If you're seeking a first-trimester appointment at a clinic in the United States, you may have to pay an average of $500. On top of that, you may have to pay for other things, such as short- or long-distance transportation to and from the clinic, a multinight hotel stay, meals, childcare for your children, and money for pain medications. You may have to pay for all of these things with your own cash because some state and federal policies ban private and public health insurance from covering abortions. If you are going to a clinic, ask if they accept insurance—some do not, so you may need to pay out of pocket anyway.

INSURANCE

If you have insurance, check to see whether your health insurance policy will cover an abortion. It may not be listed clearly. Look for language such as "outpatient surgery" or "outpatient pregnancy termination" or similar wording. You can also call your provider and ask. If you are able to use your insurance, that's great! You should, because that's what it's for. Insurance companies' network policies and billing coding can be confusing, so you may need to check to make sure that the clinic is "in-network." You can also see if your insurance policy allows you to be reimbursed for any portion of your procedure that you pay out of pocket for. Keep in mind that if you aren't the policyholder, the Explanation of Benefits (EOB) will notify the policyholder via mail or email about the services that the insurance paid for, which means that the policyholder may be notified of your abortion. Renee learned this at her appointment and didn't use her insurance because she wasn't ready for her parents, the policyholders, to know that she was having an abortion.

If you have public health insurance, such as Medicaid or Medicare, there's a federal policy called the Hyde Amendment, discussed in chapter 5 ("What's Race & Class Got to Do with It?"), that bans the use of federal money for abortion care. Although nearly twenty states override this rule and allow for their state Medicaid program to cover abortion care, most do not, and that means your insurance will not pay for your abortion. Technically, Medicaid allows for an abortion to be covered in the cases of rape, incest, or life endangerment, but in reality these exceptions rarely work. In order to access the medical exceptions, a doctor must say that the abortion is medically necessary to protect your life, but the situation has to be so dire that you're basically knocking on death's door—and no one should have to wait that long. To access the rape or incest exception, some states require you to file a police report, which isn't a safe option for everyone.

You'll also need to see whether the clinic accepts insurance. Some don't because the US insurance system is complicated and doesn't fairly compensate clinics for their services or cover patients' care without a fight and lots of paperwork. As a workaround, some clinics may take insurance for some preprocedure work such as blood tests and other exams, but not for the abortion itself. Talk to the clinic staff while booking your appointment; they'll be able to help you through the process, because they're the experts.

CLINIC DISCOUNTS

Clinics know that paying for an abortion is hard for most patients, so they have lots of options to help people afford care. Some clinics will help you contact abortion funds or have their own fund they can use to help you bridge the gap between how much you have and the full price of your abortion. A few clinics have discounts they can offer you to take a little bit off the price or payment plans so you can make smaller payments for your abortion over weeks or months.

ABORTION WISDOM: *Some clinics accept only cash to pay for your appointment—no checks, credit cards, or digital payments. Ask how the clinic accepts payment before your appointment, so you can build in time to go to an ATM or the bank, or borrow cash from a loved one.*

ABORTION FUNDS AND PRACTICAL SUPPORT GROUPS

Abortion funds are fantastic organizations all across the country that help people pay for their abortions. They are local, grassroots organizations that raise money to help people cover the gap between the cost and what they have or even the entire amount of their abortions. Your clinic can tell you about local abortion funds, or you can search online for your city or state with the words "abortion fund," and a list will come up. Sometimes a fund in the city or state you are traveling to can help pay for your appointment as well.

If you have to travel far (or even near!) to your clinic, or need help arranging or paying for childcare, a hotel stay, transportation (planes, trains, or automobiles!), or literally anything else associated with your abortion, a local abortion fund or a practical support group can help you. A practical support group is a local organization that coordinates volunteers who can give you rides to and from your appointments, hotel, or flights; offer babysitting or translation services; or just be a caring friend. The abortion fund or clinic can get you connected to a practical support group and their services. For nearly a decade, Renee has offered practical support to people traveling for their abortions. She's been a doula, offered airport and train station pickups, picked up pre- and post-appointment dinners, set up a warm place for people to lay their heads in her home, played with a patient's little ones during babysitting duties, and even served as an overnight hotel room buddy.

Because of state laws banning who can share information about abortion, some organizations may not be able to tell you about all your options such as receiving pills via telemedicine from another state, like Massachusetts. You should always do your own research, too!

Whatever you need, there's probably someone out there who is willing to be by your side. Give your local abortion fund a call, and they'll help you through everything.

ABORTION WISDOM: *Avoid payday loans as best you can! They may give you fast cash, but as We Testify abortion storyteller Tohan testified before the Senate in 2021, the loan can become its own nightmare. She took out a $600 online payday loan to pay the clinic's deposit and then another $500 from a different company to pay off the $250 balance. The payday loan companies charged her a 400 percent interest rate, and although she kept making payments, the total just kept growing. Eventually the loan cost her thousands of dollars. "It ruined my credit and has done so much damage," she testified. "It was a never-ending cycle, all because my insurance wouldn't cover it."*

MAKE YOUR APPOINTMENT

Scheduling your abortion appointment can be complicated, so you should be prepared to make a few calls back and forth with the clinic. Some clinics do abortions only on certain days of the week, so for any medical appointment, it's not as simple as calling and getting an appointment the next day. This is because abortion clinics have been shut down and states have created ridiculous restrictions, forcing people to make multiple visits, all designed to delay you and clog up the system. It is normal that you may have to wait a few weeks before you can get an appointment. It sucks, we know. If you're having a later procedure, your abortion can take several days to a week from start to finish. Be ready with your calendar and have a few dates as options for your appointment. Unfortunately, if you are traveling a long way for your appointment, you may need to take a few days off work or school. Remember to factor in recovery time, as you may want an extra day or two to feel like yourself again. Be ready to arrange childcare for your little ones. If you can trust someone to tell them the full story, you should try. But if not, you can make up a need for a small noninvasive surgery or "medical procedure" as your reasoning.

ABORTION WISDOM: *If you can afford it, take a day or two extra off work or school to do nothing but rest after your abortion appointment. We know not everyone can afford to, especially because our nation doesn't guarantee paid sick leave, but it's important for your body to recover and for you to take time to care for and center yourself.*

OVERCOME ANY LEGAL OBSTACLES

It's pretty common to have to jump through legal hoops before you can be unpregnant. The laws are pretty ridiculous and can include everything from requiring multiple appointments, to forcing you to look at an ultrasound and hear the cardiac pulses (the muscle cells that pulse and would eventually grow into a heartbeat), to hearing state-mandated unscientific statements about abortion and signing a statement that zebras are just horses in striped pajamas. (Okay, fine, that last one isn't actually a policy anywhere . . . yet.)

No matter what, there's a lot to do before your appointments, so you'll need to plan time in your calendar. Tell the clinic worker when you have to work and what else you have going on so that they can help figure out times you can come in for your appointments when it's the least disruptive for your calendar.

More Barriers for Teens

If you're under eighteen, you may have to deal with another legal hurdle: parental involvement laws. Parental involvement laws are rules that require a minor to have a parent or legal guardian be either notified of your abortion (parental notification) or give their consent to it (parental consent). The truth is that most young people do involve their parents in their decision, and those who don't have a good reason not to. But the lawmakers who made these laws don't care about the truth.

There are a few ways around this law, but they are time-consuming and complicated. (Of course, this doesn't apply to young people who are married or emancipated, but you'll need your paperwork to prove it.) One way is to travel to a nearby state that doesn't have these laws, the way Veronica and Bailey do in the book and subsequent movie *Unpregnant*. As in the novel and film, this method can be an arduous journey that takes days and days, costs a lot of money, and requires an extravagant story about where you'll be to those who will be wondering. Local abortion organizations can help you travel and coordinate all aspects of the trip.

Another way around these laws is through a judicial bypass, when you go to a judge to prove that you are *mature enough* to handle an abortion. We know how ridiculous it sounds, but we don't make the rules, unfortunately. The process can take weeks or months, because the court system is slow, and you'll need to have ultrasounds to show how far along you are and school papers to prove that you are a good student. The entire process is based on respectability and proximity to whiteness. Look to see whether there are lawyers who can help you through the process; you can connect to them through your clinic, local abortion fund, or practical support organization.

PREPARE FOR YOUR ABORTION

Having an abortion can bring up a lot of feelings and questions, especially because you may not know what to expect. Abortion wisdom from others who've been through it can be helpful.

What to Ask

It's common to feel scared or embarrassed about asking questions during a medical appointment, even when it's not an abortion. But the answers to your questions can put you at ease, so muster your courage and ask all of the questions you have so you can feel as comfortable and informed as possible.

A Few Questions You Could Ask on the Phone or at Your Appointment

* What type of procedure will I be having, and what is the process?
* *If you're having sedation:* What time should I stop eating before my procedure?
* Who will be in the room during my abortion? Who will be performing my abortion?
* How long will the procedure take? How long does recovery usually take?
* If I become worried about my health, whom can I call for advice?
* What types of pain management do you offer?
* What kind of medications can I take during my procedure? Are there any medications I should stop taking?
* Can I smoke marijuana or take a THC or CBD edible to take the edge off before or after my procedure?
* I am living with [disability]. Do you have experience treating people with [disability]? How will receiving this method of abortion interact with my disability?

* Can you tell me everything you're doing as you're doing it?
* Can we discuss where you will touch me before you do so?
* Do you have experience caring for nonbinary or trans patients?
* Can you avoid using the word [*word you don't like used to describe your body*] when you describe my body?
* Can I have a loved one or doula in the room with me during the procedure?
* Can I listen to my own music through my headphones or a speaker in the room?
* *If you're having a later abortion, especially after 18 weeks:* Can you put milk suppressant in my IV drip or write a prescription for cabergoline pills so that I don't leak milk as my body readjusts to not being pregnant?

Travel Planning

If you're traveling for your abortion, you will want to be prepared, as you may be traveling to a city or state you've never been to before. Save in one place all important phone numbers, including the numbers for the clinic, abortion fund case manager, practical support volunteer, or any other emergency contacts, in case you need to reach them in a pinch. Download maps off-line on your phone so you can get around if your cell service isn't available or is slow. Read up on the airport or train station directions so you know where you need to go to catch your ride smoothly. Don't forget to arrive early so you can be settled and grab a bite to eat before takeoff.

Getting to Your Appointment

Arranging a ride to your abortion can be complicated, because you have to trust someone else with your experience, and they may need to travel across state lines with you. If you trust them enough, this is a good opportunity for a bestie road trip. If you have the cash, you can always take a cab or use an app service to book a car, but remember there may be a digital history of your ride to the clinic, and you could end up with an extra chatty driver who asks where you're headed and why. If you need to enter a destination digitally, try choosing a spot near the clinic.

Local abortion funds and practical support organizations can arrange volunteers to offer you rides from your home, work, airport, or train station—truly wherever!—to your appointment and back.

However you get to your clinic appointment, be vigilant for police outside the clinic or ICE (Immigration and Customs Enforcement) agents, who set up traps on thoroughfares and near clinics, schools, and hospitals to detain and arrest Black and Brown people, undocumented immigrants, and other marginalized groups. This step is critical if you're crossing checkpoints or borders or if you live in or near heavily policed communities. The morning of your appointment, you might want to check with your community and trusted immigration organizations that document where ICE sets up checkpoints on the way to your destination.

When you arrive for your appointment, double-check to make sure the place you're headed to is indeed the clinic. Antiabortion crisis pregnancy centers often set up next door to abortion clinics, or an antiabortion clinic may have a name similar to the name of the exact clinic you're trying to get to. There are often antiabortion protesters outside of clinics who scream and yell at anyone walking near the abortion clinic, in hopes of scaring people out of going inside or disorienting them so they walk into the wrong place. These people are not afraid to push or shove you. Of course, you don't deserve to be treated this way; the more prepared you are, the more ready and safe you can be. Perhaps you can do a few power stances or tell yourself some encouraging mantras so you arrive at the clinic in the right headspace and their comments cannot affect your confidence.

ABORTION WISDOM: *Take some time to think about what you're unsure of and what you need to feel comfortable during your procedure. It can be hard to think about this, because you don't know what you don't know. Close your eyes. Imagine what the best possible experience would look like for you. How does that provider show up for you? What are you in control of? Write down those things and ask your provider whether any of your ideas are possible. The provider may already plan for these things as part of your treatment.*

HAVE YOUR ABORTION YOUR WAY

Call "Your Person"

As we mentioned earlier, in the first season of *Grey's Anatomy*, Dr. Cristina Yang sits at a bar with Dr. Meredith Grey as they grieve their failing love lives over snacks. Cristina is pregnant and has an abortion scheduled, but according to clinic policy, she needed to designate an emergency contact on her form, so she wrote down Meredith's name. "That's why I told you I'm pregnant," Cristina tells Meredith. "You're my person." Meredith hugs her friend, who receives the hug reluctantly. "Shut up. I'm your person," Meredith replies.

This short scene in the iconic long-running television show created a beloved shorthand for best friends who promise to show up for one another, no matter what. That it grew out of a supportive abortion decision is just the icing on the cake for us.

Like Cristina, you may want to identify "your person" to check in on you, hold your hand in the waiting room, or sit with you as you pass the pregnancy while binge-watching *Grey's Anatomy*. Ask your clinic whether you can bring a friend or loved one with you. Each clinic has different policies; some may say no, and others may say, yes, "your person" can join you in the waiting room, recovery room, or in the procedure room. You might be a little dizzy after the sedation or cramping a bit if you have an in-clinic procedure, so having someone else drive you home is definitely recommended. We Testify abortion storyteller Cazembe Murphy Jackson agrees. He suggests that you find someone who can attend the procedure with you and be with you in the days following. "Maybe plan out some restful activities that you really like to do or that will keep you happy, shows you want to watch, stuff like that. I think that would have been really helpful for me," he explained.

A lot of people who are traveling long distances for their abortions bring a friend or family member along for the journey. It's nice to have a familiar face with you through the multiday process. If you're having your abortion at home, you may want to call on someone from your community to sit with you through the process and chill out for a few days. They can help you to get to and from the toilet, clean up, make you food, and dote on you as you deserve.

Ask for What You Need

As wonderful as abortion providers are, some are still learning about how to better care for patients with disabilities, those who are fat, survivors, or nonbinary or trans people, to name a few identities. Be ready to tell your provider what you need in order to have an abortion experience that is right for you. If your body doesn't move in a particular way or you do not like your body parts to be touched or referred to in a certain way, tell your providers in advance, potentially during the counseling conversation. You may also want to remind them that your body requires a different dosage of pain medication compared with other patients. Good providers will accommodate your needs. It is unfortunate that you may have to be the one to initiate this, but some providers aren't used to caring for certain bodies or are so focused on providing abortion care that they forget to check in. You deserve an abortion experience that centers you.

Do It with a Doula

Both Cazembe and Ash Williams recommend finding a doula to attend your abortion with you. A doula is a trained caregiver who can tend to your needs and advocate for you with your provider. They are there to listen to your feelings, talk you through the process, and answer all of your questions, or even give you a massage or other physical attention that you need before, during, and after your abortion. As an abortion doula, Ash offers this care to abortion patients as well as advocacy with providers. "My abortion experience was impacted positively because I had doula support," he explained. "I want people to know that they deserve the best abortions that they can have. They deserve the sedation options, they deserve for their abortions to be paid for. They deserve care, and they deserve for people to get their pronouns right and to ask them what their pronouns are." Local abortion funds, practical support organizations, and clinics may be able to connect you with doulas who offer their services at a low cost or for free if you cannot afford their full-service prices.

WHAT TO BRING TO THE CLINIC

There are a variety of things that you may want to bring along to the clinic to ensure your appointment goes smoothly. Some items may be a matter of intuition, but others are less so. Ask your loved ones who've had abortions what they'd add.

Government-issued identification: Some clinics request identification such as a passport, green card, driver's license, or state ID for check-in. These will definitely be needed if you're traveling to your appointment by airplane or rental car, when checking in at a hotel, and sometimes for other travel.

Health insurance card: If you have health insurance, bring your cards or, at the very least, write down your policy number. Even if your insurance doesn't cover the abortion procedure, you might be able to use it for other services, such as blood tests and an ultrasound. The clinic can help you sort it out. Note that the policyholder might be notified.

Cash and cards: Plan to have some cash on hand and your debit or credit cards with you in case you need to order a meal, pay for gas, pay your final balance at the clinic, or check into a hotel.

Tickets: Traveling for your abortion? Be sure to check in for your flight the day before and arrive early for all scheduled transportation. You can also print or download your tickets, or take a screenshot of them on your phone, to save time so that you can get moving on your flight or train or bus quickly.

Medication: Bring your daily and prescription medications with you so you can take them as you travel and in case you want to show them to your provider to make sure they're okay to take during or after your procedure. Very, very few medications have contraindications with abortion medications and procedures, but it's always good to check with your providers.

More Things to Bring

One thing everyone should know about abortions is that there's a lot of waiting—waiting in the clinic lobby, waiting for the pregnancy to pass, waiting for the symptoms to subside. Waiting for hours or days, depending on how far along you are. *Waiting.* To pass the time—and to be prepared—there are lots of things you may want to bring with you to the clinic or have nearby at home.

Your phone: Your phone is critical. Not only is it important for scrolling the internet and passing the time, but you can use it to write down important things your providers share with you, take pictures of any documents or notes, and call for support. Save any important numbers you'll need. Be aware that antiabortion organizations often use geotagging services to serve ads with misinformation about abortion and adoption to people at or near abortion clinics, so you may not be completely free from the protesters' influence while scrolling social media to unwind. You can always turn off your location settings during the process and turn them back on when you're done if that would help put your mind at ease. (And it could help reduce your criminalization risk.)

Portable charger: Batteries on your devices can run down quickly. Bring a portable charger so you can plug in and recharge while on the go without an outlet.

Distraction devices: Whether a tablet, portable video game system, or e-reader, be sure to charge your favorite devices and bring them with you. Download whatever you want to watch, play, listen to, or read before leaving home, because fast, safe, and open Wi-Fi isn't always available.

Headphones: Pack your headphones so you can listen to music, movies, and podcasts at your leisure. Noise-canceling headphones are also great to drown out the sounds of protesters or other distractions when heading into your appointment.

ABORTION WISDOM: *If you're nervous about hearing the vacuum aspirator or any other medical equipment sounds during your appointment, ask your provider whether you can listen to your own music during your procedure.*

Books: Undisturbed time is the perfect opportunity to start or finish a novel you've been meaning to get lost in. Bring a book or two to read while you wait between your appointments or for the abortion pills to start working.

Your journal: A lot can come up during your abortion. Having your journal handy allows you to reflect on your feelings and write down questions you may have and want to ask someone later. Try to bring a pen, but if you forget, the clinic will probably let you borrow one.

WHAT TO WEAR

Like Renee, you might be unsure of what to wear during your abortion. Whether your abortion happens in the clinic or at home, you should feel comfortable, calm, and confident in what you wear. That said, we do have some suggestions. Soft and relaxed shirts and dark-colored pants will allow you to feel a bit freer during the clinic waits, plane/train/car rides, and long hours recovering on the couch. Layers are good because you may experience nausea and chills or may be traveling to a state with a different climate from what you are used to. Do your best to avoid tight jeans, yoga pants, and belts as they don't have much give, especially around your abdomen. Think loose, cozy clothes. Bring sneakers, clogs, or other comfortable shoes in case you have to walk long distances. If you're staying somewhere overnight, don't forget your pajamas!

If you're going to a clinic, we would also recommend bringing a sweat-shirt, cozy jacket, or another top layer and warm socks, as some clinics can be a little chilly. You should also pack a pair of sunglasses and a hat for the walk inside the clinic. There may be protesters outside, and they can help you maintain privacy and block out irritating people.

ABORTION WISDOM: *You may not want to wear your favorite pair of under-wear or pants, because bleeding and spotting is normal. When traveling for your abortion, it's a good idea to overpack on underwear and pants in case a pair gets soiled with blood and because you'll be on the road for a few days.*

CREATE AN ABORTION SANCTUARY

Whether you're having your abortion at home or in the clinic, staying overnight at a hotel, or crashing at a friend's house, it's important that you set up your abortion and recovery spaces so that you feel held and loved. This is We Testify storyteller Cynthia Gutierrez's best abortion wisdom for you. When she had her abortion in 2013, she didn't know about abortion funds or abortion doulas, and self-care wasn't a concept she had thought about for the process. She had her abortion at home with a roommate who was antiabortion and freaking out as Cynthia threw up and passed the pregnancy. In retrospect, she said she would have cherished being in a safe, comforting, loving place with all the items that felt welcoming to her spirit, such as pillows and blankets, a heating pad, scrumptious food, and her favorite shows on repeat. "I would love to have an abortion doula and have that support," she told us. "I would take time off work. I would make sure that I prioritize my physical health and my mental well-being more; drink a lot of water, eat good food, and just do whatever the hell I wanted to bring comfort and ease to my life. Literally, if I can go back in time, that's what I would do."

You can set up this kind of space for your abortion. Grab all of your favorite blankets and pillows and find a place to camp out for your at-home abortion or recovery: a bed, a snug couch, a pillow fort in front of the TV—whatever feels snuggliest to you. Cynthia recommends placing beautiful images, lavender lotion, essential oils, and flowers everywhere.

Truly make it a transformative moment for you encircled by everything you love, along with the practical items.

Nourish your body: Your ability to eat and drink before, during, and after your abortion depends on what type of abortion procedure you have and where you are in the procedure. If you're having sedation, usually you'll be advised to stop eating a certain number of hours before your appointment. If you're having an abortion with pills, usually you can eat smaller, light meals throughout the process. You're gonna feel pretty nauseated; heavy meals can make nausea worse. Talk to your medical provider or doula—they'll be able to advise you, especially if you have a medical condition or dietary restrictions.

We Testify abortion storyteller and Ohio organizer Jordyn Close is a huge abortion snack evangelist—the more snacks, the better. Ask your besties who had abortions for their snack recommendations. We suggest having snacks nearby for the times that you can eat—something light that your body can easily digest. Soups are great, as are simple sandwiches. Have nearby a water bottle, herbal tea, drinks with electrolytes such as sports drinks to keep you hydrated, and maybe ginger ale to settle your stomach. You may experience nausea or vomiting, so rehydrating yourself is critical.

Prepare for pain: Everyone's abortion experience is different, but most people experience quite a bit of cramping, especially during a medication abortion. Nancy Cárdenas Peña told us she wished she had thought more about pain management before she started her self-managed abortion with pills. (You can take ibuprofen, but not aspirin.) You may also want to have a heating pad, pain relief patches, a hot-water bottle, or cooling pain-relief ointment as the cramps become more intense.

ABORTION WISDOM: *As your body prepares for a pregnancy, it naturally begins to prepare for lactation during the second trimester. Abortion storyteller Beth Vial had a later abortion; her advice is to freeze cabbage leaves and place them on your nipples to help speed up the cessation of milk production.*

Ready your restroom: If you haven't spent a whole lot of time in your bathroom, get ready to—especially if you're having a medication abortion. Be ready to sit on the toilet for a long time and maybe even throw up. If you have the time and energy, clean the bathroom in preparation for your abortion—or outsource this task to a caring friend!

Stock up on period pads, toilet paper, and facial tissue: In case you haven't figured it out by now, there will be blood during and after your abortion. It's normal. Your body is expelling the pregnancy and all of the blood with it as it resets. Have period pads—not tampons!—of all sizes ready, especially the super thick ones. You'll need the thick ones at the start of your abortion and then the thinner ones as your bleeding and spotting tapers off. Some people like to use their menstrual cup, too! Facial tissue is great for catching tears or any other bodily fluids as you run to the toilet. Stocking your bathroom with toilet paper is also a good call, so you're not searching for a stashed roll at the last minute.

Pamper yourself: It's not often that you can take a moment to honor yourself and all you've endured and reflect on your journey. It's a good idea to pamper yourself with a face mask, a relaxing hot bath, or scented lotions. Remember Favianna Rodriguez, the artist and activist who made her self-managed abortion a ritual? She enjoyed an herb-filled bath and yoni steam courtesy of her doula. You deserve softness.

AFTER YOUR ABORTION

Medically, it will usually take a few days or weeks to feel that you're back to normal after your abortion. The bleeding should subside within a few days, turning to spotting, as after a period, rather than full-on bleeding, whether you've had a procedural or medication abortion. But with medication and herbal abortions, the bleeding can last for days, on average two weeks. You should be able to resume your normal activities and get back to life, whatever that looks like for you. Some people feel resistance to sex after their procedure. Medically, there's no reason for you to not resume sex, but of course that doesn't always match up with the feelings you may hold about how you became pregnant and everything else. Trust your instincts. Trust your body. When you're ready, if you are ready, you'll know. Everything you feel after your abortion is right, whatever that is. For Renee, relief followed by feeling guilty for not feeling guilty were the first emotions. She was ready to get back to her life and whatever followed. But she wasn't ready to talk about her abortion and didn't for six years. (Obviously, she hasn't stopped since!) It's not that she wasn't ready to talk about it because she was ashamed; it's that she wasn't in the mood to hold other people's potential feelings about her decision, especially if those feelings were disappointment or anger. Renee was happy with her decision, and that was all that mattered.

In her book *The Turnaway Study*, Diana Greene Foster writes about her research following nearly a thousand women over ten years and analyzing what happened to those who were able to have abortions and those who were not because they hit their state's gestational limit and were thus turned away. Many studies shaped the book, including one finding that 95 percent of women believed they had made the right decision. They had a mixture of feelings, including happiness, sadness, regret, relief, and more, but the positive emotions outweighed the negative ones. And the negative ones weren't as simple as they're made out to be in the conversation surrounding abortion. A feeling of regret didn't necessarily mean that someone regretted the abortion. In fact, it was that they regretted the situation they were in that had led them to need the abortion. From our experiences talking to people who had abortions, as well as from our own personal experiences, that's a really common feeling, which can make talking about our feelings even more difficult for fear that we will be misinterpreted, misunderstood, and maligned. It's also difficult to parse out our own feelings when we aren't given the open space to do so because abortion is so deeply entrenched in partisan politics and under attack. We've talked with people who've had less-than-stellar clinic experiences but who were uncomfortable talking about them because antiabortion activists would say that these bad instances prove their point. We've talked with people who've experienced mental health crises during their abortions and were afraid that people would think that the crises were caused by their abortions. It can take time to separate your own feelings from what the world puts on you. You deserve the space to figure out your feelings, on your own timeline, no matter what's happening with abortion politically.

You may want to talk about your abortion at some point. Some are ready to talk about it soon afterward, and others never want to talk about it or want to wait a period of time. There's no wrong way to feel after your abortion. There's no wrong way to behave. Our reactions to our abortion experiences reflect the constellation of emotions, experiences, and moments that make up who we are. But because we're socialized to not talk about and to be ashamed of our abortions, it may take some time to undo that negative teaching. There's no perfect way to do so, but we can share some abortion wisdom that may help you arrive to that peace.

Explore your feelings: For a lot of people, abortions happen as they're in the midst of a bunch of other equally important crises and life decisions. Take time to feel your feelings when you're ready. You may need to compartmentalize just so you can make it through the next day. You may want to process in the immediate aftermath. They're your emotions, so it's your timeline. It's also possible that you have no emotions to process whatsoever. That is absolutely fine, too. We know there are folks who feel deeply separated from the abortion feelings conversation because they simply didn't have any emotions to feel. Whatever you feel (or don't feel!) is right.

Affirm yourself: Author of *Baking by Feel*, abortion storyteller, and creator of the Instagram account @TheSweetFeminist Becca Rea-Tucker creates wonderful videos of abortion affirmations, in which she says kind things affirming what we need to hear before, during, and after our abortions. Because we are all different, she encourages viewers to take what resonates with them and leave the rest behind:

You deserve compassion and respect.

You can talk about your abortion however you want to.

I'm so sorry that you weren't safe around the medical staff who have a responsibility to care for you.

You are totally allowed to feel excited about this pregnancy if you've had abortions before.

I'm so sorry this took a heavy financial toll on you.

It's okay to choose yourself.

What's the affirmation you would say to yourself? If you want to read words that people who've had abortions can offer you, flip to chapter 12 and see the poetic affirmations they have for you.

Honoring your abortion: Every year, on the anniversary of her abortion, Renee takes the day off work and does whatever feels right. Sometimes it's taking herself out for a scrumptious meal, luxuriating at a spa, or just reflecting on how far she's come in the nearly two decades since her abortion. For her, it's a day of reflection with a bit of self-indulgence. When she started We Testify, she instituted "abortionaversaries," with employees having days off on the anniversaries of their abortions. There's no rule for how to spend your abortionaversary. It's a day (or several days if you've had more than one abortion) to pause and reflect on how far you've come.

Lots of We Testify storytellers observe their abortionaversaries. Some treat the anniversary as a serene day of reflection, and others celebrate it as a momentous occasion. Some years, people mark the abortionaversary differently from the way they observed it in other years. However you commemorate your abortionaversary is wholly up to you.

One We Testify abortion storyteller, Alejandra Pablos, wanted to build joy and celebration around her abortions, so she created the "abortion shower," an in-person or virtual event that celebrates one person's abortion journey with friends, decorations, cakes, gifts, songs, and games. Some of the abortion showers raise money for local organizing or future showers for people who have abortions, and guests at others can pitch in to make abortion care packages for people going through the experience in their community. Abortion showers are designed as a safe space for people to be able to share their abortion stories and feel the love, camaraderie, and support they may not have had during their abortion.

Sharing your story: At We Testify, Renee and her team say the first rule of abortion storytelling is "You don't have to share your story." Abortion storytelling is everywhere. The staff often hears people say, "I know I should share my abortion story to convince people abortion should be legal," but to us, that's the last reason someone *should* share their abortion story. If and when you want to share, it should be because *you* want to.

Share your story on your own terms, with whomever feels safest for you. It may take you years to feel ready to share, and that's okay. If you do decide to share, you may want to be discerning about whom you share with. Feel the person out first to see how they feel about abortion, to make sure you'll feel safe disclosing to them and that they'll hold your story with kindness.

We Testify storyteller Sal Alves offers a good reminder: although we may want to share our stories and destigmatize abortion for loved ones, it's not our job to convince people who are antiabortion of our humanity. "Just know your experience as someone who has had an abortion does not mean you have to be a spokesperson out here in these streets to try to get these antis to come over to our side." Sal wants to give you permission to share what you want; the rest is your story to keep, especially because some people support abortion only in certain circumstances and may judge your reason. If your reason is simply "I did not want to follow through with my pregnancy," that's okay.

If you do want to share your abortion story loud and proud, just do it! You can start by talking with your nearest and dearest humans and then start telling others in your community through art, poetry, rally speeches, and social media or whatever feels right for you. Find your community. There are abortion storytellers nearby who are willing to show you the ropes and help you amplify your voice to your community and beyond. And We Testify is always ready to support you!

Whatever your reason for having an abortion, know that you'll be okay. As We Testify storyteller Jack Qu'emi Gutiérrez said, "I don't want to say don't worry, but don't worry."

HOW TO SHOW UP FOR YOUR LOVED ONES

Some of you who are reading this book may not have had an abortion yet but may find yourselves supporting someone who is going to have an abortion. It's critical that you learn how to support that person to ensure they are validated and centered during their experience. It is an honor to be invited into someone's abortion experience. They are trusting you to show up for them in a vulnerable moment. It's possible that you're the only person they feel safe telling about their abortion. Honor that trust by putting their needs first and respecting their boundaries. We have a few suggestions for how you can approach showing up for their experience.

Maintain confidentiality: In movement organizing spaces, activists say, "What's said here stays here—what's learned here leaves here." The things people say, the conversations you have, and the details of the experience should stay confidential. But the lessons learned and the way you're inspired to support others can leave the confidential space and inform how you show up for others. Your loved one deserves to know that their experience, all of their feelings, and what happens to them won't become a story you share with other friends or fodder for a social media post. Keep your loved one's confidence and earn their trust.

Be ready for all feelings: Your loved one may exhibit a lot of different feelings before, during, and after their abortion. That is normal. The most common feeling after an abortion is relief, but a lot of other feelings can come and go. Be ready for your loved one to show you all their feelings, and be ready to hold them and listen.

Let them make their own decisions: We know you love your friend. We know you have thoughts about what they should or shouldn't do. But this moment isn't about you. It's about your loved one and their decisions. The most powerful thing you can do is to let your friend come to their decisions on their own terms.

The trainers at All-Options explain it this way: Remember the movie *Dirty Dancing*? When Johnny is explaining dance space to Baby, he critiques her spaghetti arms and asks her to hold her arms tight to protect her dance space. They each have a dance space; for the dance to work, they both have to hold their frames steady and dance only in their respective dance space. Supporting someone through an abortion is similar. You have to know where your own dance space begins and ends. Know where your feelings, emotions, bias, and beliefs begin and end, and hold a separate space for your loved one's own dance space. You can still be there to listen and reflect what your friend is saying back to them. But let them work through those decisions on their own. Ask open-ended questions so they can talk through their feelings and come to their own resolution. Avoid sharing other people's stories or layering your own feelings over their experience. It's theirs to experience and share when they are ready, on their own terms. Respect that.

It's okay not to know everything: There can be a lot to know about the abortion process. It's okay if you don't know everything. Don't make up anything. Pause. Think. Call a medical provider or research the question on a reputable medical website. Support your loved one in finding the answers.

Cook, clean, care: You know how wonderful it is when someone anticipates your every need? That's exponentially magical when someone is having an abortion. Cook or order their favorite meals. Clean up their space so they're not worried about emptying the trash full of used pads. Bring over their favorite things and extras of the must-have items we've outlined. Create a caring space where your loved one is pampered and can rest and recover.

Love unconditionally: The best thing you can do is love your friend, unconditionally. Having an abortion can be very difficult—mostly because people having an abortion often have few people in their lives they can turn to about it. Unfortunately, they're going to experience stigma and shame from the world around them and from other people they love. The most radical thing you can do is love them unconditionally.

Affirmations for People Who Will Have Abortions

... From People Who Have Had Abortions

PAULA ÁVILA-GUILLÉN (SHE/HER)

Abortion can feel right, abortion can feel okay, and that is good. Don't ever feel guilty because you feel relief because of your abortion. Abortion can be liberating and it can be very powerful. So if it felt right for you, then that was the right thing for you. Just follow your heart.

US CONGRESSWOMAN CORI BUSH (SHE/HER)

If you need an abortion, even if you live in a state where abortion is no longer legal, there is still access to abortion. There are people and organizations that can help. There are resources out there: there are medication abortions [and] there are organizations and funds that have the resources to help you get the services that you need. So get the help that you need. Get the resources, the services that you need for yourself. This country should not be able to dictate what you do with your own body. You have been managing your body all of this time. You manage your present, you manage your future. Walk in that and hold your head up and your shoulders back, because there's nothing wrong with you. There is no shame in considering an abortion and there is no shame in having an abortion. The shame is this country [and the] people in this country making the decision that you should feel shame. [But] you should have the right to your own body while knowing that you are doing the best for you, for your family, for your community—whoever it is that you are doing this for, or if you're just doing this for yourself. This is the best decision for you. And if you are one of those people, and you feel like not only can I do this, but I want to go out and I want to advocate and I want to go help fight this fight, we need you to join this movement. We need you to be a part of this work, because we are going to end these draconian laws that are completely traumatizing, for lack of a better word, our communities. Whether it's through an organization and people that you know or a local elected official, get involved. We need people at every level—the municipal level, the state level, the federal level. Get involved and let's get to work. Because when we win, it will save lives.

NANCY CÁRDENAS PEÑA (SHE/HER)

Folks should understand that it's about having as many options as you can for abortion care, including self-managed abortion, and not being limited to whatever the state is providing you.

MARGARET CHO (SHE/HER)

Hell yea! We did it! We did this shit! It's a high-five moment. It's a very triumphant thing. We don't have to do what's planned for us. We don't have to be a victim of circumstances. We can take charge and do what we want with our lives and our bodies.

SHEILA DESAI (SHE/HER)

For someone who's about to have an abortion, know your decision to have an abortion is valid and worthy, no matter the reason or what other people may think or say. Trust yourself to know what is best for you and know that you are not alone. And for others who've had abortions, including those who've shared their stories, I have so much pride, gratitude, and love for you all. Thank you for reminding me every day that I am not alone.

CYNTHIA GUTIERREZ (SHE/HER)

You are not alone. Even if you're physically alone, you have the guidance of your ancestors, your spirits, the energy of other people who've had abortions. You are not alone.

You are loved. You are making the best decision for your life. You are empowered. You are safe. Any discomfort that you have is hopefully temporary. You are divine. You are magical. You are doing exactly what you need to do for your well-being.

JACK QU'EMI GUTIÉRREZ (THEY/THEM)

Abortions are bad bitch behavior. Bad bitch behavior. Abortions are bad bitch behavior. A hundred percent. I've done amazing things because of my abortion in my personal and professional life. It's only going up from there.

Talk about your abortion. Bring it up in casual conversation. Bring it up in spaces where you're like, this might not be polite. Bring it up. Bring it up. Normalize this shit. Because you don't even realize how many people are really like, Oh, bitch, me too. I went back to Florida a year ago, bumped into my childhood friend, mentioned she had seen some of the articles or whatever that We Testify put out and saw me, and was like, Bitch, I had an abortion too. I was like Bitch, twins. Your community is only going to get stronger. Normalize this shit. Abortion is bad bitch behavior. I'm going to get that tattooed on my ass.

CAZEMBE MURPHY JACKSON (HE/HIM)

Congratulations on making a choice for your own life. I'm grateful that you had the ability to be able to make that choice for your life. And I really hope that your abortion is as good for you and your life as my abortion was for me.

SARAH JONES (SHE/HER)

I'm so proud of you for taking care of yourself and so proud of you for talking about taking care of yourself.

SHIVANA JORAWAR (SHE/THEY)

You did nothing wrong. You are making the right decision for you and I'm so proud of you. There is nothing shameful about having an abortion, and it's actually so normal! One out of every four people who can get pregnant will have an abortion in their lifetime. It isn't dangerous for your body—abortion methods are very safe—and this isn't our grandmother's time. Don't be scared. You are not alone.

ELNORA BRACEY (SHE/HER)

You have the right to decide what's best for you to survive in this world.

US CONGRESSWOMAN BARBARA LEE (SHE/HER)

If you feel comfortable, speak out. Help others. Normalize this; abortion is health care. But that's only if you feel comfortable in doing that because I know what it's like. I just encourage the dialogue and the discussion, because that's the only way that the solidarity will be tighter among people who've had abortions; but that's also a way to empower.

RACHAEL LORENZO (THEY/THEM)

My affirmation is that just because I love abortion—I think about abortion all day, before I go to sleep, every day of my life—does not mean that someone who is contemplating abortion or who has had an abortion who has complicated feelings needs to feel the way that I do. We don't all have to. It is absolutely something to celebrate, and we should be changing the narrative of how we talk about it. And there's room in this movement to honor complicated feelings. So if someone has complicated feelings or is still working through their own experience, this isn't a sprint, it's a marathon, right? Number one, please just leave us the fuck alone and let us make our own decisions. And on the other hand, let's make space for that and however someone feels. I'm just here to help you get an abortion.

SARAH MICHAL HAMID (SHE/THEY)

You are so worth it, and rock on. We're so worthy of all the things that led us to have abortions, of all the things that come after our abortions. We're worth it.

US CONGRESSWOMAN GWEN MOORE (SHE/HER)

You're not alone. . . . There's nothing wrong with having a baby and there's nothing wrong with not having one. This is your life, and at the end of the day, no matter what, it is your decision because this is your consequence.

BRITTANY MOSTILLER (SHE/HER)

I see you, I affirm you, I love you.

When I'm saying that, it's with the hope that people start to feel love, that they feel seen and heard, and then feel validated. I don't give a fuck what your profession is or what movement you in—it's none of that. At the end of the day, we are people. Yeah, we are having abortions and fucking and doing all the things, making mistakes and all that, but we're still people and we all want to feel seen and we all want to be loved. And that's your birthright; being loved is your birthright. This world is very, very fucked up. It's why you hold on to the moments of joy and love when you're in them. To quote Mariame Kaba, she says something to the effect of, beautiful things have always happened alongside the terrible. So even when life feels shitty, and people are being shitty to you, love is your birthright. Abortion is just you having an abortion. Whatever is wrapped up in there that you probably want to dig into or get to the bottom of, or whatever core beliefs, do that on your own time. You can do that. Because I know it's not just "I had an abortion" for some folks—like it's a really deep thing and that's okay to feel. I still love you. You still deserve love. You still deserve respect. You still deserve to be treated with dignity.

LAYIDUA SALAZAR (SHE/HER)

I'm proud that you are making a decision that feels good for you and your body and happy that hopefully this process is as simple and uncomplicated as it can be.

DIANE SHERMAN (SHE/HER)

Trust your gut. Trust yourself. Trust what you know, and trust the people who love you. Find a safe place to do what you need to do, take care of your mental health and your spiritual self, and then do what you need to do and know that everything is okay. It's as it's supposed to be in this moment.

GLORIA STEINEM (SHE/HER)

The womb gives us the power to create and the power to give birth to ourselves.

ASH WILLIAMS (HE/HIM)

I'm so proud of you for doing what's right for yourself. I'm so proud of you for choosing yourself in this moment. And I hope that you can remember that this choice is one of the most important ones that you can make.

DR. YING ZHANG (SHE/HER)

You did what you needed to do to take care of yourself and your family. You are loved, so love yourself. Abortion is health care, and everyone should have the right and choice to health care.

Liberating Abortion

When we win, it will save lives.

—US CONGRESSWOMAN CORI BUSH

For nearly forty years, Elnora Bracey didn't talk about her abortion. Only her sister and boyfriend knew she had had one, and since then, she hadn't really thought about it much. She'd met a Philadelphian in the Virgin Islands, and they began dating. He was a dreamer who lived in but contributed little to the rent of her Chicago apartment, she told us. Elnora had dreams, too: she wanted to be a nurse. When she realized she was roughly six weeks pregnant, she knew quite quickly that she wanted an abortion. She wasn't ready to be a parent, but she also heard her mother's warning echoing in her head: "I'm done raising children. Don't be bringin' any babies home here."

She scheduled an abortion at a Planned Parenthood in downtown Chicago. Although she was glad to have access to abortion care, Elnora, who is Black, felt uncomfortable when the providers shamed her for using the rhythm method and told her that not using contraceptives, and potentially needing additional abortions, would be bad for her health. "There was this guilt feeling I felt when they said that," she said. Once the abortion was over, she broke up with the boyfriend and started moving on with her life. Although she loved her mother deeply, Elnora wanted a life different from hers. She saw how her mother's lack of autonomy over her reproduction kept her tied to Elnora's father, who cheated on her constantly and dictated how every dollar in the house was spent. A few years later, while in nursing school, she met another student with whom she fell in love and had children when she was ready, on her own terms.

In July 2022, nearly fifty years after her abortion, Elnora felt that her decision came full circle. Less than a month after the Supreme Court overturned the right to an abortion, she was sitting with her husband watching a congressional hearing on the impact of abortion bans. As the first speaker shared her abortion story, she began to cry. "I owe my life to abortion; not only my own but because, shortly after *Roe v. Wade*, a Black woman was able to have an abortion in Illinois," Renee testified. "She was in a relationship that wasn't right for her, and her abortion allowed her to move on, attend nursing school, marry a fellow student, and have a child with him. That child was me. As my mother told me, 'Renee, I chose you.' That's exactly what abortion is about: the ability for all of us to choose if, when, and how to create our families, on our own terms."

As Elnora watched her daughter make history as the first person to share the self-managed abortion protocol before Congress, she broke down. "I felt like you were my voice. You were able to speak it for me and say all of the things I wish I had the ability to say," Elnora told Renee in an interview. "When you spoke, it was like it was coming out of my mouth because you are me. You are a part of me."

When Renee began sharing her abortion story, she knew of only one family member, her cousin Nora, who'd had an abortion, which left Renee feeling isolated and alone. It wasn't until she had been pioneering abortion storytelling methods for several years that one summer afternoon in 2014 her mother finally told Renee that she, too, had had an abortion. Renee was working on her first abortion storytelling guide, *Saying Abortion Aloud*, when her mother asked what should happen for people who don't want to share their abortion stories. Without looking up, Renee said that they didn't have to share their stories, of course.

"Well, I don't want to share mine," Elnora replied hesitantly. Renee was floored. How had she been doing this work without even knowing that her own mother had had an abortion? Elnora felt similarly. "My daughter's doing all this work and I can't even tell her that I've had one. What's wrong with me?"

Renee knew her mother supported abortion because as a teenager she'd heard Elnora say that it was a viable option for an unintended pregnancy. But still, Renee didn't feel comfortable going to her mother for support when she had her abortion. Renee had heard her mother say she was proud of getting Renee through high school without getting pregnant, and Renee didn't want to ruin that image. As Renee began doing abortion organizing, her mother told her that she had helped her niece Katherine pay for a flight to get a twenty-week abortion in New York City in 1983, but Elnora did not share her own abortion story. "If you had told me that you'd had an abortion, I would have gone to you for help," Renee told her mother that day in 2014. "I was afraid I would be a disappointment to you. That's why I do this work—to open up lines of communication like this." In hindsight, Elnora said, she should have said something to Renee about her abortion, but she was struggling with the stigma of having an abortion and didn't know how to verbalize it. "I felt like a failure, too," she told Renee during an interview. "I am so sorry that I made you feel like a failure by not discussing it with you."

Since writing this book, Renee has learned of more loved ones who've had abortions—several of whom appear in these pages. Her mother's sister, Vera, had an abortion in the late 1970s because she already had two children and was working night shifts as a nurse. Renee's cousin Katherine, Vera's daughter, estimates that she had ten abortions in between having her two sons. They spoke candidly about the support Renee's mother provided Katherine when she first became pregnant with her son as a teen and was afraid to tell her parents and when she needed subsequent abortions and help parenting. Renee and Katherine found similarities in their stories, including their fear of disappointing their mothers and their consideration of unsafe methods such as throwing themselves down the stairs or using unsafe substances to cause an abortion. These were things they'd never uttered to other family members until then. Talking about abortion opened up something among all of them. For Renee, she felt a deeper connection to her kin, and an invisible weight of fear and shame was lifted off her shoulders. She and her mother were liberated by sharing their abortion stories.

* * *

Imagining liberation can feel like a lofty vision. It means envisioning a perfect society, in which everyone has what they need when they need it and feels loved and supported in achieving their abortion. And yet, imagining the liberation of abortion is something we have been doing for thousands of years, from the first people who figured which concoction of savin or peacock flower or cotton root bark would do the trick most effectively, to the midwives and Brazilian women and pharmacists who tried all sorts of drugs to safely end pregnancies. We have always been on a journey to ensure everyone is able to safely end their pregnancies and determine their futures on their own terms. Liberating abortion is an unrealized goal, passed on through generations for centuries.

When the Supreme Court overturned *Roe v. Wade*, many began to panic. *What do we do? We're going back to the Dark Ages! We've never been through this before!* they cried. The moment was scary—terrifying, actually. And we had to take a deep breath and remind ourselves that we've been here before, many times over. That's why we decided to write this book. We saw the writing on the wall spelling the end of *Roe* more than a decade ago, and although we may not have had the ability to stop it, we knew that the audacity of our ancestors and education for the masses would be needed to take us into whatever would come next. We knew everyone would need to think radically different about abortion in order to rebuild after the fall of *Roe*. We need to liberate abortion for real this time, with everyone who needs access included.

Liberating abortion won't come easy. In fact, it will be a struggle. We will need to demand engagement and accountability from pro-choice politicians and those in our community who are open to exceptions in abortion laws, privileging some over others. Over the course of writing this book, Renee launched a campaign, Did Biden Say Abortion Yet?, to get President Biden to even say the word "abortion." He was 468 days into his administration before he said it for the first time, after *Roe* had been overturned, and even now he says it once in a blue moon. Rather, he prefers to tout his plan to "fund the police," an offensive call to invest in brutalizing police forces—the very officers that are used to criminalize people for the outcomes of their pregnancies. We have pro-choice politicians championing policies that would restore abortion access, but leave out young people, later abortion patients, incarcerated people, immigrants, people enrolled in Medicaid, and anyone else who can't afford it. As much as people say they don't want to go back to the past, they aren't willing to make the large-scale changes that would move us forward toward a more just future of abortion access.

We wrote this book for all of you who yearn for a better world for people who have abortions. In order to get there, we have to start sharing these stories and the truth about abortion in our communities, going back centuries.

Building on the vision of the founders of reproductive justice, we believe it's critical to embrace that framework but also deepen that work so we can continue the journey toward liberation.

Reproductive justice started as an idea in response to a Democratic administration's health policy that would be detrimental to Black and Brown communities and increase surveillance and policing while failing to adequately care for families. The founding mothers of reproductive justice knew that centering Black liberation and the reproductive needs of Black people would be the key to reproductive freedom for all of us. They theorized that if we could connect all of the issues oppressing us, centering on how they impacted our ability to decide if, when, and how to grow our families, we could unlock a better world for all families.

A world without anti-Black capitalist hierarchies would not only free us from the chains of reproductive oppression that make it impossible to exercise bodily autonomy and agency and to parent our children in safe and sustainable communities, it would also ensure protections for everyone impacted by those harmful systems.

We believe the path to liberation is a fundamental shift in the role reproductive justice plays in our lives. Reproductive justice must become the air we breathe, replacing abortion stigma and all the ways it shows up in our systems, conversations, media, and interpersonal relationships. Reproductive justice is a way of being. It asks us to consider all that we, and those around us, are coming to the table with, and how we can ensure everyone has the education and resources they need to choose their own destiny, understand their body, and have the sexual satisfaction and pleasure they desire. How can we create a world in which everyone has what they need to see themselves in their best light with the most confidence in their body, sexuality, and mind?

When We Testify storyteller Nancy Cárdenas Peña learned that she was pregnant, she knew that she would have an abortion. "I don't ever picture myself being a parent," she told us. "I definitely wasn't ready to be a parent then." Nancy, who is Latina, was in a relationship that she wanted to leave at the time, and she didn't tell her loved ones that she was pregnant or about her decision to terminate the pregnancy. Since she was involved in local immigration and abortion politics in Austin, Texas, she didn't want to go to a clinic and risk seeing people she knew and face clinic protesters. "I wanted as much power as I could get over this decision." She already had access to information and resources on medication abortion. She knew what she wanted and was able to have complete control over her decision. "I don't think I would have preferred anything else," Nancy told us.

As empowering as Nancy's abortion experience was, it fell apart when her ex-partner told her story in a legal complaint filed against her. "A lot of people [now] knew that I had an abortion, and it felt like my power had been stripped from me," Nancy said. "But, thanks to We Testify, I felt like I could reclaim my story—and I did."

Her experience now informs her work and the emphasis she puts on advocating for self-managed abortion. She wants everyone to know that it's okay to have an abortion and it's okay to have it on your own terms, inside of a clinic or out. "I've fought very hard for folks to understand that it is about having as many options as you can have for abortion care and not being limited to whatever the state was providing you."

Similarly, full-spectrum doula and We Testify abortion storyteller Sarah Michal Hamid was able to access an abortion as a minor without impediments, particularly without having to tell her parents or having to use their insurance plan, which would have sent them a claim showing what the company had covered. California's Medicaid program, Medi-Cal, allowed the then-sixteen-year-old Sarah to walk into her abortion appointment, mark on the clinic's intake forms that she didn't have insurance and had $0 in income, and receive presumptive eligibility for the state program, which covers abortions as basic health care. "If I had had to go through a judicial bypass process, I don't know what would have happened to me, because I was so mentally unwell and so desperately just wanted to not be pregnant anymore," Sarah told us. The majority of states have a judicial bypass process, allowing minors in those states to get an abortion without notifying their parents, but only if a judge believes they are mature enough and grants a waiver. It is an infantilizing process that can be grueling for the minors who are forced into it. "It would have just made me feel like a bad person for wanting something that I knew was the right decision," Sarah explained. Sarah received Medi-Cal benefits on the spot—benefits she said that she still uses today—which meant she could get the abortion she wanted safely and privately in a time frame that didn't derail her life.

In these examples, we can see pathways toward abortion liberation. Despite stigma and slight barriers, both Nancy and Sarah were able to have their abortions on their own terms, using the method of their choosing, for little to no cost. Of course their experiences weren't perfect, but they help us imagine what policies and community support could look like for those who want to have abortions and reclaim their stories. Their experiences remind us of the women of Jane. They offered free or low-cost safe abortions and dreamed of centers where the people who came to them not only received abortions but also learned about their bodies and sexuality. How different does the world look when every pregnancy is met with compassion and care?

As you read the stories in this book, we hope you noticed not only the injustices that the abortion storytellers faced but also the opportunities—the points at which they advocated for themselves; the moments when they realized they could change the system; the times they created something new so that no one else after them had to go through what they went through. That is what our ancestors have done for us: they've shared abortion wisdom that makes the journey a little easier for the next generation. But that is only possible if we know our history and continue to share our abortion stories. In Renee's family, sharing abortion stories, even decades later, has allowed the shame to be erased, relationships to be repaired, and new connections to be built. Our stories are the best road map we have toward envisioning abortion liberation.

When we share our stories, we open ourselves up to connect with others in a vulnerable way that transforms us. We trust each other with our deepest desires about our bodies and our futures.

But we cannot liberate abortion with just feel-good vibes and caring for one another on an individual level. We actually have to change our society to work for all of us. For that, we believe reproductive justice and abolition are the keys to liberating abortion. Liberation calls for an investment in people and families. Our policies have been built on lies about all of us and our worthiness. Learning our history allows us to confront those untruths and demand retribution for the harm caused. We must open our eyes and realize that all of the problems in our society are created by a disinvestment in families and our refusal to care for one another.

To liberate abortion, we must change the way we see parenting in this country and around the world. Being a parent cannot be a role people take on through happenstance or because they couldn't afford to make any other decision. It should be a role people step into feeling confident and supported. It must be a role that people are supported in taking on, by creating the conditions in which everyone can build a family on their own terms. That includes free access to reproductive technologies for low-income, queer, trans, disabled, single, and older people alongside everyone else. That means investing in keeping families together, regardless of immigration status, age, or how much money they have. It's an investment in communities to build our families collectively, with all the monetary and physical resources we need. Family building must not be based on bank accounts. We have all that we need right now; it's just being invested in the wrong things.

We must begin diverting tax dollars away from systems such as the family policing system, police departments, and the military and into universal health care, childcare, housing, and basic income. In order to liberate abortion, police must cease to exist. There is no way anyone can freely decide if, when, and how to grow their family so long as state-sanctioned violence and state coercion exist. Reproductive freedom cannot exist so long as police are funded to investigate people suspected of self-managing their abortions, having miscarriages, trading sex for money or resources, or neglecting their children simply because they can't afford childcare or to put food on the table. Everyone must feel safe and supported enough to obtain an abortion without being forced to involve police or anyone who could force them to engage with the carceral system. This vision also calls for the abolition of prisons. There is no freedom so long as our loved ones can be kept in cages for seeking healthcare or are forced to parent behind bars. We must end the practice of separating families and isolating people. People would no longer be separated from their loved ones. Rather, restorative justice practitioners would step in when conflict interventions are needed and treatment programs would be available for pregnant and parenting people who live with addictions and illnesses.

Abortion liberation forces us to see those who are impacted by unjust and unequal systems: the majority of us are people of color, the majority are already parenting, the majority are religious or spiritual, and the majority are struggling financially. We are trans and nonbinary people, disabled folks, immigrants, and young people. We are groups of people who are forgotten about when under attack because people look at us and say: *Oh, that's not me. I'll never need this. It's not my life. It's not my loved ones.*

Abortion impacts all of us. How our society treats people who have abortions is a reflection on our values.

But that's why our abortion stories are so important—because our voices change the conversation and challenge the myths and disinformation that are spread about who we are, what our lives are like, and why we had abortions. Our abortion stories reveal the ways current political systems don't support our ability to decide if, when, and how to grow our families. Our stories reveal how our health insurance system denies people humanity when they're pregnant and need support, and our low minimum wages make it impossible for people to afford birth control, abortions, and children, often forcing the decision for us. Our abortion stories are a reflection of what's wrong in society—not what's wrong with us.

There's nothing more powerful than seeing someone feel confident—not just in making their decision about whether or not to carry their pregnancy to term, with support and love, but also in being able to talk about it without being burdened by shame and stigma. It's beautiful to see someone feeling confident in their bodies and expressing their sexuality and gender in their most authentic and joyful way.

Our vision for abortion liberation is to build a world where everyone is free to make their own decisions without feeling terrible about themselves and their options. We hope that they can make those decisions surrounded by loved ones and with real information. We hope it can be part of a journey to learn more about their bodies and themselves.

We have never had a world where everyone is able to make free and liberated decisions about their pregnancies, bodies, or sexuality. There are no communities where everyone feels that freedom. The world we want to create doesn't exist yet—we have to imagine it. It's possible we'll never get to experience the world we're building toward, but even if we can make a difference for a few people here and now, that will affect the next generation to come.

After reading the stories in this book, what would that liberation look like to you? What resources do you see in your communities? What programs do you see that are available to everyone who is pregnant? What does the love in our homes look like? What does that love feel like? What would it take to create that world? How would you tell that story to someone else so that they'd join you on the journey to build toward abortion liberation?

* * *

Most important, think about the work you have to do on yourself to make that world possible. What are you committed to learning to educate yourself deeper? What are you committed to doing to change your life and the experience of someone else you care about? How are you going to challenge yourself to appreciate the expansiveness of our identities and life paths? What about yourself are you going to change so that you don't continue to perpetuate the stigma that's holding us all back from liberation? With whom in your family do you want to talk, to unlock those untold stories? What do you want to learn about your body to know you better? What do you need to feel your sexiest self?

Abolition is not just the divestment of resources from harmful systems. It's also about the investment in systems that support all of our families. It's the presence of love and resources. It's the presence of stability and support. A future that fully liberates abortion delivers on the original promise of reproductive freedom outlined in the 1989 "We Remember" brochure: "Reproductive freedom gives each of us the right to make our own choices, and guarantees us a safe, legal, affordable support system."

Abortion liberation can be what we want it to be when we work together to love on and support one another and create the abortion experiences we desire for ourselves and others. Abortion is ours. This has always been our movement. This has always been our journey. There are millions like us. And when we show up for one another with love and dignity, we win.

Acknowledgments

Liberating Abortion would not have been possible without our loved ones, friends, and colleagues who supported us every step of the way. Our deepest appreciation to Tanya McKinnon and Carol Taylor at McKinnon Literary for seeing our vision to write a book unapologetically for us. We are thankful to Jennifer Baker for creating a future for this book, acquiring it, and being our book doula. Thank you to the unionized team at Amistad/HarperCollins, especially our editors Gabi Page-Fort and Ryan Amato for their encouragement and guidance in making this book a reality. Gratitude to The Omega Institute, Pop Culture Collaborative, Harness, and Smith College for their support. Appreciations to The Meteor for offering us space to think through our ideas in our podcast, *The A Files: A Secret History of Abortion*. We are grateful to the talents of Adrianne Wright (publicity), Alma Beauvais (fact-checking), Jamilla Okubo (cover art), Emma Hernández (illustrator), and Jenni Kotting (website design).

RENEE
I would like to thank my friends who held me, including Jasmine, Amber, Elizabeth, Julia, Lauren, Daniela, Edwith, Melissa, Amy, Lindsay,

Jenni, Natasha, and Stephanie in Sweden. To Beyoncé & Solange for their art and my teachers for instilling a love of learning. To my abortion providers for their care. To my research assistants whose friendship made me love data: Drs. Daniel Grossman, Gretchen Sisson, and Caitlin Gerdts. I am grateful to Dr. Tracy Weitz, whose mentorship has been the architect of my dreams. To the We Testify staff and storytellers for their creativity and brilliance: Kenya, Emma, Aryn, Tunisia, and Beth, and especially Nikiya for her unwavering partnership. To my family for their love. Nora, Ivy, and Athena: thank you for your ideas and joy. To my brothers Mark and Matthew and their babies Graham and Natalie, for the smiles. To my father for teaching me to never accept injustice. To my mother: thank you for the sacrifices you made to make my life possible.

REGINA

I would like to thank my partner, Nick, who listened to me talk about everything I was reading with curiosity at all hours of the day and night. I am indebted to siblings, their partners, and their children who babysat on the busiest days; thank you, Simone, Keisha, Stevon, Jennifer, Andre, Bobby, Stephanie, Dustin, Tiffany, and Melinda and Ayelle, and so many other beloveds who virtually sent support. To my mom and mother-in-law, thank you for making it possible for us to build our family when we were ready. Thank you, Dad, for loving me unconditionally. So much love to my *Nation* colleagues and writing-while-parenting book friends, Candace and Sara, for their abundant support and encouragement. To my best friends—Helena, Kat, Mary Ann, and Sarah—thank you for always seeing me. Kieran and Olivia, just as much as I chose you, thank you for choosing me: You are my air, and I am so lucky to get to build a better world for you.

* * *

Finally, thank you to the founders of reproductive justice and all of you who shared your abortion stories with us. Thank you for trusting us. We love you.

Works Cited

INTRODUCTION

Bailey, Moya. *Misogynoir Transformed: Black Women's Digital Resistance*. New York: New York Univ. Press, 2021.

Carruthers, Charlene A. *Unapologetic: A Black, Queer, and Feminist Mandate for Radical Movements*. Boston: Beacon Press, 2018.

Collins, Patricia Hill. *Black Feminist Thought: Knowledge, Consciousness, and the Politics of Empowerment*. New York: Routledge, 2022.

Goodwin, Michele. *Policing the Womb: Invisible Women and the Criminalization of Motherhood*. Cambridge: Cambridge Univ. Press, 2020.

Jones, Rachel K., Doris W. Chiu. "Characteristics of Abortion Patients in Protected and Restricted States Accessing Clinic-Based Care 12 Months Prior to the Elimination of the Federal Constitutional Right to Abortion in the United States." *Perspectives on Sexual and Reproductive Health* 55, no. 2 (June 2023).

Kimport, Katrina, Kira Foster, and Tracy A. Weitz. "Social Sources of Women's Emotional Difficulty After Abortion: Lessons from Women's Abortion Narratives." *Perspectives on Sexual and Reproductive Health* 43, no. 2 (June 2011). https://doi.org/10.1363/4310311.

CHAPTER 1: WHAT IS AN ABORTION?

Bearak, Jonathan M., Anna Popinchalk, Cynthia Beavin, Bela Ganatra, Ann-Beth Moller, Özge Tunçalp, Leontine Alkema. "Country-Specific Estimates of Unintended Pregnancy and Abortion Incidence: A Global Comparative Analysis of Levels in 2015–2019." *BMJ Global Health* 7, no. 3 (March 2022). https://doi.org/10.1136/bmjgh-2021-007151.

The Centers for Disease Control and Prevention. "U.S. Pregnancy Rates Drop During Last Decade." April 12, 2023. https://www.cdc.gov/nchs/pressroom/nchs_press _releases/2023/20230412.htm.

Chiu, Doris W., Emma Stoskopf-Ehrlich, Rachel K. Jones. "As Many as 16% of People Having Abortions Do Not Identify as Heterosexual Women." Guttmacher Institute. June 2023. https://www.guttmacher.org/2023/06/many-16-people-having-abortions -do-not-identify-heterosexual-women.

Gatter, Mary, Katrina Kimport, Diana Greene Foster, Tracy A. Weitz, and Ushma D. Upadhyay. "Relationship Between Ultrasound Viewing and Proceeding to Abortion." *Obstetrics and Gynecology* 123, no. 1 (January 2014): 81–87. https://doi .org/10.1097/AOG.0000000000000053.

Gilloly, Jane, director. *Leona's Sister Gerri*. PBS POV, 1995. 57 minutes. https://www .pbs.org/pov/films/leonassistergerri.

Goodwin, Michele. *Policing the Womb: Invisible Women and the Criminalization of Motherhood*. Cambridge: Cambridge Univ. Press, 2020.

Gratz, Roberta Brandes. "Never Again." *Ms. Magazine*, April 1973.

Grossman, Daniel, Sarah E. Baum, Denitza Andjelic, Carrie Tatum, Guadalupe Torres, Liza Fuentes, and Jennifer Friedman. "A Harm-Reduction Model of Abortion Counseling About Misoprostol Use in Peru with Telephone and In-Person Follow-Up: A Cohort Study." *PLoS ONE* 13, no. 1 (January 10, 2018): e0189195. https://pubmed.ncbi.nlm .nih.gov/29320513/.

Guttmacher Institute. "Induced Abortion in the United States." September 2019. https://www.guttmacher.org/fact-sheet/induced-abortion-united-states.

Jayaweera, Ruvani, Ijeoma Egwuatu, Sybil Nmezi, Ika Ayu Kristianingrum, Ruth Zurbriggen, Belén Grosso, Chiara Bercu, Caitlin Gerdts, and Heidi Moseson. "Medication Abortion Safety and Effectiveness with Misoprostol Alone." *Obstetrics and Gynecology* (October 27, 2023). https://jamanetwork.com/journals/jamanet workopen/fullarticle/2811114.

Jones, Rachel K. "People of All Religions Use Birth Control and Have Abortions." Guttmacher Institute. October 2020. https://www.guttmacher.org/article/2020/10 /people-all-religions-use-birth-control-and-have-abortions.

Jones, Rachel K., and Amy Friedrich-Karnik. "Medication Abortion Accounted for 63% of All US Abortions in 2023—An Increase from 53% in 2020," Guttmacher Institute, March 2024. https://www.guttmacher.org/2024/03/medication-abortion -accounted-63-all-us-abortions-2023-increase-53-2020.

Jones, Rachel K., and Doris W. Chiu. "Characteristics of Abortion Patients in Protected and Restricted States Accessing Clinic-Based Care 12 Months Prior to the Elimination of the Federal Constitutional Right to Abortion in the United States." *Perspectives on Sexual and Reproductive Health* 55, no. 2 (June 2023).

Jones, Rachel K., Jesse Philbin, Marielle Kirstein, Elizabeth Nash, and Kimberley Lufkin. "Long-Term Decline in US Abortions Reverses, Showing Rising Need for Abortion as Supreme Court Is Poised to Overturn Roe v. Wade." Guttmacher Institute. June 2022. https://www.guttmacher.org/article/2022/06/long-term-decline-us-abortions -reverses-showing-rising-need-abortion-supreme-court.

Mahone, Regina. "Notes on Language: Why We Stopped Using 'Surgical Abortion' at

Rewire News Group." Rewire News Group, April 16, 2020. https://rewirenewsgroup
.com/2020/04/16/notes-language-stopped-using-surgical-abortion/.

Moseson, Heidi, Laura Fix, Caitlin Gerdts, Sachiko Ragosta, Jen Hastings, Ari
Stoeffler, Eli A. Goldberg, Mitchell R. Lunn, Annesa Flentje, Matthew R. Capriotti,
Micah E. Lubensky, Juno Obedin-Maliver. "Abortion Attempts Without Clinical
Supervision Among Transgender, Nonbinary and Gender-Expansive People in the
United States." *BMJ Sexual & Reproductive Health* 48, no.1 (January 2022): 22–30.
https://doi.org/10.1136/bmjsrh-2020-200966.

Moseson, Heidi, Laura Fix, Sachiko Ragosta, Hannah Forsberg, Jen Hastings, Ari
Stoeffler, Mitchell R. Lunn, Annesa Flentje, Matthew R. Capriotti, Micah E. Lubensky,
Juno Obedin-Maliver. "Abortion Experiences and Preferences of Transgender,
Nonbinary, and Gender-expansive People in the United States." *American Journal of
Obstetrics and Gynecology* 224, no. 4 (April 2021). https://doi.org/10.1016/j.ajog
.2020.09.035.

Murtagh, Chloe, Elisa Wells, Elizabeth G. Raymond, Francine Coeytaux, and Beverly
Winikoff. "Exploring the Feasibility of Obtaining Mifepristone and Misoprostol
from the Internet." *Contraception* 97, no. 4 (April 2018): 287–91. https://www
.sciencedirect.com/science/article/pii/S0010782417304754?via%3Dihub.

Riddle, John M. *Contraception and Abortion from the Ancient World to the Renaissance.*
Cambridge, MA: Harvard Univ. Press, 1994.

Sedgh, Gilda, and Irum Taqi. "Mifepristone for Abortion in a Global Context: Safe,
Effective and Approved in Nearly 100 Countries." Guttmacher Institute, July 2023.
https://www.guttmacher.org/2023/07/mifepristone-abortion-global-context-safe
-effective-and-approved-nearly-100-countries.

Society of Family Planning. "#WeCount Public Report," February 28, 2024. https://
doi.org/10.46621/675707thmfmv.

Theobald, Brianna. *Reproduction on the Reservation: Pregnancy, Childbirth, and Colonialism
in the Long Twentieth Century.* Chapel Hill: Univ. of North Carolina Press, 2019.

White, Kari, Sarah E. Baum, Kristine Hopkins, Joseph E. Potter, and Daniel
Grossman. "Change in Second-Trimester Abortion After Implementation of a
Restrictive State Law." *Obstetrics & Gynecology* 133, no. 4 (April 2019): 771–779.
https://doi.org/10.1097/AOG.0000000000003183.

CHAPTER 2: "JANE . . . NEVER LEFT ME": THE BLACK WOMEN OF JANE

Kaplan, Laura. *The Story of Jane: The Legendary Underground Feminist Abortion Service,*
2nd ed. (Chicago: Univ. of Chicago Press, 1997). First edition published 1995.

Lessin, Tia, and Emma Pildes, directors. *The Janes.* HBO, 2022. 1 hour, 42 minutes.
https://www.hbo.com/movies/the-janes.

"Lib Groups Linked to Abortions." *Chicago Tribune,* May 5, 1972. https://www
.newspapers.com/article/chicago-tribune/57649992/.

McDuffie, Candace. "This Activist's Life Shows Abortion Access Is Not Just a 'White
Woman's Movement.'" WBEZ Chicago, January 31, 2023. https://www.wbez
.org/stories/marie-leaner-on-being-a-black-jane/af19365b-ea29-418e-8eb2
-1c416f824dc1.

Reagan, Leslie J. *When Abortion Was a Crime: Women, Medicine, and Law in the United States, 1867–1973*. Berkeley: Univ. of California Press, 1996.

CHAPTER 3: "WE TOOK THE TEA": ABORTION METHODS THROUGHOUT HISTORY

Grescoe, Taras. "This Miracle Plant Was Eaten Into Extinction 2000 Years Ago—Or Was It?" *National Geographic*, September 23, 2022. https://www.nationalgeographic .com/premium/article/miracle-plant-eaten-extinction-2000-years-ago-silphion.

Horner, Daena, Molly Dutton-Kenny, Ember Peters, Cheré Suzette Bergeron, and Amanda Jokerst. "A Place for Herbal Abortion in Clinical Herbalism." *Journal of the American Herbalists Guild* (Fall 2022). https://static1.squarespace.com/static /627b15a2f27eab1ffabdde6d/t/63eb9bd5d9046a5e4922c1f5/1676385240849 /A+Place+for+Herbal+Abortion+in+Clinical+Herbalism.pdf%5C.

Jefferson, Thomas. *Notes on the State of Virginia*. London: Printed for John Stockdale, 1787.

Jones, Rachel K., and Amy Friedrich-Karnik. "Medication Abortion Accounted for 63% of All US Abortions in 2023—An Increase from 53% in 2020." Guttmacher Institute, March 2024. https://www.guttmacher.org/2024/03/medication-abortion -accounted-63-all-us-abortions-2023-increase-53-2020.

Löwy, Ilana, and Marilena Cordeiro Dias Villela Corrêa. "The 'Abortion Pill' Misoprostol in Brazil: Women's Empowerment in a Conservative and Repressive Political Environment." *American Journal of Public Health* 110, no. 5 (May 2020): 677–84. https://www.ncbi.nlm.nih.gov/pmc/articles/PMC7144453/.

Nikolajsen, Tine. "Uterine Contraction Induced by Tanzanian Plants Used to Induce Abortion." *Journal of Ethnopharmacology* 137, no. 1 (May 2011): 921–25. https:// www.researchgate.net/publication/51195786_Uterine_contraction_induced_by _Tanzanian_plants_used_to_induce_abortion.

Riddle, John M. *Contraception and Abortion from the Ancient World to the Renaissance*. Cambridge, MA: Harvard Univ. Press, 1994.

———. *Eve's Herbs: A History of Contraception and Abortion in the West*. Cambridge, MA: Harvard Univ. Press, 1999.

Roberts, Dorothy. *Killing the Black Body: Race, Reproduction, and the Meaning of Liberty*. New York: Pantheon, 1997.

Schiebinger, Londa. *Plants and Empire: Colonial Bioprospecting in the Atlantic World*. Cambridge, MA: Harvard Univ. Press, 2007.

CHAPTER 4: THE FIRST TIME ABORTION WAS A CRIME

"The Abortion Menace." *EBONY Magazine*, January 1951, 21–26.

"Abortion Racket." *Our World Magazine*. November 1947.

Chisholm, Shirley. *Unbought and Unbossed*. New York: Avon, January 1971.

Gutierrez-Romine, Alicia. *From Back Alley to the Border: Criminal Abortion in California, 1920–1969*. Lincoln: Univ. of Nebraska Press, 2020.

Jergens, Marianne. "I Performed an Abortion on My Sister." *Bronze Thrills*, February 1971.

Kaplan, Sara Clarke. "After Roe: Race, Reproduction, and Life at the Limit of Law." *WSQ: Women's Studies Quarterly* 51, no. 12 (2023): 117–30. https://doi.org/10.1353/wsq.2023.0006.

Keemer Jr., Dr. Edgar Bass. *Confessions of a Pro-Life Abortionist*. Detroit: Vinco Press, 1980.

King Jr., Martin Luther. "The Social Organization of Nonviolence," *Liberation* 4 (October 1959): 5–6. https://kinginstitute.stanford.edu/king-papers/documents/social-organization-nonviolence.

Miller, Lynn E., and Richard M. Weiss. "Revisiting Black Medical School Extinctions in the Flexner Era." *Journal of the History of Medicine and Allied Sciences* 67, no. 2 (2012): 217–43. http://www.jstor.org/stable/24632042.

Mohr, James. *Abortion in America: The Origins and Evolution of National Policy*. Oxford: Oxford Univ. Press, 1979.

Reagan, Leslie J. *Dangerous Pregnancies: Mothers, Disability, and Abortion in Modern America*. Berkeley: Univ. of California Press, 2010.

Roberts, Dorothy. *Killing the Black Body: Race, Reproduction, and the Meaning of Liberty*. New York: Pantheon, 1997.

Storer, Horatio Robinson. *Why Not? A Book for Every Woman*. 1866.

Tunc, Tanfer Emin. "The Mistress, the Midwife, and the Medical Doctor: Pregnancy and Childbirth on the Plantations of the Antebellum American South, 1800–1860." *Women's History Review* 19, no. 3 (2010), 395–419. https://www.doi.org/10.1080/09612025.2010.489348.

Werbel, Amy. "Anthony Comstock and the Rise (and Fall) of Obscenity Prosecutions." In *The Cambridge History of Sexuality in the United States*, vol. 2, edited by Jen Manion and Nick Syrett. New York: Cambridge Univ. Press, forthcoming.

West, Emily, and Erin Shearer. "Fertility Control, Shared Nurturing, and Dual Exploitation: The Lives of Enslaved Mothers in the Antebellum United States." *Women's History Review* 27, no. 6 (2018): 1006–20. https://www.doi.org/10.1080/09612025.2017.1336849.

Wright, Jennifer. *Madame Restell: The Life, Death, and Resurrection of Old New York's Most Fabulous, Fearless, and Infamous Abortionist*. New York: Hachette Books, 2023.

CHAPTER 5: WHAT'S RACE & CLASS GOT TO DO WITH IT?

Barot, Sneha. "Abortion Restrictions in U.S. Foreign Aid: The History and Harms of the Helms Amendment." *Guttmacher Policy Review* 16, no. 3 (September 13, 2013). https://www.guttmacher.org/gpr/2013/09/abortion-restrictions-us-foreign-aid-history-and-harms-helms-amendment.

Briggs, Laura. *Taking Children: A History of American Terror*. Berkeley: Univ. of California Press, 2021.

Chavez, Nicole. "Texas Woman Died After an Unsafe Abortion Years Ago. Her Daughter Fears Same Thing May Happen Again." CNN, October 11, 2021. https://www.cnn.com/2021/10/11/us/texas-abortion-rosie-jimenez/index.html.

"Epidemiologic Notes and Reports: Cluster of Abortion-Related Complications—Texas." *Morbidity and Mortality Weekly Report*, March 3, 1978. https://stacks.cdc.gov/view/cdc/1207/cdc_1207_DS1.pdf.

Frankfort, Ellen. *Rosie: The Investigation of a Wrongful Death*. New York: Dial Press, January 1979.

Garcia, Laura. "Rep. Barbara Lee Talks About Her Experiences with Abortions." Video. NBC Bay Area, May 5, 2022. https://www.nbcbayarea.com/news/local/watch-rep -barbara-lee-talks-about-her-experiences-with-abortions/2882649/.

Garcia-Ditta, Alexa. "Reckoning with Rosie." *Texas Observer*, November 3, 2015. https://www.texasobserver.org/rosie-jimenez-abortion-medicaid/.

Haddad, Lisa B., and Nawal M. Nour. "Unsafe Abortion: Unnecessary Maternal Mortality." *Reviews in Obstetrics and Gynecology* 2, no. 2 (Spring 2009): 122–26. https://pubmed.ncbi.nlm.nih.gov/19609407/.

"House Hearing on Abortion Affordability." Video. C-SPAN, December 8, 2020. https://www.c-span.org/video/?507083-1/house-hearing-abortion-affordability.

KFF. "State Health Facts: Distribution of the Nonelderly with Medicaid by Race/ Ethnicity, 2022." Accessed March 3, 2024. https://www.kff.org/medicaid/state -indicator/medicaid-distribution-nonelderly-by-raceethnicity.

———. "The U.S. Government and International Family Planning and Reproductive Health: Statutory Requirements and Policies." *Global Health Policy*, October 27, 2023. https://www.kff.org/global-health-policy/fact-sheet/the-u-s-government-and -international-family-planning-reproductive-health-statutory-requirements-and -policies/.

Kimport, Katrina. *No Real Choice: How Culture and Politics Matter for Reproductive Autonomy*. New Brunswick, NJ: Rutgers Univ. Press, 2021.

Lee, Barbara. *Renegade for Peace and Justice: Congresswoman Barbara Lee Speaks for Me*. New York: Rowman & Littlefield, 2008.

Maloni, Judith A., Ching-Yu Cheng, Cary P. Liebl, and Jeanmarie Sharp Maier. "Transforming Prenatal Care: Reflections on the Past and Present with Implications for the Future." *JOGNN* 25, no. 1 (January 1996): 17–23. https://www.jognn.org /article/S0884-2175(15)33326-8/pdf.

Monira Farin, Sherajum, Lauren Hoehn-Velasco, and Michael F. Pesko. "The Impact of Legal Abortion on Maternal Mortality." IZA DP No. 15657. October 2022. https:// docs.iza.org/dp15657.pdf.

Navas, Celeste Melissa. Rosie's Choice: The Politics of Abortion and Feminist Martyrdom thesis. https://escholarship.org/content/qt1s96x2t3/qt1s96x2t3_noSplash_7d81f4b5 5e4c2aa8c7cdf6160bd4266f.pdf?t=r719nj.

Roberts, Dorothy. *Killing the Black Body: Race, Reproduction, and the Meaning of Liberty*. New York: Pantheon, 1997.

Shapiro, Isaac, Danilo Trisi, and Raheem Chaudhry. "Poverty Reduction Programs Help Adults Lacking College Degrees the Most." Center on Budget and Policy Priorities, February 16, 2017. https://www.cbpp.org/research/poverty-and-inequality/poverty -reduction-programs-help-adults-lacking-college-degrees-the#.

Somers, Sarah, and Jane Perkins. "The Ongoing Racial Paradox of the Medicaid Program." *Journal of Health and Life Sciences Law* 16, no. 1 (May 23, 2022): 96–112. https://healthlaw.org/wp-content/uploads/2022/05/The-Ongoing-Racial-Paradox -of-the-Medicaid-Program.pdf.

Taladrid, Stephania. "Dispatch: In the Post-Roe Era, Letting Pregnant Patients

Get Sicker—by Design." *New Yorker*, May 2023. https://www.newyorker.com /news/dispatch/in-the-post-roe-era-letting-pregnant-patients-get-sicker-by -design.

Wattleton, Faye. *Life on the Line*. New York: Ballantine Books, 1998.

CHAPTER 6: ABORTIONSPLAINING

"Book Reviews." *Socialism and Democracy* 20, no. 2 (2006): 165–218. https://doi. org/10.1080/08854300600691806.

Bracey, Earnest N. *Fannie Lou Hamer: The Life of a Civil Rights Icon*. Jefferson: McFarland & Company, 2011.

Bracey Sherman, Renee, and Lizz Winstead. "Patriot Front's Anti-abortion Advocacy at March for Life Sends a Clear Message." NBC News, January 24, 2022. https://www .nbcnews.com/think/opinion/patriot-front-s-antiabortion-advocacy-march-life -sends-clear-ncna1287952.

Crawford, S. Cromwell. *Dilemmas of Life and Death Hindu Ethics in a North American Context*. Albany: State Univ. of New York Press, 1995.

Daniels, Cynthia. R., Janna Ferguson, Grace Howard, and Amanda Roberti. "Informed or Misinformed Consent? Abortion Policy in the United States," *Journal of Health Politics, Policy and Law* 41, no. 2 (2016): 181–209. https://doi.org/10.1215/03616878 -3476105.

Federici, Silvia. *Caliban and the Witch: Women, the Body and Primitive Accumulation*. New York: Autonomedia, 2004.

Feldman, David M. *Marital Relations, Birth Control, and Abortion in Jewish Law*. New York: Schocken, January 1987.

Foster, Diana Greene. *The Turnaway Study: Ten Years, a Thousand Women, and the Consequences of Having—or Being Denied—an Abortion*. New York: Scribner, 2021.

Greenberg, Zoe. "California Assemblywoman: Drought Represents God's Wrath over Abortion." Rewire News Group, June 10, 2015. https://rewirenewsgroup.com/2015 /06/10/california-assemblywoman-drought-represents-gods-wrath-abortion/.

Gurr, Barbara. *Reproductive Justice: The Politics of Health Care for Native American Women*. New Brunswick: Rutgers Univ. Press, 2015.

"Hearing on Texas Abortion Law." Video. C-SPAN, November 4, 2021. https://www .c-span.org/video/?515843-1/hearing-texas-abortion-law#!.

Holland, Jennifer L. *Tiny You: A Western History of the Anti-abortion Movement*. Berkeley: Univ. of California Press, 2020.

Jaffe, Sarah. *Work Won't Love You Back: How Devotion to Our Jobs Keeps Us Exploited, Exhausted, and Alone*. London: Hurst Publishers, 2021.

Jefferson, Thomas. *Thomas Jefferson's Farm Book: With Commentary and Relevant Extracts from Other Writings*. Princeton: Princeton Univ. Press, 1953.

Joffe, Carole. "What Abortion Counselors Want from Their Clients." *Social Problems* 26, no. 1 (October 1, 1978): 112–21. https://academic.oup.com/socpro/article-abstract /26/1/112/1669334.

Kai Lee, Chana. *For Freedom's Sake: The Life of Fannie Lou Hamer*. Champaign: Univ. of Illinois Press, 1999.

Kelly, K. "The Spread of 'Post Abortion Syndrome' as Social Diagnosis." *Social Science & Medicine* 102 (2014): 18–25. https://doi.org/10.1016/j.socscimed.2013.11.030.

Kelly, Mary Louise. "Sociologist Says Women Are More Likely to Choose Abortion over Adoption." NPR, December 3, 2021. https://www.npr.org/2021/12/03/1061333491 /sociologist-says-women-are-more-likely-to-choose-abortion-over-adoption.

Kennedy, Florynce, and Diane Schulder. *Abortion Rap: Testimony by Women Who Have Suffered the Consequences of Restrictive Abortion Laws*. New York: McGraw-Hill, 1971.

Keown, Damien (editor). *Buddhism and Abortion*. Honolulu: Univ. of Hawai'i Press, 1999.

Kimport, Katrina, Ushma Upadhyay, and Diana Greene Foster. "Ultrasound Viewing." Advancing New Standards in Reproductive Health, University of California, San Francisco. Accessed March 7, 2024. https://www.ansirh.org/research/ongoing /ultrasound-viewing.

Kumar, Anuradha. "Disgust, Stigma, and the Politics of Abortion." *Feminism & Psychology* 28, no. 4 (2018): 530–538. https://doi.org/10.1177/0959353518765572.

Lombardo, Paul A. *Three Generations, No Imbeciles: Eugenics, the Supreme Court, and Buck v. Bell*. Baltimore: Johns Hopkins Univ. Press, 2008.

Mason, Carol. *Killing for Life: The Apocalyptic Narrative of Pro-Life Politics*. Ithaca: Cornell Univ. Press, 2002.

Morrison, Toni. *Beloved*. New York: Vintage, 2004.

Nelson, Jennifer. "'Abortions Under Community Control': Feminism, Nationalism, and the Politics of Reproduction Among New York City's Young Lords." *Journal of Women's History* 13, no. 1 (Spring 2001): 157–80. https://doi.org/10.1353/jowh.2001.0031.

Pew Research Center. "Views About Abortion." Accessed March 7, 2024. https://www .pewforum.org/religious-landscape-study/views-about-abortion/.

"The Prevention and Treatment of Abortion." *JAMA* LIV, no. 13 (1910): 1080. https:// doi.org/10.1001/jama.1910.02550390062024.

Proctor, Robert N. *Racial Hygiene: Medicine Under the Nazis*. Cambridge: Harvard Univ. Press, 1988.

Quraishi-Landes, Dr. Asifa (editor). *The Sex Talk: A Muslim's Guide to Healthy Sex & Relationships*. HEART to Grow, 2022.

Raymond, Elizabeth G., and David A. Grimes. "The Comparative Safety of Legal Induced Abortion and Childbirth in the United States." *Obstetrics and Gynecology* 119, no. 2, pt. 1 (February 2012): 215–19. https://www.doi.org/10.1097/AOG .0b013e31823fe923.

Reed, Miriam. *Margaret Sanger: Her Life in Her Words*. Fort Lee, NJ: Barricade Books, 2004.

Roberts, Dorothy. *Killing the Black Body: Race, Reproduction, and the Meaning of Liberty*. New York: Pantheon, 1997.

Roth, Cassia. *A Miscarriage of Justice: Women's Reproductive Lives and the Law in Early Twentieth-Century Brazil*. Stanford: Stanford Univ. Press, 2020.

Sanger, Margaret. "The Pope's Position on Birth Control." *The Nation*, January 27, 1932.

Schaeffer, Francis A., and C. Everett Koop. *Whatever Happened to the Human Race?* Old Tappan, NJ: F. H. Revell, 1979

Schwartz, Marie Jenkins. *Birthing a Slave: Motherhood and Medicine in the Antebellum South*. Cambridge, MA: Harvard Univ. Press, 2006.

Sisson, Gretchen. *Relinquished: The Politics of Adoption and the Privilege of American Motherhood*. New York: St. Martin's Press, 2024.

Stephens, Moira, Christopher Jordens, Ian Kerridge, and Rachel A. Ankeny. "Religious Perspectives on Abortion and a Secular Response." *Journal of Religion and Health* 49, no. 4 (2010): 513–35. https://doi.org/10.1007/s10943-009-9273-7.

Upadhyay, Ushma D., Sheila Desai, Vera Zlidar, Tracy A. Weitz, Daniel Grossman, Patricia Anderson, and Diana Taylor. "Incidence of Emergency Department Visits and Complications After Abortion." *Obstetrics and Gynecology* 125, no. 1 (January 2015): 175–83. https://www.doi.org/10.1097/AOG.0000000000000603.

Usborne, Cornelie. *Cultures of Abortion in Weimar Germany*. New York: Berghahn Books, 2007.

Washington, Harriet A. *Medical Apartheid: The Dark History of Medical Experimentation on Black Americans from Colonial Times to the Present*. New York: Vintage, 2008.

Williams, Maxine. "Why Black Women Support the Abortion Struggle." 1971, Newspaper Ephemera.

CHAPTER 7: EVERYBODY NEEDS REPRODUCTIVE JUSTICE

Black Woman's Voice II, no. 2 (January/February 1973). https://collections.barnard.edu/public/repositories/2/archival_objects/6849.

Bracey Sherman, Renee. "Choice Under Fire: Issues Surrounding African American Reproductive Rights." *EBONY Magazine*, November 2, 2015. https://www.ebony.com/choice-under-fire-issues-surrounding-african-american-reproductive-rights/.

Bracey Sherman, Renee, and Regina Mahone. "Pro-Choice, But Not Pro-Everybody?" *The A Files: A Secret History of Abortion* (The Meteor), February 14, 2024. Podcast, website, 40:42. https://the-a-files.simplecast.com/episodes/pro-choice-but-not-pro-everybody.

Chiu, Doris W., Emma Stoskopf-Ehrlich, Rachel K. Jones. "As Many as 16% of People Having Abortions Do Not Identify as Heterosexual Women." Guttmacher Institute. June 2023. https://www.guttmacher.org/2023/06/many-16-people-having-abortions-do-not-identify-heterosexual-women.

The Combahee River Collective Statement. April 1977. https://www.loc.gov/item/lcwaN00 28151/.

Desai, Sheila, Mary Huynh, and Heidi E. Jones. "Differences in Abortion Rates Between Asian Populations by Country of Origin and Nativity Status in New York City, 2011–2015." *International Journal of Environmental Research and Public Health* 18, no. 12 (June 8, 2021): 6182. https://doi.org/10.3390/ijerph18126182.

Picardi, Phillip. "A Divine Abortion Story," *Unholier Than Thou* (Crooked Media), September 11, 2020. Podcast, website, 40:34. https://www.crooked.com/podcast/a-divine-abortion-story/.

Religious Landscape Study. Pew Research Center, 2015. https://www.pewresearch.org/religion/religious-landscape-study/.

"Rep. Cori Bush: In 1994 'I Was Raped, I Became Pregnant and I Chose to Have an Abortion.'" Video. C-SPAN, September 30, 2021. https://www.youtube.com /watch?v=RebXsll-awc.

Rodriguez, Luz, interview by Joyce Follet, Voices of Feminism Oral History Project. Sophia Smith Collection, Smith College, June 16–17, 2006. https://www.smith .edu/libraries/libs/ssc/vof/transcripts/Rodriguez.pdf.

Ross, Loretta, Lynn Roberts, Erika Derkas, Whitney Peoples, and Pamela Bridgewater Toure, eds. *Radical Reproductive Justice: Foundation, Theory, Practice, Critique*. New York: Feminist Press, 2017.

Ross, Loretta, and Rickie Solinger. *Reproductive Justice: An Introduction*. Berkeley: Univ. of California Press, 2017.

Scott, Cherisse. "Tennessee Lawmakers Cut Off My Mic, but I Won't Be Silenced." Rewire News Group, September 11, 2019. https://rewirenewsgroup.com/2019/09/11 /tennessee-lawmakers-cut-off-my-mic-but-i-wont-be-silenced/.

Silliman, Jael, Marlene Gerber Fried, Loretta Ross, and Elena Gutierrez. *Undivided Rights: Women of Color Organizing for Reproductive Justice*. Boston: South End Press, 2004.

Simpson, Monica. "Reproductive Justice and 'Choice': An Open Letter to Planned Parenthood." Rewire News Group, August 5, 2014. https://rewirenewsgroup.com /2014/08/05/reproductive-justice-choice-open-letter-planned-parenthood/.

Watts, Kyra. "Roe v. Wade Decision Might Go, but Cherisse Scott's Story Shows Why Women Deserve a Choice." *The Tennessean*, May 3, 2022. https://www.tennessean .com/story/opinion/2022/05/03/roe-v-wade-cherisse-scott-abortion-reproductive -rights-women-choice/7370705001/.

CHAPTER 8: OUR RIGHT TO PARENT

Cheung, Nicole. "Miscarriages in Gaza Have Increased 300% Under Israeli Bombing." *Jezebel*, January 17, 2024. https://www.jezebel.com/miscarriages-in-gaza-have -increased-300-under-israeli-1851168680.

"Child Care Costs in the United States." Economic Policy Institute. Accessed March 10, 2024. https://www.epi.org/child-care-costs-in-the-united-states/#/NY.

Cooper, DeMareo. "America Needs Social Housing." *The Nation*, March 24, 2022. https://www.thenation.com/article/society/america-housing-crisis/.

Diepenbrock, George. "Flint Water Crisis Led to Lower Fertility Rates, Higher Fetal Death Rates, Researchers Find." *KU News* (University of Kansas), September 20, 2017. https://news.ku.edu/news/article/2017/09/15/flint-water-crisis-led-lower -fertility-rates-higher-fetal-death-rates-researchers-find.

El-Rifae, Yasmin. "Abortion in Palestine: How to Get Past Checkpoints." *Lux*, no. 8 (Fall 2023). https://lux-magazine.com/article/abortions-palestine/.

Foster, Diana Greene, M. Antonia Biggs, Lauren Ralph, Caitlin Gerdts, Sarah Roberts, and M. Maria Glymour. "Socioeconomic Outcomes of Women Who Receive and Women Who Are Denied Wanted Abortions." *American Journal of Public Health* 108, no. 3 (March 2018): 407–13. https://www.ncbi.nlm.nih.gov/pmc/articles /PMC5803812/.

Froio, Nicole. "Reproductive Rights Organizations Are Failing Palestinians." *Prism*, February 13, 2024.

Lee, Christine, Denise Yen Tran, Deanna Thoi, Melissa Chang, Lisa Wu, and Sang Leng Trieu. "Sex Education Among Asian American College Females: Who Is Teaching Them and What Is Being Taught." *Journal of Immigrant and Minority Health* 15, no. 2 (April 2013): 350–56. https://www.doi.org/10.1007/s10903-012-9668-5.

Mari, Francesca. "Imagine a Renters' Utopia. It Might Look Like Vienna." *New York Times*, May 23, 2023. https://www.nytimes.com/2023/05/23/magazine/vienna-social-housing.html.

Perry, Andre M., Hannah Stephens, and Manann Donoghoe. "Black Wealth Is Increasing, but So Is the Racial Wealth Gap." Brookings, January 9, 2024. https://www.brookings.edu/articles/black-wealth-is-increasing-but-so-is-the-racial-wealth-gap/.

Purnell, Derecka. *Becoming Abolitionists: Police, Protests, and the Pursuit of Freedom*. New York: Astra House, 2021.

"QuickFacts, New York." United States Census Bureau. Accessed March 20, 2024. https://www.census.gov/quickfacts/fact/table/NY/INC110222.

Reece, Kevin, and William Joy. "North Texas Parents Demanding Return of Newborn Taken by CPS over Concerns About Jaundice." WFAA, April 6, 2023. https://www.wfaa.com/article/news/local/north-texas-parents-demand-cps-return-newborn-daughter/287-c258a72f-019f-412f-b8c9-ba8682428612.

Roberts, Dorothy. *Torn Apart: How the Child Welfare System Destroys Black Families—and How Abolition Can Build a Safer World*. New York: Hachette Book Group, 2022.

Upadhyay, Ushma D., M. Antonia Biggs, and Diana Greene Foster. "The Effect of Abortion on Having and Achieving Aspirational One-Year Plans." *BMC Women's Health* 15, no. 102 (2015). https://doi.org/10.1186/s12905-015-0259-1.

Winston, Kay. "Medication and My Abortions Were the Mental Health Care I Needed to Parent." Rewire News Group, May 3, 2021. https://rewirenewsgroup.com/2021/05/03/medication-and-my-abortions-were-the-mental-health-care-i-needed-to-parent/.

CHAPTER 9: FEELIN' OURSELVES: SEXUALITY & PLEASURE

Chung Hayashi, Mary. *Far From Home: Shattering the Myth of the Model Minority*. Littleton, MA: Tapestry Press, 2003.

Dreifus, Claudia. "Joycelyn Elders." Interview. *New York Times*, January 30, 1994. https://www.nytimes.com/1994/01/30/magazine/joycelyn-elders.html.

Dutta, Daisy, Chhanda Chakraborti, and Pulak Mishra. "Tuloni Biya and Its Impact on Menstrual Health: A Qualitative Exploration of the Menstrual Experiences of Adolescent Girls in Assam." *Development Policy Review* 41, no. 5 (March 2, 2023). https://onlinelibrary.wiley.com/doi/abs/10.1111/dpr.12699.

Ellington Taylor D., Jacqueline W Miller, S. Jane Henley, Reda J. Wilson, Manxia Wu, and Lisa C. Richardson. "Trends in Breast Cancer Incidence, by Race, Ethnicity, and Age Among Women Aged ≥20 Years—United States, 1999–2018." *Morbidity and Mortality Weekly Reporter* 71, no. 2 (2022): 43–47. https://pubmed.ncbi.nlm.nih.gov/35025856/.

Evans, Jonathan, Neha Sahgal, Ariana Monique Salazar, Kelsey Jo Starr, and Manolo Corichi. "How Indians View Gender Roles in Families and Society." Pew Research Center, March 2, 2022. https://www.pewresearch.org/religion/2022/03/02/how -indians-view-gender-roles-in-families-and-society/.

"Federally Funded Abstinence-Only Programs: Harmful and Ineffective." Guttmacher Institute, May 2021. https://www.guttmacher.org/fact-sheet/abstinence-only -programs.

History of Sex Education. SIECUS, March 8, 2021. https://siecus.org/wp-content/ uploads/2021/03/2021-SIECUS-History-of-Sex-Ed_Final.pdf.

Hu, Cathy. "What We Know About Intimate Partner Violence in Asian American and Pacific Islander Communities." Urban Institute, May 31, 2018. https://www.urban .org/urban-wire/what-we-know-about-intimate-partner-violence-asian-american -and-pacific-islander-communities.

Lee, Christine, Denise Yen Tran, Deanna Thoi, Melissa Chang, Lisa Wu, and Sang Leng Trieu. "Sex Education Among Asian American College Females: Who Is Teaching Them and What Is Being Taught." *Journal of Immigrant and Minority Health* 15, no. 2 (April 2013): 350–56. https://www.doi.org/10.1007/s10903-012-9668-5.

"M. Joycelyn Elders, Controversial Views on Sex Education." Video. Interview by the National Visionary Leadership Project, March 17, 2010. https://www.youtube.com /watch?v=1bMk8oAyUiE

McCammon, Sarah. "Abstinence-Only Education Is Ineffective and Unethical, Report Argues." NPR, August 23, 2017. https://www.npr.org/sections/health-shots /2017/08/23/545289168/abstinence-education-is-ineffective-and-unethical-report -argues.

McVean, Ada. "The American Plan to Win World War I: Incarcerate Promiscuous Women." McGill Office for Science and Society, February 17, 2023. https:// www.mcgill.ca/oss/article/history/american-plan-win-world-war-ii-incarcerate -promiscuous-women.

Nelson, Kate. "Sacred Rites." *New Mexico Magazine*, June 25, 2019. https://www .newmexicomagazine.org/blog/post/mescalero-rites/.

Pember, Mary Annette. "'Honoring Our Monthly Moons': Some Menstruation Rituals Give Indigenous Women Hope," Rewire News Group, February 20, 2019. https:// rewirenewsgroup.com/2019/02/20/monthly-moons-menstruation-rituals-indigenous -women/.

"The Puerto Rico Pill Trials." *American Experience*. PBS. Accessed March 10, 2024. https://www.pbs.org/wgbh/americanexperience/features/pill-puerto-rico-pill-trials/.

Rodriguez, Michael A., and Robert Garcia. "First, Do No Harm: The US Sexually Transmitted Disease Experiments in Guatemala." *American Journal of Public Health* 103, no. 12 (December 2013): 2122–26. https://www.ncbi.nlm.nih.gov/pmc /articles/PMC3828982/.

Sex Ed State Law and Policy Chart. SIECUS, July 2022. https://siecus.org/wp-content /uploads/2021/09/2022-Sex-Ed-State-Law-and-Policy-Chart.pdf.

"State of the Period 2023." Thinx, Inc. and PERIOD. Accessed March 7, 2024. https:// period.org/uploads/2023-State-of-the-Period-Study.pdf.

Vargas, Theresa. "Birth Control Pill History." *Washington Post*, May 9, 2017. https://www.washingtonpost.com/news/retropolis/wp/2017/05/09/guinea-pigs-or-pioneers-how-puerto-rican-women-were-used-to-test-the-birth-control-pill/.

Wexler, Tanya, dir. *Hysteria*. Amazon Prime Video: Sony Pictures Classics, 2011, https://www.amazon.com/Hysteria-Hugh-Dancy/dp/B009CPGQHA.

CHAPTER 10: SEEING OURSELVES: ABORTION ON-SCREEN

Allport, Gordon W. *The Nature of Prejudice*. Cambridge, Massachusetts: Addison-Wesley Pub. Co, 1954.

Azeem, Saleha, Biah Mustafa, Aman Salaam Ahmad, Sumara Rashid, Minaam Farooq, Tariq Rasheed. "Impact of Medical TV Shows on the Surgical Knowledge of Non-Healthcare Students of Lahore, Pakistan." *Advances in Medical Education and Practice* 21, no. 13 (2022): 1341–1349. https://doi.org/10.2147/AMEP.S377808.

Bonavoglia, Angela. *The Choices We Made: Twenty-Five Women and Men Speak Out About Abortion*. New York: Random House, 1991.

Bracey Sherman, Renee. "Hollywood Rarely Tells the Truth About Abortion. 'Little Woods' Is Different." *Washington Post*, April 23, 2019. https://www.washingtonpost.com/opinions/2019/04/23/hollywood-rarely-tells-truth-about-abortion-little-woods-is-different/.

Chow, Ronald, Jaclyn Viehweger, Kehinde Kazeem Kanmodi. "Many Hours of Watching Medical TV Shows Is Associated with Greater Medical Knowledge." International Journal of Adolescent Medicine and Health, 33, no. 1 (September 2018): https://doi:10.1515/ijamh-2018-0026.

Condit, Celeste Michelle. *Decoding Abortion Rhetoric: Communicating Social Change*. Urbana and Chicago: Univ. of Illinois Press, 1990.

Conteh, Mankaprr. "It's Quinta Brunson's World and We're All Just Laughing in It." *Rolling Stone*, June 28, 2022. https://www.rollingstone.com/tv-movies/tv-movie-features/quinta-brunson-abbott-elementary-interview-1367384/.

Crenshaw, Kimberle. "Mapping the Margins: Intersectionality, Identity Politics, and Violence against Women of Color." *Stanford Law Review* 43, no. 6 (1991): 1241–1299. https://doi.org/10.2307/1229039.

Fang, Marina. "Shonda Rhimes' Shows Treated Abortion Matter-of-Factly When Few Shows Did." *HuffPost*, June 15, 2022. https://www.huffpost.com/entry/shonda-rhimes-abortion-greys-anatomy-scandal_n_62a6b9a7e4b0cdccbe5214ba.

Flores, MJ. "Naya Rivera: Because You Told Your Abortion Story, I'm Telling Mine," Rewire News Group, August 30, 2016. https://rewirenewsgroup.com/2016/08/30/naya-rivera-abortion-story-telling-mine/.

Gomez, Stephanie L., and Megan D. McFarlane. "'It's (Not) Handled': Race, Gender, and Refraction in Scandal." Feminist Media Studies 17, no. 3 (2017): 362–76. doi: 10.1080/14680777.2016.1218352.

Greene, Bryan. "The Unmistakable Black Roots of 'Sesame Street.'" *Smithsonian Magazine*, November 7, 2019. https://www.smithsonianmag.com/history/unmistakable-black-roots-sesame-street-180973490/.

Guttmacher Institute. "Induced Abortion in the United States." September 2019. https://www.guttmacher.org/fact-sheet/induced-abortion-united-states.

Harrington, Anne. "Psychiatry, Racism, and the Birth of 'Sesame Street.'" *Undark*, May 17, 2019. https://undark.org/2019/05/17/psychiatry-racism-sesame-street/.

Herold, Stephanie, Natalie Morris, M. Antonia Biggs, Rosalyn Schroeder, Shelly Kaller, and Gretchen Sisson. "Abortion Pills on TV: An Exploratory Study of the Associations Between Abortion Plotline Viewership and Beliefs Regarding In-Clinic and Self-Managed Medication Abortion." *Contraception*, February 29, 2024. https://doi.org/10.1016/j.contraception.2024.110416.

Herold, Stephanie, and Gretchen Sisson, "You Can't Tell This Story Without Abortion": Television Creators on Narrative Intention and Development of Abortion Stories on Their Shows." Communication, Culture and Critique, 16, no. 3 (September 2023): 190–197. https://doi.org/10.1093/ccc/tcad016.

Herold, Stephanie, Gretchen Sisson, and Renee Bracey Sherman. "'I Can't Believe Your Mixed Ass Wasn't on the Pill!': Race and Abortion on American Scripted Television, 2008–2019." *Feminist Media Studies* 22, no. 4 (December 7, 2020): 932–948. https://www.tandfonline.com/doi/full/10.1080/14680777.2020.1856908.

Israel, Lee. *Miss Tallulah Bankhead*. G.P. Putnam's Sons, 1972.

Jones, Rachel K., and Doris W. Chiu. "Characteristics of Abortion Patients in Protected and Restricted States Accessing Clinic-Based Care 12 Months Prior to the Elimination of the Federal Constitutional Right to Abortion in the United States." *Perspectives on Sexual and Reproductive Health* 55, no. 2 (June 2023).

Lauzen, Dr. Martha M. "The Celluloid Ceiling: Employment of Behind-the-Scenes Women on Top Grossing U.S. Films in 2023." Center for the Study of Women in Television and Film, January 1, 2024. https://womenintvfilm.sdsu.edu/wp-content/uploads/2024/01/2023-Celluloid-Ceiling-Report.pdf.

Martins, Nicole, and Kristen Harrison. "Racial and Gender Differences in the Relationship Between Children's Television Use and Self-Esteem: A Longitudinal Panel Study." Communication Research 39, no. 3 (2012): 338–357. https://doi.org/10.1177/0093650211401376.

Moreno, Rita. *Rita Moreno: A Memoir.* New York: Celebra, 2014.

"nobody came/cuz nobody knew": Shame and Isolation in Ntozake Shange's "abortion cycle #1," *College Language Association Journal* 62, no. 1 (March 2019): pp. 22–40. https://doi.org/10.34042/claj.62.1.0022.

Ralph, Lauren J., Diana Greene Foster, Katrina Kimport, David Turok, Sarah C.M. Roberts. "Measuring Decisional Certainty Among Women Seeking Abortion," *Contraception* 95, no. 3 (2017): 269–278. https://doi.org/10.1016/j.contraception.2016.09.008.

Rivera, Naya (@NayaRivera), "Beautifully written 💟 xo," X, August 30, 2016, 3:27 PM, https://twitter.com/NayaRivera/status/770704561254174720.

Shabo, Vicki, and Stephanie Herold. "Re-Scripting Depictions of Abortion on Screen." Better Life Lab at New America and Abortion Onscreen, October 19, 2023. https://www.newamerica.org/better-life-lab/briefs/re-scripting-depictions-of-abortion-on-screen/.

Shange, Ntozake. *For Colored Girls Who Have Considered Suicide / When the Rainbow Is Enuf*. Scribner, 1997.

Sisson, Gretchen, and Stephanie Herold. "Abortion Onscreen." Advancing New Standards in Reproductive Health, University of California, San Francisco. https://www.ansirh.org/research/ongoing/abortion-onscreen.

Sisson, Gretchen, and Brenly Rowland. "I Was Close to Death!": Abortion and Medical Risk on American Television, 2005–2016." *Contraception* 96, no. 1 (2017): 25–29. https://doi.org/10.1016/j.contraception.2017.03.010.

Sisson, Gretchen, Nathan Walter, Stephanie Herold, and John J. Brooks. "Prime-Time Abortion on Grey's Anatomy: What Do US Viewers Learn From Fictional Portrayals of Abortion on Television?" *Perspectives on Sexual and Reproductive Health* 53, no. 1–2 (2021): 13–22. https://doi.org/10.1363/psrh.12183.

UCLA Social Sciences. "The Hollywood Diversity Report 2020, Part 2: Television," October 22, 2020. https://socialsciences.ucla.edu/hollywood-diversity-report-2020/.

Warner, Kristen J. "The Racial Logic of Grey's Anatomy: Shonda Rhimes and Her 'Post-Civil Rights, Post-Feminist' Series." *Television & New Media*, 16, no. 7 (2015): 631–647. https://doi.org/10.1177/1527476414550529.

Washington, Kerry. *Thicker Than Water: A Memoir*. New York: Little, Brown Spark, 2023.

Weingarten, Karen. *Abortion in the American Imagination Before Life and Choice, 1880–1940*. Rutgers University Press, 2014.

The Writers Guild of America West. "Inclusion & Equity Report 2022." April 7, 2022. https://www.wga.org/uploadedfiles/the-guild/inclusion-and-equity/Inclusion-Report-2022.pdf.

CHAPTER 11: WHAT TO EXPECT WHEN YOU'RE EXPECTING AN ABORTION

Henkel, Andrea, Sarah A. Johnson, Matthew F. Reeves, Erica P. Cahill, Paul D. Blumenthal, Kate A. Shaw. "Cabergoline for Lactation Inhibition After Second-Trimester Abortion or Pregnancy Loss: A Randomized Controlled Trial." *Obstetrics and Gynecology* 141, no. 6 (2023): 1115–1123. https://doi.org/10.1097/AOG.0000000000005190.

"State Funding of Abortions Under Medicaid," KFF, accessed May 6, 2024, https://www.kff.org/medicaid/state-indicator/abortion-under-medicaid/?currentTimeframe=0&sortModel=%7B%22colId%22:%22Location%22,%22sort%22:%22asc%22%7D.

CHAPTER 12: AFFIRMATIONS FOR PEOPLE WHO WILL HAVE ABORTIONS

Rea-Tucker, Becca. *Baking by Feel: Recipes to Sort Out Your Emotions (Whatever They Are Today!)*. New York: Harper, 2022.

About the Authors

RENEE BRACEY SHERMAN is a reproductive justice activist, abortion story-teller, and writer. She is the founder and coexecutive director of We Testify, an organization dedicated to the leadership and representation of people who have abortions and share their stories at the intersection of race, class, and gender identity. She is also an executive producer of *Ours to Tell*, an award-winning documentary elevating the voices of people who've had abortions, and cohost of *The A Files: A Secret History of Abortion*, a podcast from The Meteor. She lives in Washington, DC.

REGINA MAHONE is a writer and editor whose work explores the inter-sections between race, class, and reproductive rights. As a senior editor at *The Nation* magazine, she edits articles on a range of topics, including national politics, and runs *Repro Nation*, a monthly newsletter about global efforts to protect reproductive freedom. She and her coauthor, We Testify Founder and Executive Director Renee Bracey Sherman, are cohosts of the podcast *The A Files: A Secret History of Abortion* from The Meteor. Regina has written for publications including *Cosmopolitan*, *Elle*, *Rewire News Group*, *Romper*, *The Nation*, and *Truthout*. She lives in New Jersey with her partner and two children.